FOREIGN POLICY
AND
U.S. PRESIDENTIAL
ELECTIONS

1940
1948

FOREIGN POLICY
AND
U.S. PRESIDENTIAL
ELECTIONS

1940
1948

BY ROBERT A. DIVINE

NEW VIEWPOINTS
A Division of Franklin Watts, Inc.
New York
1974

To Kirk

Cover design by Nicholas Krenitsky
Book design by Rafael Hernandez

Library of Congress Cataloging in Publication Data

Divine, Robert A.
  Foreign policy and U.S. presidential elections,
1940–1948.

  Bibliography: p.
  1. Presidents—United States—Election—1940.
2. Presidents—United States—Election—1944.
3. Presidents—United States—Election—1948.
4. United States—Foreign relations—1933–1945.
5. United States—Foreign relations—1945–1953.
I. Title.
E811.D53   329′.023′7309   73-10464
ISBN 0-531-05357-1
ISBN 0-531-06495-6 (pbk.)

CONTENTS

PREFACE

"Politics stops at the water's edge," runs the popular saying about foreign policy and the political process. Like most clichés, this one has a superficial validity, especially for the years before World War II. Throughout most of the early history of the United States, foreign policy has been a secondary consideration in presidential politics, ranking far below such fundamental considerations as westward expansion, economic growth, and the race issue. It is true that in the 1790's a sharp division of opinion over the French Revolution played an important part in the development of the first political parties: the Federalists, strongly pro-English in sentiment, and the Jeffersonian Republicans, who favored revolutionary France. But in the nineteenth century, once the defeat of Napoleon at Waterloo had restored peace in Europe, American political parties tended to ignore world issues in their struggles for the presidency. James K. Polk, with his vigorous call for expansion into Texas and Oregon in 1844, is one of the few Presidents in this era who made foreign policy the basis of his election campaign. Usually, the candidates focused on domestic issues that touched more directly on the lives of voters, such as land, jobs, and corruption in government.

Even the rise to world power in the 1890's did not elevate foreign policy into a primary political concern. Hawks in both parties called for war against Spain in 1898, and though Bryan tried to make imperialism an issue in 1900, McKinley won by a broad-based appeal that stressed economic prosperity. The demand for reform raised by the Progressives dominated presidential politics in the first two decades of the twentieth century. Woodrow Wilson barely touched on world affairs in his New Freedom campaign in 1912, and though the Democrats played up the slogan "He Kept Us Out of War" in 1916, Progressive reform played an even more important part in his reelection than the peace theme. Wilson hoped that the election of 1920 would be "a solemn referendum" on the League of Nations, but Democratic candidates James Cox and Franklin D. Roosevelt soon found that the voters were apathetic toward further appeals for a strenuous world role. Domestic considerations prevailed in Harding's landslide triumph, and for the next two decades foreign policy virtually disappeared as the nation became preoccupied first with the joy of prosperity and then with the agony of depression. Franklin Roosevelt dismissed the world with a single sentence in his inaugural address in 1933; when he ran for reelection in 1936, he devoted only one speech, the famous Chautauqua address denouncing war, to international affairs.

World War II brought foreign policy to the forefront of American presidential politics, and the Cold War has kept it there ever since. Diplomacy ceased to be the exclusive domain of a foreign policy elite after 1940 as world events impinged directly on the lives of individual Americans. Three generations of youth marched off to battle in Europe, the Pacific, Korea, and Vietnam, and the entire nation learned to live under the threat of nuclear destruction. Foreign policy became a "gut" issue as peace now rivaled prosperity as the politician's favorite promise.

In this book, I have concentrated on the impact of that startling transformation on American presidential politics. My purpose is to show the central role that foreign policy has played in presidential elections since 1940, when Hitler's dramatic victories in Europe cut short the debate over the New Deal and focused American attention on events overseas. At the outset, I intended to show the interaction of politics and diplomacy—the way positions taken during a campaign influenced subsequent diplomacy as well as the way in which foreign policy stands affected the election outcome. But I found that, with rare exceptions, the campaign statements and promises did not have an appreciable impact on the future course of American diplomacy. FDR's pledge in 1940 not to send American boys into a foreign war did not prevent our entry into World War II; Truman's abortive attempt to send Chief Justice Vinson on a peace mission to Moscow did not lead to an effort to reach a detente with the Soviet Union. I was driven to the inescapable conclusion that politicians treat foreign policy as an elaborate charade, raising issues that promise them votes rather than ones that reveal their future intentions in world affairs. Presidential candidates, in short, play politics with foreign policy; they exploit crises overseas in exactly the same way they capitalize on economic, racial, and social problems at home.

At the same time, I discovered that foreign policy played an even larger role in the electoral process than I had suspected. Since the advent of World War II, American Presidents and their challengers have made it a major political battleground in their quest for votes. They have placed heavy emphasis on the question of war or peace, realizing that in recent American experience developments abroad affect the lives of voters as deeply as any domestic issue. In tracing the role of foreign policy in the campaigns, I have been aware of the danger of distorting the political process by my deliberate neglect of the significant domestic factors that also influence the outcome of presidential elections. I make no claim that foreign policy alone determines who is elected. Rather, I intend only to lift international considerations out of the relative obscurity to which historians and political scientists have consigned them in modern American politics.

I begin in 1940 because World War II brought foreign policy directly into the contest between Franklin Roosevelt and Wendell Willkie. This volume ends with the 1948 election, one usually treated exclusively in domestic terms but one in which I believe foreign policy played a highly significant role. A second volume traces the same theme from Eisenhower's triumphant crusade in 1952 through John F. Kennedy's narrow victory over Richard Nixon. I have not examined the elections after 1960, but one could well argue that concern for world affairs was largely responsible for the landslide victories of Lyndon Johnson in 1964 and Richard Nixon in 1972, and that it was the disaster in Vietnam that drove LBJ out of office in 1968 and thereby paved the way for Nixon's first triumph. I simply wished to limit my study to a feasible scope, leaving the subsequent elections for others to treat.

In the pages that follow, I have tried to tell the story dispassionately, letting the actors in the historical drama speak for themselves. I have no strong views I wish to impose on my reader, and I feel deeply that the attempt, especially in the last decade, to channel history along rigid ideological lines has retarded rather than advanced our understanding of the recent past. Yet I cannot help commenting on the essentially negative conclusions that flow from my study. Ideally, a presidential campaign should be a great educational experience, in which would-be leaders make clear the issues confronting the nation and offer positive programs to the voters. In fact, the process rarely is so rational and constructive. The picture that emerges from these pages is more often that of a contest between men who seek to exploit foreign policy issues to gain maximum political advantage. Their goal is not to enlighten the voter, but instead to appeal to his emotions by oversimplifying and frequently distorting complex world problems. Once elected, they turn diplomatic issues back to the small cadre of experts who repair the damage and strive to preserve their domain from the ravage of political discussion for another four years.

Yet despite this dismaying tendency, I believe that in the years from 1940 to 1948 the American electorate displayed an innate wisdom in choosing its Presidents for qualities of international leadership. The people tended to cut through the charges and countercharges to seek the man they felt was most capable of leading the nation in a hazardous world. Voters may never have fully understood all the issues involved in American entry into World War II, in the movement for the creation of the United Nations, or in the conduct of the Cold War with the Soviet Union, but they did make their decisions about the relative quality of leadership of Franklin D. Roosevelt and Harry Truman. Their defeated rivals, Wendell Willkie and Thomas Dewey, might well have proved as capable in office, but neither candidate offered demonstrably better credentials in foreign policy. Thus whatever the faults of the political process, the American voter from 1940 to 1948 proved his ability to make a reasonably informed choice and to elect Presidents equipped to guide the nation safely through the perils of both World War II and the early stages of the Cold War.

I have incurred many debts in the course of the research and writing of this book. A grant from the Penrose Fund of the American Philosophical Society made it possible for me to examine manuscript collections and presidential libraries; the University of Texas Research Institute provided a semester's leave which enabled me to do most of the writing. I am grateful for the assistance of archivists at the Manuscripts Division of the Library of Congress, the Princeton University Library, the Clements Library at the University of Michigan, and especially the extremely helpful and courteous staffs of the Franklin D. Roosevelt and Harry S. Truman presidential libraries. I wish also to thank the many dedicated librarians at the University of Texas who have served me so competently in the course of my research. I am grateful to Mrs. Laura Bodour for typing the manuscript so efficiently. My wife, Barbara Renick Divine, has sustained an unflagging interest in this project for five years, enduring my absences for research as well as the frequent mental aberrations of a spouse lost in the past. Once again, she has demonstrated her unfailing gift for editorial judgment and thereby helped give this book whatever stylistic grace it may possess.

R. A. D.
Austin, Texas
July, 1973

FOREIGN POLICY
AND
U.S. PRESIDENTIAL
ELECTIONS

1940
1948

1940

1234567

As the election year of 1940 opened, Franklin D. Roosevelt found himself in an unusual position—politically vulnerable and uncertain of his course. Only four years before, he had won a triumphal reelection, swamping the hapless Alfred M. Landon and leading his party to renewed control of Congress. But then he suffered a steady series of political setbacks. The attempt to pack the Supreme Court, so as to end its resistance to New Deal measures, opened up wounds within the Democratic party that never fully healed. His subsequent effort to purge conservatives within the party proved equally disastrous, and in the 1938 elections helped a revitalized Republican party make serious inroads into the Democratic majorities in Congress. Even his claim to economic leadership based on overcoming the depression was called into question when a sharp downturn in 1937 and 1938 was quickly dubbed "the Roosevelt recession." When the new Congress met in January 1939, a conservative coalition of southern Democrats and northern Republicans fought Roosevelt on nearly every issue in order to block further efforts at reform and thus bring the New Deal era to an end. Gaining in confidence, conservative Democrats began dismissing talk of a third term for Roosevelt while they mounted a budding campaign for Vice-President John Nance Garner as the party's candidate.[1]

Bleak as this picture appeared, Roosevelt was not yet finished politically. A group of stalwart New Dealers, led by Harold L. Ickes and Harry L. Hopkins, fought within party ranks to contain the conservative attacks and to advance the precedent-shattering idea of a third term for FDR. Although they acted and spoke in terms of the reform ideology of the New Deal, they gained their most significant support from the big-city bosses who knew that Roosevelt was responsible for the Democratic successes of the 1930's. Men like Mayor Kelly of Chicago, Ed Flynn of the Bronx, and Frank Hague of Jersey City realized that FDR alone possessed the political leadership to ensure victory in 1940. Neither Garner nor the other possible candidates—Cordell Hull, James A. Farley, and Paul V. McNutt—developed any substantial popular following, while Roosevelt continued to receive the support of more than three-quarters of the Democratic voters, according to the Gallup poll.[2] Roosevelt's difficulties with Congressional conservatives stalled his legislative program, but the party leaders were aware that he still had broad appeal to the American people.

Roosevelt's own position on the crucial question of a third term did nothing to clarify this confusing situation. From 1937 on, he steadfastly refused to discuss the possibility of his running again, but he took great care to leave this alternative open. Instead of selecting one man and grooming him as a successor, Roosevelt was generous with his endorsements, building up a number of possible candidates with his ambiguous encouragement and then letting them kill each other off. At various times, he had seemed to give his nod of approval to Harry Hopkins, Paul McNutt, James Farley, and Cordell Hull. By these devious tactics, Roosevelt kept both friends and foes guessing, with no one sure what he would finally decide to do. Shrewd as these moves were, it is doubtful if FDR himself knew his future course of action; those closest to him felt that he was genuinely undecided.[3] The struggle with a recalcitrant Congress had taken much of the joy out of the presidency, and he looked forward to a return to Hyde Park and a quiet retirement. Yet he had always responded to the call of duty and, like many famous men, had difficulty imagining that anyone else would provide the leadership he knew he could supply.

The outbreak of World War II in September 1939 added a new dimension to Roosevelt's dilemma, and in the long run it provided the ultimate solution. Although Roosevelt, like most informed Americans in the 1930's, realized the possibility of war long before it occurred, the actual conflict came as a shock to him. He quickly invoked the Neutrality Acts to keep the war away from America, but in a fireside chat he carefully pointed out that he did not expect people to be neutral in thought. He called Congress into special session to repeal the mandatory arms embargo, which prevented the sale of munitions to the Allies, and to replace it with a cash-and-carry system which in effect provided for extensive trade with England and France under the guise of continued neutrality. After Hitler's conquest of Poland, concern over the European war gradually died down as the fighting gave way to a war of nerves during the winter months. Yet Roosevelt was alive to the political implications of the European conflict. In his January 1940 message to Congress he was careful to remind his listeners that "The time is long past when any political party or any particular group can curry or capture public favor by labeling itself the peace party." And he must have been aware that the course of the war in Europe would go far toward determining the outcome of the 1940 election. Any dramatic turn in the conflict was likely to rally the nation behind his leadership, while a continued stalemate would help the Republicans, who focused on domestic discontent. As Kenneth Crawford commented in February 1940, "The worse the world turmoil, the greater will be the demand for retention of the party, the policies, and the men who have kept this country free of it." [4]

The war left the Democrats with Secretary of State Cordell Hull as the only serious alternative to Roosevelt. Garner, a veteran of Congressional politics, had neither the experience nor the personality to cope with a foreign crisis. By May he was effectively removed from the race when Roosevelt supporters in Texas, led by Under Secretary of the Interior Alvin Wirtz and Congressman Lyndon B. Johnson, forced him to accept a favorite-son role at the Democratic convention, with the Texas delegation pledged for Roosevelt after a token first ballot vote for Garner. James Farley, the Postmaster General and architect of Roosevelt's winning campaigns in 1932 and 1936, had no experience in foreign policy. Although he announced in March that he would let his name go before the convention, he set his sight on the vice-presidency and began now to align himself behind the still-reluctant Cordell Hull. The aging Tennesseean had formally presided over Roosevelt's foreign policy since 1933, but in fact FDR had personally conducted diplomacy on matters he considered important, leaving Hull to keep peace with Congress and devote himself to his reciprocal trade agreements program. Hull opposed a third term on principle, but he did not believe it fitting for him to seek the nomination actively. And so he sat quietly in his State Department office, telling those who encouraged him to run that "I am not in politics," and finally, in early June, made public a letter to a political supporter in Tennessee requesting that "my name be not used in connection with any proposed political recognition, either conditional or unconditional." Roosevelt carefully led Hull to believe that he would back him if he himself did not run. Thus Hull, without a campaign organization or any pledged delegates, became, as James MacGregor Burns says, "utterly dependent on the President." [5]

I

In the early morning hours of April 9, 1940, the German army moved swiftly into neighboring Denmark and quickly forced a bloodless surrender. Meanwhile, troops smuggled in on coal barges began a surprise attack on Norway and met with stiffer resistance, particularly at Oslo, where hard-fighting Norwegians delayed the German advance and permitted the king to escape. Despite a belated British landing at Narvik in the north, Germany soon spread its control over all Norway, and thus demonstrated again the superiority of its armed forces.[6]

Americans watched the renewal of the European fighting both with sympathy and admiration for those resisting Nazi aggression and a profound sense of relief at American noninvolvement. A few outspoken interventionists, such as Freda Kirchwey, editor of the *Nation,* warned that the battles at Oslo and Narvik were of vital importance to the United States. "If these struggles look remote to isolationists," she wrote, "it is only because they are afflicted with a convenient nearsightedness." At the other extreme, George Soule, a liberal economist, saw the Scandinavian campaign as indicating a likely German victory in the war, but he thought the idea that a victorious Hitler would then attack the United States was "too fantastic to be seriously considered." [7]

Roosevelt, vacationing at Hyde Park when the Nazi offensive started, wanted to deliver a blistering denunciation of the German aggression, but Secretary Hull persuaded him to wait and see how events unfolded. On April 13, the President finally issued a public condemnation of Hitler's invasion of Norway and Denmark, expressing his government's "disapprobation of such unlawful exercise of force." Five days later, speaking off the record to the nation's newspaper editors, Roosevelt gave a more candid and personal sense of his concern. "I think every man, woman, and child," he said, "ought to ask themselves the question 'What is going to happen to the United States if dictatorship wins in Europe and the Far East?' " Washington observers believed that the publication, in late April, of *American White Paper* by journalists Joseph Alsop and Robert Kintner gave an even clearer indication of Roosevelt's alignment with the European democracies. The book, based on secret State Department material leaked by Assistant Secretary Adolf A. Berle, Jr., traced the President's efforts to help England and France prevent the outbreak of war in 1939 and suggested that Roosevelt privately was disposed to extend all possible help to those fighting against the Axis.[8]

There was growing evidence by the end of April that a majority of the American people shared Roosevelt's sympathy for the Allies. A Gallup poll taken in early May showed that two-thirds of those questioned preferred a presidential candidate willing "to give England and France all the help they want, except sending our army and navy" to one who "promises to keep us out of war and refuses to give any more help to England and France than we are now giving." Surprisingly, slightly more voters thought that the Democrats could do a better job than the Republicans in keeping the nation out of war, though nearly as many thought that the issue of war or peace did not turn on the question of which party was in power. The German chargé d'affaires in Washington, Hans Thomsen, reported back to Berlin that the invasion of Norway had intensified interventionist sentiment in the United States. Noting that the Republicans had committed themselves to an isolationist policy, Thomsen concluded, "The prospects for Roosevelt's re-election have improved considerably." And yet as astute an observer of the contemporary scene as Turner Catledge commented in the *New York Times* on May 5 that antiwar sentiment was so dominant that neither party would risk taking a pro-Allied stand. "So, unless some wholly unforeseen event, of calamitous proportions, takes place in the next few weeks, 'isolation' as such will be hardly a controversial issue in the forthcoming political campaign," Catledge predicted. "All office seekers will be for it, by one name or another." [9]

The unexpected calamity came just five days later, when Hitler unleashed his great *Blitzkrieg* on the western front. On May 10, German units invaded both Belgium and Holland, quickly capturing key points and forcing the British and French to rush reinforcements into the low countries. Then the *panzer* divisions knifed through the Allied lines in the Ardennes region, opening a huge hole through which armored columns moved to cut off the British from the sea. Although the bulk of the English troops escaped at Dunkirk in late May, they left behind their equipment and a demoralized French ally, unprepared for the next German onslaught. In less than three weeks, Germany had upset the European balance of power upon which American security had rested for over a century. [10]

The American people were bewildered and frightened by this amazing turn of events, and at first Roosevelt seemed to reflect the same feeling. In a press conference on May 10, he ducked a question about possible entry into the conflict, and when asked about the Nazi blitz, he commented, "There isn't very much that I can say about the situation. I think it speaks for itself." As news of the German victories dominated the headlines for the next few days, Roosevelt moved quickly to reassure the American people. Aware of the tension between interventionists and isolationists, he concentrated on national defense, a cause on which all Americans could agree. On May 16, he went before Congress to ask for over one billion dollars in emergency defense appropriations, and before he could speak, congressmen and senators leaped to their feet and gave him a wild outburst of cheering, something he had not heard from these men in years. Waves of applause greeted each of his requests, the greatest coming for his call for 50,000 airplanes for the armed forces, and afterward Republicans demonstrated their approval with promises of support for all his defense measures. In the next few weeks, the House and Senate voted for nearly $3 billion in defense funds in an impressive demonstration of national unity.[11]

The growing sense of crisis led inevitably to new pressure on Roosevelt to run for a third term. Just before the blitz began, Rexford Tugwell issued a call to liberals to draft Roosevelt as the only man who could lead the nation through the "worldwide trial of force" that "is now going on." The day after the German invasion of the low countries, four senators, led by independent George Norris of Nebraska, declared that the war had made Roosevelt's renomination essential. "Europe developments compel the President to run for a third term," Norris announced, "regardless of the wishes of himself, his friends or his enemies." The *Nation* launched a campaign to organize liberal support for Roosevelt, with Freda Kirchwey claiming that FDR alone stood out as "a symbol of the will to make democracy live" and Max Lerner labeling him a "crisis President" who was "great enough to match the great times." Even Dorothy Thompson, a Republican and long an opponent of Roosevelt's domestic program, came out for a third term in mid-May. "The President has been right," she wrote in her column. ". . . [T]he fall of Roosevelt in America would be worse for the cause of democracy and freedom than the Nazi occupation of Switzerland." In the State Department, Hull's aide and confidant, Breckinridge Long, concluded that his chief's chances for the Democratic nomination were doomed, and confided in his diary, "The developments as of today will cause the President to be nominated by acclamation at the Convention." *Time* magazine summed up the prevailing belief that the European crisis meant a third term for Roosevelt by commenting that "the Republican Party was the first U.S. casualty in World War II." [12]

Isolationists viewed the drift to Roosevelt ominously. Oswald Garrison Villard, in his last column in the *Nation,* a journal he once edited, warned that war would end the New Deal and perhaps even transform America into a totalitarian state as a result of betrayal "in the White House." Claiming that a war mania was sweeping the country, John T. Flynn spoke out against presidential candidates who gave lip service to staying out of war but called for increased defense spending. In his acid biography of Roosevelt, *Country Squire in the White House,* written in the spring of 1940, Flynn declared that FDR was likely to engage in a "military adventure." "The simple truth is—though Americans have not realized it—that we have a militarist in the White House," Flynn concluded.[13]

The American people ignored these warnings. By late May, Roosevelt had won the support of more than half the delegates to the Democratic convention, thereby ensuring his renomination if he chose to run. More significantly, a Gallup poll taken in mid-May, after the Nazi blitz began, revealed a dramatic rise in Roosevelt's political strength. Where earlier only 47 percent of those polled favored a third term for the President, now 57 percent, a clear majority, indicated they would vote for FDR if he ran again in 1940. When voters were asked in early June if they thought Roosevelt had done a "good job or a poor job in dealing with the war crisis in Europe," 79 percent responded "good job," with even 60 percent of Republican voters agreeing. Yet at the same time polls showed that an overwhelming majority of the American people wanted the government to "keep us out of war, unless we are attacked, no matter what happens abroad." [14]

The war thus transformed the fluid political situation facing Roosevelt in the spring of 1940. The man who had first risen to greatness in the crisis of depression now had an opportunity to restore his tarnished reputation and demonstrate anew his ability as a leader. Though he continued to keep his political plans quiet, not even revealing his intentions to his intimates, the war crisis was inevitably inclining him toward a third term. He felt deeply about the issues at stake on the continent, and he had long been aware, as many of his countrymen had not, that American security depended on a stable and friendly Europe. In an off-the-record talk to the Business Advisory Council on May 23, he commented on the importance of the French army and the British fleet to American security. "If those two are removed, there is nothing between the Americas and those new forces in Europe." [15] Given that concern, it is difficult to conceive of Roosevelt turning his back on the nation and retiring quietly to Hyde Park.

A decision to run for a third term was bound to make foreign policy a major issue in the fall election. As long as Roosevelt emphasized national defense, he could count on nearly unanimous support, but sooner or later he would have to face the more controversial issues of how much aid to extend to those fighting aggression and how far America should become involved, short of actual entry into the conflict. "The American people are divided between their desire to take advantage of the President's experience," commented the *New Republic,* "and the fear that he may get them into war." [16] Roosevelt had consistently been more interventionist than the American people in his approach to the European war. Though they rallied behind his leadership when the storm broke in May, there remained a residue of distrust which isolationists would be certain to play upon in the months ahead. The challenge facing his political opponents would be to exploit this fear of war without undermining American security in a time of grave world crisis.

II

In early 1940, the Republicans, in contrast to the Democrats, looked forward to the coming election with considerable optimism. The party had made a miraculous recovery after Landon's disastrous defeat in 1936 and GOP leaders thought they had a good chance of regaining the presidency in the fall. They viewed the party's gains in the House and Senate in 1938 and the dominance of a conservative coalition in Congress as signs that the public had turned against the New Deal. Planning a campaign that focused on domestic issues, Republicans realized that the outbreak of the European war meant that foreign policy questions could not be avoided. Nevertheless, they still hoped to minimize them, since they knew that the war issue tended to divide eastern internationalists within the party from midwestern isolationists and that Roosevelt could well capitalize on a foreign crisis to overcome the developing sentiment against a third term.[17]

The chief uncertainty facing the Republicans was the choice of a candidate who could defeat Roosevelt or his hand-picked successor. Early in the year, Thomas E. Dewey, the thirty-eight-year-old district attorney of New York County, emerged as the front runner, much to the surprise and consternation of party leaders. Though conservative in his political views, Dewey had ties with neither the eastern financial establishment nor the party's old guard, which centered in the midwest. With Ruth Hanna McCormick Simms directing his campaign, Dewey swept to early primary victories and in March led in the Gallup preference poll with 43 percent, nearly twice the support of his nearest contender. This popularity with the rank-and-file forced party professionals to begin considering him as a serious possibility.[18]

Dewey had made a meteoric rise. Born in modest circumstances in Michigan, his early years were a classic American success story. He worked his way through the University of Michigan and Columbia University Law School by singing in his rich baritone voice. He turned down a possible operatic career to pursue the law, became an assistant United States attorney in New York City in 1931, and then won national fame as a special prosecutor in New York in the mid-1930's, breaking up a gang of notorious racketeers in the city and using his success to win election as district attorney in 1938. Later that year, he met his first defeat, losing a bid for the governorship to incumbent Herbert Lehman by 65,000 votes. Yet the narrowness of his defeat by an experienced and popular governor served to enhance his popularity. His mellow, resonant speaking voice, his aggressive political style, and above all his reputation as a successful crime fighter at a time when the nation was crime-conscious were his chief political assets. Those associated closely with him complained of an arrogance and egotism that led him to take all the credit for what were often group achievements, and reporters found him aloof and cold.[19] Yet his public image as a young and courageous prosecutor willing to take on all comers, even FDR, gave him an irresistible political appeal as a young David in search of a Goliath.

Dewey's gravest weakness lay in the area of foreign policy. Totally without experience in international affairs, he would have to convince the American people that he was competent to direct the nation's diplomacy in a world at war. First, he had to make clear his views, and in doing so he let political expediency dictate his course. In his first major speech on foreign policy, delivered in New York City to the Women's National Republican Club in January, he associated himself with the party's internationalist tradition pioneered by Elihu Root and Henry Stimson. He expressed general agreement with Roosevelt's conduct of diplomacy, saying that FDR had wisely followed policies laid down by the Republican presidents of the 1920's, except for the recognition of the Soviet Union in 1933, which Dewey labeled a serious departure. He voiced a mild sympathy for England and France and suggested that "we must search for the moment when we might, without entanglement, use our good offices to effect a genuine peace." At the same time, Dewey made it clear that he was no interventionist, promising his audience that "we shall send no American to die on the battlefields of Europe." Two months later, campaigning in the Wisconsin primary, Dewey turned his back on this mild internationalist position and spoke like a confirmed isolationist. Accusing Roosevelt of harboring designs for American entry into the conflict, Dewey told his midwestern audiences that it was "imperative" that the United States "not become involved directly or indirectly in foreign wars." On March 31, he told a cheering crowd at Madison, "I am convinced the only way this country can remain genuinely neutral is for the government to give its full attention to procuring domestic recovery and to keep its hands wholly out of the European war. . . ." [20]

The German blitz caught Dewey off balance. During the Scandinavian campaign, he continued to preach the isolationist line, telling reporters that after a trip to the West he was convinced the nation was "solidly, without a single exception, against war involvement." After the invasion of the low countries, he called for a massive defense build-up, charging that Roosevelt had not prepared the nation for the present emergency, but he still stressed his determination "that no American forces shall ever again be sent to fight in Europe." By late May, while still affirming noninvolvement, Dewey expressed sympathy for the Allies and suggested sending planes to England and France, a position identical with Roosevelt's policy of aid to the Allies short of war. [21]

Dewey's flexibility in foreign policy demonstrated his political skill, but it could hardly offset the damaging blow the world crisis had delivered to his chances. Although Republican voters in late May ranked him second only to former President Herbert Hoover among men they thought could best handle the nation's foreign policy, most observers felt that his youth and inexperience ruled him out of serious consideration at a time of dire national emergency. He began to slip in the Gallup poll, and though he still led both in popularity and in pledged delegates, he had lost his opportunity for a quick and dramatic convention victory. In attempting to account for this decline, TRB, the *New Republic*'s veteran Washington reporter, commented, "It is based on sheer inability to imagine this country in the midst of a world crisis under the leadership of a thirty-eight-year-old gangbuster." [22]

Dewey's loss of momentum aided neither of the two men who were viewed as his leading rivals during the spring. Senator Robert A. Taft of Ohio ran second in the polls and first in the hearts of the old guard. Carefully avoiding the primaries, where his abrasive personality and scraggly appearance alienated voters, Taft had carefully cultivated the party leaders, winning delegates who admired his unbending opposition to the New Deal, which he had fought since his election to the Senate in 1936. In his infrequent public speeches, Taft stressed domestic issues and remained silent about the war in Europe, except to suggest that American involvement would endanger democracy at home more than a victory by the dictators abroad. Although Taft had been one of only eight Republican senators who had supported Roosevelt on the repeal of the arms embargo in late 1939, he took a moderate isolationist position after the German offensive began in the spring. He voted for defense expenditures, but he continued to warn against American involvement in the war, regardless of the outcome. As the American people identified more and more with the beleaguered Allies, Taft became an even less likely choice for the Republican nomination.[23]

Senator Arthur H. Vandenberg of Michigan, once rated a strong presidential possibility, gradually dropped out of contention. One of the few Republicans to survive the Democratic sweep of Congress in 1934, Vandenberg had taken a moderate stand on the New Deal while becoming the leading Republican isolationist after the death of William Borah in early 1940. He refused to campaign actively for the GOP nomination, but he did let a group of supporters in Michigan organize a movement for him and enter his name in the Wisconsin primary, where Dewey defeated him decisively. The renewal of fighting in Europe doomed whatever slight chance Vandenberg still had, since he was known as an outspoken isolationist. Yet in May, Vandenberg, stirred by the war, spoke out finally in his own behalf, calling himself an "insulationist" rather than an isolationist, and explaining to a friend, "As an 'insulationist' it seems to me that we must continue to keep out of this war abroad and here develop as swiftly as possible an impregnable national defense." Whatever he called himself, Vandenberg remained at best a dark-horse candidate, the man the Republicans might turn to if they became deadlocked and were willing to make foreign policy the primary issue in the campaign.[24]

As Dewey, Taft, and Vandenberg stalled, the war crisis accelerated the phenomenal candidacy of the longest shot of all —Wendell Willkie. A lifelong Democrat who had never before run for political office, Willkie took advantage of the vacuum in Republican ranks and his own dynamic career as a lawyer, utility company executive, and business foe of the New Deal in offering himself as the man who could "take on the champ," as he called FDR. Willkie had grown up in a small Indiana town, the grandson of German immigrants, had practiced law in Ohio, and had then moved to New York City in 1929 where he joined a law firm which represented Commonwealth and Southern, a utility holding company. Within four years, Willkie had risen to the presidency of the company and was soon engaged in a hectic struggle with the Tennessee Valley Authority. Though he lost the legal battle to TVA, he established his reputation as a rugged advocate of free enterprise and an effective critic of the New Deal. A big, tousled man with rumpled hair and suits that always looked unpressed, Willkie was a dynamic and attractive individual who combined midwestern rural charm with a shrewd understanding of economic and social issues. Above all, he was a vibrant human being, a man of restless energy and great drive who radiated faith in traditional American ideals and who yearned to play a decisive role in national life.[25]

Willkie's name first began to appear in the press as a presidential possibility in mid-1939. As the idea seemed to spread, a small group of easterners active in business, finance, and publishing began a concerted effort to win the Republican nomination for Willkie. They included Russell Davenport of *Fortune* magazine and Mrs. Helen Ogden Reid, publisher of the *New York Herald Tribune;* Charlton MacVeagh and Frank Altschul, both active financiers with important positions within the Republican party; and Samuel Pryor, Republican national committeeman from Connecticut, and John D. M. Hamilton, outgoing GOP national chairman. Later, Oren Root, Jr., a young New York attorney, organized a nationwide network of Willkie for President clubs, thus giving the movement an amateur, grass-roots character which disguised its establishment origins.[26]

Willkie became an active candidate in the early spring of 1940 with the publication of an article entitled, "We, the People," in *Fortune.* Focusing primarily on domestic problems, Willkie called on the people to rise up and join him in a fight to limit the power of the federal government. He made only casual references to foreign policy, though he did assert his interest in stimulating American trade in the world and his desire "to cooperate with and assist genuinely democratic nations." The article touched off a drive for Willkie that developed into a boom after he made an impressive appearance on the popular radio program *Information, Please* in early April. His showing in the Gallup poll, nonexistent in March, shot up as his managers carefully kept him out of the primaries but arranged for a series of well-publicized speeches at civic and party functions across the nation.[27]

Willkie's candidacy, conceived of and developed almost entirely for domestic reasons, hit full stride with the outbreak of the Nazi offensive in Europe. Speaking at a New York banquet the day after Germany invaded Norway and Denmark, Willkie forthrightly declared, "There is one thing we are all agreed upon, and that is that the British and French way of life shall continue in this world." In a newspaper interview on May 4, he likened isolationists to ostriches hiding their heads in the sand, and he called for a policy of "helping the democracies in every way possible, within the limits of international law." After the German blitz began on May 10, he became even more outspoken in calling for "anything short of war which would strengthen the forces of France, England, Holland and Belgium." He openly criticized other Republicans for their isolationist views and accused Roosevelt of being too secretive in conducting his foreign policy. Willkie's boldest stand came in a speech to the American Legion in Akron, Ohio, on May 28, where he claimed that England and France "constitute our first line of defense against Hitler." Charging that Roosevelt was slow in supplying aid to the Allies, Willkie called upon Secretary of State Hull "to ask the democracies, publicly and openly in the name of the American people, what help—short of troops—the American people can give." [28]

Willkie's forthright stand in favor of the Allies greatly enhanced his popularity. Though most Republicans still preferred Dewey, Willkie tripled his standing in the Gallup preferential poll in May, going from 3 to 10 percent in three weeks' time. Dewey's straddle on foreign policy began to erode his support, and the unrelieved isolationism of Taft and Vandenberg made them unacceptable alternatives. Among the Republicans, only Willkie seemed to offer the qualities of leadership and concern for the Allies that the American people wanted. He gave the impression of being a strong man in a crisis, commented Dorothy Thompson, who suggested that the two parties form a coalition and run FDR for President and Willkie for Vice-President. In early June, David Lawrence, who earlier had termed Willkie's nomination "inconceivable," now wrote that it "is decidedly within the realm of a possibility today." William Allen White, the Kansas Republican who headed the recently formed Committee to Defend America by Aiding the Allies, boosted Willkie as "the best prospect" for the Republican nomination, though he expressed fear that isolationists within the party would try to stop him.[29]

As he began to forge ahead, Willkie and his managers became cautious. They were aware that however much the public admired his bold statements, his fate rested with the delegates to the convention, many of whom reflected the isolationism that had pervaded the Republican party in the past. In the week before the Republican convention opened, Willkie toned down his foreign policy views in a speaking tour of New England and New York. In Boston, while affirming aid for the Allies, he stressed the importance of staying out of the conflict. "It is the duty of the Chief Executive to prevent war if he can possibly do so," he proclaimed, adding, ". . . I have been against getting in this war, or any other war, and I still am." The next day, he told a Connecticut audience that talk of sending American boys to Europe was "sheer nonsense." In his last preconvention speech, in Brooklyn on June 18, Willkie went out of his way to reassure isolationists when he announced, "It is the duty of the President of the United States to recognize the determination of the people to stay out of war and to do nothing by word or deed to undermine that determination." [30]

Thus even Willkie, the most outspoken Republican candidate on foreign policy, found it necessary to hedge on the vital issue of peace and war. He realized that the Nazi blitz had shaken the American people out of their earlier complacency, but, like Roosevelt, he knew that they still wanted to avoid entry into the conflict despite their strong sympathy for England and France. Once he had distinguished himself from the other Republican contenders on foreign policy, he quickly retreated to the safety of the Rooseveltian formula of all aid short of war, with a decided emphasis on the last three words. Even so, he stood out clearly as the only Republican candidate who was in tune with the new public consensus which viewed aid to the Allies as vital to American security.

III

While Willkie was emerging as the most promising Republican candidate, Franklin Roosevelt returned to an old idea which now had new political appeal—the appointment of prominent Republican leaders to his Cabinet. As far back as the Munich crisis in 1938, he had considered asking Alfred Landon and Frank Knox, the defeated Republican candidates in 1936, to join his administration as Secretary of War and Secretary of the Navy. He dropped this idea, but in December 1939 he asked Knox to serve as Secretary of the Navy. Although the Chicago publisher was tempted, since he supported FDR's foreign policy, he declined, adding that he might reconsider if the war crisis became serious. After the Nazi blitz, Roosevelt decided the time had come to act. Secretary of the Navy Charles Edison was resigning to run for the governorship of New Jersey, and Secretary of War Harry A. Woodring had long since lost Roosevelt's confidence. The President needed strong, vigorous leaders in these vital posts, and though national defense was probably uppermost in his mind, he could not have been blind to the political implications. The appointment of prominent Republicans would further the sense of national unity and prevent the GOP from attacking the Democrats as the war party in the fall campaign.[31]

In mid-May, Roosevelt invited Alfred Landon, the former governor of Kansas, to lunch with him at the White House. News of the forthcoming meeting leaked out and sparked rumors in the press that Roosevelt was thinking of inviting Republicans to join in a coalition government, perhaps along the lines Dorothy Thompson had suggested, with Willkie as Vice-President and a number of Republicans in the Cabinet. Since this implied a break in the two-party tradition, and possibly even the suspension of the fall election, Roosevelt was quick to deny the rumors, claiming they were "made out of whole cloth" by inventive journalists. Embarrassed by the public discussion, he postponed the meeting with Landon for several days, but finally met with him on May 23. Roosevelt apparently never offered him the post of Secretary of War, but Landon informed him that Knox, who had kept the Kansan fully informed of his contacts with the President, was ready to accept the position of Secretary of the Navy if Roosevelt would appoint another Republican to head the War Department. Undoubtedly Landon told FDR in private what he told the press afterward—that the only way to insure national unity and bipartisan cooperation would be for Roosevelt to renounce a third term. Angry at Landon's demand, the President released a statement saying simply that he had no time for political statements since he was "too busily engaged with problems of far greater national importance." Thus Landon, who had consulted in advance with Senator Taft and GOP House Leader Joseph W. Martin of Massachusetts, deftly blocked FDR's first attempt to outflank the Republicans on the war issue. Roosevelt wisely let the issue drop, waiting for a more propitious time to take it up again.[32]

By early June, the war had taken an even more ominous turn. After the British retreat from the continent at Dunkirk, the German army regrouped for a new offensive against France. With astonishing speed, the *panzer* divisions again broke through the crumbling French lines and began to drive deep into the country. On June 10, Mussolini brought Italy into the war to gain a belated share in the victory, and four days later the German army marched triumphantly into Paris. It was only a matter of days before all France would be in German hands.

Roosevelt responded by making a bold commitment of American aid to the Allies. Speaking at the commencement exercises at the University of Virginia in Charlottesville, he warned that the "military and naval victory for the gods of force and hate" endangered "the institutions of democracy in the Western World," and he declared that "the whole of our sympathies lies with those nations that are giving their life blood in combat against these forces." Then the President committed the nation to a twofold policy of increased national defense and extending "to the opponents of force the material resources of this nation." Although the press paid greatest attention to his dramatic denunciation of Italy's attack on France—"the hand that held the dagger has struck it into the back of its neighbor"—the Charlottesville speech marked Roosevelt's willingness to make public his program of all-out aid to the Allies short of war.[33]

Interventionists were delighted with Roosevelt's speech. Felix Frankfurter, a recent appointee to the Supreme Court and ardent foe of Hitler, told FDR the words were "a grand tonic." "We need that kind of moral summons," Frankfurter commented. *Newsweek* called it "the President's strongest blast ever at the dictators," while TRB proclaimed joyously in the *New Republic,* "We are openly on the side of the Allies." Isolationist newspapers found it too belligerent in tone, however, and Republicans were quite skeptical. Dewey said the Charlottesville speech "gives cause for grave concern," and went on to warn, "If the President intends to involve us in this war, he should say so openly." When reporters asked Willkie for his views, he dodged a direct comment, but he did criticize the President for being "too secretive and too emotional about the details of his foreign policy." [34]

Those who worried about Roosevelt leading the nation into war mistook their man. Although he spoke out boldly at Charlottesville, he acted cautiously when the French, facing certain defeat, made an eleventh-hour appeal for help. In secret notes, Roosevelt continued to express his sympathy, but he carefully informed the French government: "I know that you will understand that these statements carry with them no implication of military commitments. Only the Congress can make such commitments." Cordell Hull, who had drafted this note, felt that he had effectively protected Roosevelt from "getting implicated in the difficulties with France." [35]

On June 20, Roosevelt startled the nation by announcing the appointment of Frank Knox as Secretary of the Navy and seventy-two-year-old Henry L. Stimson as Secretary of War. After the May meeting with Landon, Roosevelt had quietly continued his search for a prominent Republican to head the War Department while Knox stood by. Grenville Clark, a New York Republican active in a growing movement for conscription, first suggested Stimson, a distinguished public servant who had not only been Secretary of War briefly under William Howard Taft but had also served as Hoover's Secretary of State. Felix Frankfurter became his strongest advocate. Pointing out to Roosevelt that Stimson was known to be "out of sorts" with his own party, he said his appointment would not revive talk of a bipartisan coalition; and when Roosevelt questioned his age, Frankfurter arranged for Robert Patterson to serve as Stimson's chief assistant. Stimson himself had doubts about his vitality, but after a thorough medical checkup, and assurances from Roosevelt that the War Department would be kept out of politics, he indicated his willingness to serve. Roosevelt called Stimson on the morning of June 19 to make the offer official, and when Stimson accepted, the President released the news of the two appointments to the press.[36]

Republican officials, gathering in Philadelphia for the party's convention which was due to open in three days, were stunned by the news. National Chairman John Hamilton read Stimson and Knox out of the party, claiming that they were no longer "qualified to speak as Republicans." "Since Colonel

Knox and Colonel Stimson have long desired to intervene in the affairs of Europe and the Democratic party has become the war party," Hamilton asserted, "we may accept that issue at its face value." Taft echoed Hamilton in labeling the Democrats "the war party," and Dewey called the appointments "a direct step toward war." Only Willkie sidestepped the issue, saying simply that each individual had to follow "the dictates of his own conscience." Democratic isolationists were equally irate, criticizing both Stimson and Knox as interventionists. But public opinion strongly supported the appointments; the Gallup poll showed Republicans as well as Democrats in favor of them, and despite threatened opposition, the Senate quickly confirmed both men in early July.[37]

The appointment of Stimson and Knox proved to be a brilliant political triumph for FDR. While national defense may have been uppermost in his calculations, the Republican outcry played directly into his hands. If GOP leaders had praised the President for turning to distinguished Republicans in a time of crisis, they could have neutralized the political impact. Instead, by protesting, they took an isolationist stance at a time when the nation was clearly moving in the opposite direction. Criticizing his party, interventionist William Allen White warned that if the Republicans became the "peace party," they would not even carry Maine or Vermont in November. Roosevelt, carefully refraining from any comment on the appointments, seemed to agree.[38] On the eve of the party conventions, he once again proved to be master of the political situation, placing the Republicans on the defensive and assuming a new role as the national leader who stood above the partisan battle, ready to lead the nation through the unknown hazards that lay ahead. Though he had not yet formally announced his candidacy for a third term, by the end of June it was evident that Roosevelt had let events make the decision for him.

IV

Republicans began streaming into Philadelphia in a gloomy mood for the convention that was to open on June 24. On Saturday, June 22, the French signed an armistice with Germany, thus leaving England alone to carry on the uneven struggle against Hitler. GOP leaders were still shaken by the recent defection of Stimson and Knox from their ranks. They realized that Roosevelt was almost certain to run again and that he would be difficult to defeat. Above all, Republicans agonized over the foreign policy dilemma. Should they continue to attack FDR as a warmonger and base their hopes for victory on a peace theme, or should they simply second the Democrats' call for aid to the Allies and a strong national defense? On a nationwide radio broadcast on June 21, Thomas Dewey chose the first alternative in a blistering attack on Roosevelt. Though he called for "all proper aid" to victims of aggression, Dewey accused the President of "edging the country toward participation in the European war" at a time when the nation was totally unprepared to fight. "We in this country are facing a choice between new leadership and war," Dewey concluded. Though Dewey had now slipped down to 47 percent in the Gallup preferential poll, the delegates seemed to share his isolationist sentiments.[39]

Willkie arrived in Philadelphia on June 22, and he quickly gave anxious Republicans the lift they needed. Buoyed by a steady rise in the polls and confident of his nomination, as always, Willkie called an impromptu press conference and radiated optimism as he answered all questions with refreshing candor. He played down foreign policy questions, telling a Taft supporter that the European conflict had made his support for Hull's reciprocal trade program academic, and sticking to the safe formula, "I favor all possible aid to the Allies without going to war." Willkie had evidently decided not to challenge the prevailing isolationism within the party, but instead hoped to win over the reluctant delegates with his dynamic charm, while behind the scenes his managers, who now included keynoter Harold Stassen and convention chairman Joseph Martin, employed traditional political maneuvers to secure his nomination. [40]

The real battle took place within the Resolutions Committee, which was attempting to write a platform to please all elements within the party. Alfred Landon was the leading interventionist spokesman on the committee, and though he was not committed to any candidate, his views drew him toward the Willkie camp. Appointed chairman of the subcommittee charged with drafting the foreign policy plank, Landon felt confident that he could secure acceptance of one which read, "We favor all proper aid to the Allies that does not involve any commitment that will take us into war unless the vital interests of America are threatened in a tangible and concrete way." Then the appointment of Stimson and Knox touched off a rebellion led by Illinois Senator C. Wayland ("Curly") Brooks, an inveterate isolationist, who demanded that the Republicans ignore the issue of aid to the Allies and instead make an ironclad pledge to keep the United States out of the war. Hans Thomsen, the German chargé in Washington, paid the expenses of some twenty-two isolationist Republican congressmen who traveled to Philadelphia under the leadership of Representative Hamilton Fish of New York to testify before the subcommittee "in favor of an isolationist foreign policy." On the second day of the convention, the German Embassy paid for a full-page ad in newspapers around the nation in which the Fish group called on voters and delegates to "Stop the March to War! Stop the Interventionists and Warmongers! Stop the Democratic Party!" [41]

Worried by this isolationist resurgence, Landon adjourned his group for several days, playing for time while he searched for a flexible formula that would disguise the gulf within the party on foreign policy. Meanwhile, the convention opened with Harold Stassen, the young Minnesota governor, delivering the keynote address. Focusing mainly on domestic issues, Stassen carefully refrained from entering into the foreign policy debate. He did attack Roosevelt for failing to inform the people of developments in Europe in the 1930's and for not preparing the nation for the present emergency, but there were no charges of warmongering or undue aid to the Allies. All Stassen promised was that the Republicans "have the earnest hope to keep this nation out of war." In his speech accepting the role of permanent chairman, Joe Martin was equally vague on the subject. Apparently the Willkie forces had decided to try to bury the foreign policy issue which they feared would hurt their candidate.[42]

Landon's subcommittee finally reported a moderate plank and submitted it to the full Resolutions Committee. Curly Brooks and Senator Henry Cabot Lodge of Massachusetts immediately attacked it as too weak on the vital issue of peace or war. They proceeded to rewrite the plank, striking out interventionist phrases and ending up with a much more isolationist document. Landon, aided by Governor Walter Edge of New Jersey, fought back, eventually winning inclusion of a grudging statement on aid to those "fighting for liberty"; but they both finally gave in and accepted the revised plank just before midnight on the second day of the convention. Some of the more ardent interventionists wanted to take the issue to the floor, but the Willkie forces, fearful of antagonizing the isolationists, counseled against such a move, and Landon reluctantly agreed to accept the committee's decision as final.[43]

The next day the convention routinely approved a platform which began, "The Republican party is firmly opposed to involving this Nation in foreign war." The plank went on to blame the "New Deal" for "our unpreparedness and for the consequent danger of involvement in war." The Republicans promised to support a vigorous defense program, but they deplored "explosive utterances by the President directed at other governments which serve to imperil our peace." Near the end, they included the expression of sympathy and aid for those "fighting for liberty," with the stipulation that the aid "shall not be in violation of international law or inconsistent with the requirements of our own national defense." [44]

Although Senator Brooks gave a brief speech explaining that his own views were more isolationist than the platform plank, most observers felt that the Republicans had gone too far in appeasing the isolationists. The *New York Times* called it a "non-interventionist" plank, foreign correspondent Anne O'Hare McCormick termed it a "patch-up compromise," and *Time* dismissed it as "a somersaulting weasel." The irrepressible H. L. Mencken commented on its ambiguous nature, saying, "It is so written that it will fit both the triumph of democracy and the collapse of democracy, and approve both sending arms to England or sending only flowers." Hamilton Fish hailed it as proof that "the Republican party is determined to keep the country out of war," and Hans Thomsen reported back to Berlin that his efforts had led to the adoption of an isolationist platform with a clear-cut pledge not to enter the war. [45]

It is doubtful whether even a full floor fight would have changed the outcome. Though perhaps a majority of the delegates were not isolationists, most were still smarting from Roosevelt's appointment of Stimson and Knox, and they wanted to take up the President's challenge on foreign policy. The Willkie forces, realizing that the candidate was not bound by the platform, wisely decided to let the delegates enjoy the emotional release afforded them by an isolationist foreign policy plank, rather than risk alienating men and women whose votes they needed.

With the platform fight resolved, the balloting got under way on Thursday. Charles Halleck, a veteran Indiana congressman with an isolationist voting record, placed Willkie's name before the convention in a speech written by Russell Davenport which ignored foreign policy in stressing Willkie's career as a businessman and foe of the New Deal. Though Halleck's speech fell flat, a Willkie boom developed as telegrams from across the country demanding his nomination poured into Philadelphia and the crowded gallery began the rhythmic cry, "We Want Willkie!" On the first ballot, Willkie ran third behind Dewey and Taft, polling just over one hundred votes. But on succeeding tallies, Dewey slipped badly as Willkie steadily gained support, taking the lead over Taft on the third ballot and sweeping on to victory on the sixth.[46]

Many observers attributed Willkie's triumph to the war in Europe. The German victories, culminating in the fall of France on the eve of the Republican convention, compelled the Republicans to turn from one of their drab, isolationist-leaning regulars to a bold new leader who could meet the challenge of the world crisis. Yet in fact Willkie won the nomination by playing down his controversial foreign policy views. His managers carefully avoided a floor fight on the platform: they had an isolationist congressman nominate him without reference to his stand on the war. When he won, they agreed to make Senator Charles McNary of Oregon, a man with a consistently isolationist voting record, his running mate. Though Willkie never repudiated his earlier call for aid to the Allies, he stressed the need to stay out of war in his public statements just before the convention. ". . . [T]he full extent of Willkie's views on the war," commented Joseph Martin in his memoirs, "[was] not too widely understood by Republicans." As a newcomer to politics, Willkie was able to gain the votes of interventionist delegates on the basis of his spring speeches; yet at the same time his lack of a voting record and last-minute hedging allowed him to secure the support of enough isolationists to gain the nomination.[47]

In essence, Willkie won because he proved himself to be the strongest possible candidate the Republican party could put forward in 1940. Unblemished by the GOP defeats of the

1930's, he could offer himself to the people as a man running on his convictions and not simply as a politician out for partisan ends. Though he had the weaknesses of the amateur in politics—too sure of his own judgment and innocent of the need for detailed organizational effort at the precinct level— he alone had the qualities to appeal to dissident Democrats and to independents, whose votes were essential for a minority party to win. Above all, he possessed his own brand of personal magnetism to match FDR's fabled charm and thus promised to neutralize the President's greatest asset. Bruce Bliven commented that the Republicans had paid Roosevelt the ultimate compliment by choosing a candidate with the same kind of personality. "The two men are similar in their quick sense of humor, their intuitive response to the attitudes and emotions of those about them," noted Bliven. "Both have a sure feeling for the dramatic, for good theater." A race between two such attractive candidates promised an exciting contest for the hearts as well as the minds of American voters.[48]

V

Willkie's nomination virtually guaranteed that Roosevelt would run again. Democrats who had earlier opposed a third term dropped their objections as they realized that FDR was the only candidate who had the broad public support to stop Willkie. The President himself, though relieved that the Republicans had not chosen an isolationist who would challenge the administration's foreign policy, recognized Willkie's appeal to progressive voters and admitted that he would be a hard man to defeat. A Gallup poll taken right after the Republican convention confirmed the prospect of a close race, showing that if Roosevelt ran, he would have only a narrow 53–47 percent edge over Willkie.[49]

The President continued to remain silent about his plans,

and though nearly all those close to him believed that the German blitz and the fall of France had convinced him he must run, they continued to apply intense pressure in early July. Felix Frankfurter sent the President a handwritten memorandum urging him to make the race, and enclosed a longer one from Archibald MacLeish designed to rebut charges that FDR was interested only in enhancing his personal power. "In the face of the danger which confronts our time," MacLeish argued, "no individual retains or can hope to retain the rights of personal choice which free men can enjoy in times of peace." Supreme Court Justice William O. Douglas was even more candid in his advice to Roosevelt. In a long memorandum, Douglas told the President, "You are the only one who can beat Willkie." The President had to run, Douglas continued, because of the "foreign issue." If Hitler won in Europe, Roosevelt could rally the rest of the world against him, but "Willkie could not and would not. He would walk into the arms of Hitler as did the Cliveden set." [50]

These appeals probably only reinforced Roosevelt's decision to make the race. On July 7, he met at Hyde Park for over an hour with James Farley, by now his only avowed rival for the nomination. With characteristic indirection, Roosevelt indicated to Farley that he planned to run again without ever saying so explicitly. Stephen Early, FDR's press secretary, drove Farley around for an hour after this meeting to allow him to cool down before he returned to Poughkeepsie and talked with reporters. Farley regained his composure and, when he faced the press, said simply that FDR had told him his plans but that he was pledged to secrecy. Although Farley said the conversation was "entirely satisfactory," reporters sensed his bitterness and concluded that Roosevelt had told him he planned to seek a third term. The President continued to parry all questions about his political plans, but, from this time on, the nation's press assumed that Roosevelt would again be the Democratic candidate.[51]

Senator Burton K. Wheeler of Montana, a progressive Democrat, remained the final obstacle to a third-term nomination. An outspoken liberal who had supported nearly all Roosevelt's early New Deal measures, Wheeler had broken with FDR on the Supreme Court issue, and though subsequently their relations improved, the two men regarded each other as antagonists. Wheeler, known for his skill in debate and his acid tongue, was a staunch isolationist, and it was his foreign policy views which led him to lay down a challenge to the President. In the course of a Senate speech on June 13, Wheeler declared that he stood with the overwhelming majority of the American people who opposed entry into the war, and that if necessary he would break with the Democratic party on this issue. "I want everyone who is interested in the matter to know that I am not going to support any candidate for President of the United States of America—no matter who he may be—who is going to try to get us into this war," Wheeler announced.[52]

Republicans quickly tried to exploit Wheeler's threat to bolt his party by consulting with him on the text of their foreign policy plank. But Wheeler felt the GOP had not gone far enough in its antiwar statement, and he denounced Willkie as a Wall Street lawyer who "openly espoused the policy of American intervention in Europe's bloodbaths until a few weeks—if not days—ago." In speeches and public statements in late June and early July, Wheeler threatened to head a third-party ticket unless the Democrats went much further than the Republicans (the party of "the warmakers," as he termed them) in promising to keep the United States out of the conflict. Other isolationist Democrats began to take up the theme of a third-party movement, and rumors spread that John L. Lewis, the head of the CIO, would back Wheeler on an isolationist ticket. Wheeler kept insisting that all he wanted was a firm Democratic stand against involvement in the war, but he added that if the party refused to make such a pledge, "there will be a tremendous demand for a strong, liberal peace party which will give the people a chance to vote on war or peace." [53]

Roosevelt realized the seriousness of Wheeler's threat, and he moved quickly to make the necessary concession. On July 10, less than a week before the Democratic convention was due to open, the President sent a special message to Congress requesting almost $5 billion more in defense spending. Stating his opposition to war, Roosevelt told the Congress, "We will not use our arms in a war of aggression; we will not send our men to take part in European wars." For the first time, Roosevelt had made a clear-cut antiwar pledge, and the isolationists were jubilant as they welcomed the President into the ranks of the noninterventionists. Reporters quickly noted that the statement appeared to lay the basis for the peace plank in the party's platform which Wheeler demanded, and the Montana senator accepted it as satisfactory, announcing that he would no longer oppose FDR's nomination. [54]

A sharp struggle over the wording of the foreign policy plank then took place within the Resolutions Committee, chaired by Senator Robert Wagner of New York. The State Department supplied Wagner with a draft plank prepared by Adolf A. Berle which emphasized the administration's efforts to prevent the outbreak of war and promised only to try to "limit, wherever possible, the spread of war." On July 9, Berle gave Wagner a new draft embodying FDR's promise to Congress not to send troops to Europe. Senator Wheeler, however, decided this pledge did not go far enough and told the Resolutions Committee that he would insist on a plank that stated, "We will not participate in foreign wars, and we will not send our army, naval or air forces to fight in foreign lands outside of the Americas." Senator James Byrnes of South Carolina, FDR's spokesman on the Resolutions Committee, opposed this wording as placing crippling restrictions on American foreign policy, and Wagner then appointed a subcommittee to work out a compromise.[55]

The subcommittee met nearly all day on Tuesday, July 16, the second day of the Democratic convention. Wheeler and senators Pat McCarran and David Walsh held out for the antiwar pledge, while Byrnes tried to substitute more elastic wording. Neither Breckinridge Long, Hull's representative at the convention, nor Senator Key Pittman, chairman of the Foreign Relations Committee, was permitted to take part in the discussions, which at one point were adjourned to a ladies' rest room in quest of privacy. Faced with threats by Wheeler and McCarran to walk out of the convention unless their plank was adopted, Byrnes finally called Roosevelt at Hyde Park to report the impasse. FDR and his chief speech-writer, Samuel Rosenman, discussed the question at length, and finally Roosevelt came up with an amendment to the antiwar pledge which read, "except in case of attack." After checking with Cordell Hull, who gave his grudging assent, Roosevelt called Byrnes back and told him he would accept the Wheeler wording with his amendment attached. Wheeler had no objection to Roosevelt's qualification, and the next day the Resolutions Committee adopted the revised draft, which the convention then approved without further discussion.[56]

"The American people are determined that war, raging in Europe, Asia and Africa, shall not come to America," the Democratic platform declared. "We will not participate in foreign wars, and we will not send our army, naval or air forces to fight in foreign lands outside of the Americas, except in case of attack." The platform went on to praise Roosevelt for warning the nation of the danger from aggression overseas and for taking the lead in preparedness. Expressing sympathy for "the peace-loving and liberty-loving peoples wantonly attacked by ruthless dictators," the Democrats promised to extend aid to them "consistent with law and not inconsistent with the interests of our own national self-defense." [57]

Thus the isolationists had succeeded in forcing Roosevelt to accept their point of view. The platform contained a stricter antiwar pledge than the Republican platform had made, and the promise of aid to the Allies was carefully qualified. Representatives of the interventionist Committee to Defend America by Aiding the Allies protested to Harry Hopkins, who was leading the movement to nominate Roosevelt, but there was little Hopkins could do to placate them. Liberal commentators, unhappy with the plank, contented themselves with the observation that platform promises did not mean much. Thus Marquis Childs dismissed the antiwar pledge as "an obeisance to isolationist emotions," while Robert Bendiner reminded his readers that platforms "have a life expectancy of about one week." Clearly Roosevelt had lost few supporters in making his peace with isolationists within his party.[58]

Meanwhile, the convention proceeded toward the inevitable nomination of Roosevelt, with relatively little mention of foreign policy issues. Unlike the week of the Republican convention, there was a lull in the war as Germany consolidated its position after the fall of France. The keynoter, Speaker of the House William Bankhead of Alabama, and outgoing National Chairman James Farley, both struck an antiwar note in their addresses, praising Roosevelt for keeping the nation out of the European conflict. The suspense over Roosevelt's willingness to run continued until Tuesday evening, July 16, when Senator Alben Barkley concluded his address to the convention by reading a statement Roosevelt had prepared in which he disclaimed any desire to continue as President and told the delegates that they were free "to vote for any candidate." This statement was designed to touch off a demand that Roosevelt be drafted. Mayor Ed Kelly of Chicago, leaving nothing to chance, arranged for his leather-lunged superintendent of sewers to begin a chant over the loudspeaker system: "We Want

Roosevelt," "Everyone Wants Roosevelt," "The World Wants Roosevelt." A "spontaneous" demonstration then went on for more than an hour, and there no longer was any doubt about the outcome. The next day the great majority of delegates voted for Roosevelt on the first ballot, with a scattering of support for Farley and Garner. Farley then graciously moved to make the nomination unanimous.[59]

The real fight came the next day, when Roosevelt insisted on making Secretary of Agriculture Henry A. Wallace his running mate. Cordell Hull, the delegates' first choice, refused to become an active candidate, preferring to remain as Secretary of State. When Hopkins got the news of FDR's choice, he warned that the delegates might rebel, saying, "So far there must be at least ten candidates who have more votes than Wallace." Most Democrats viewed Wallace as a dreamy New Dealer with little political appeal to add to the ticket and ill suited to succeed Roosevelt if anything should happen to him. Most of all, they resented dictation from the White House, and the next day Roosevelt's men had their hands full as seven other names were presented to the convention for the vice-presidency. After a hard fight, during which Roosevelt privately threatened to withdraw if his choice was not honored, Wallace finally won out over Speaker Bankhead.[60]

In his acceptance speech, delivered to the delegates by radio, Roosevelt sought to soothe the wounds and rally the party for the coming election. For the first time, he explained why he was willing to seek a third term. Using parts of the memorandum Archibald MacLeish had prepared for him early in the month, Roosevelt confessed that before the outbreak of the European war he had decided to retire at the end of his second term. But then he realized that as Commander-in-Chief he could not ask others to serve their country unless he heeded the call of duty himself. Declaring that it was "not an ordinary war" but "a revolution imposed by force of arms, which threatens all men everywhere," Roosevelt offered his services "in the defense of our institutions of freedom." He went on to say that he would not campaign in the usual sense, though he would speak out to "call the attention of the nation to deliberate or unwitting falsifications of fact, which are sometimes made by political candidates." Then Roosevelt proceeded to defend his record on foreign policy, claiming that he had used "every peaceful means" to halt the spread of dictatorship abroad. Those who criticized him for condemning acts of aggression he dismissed as "appeaser fifth-columnists," and declared, "I felt it my duty, my simple, plain, inescapable duty, to arouse my countrymen to the danger of the new forces let loose in the world." He concluded with a plea for the nation to resist "the false lullaby of appeasement," expressing the hope that if a new administration took office, "they will not seek to substitute appeasement and compromise with those who seek to destroy all democracies everywhere, including here." [61]

With one brilliant speech, Roosevelt had regained the political initiative. He had carefully avoided any reference to the antiwar pledge in his party's platform, and instead had stressed his determination to stand fast against the totalitarian forces in the world. By reminding voters that he stood on his own record of aid to the Allies short of war, rather than on a platform dictated by the isolationists, the President challenged the Republicans to debate his foreign policy. And by suggesting that the opposition party might fall prey to appeasement, he placed Willkie on the defensive.

The conventions were now over, and the two political parties had ended up in remarkably similar positions. Both had catered to isolationist sentiment within their ranks by adopting antiwar platforms, yet both had selected presidential candidates who were clearly in the interventionist camp. It seemed to many that foreign policy was thereby removed from the forthcoming campaign. Since Roosevelt and Willkie agreed on the formula of all-out aid to the Allies short of war, there was no issue between them. The British in particular were relieved, feeling that the basic policy of assistance to England would continue regardless of the election outcome. Thus a David Low cartoon showed the two candidates flipping a coin while Hitler watched from behind a tree. The caption read, "Heads we win, tails he loses." German diplomats, much less happy over developments, reached the same conclusion. "Willkie's nomination shifts the ground of the contest for the presidential election between him and the candidate of the Democratic party to purely domestic political issues," Hans Thomsen reported to Berlin. "In matters of foreign policy, the present difference between Willkie and Roosevelt is at most one of methods and not of belief." [62]

The continuing sense of crisis engendered by the war in Europe was bound to influence the coming campaign, however. No matter how much the candidates might agree in principle, they were likely to take different stands on the specific issues that were sure to arise. More important, President Roosevelt was in a far better position than Willkie to exploit the foreign policy crisis. "Fear is on the President's side," commented TVA director David Lilienthal in his diary. "A people who are afraid are not likely to seek a change if their leader is a strong and familiar person." Breckinridge Long expressed it more bluntly: "The issue in the campaign is foreign policy, and we are running it." Roosevelt would make the decisions in the months that lay ahead, and he had the ability to shape American policy to advance his own political cause, while Willkie could only protest from the sidelines. [63]

The real question was not whether foreign policy would enter into the campaign, but how responsible the two candidates would be in dealing with it. For Willkie, the great temptation would be to try to preempt the peace issue and accuse Roosevelt of leading the nation into war. Roosevelt, on the other hand, would have to restrain his natural desire to win by running against Adolf Hitler rather than Wendell Willkie. As early as May, TRB had warned that the 1940 campaign might become "a warm, sticky bath of hypocrisy." "The trick," he told his *New Republic* readers, "is to seem to stand for keeping our boys from dying on the battlefields of Europe and, at the same time, to be in favor of world democracy and against Hitler." [64]

2 34567

The election of 1940 would turn primarily on the nature and quality of the campaign Wendell Willkie waged against FDR, the acknowledged champ. At the outset, Willkie was confident. His dramatic upset-victory in Philadelphia had won him national acclaim, and a Gallup poll taken in midsummer showed him leading the President in electoral votes. Experienced politicians, however, knew that early polls meant very little (in August 1936 Landon had led Roosevelt), and they wondered how long it would take the Republican candidate to discard his amateur approach and master the difficult and subtle complexities of American presidential politics.[1]

Willkie first tackled the problem of organization. Going against the advice of professionals, he dismissed John D. M. Hamilton from the national chairmanship and proposed replacing him with a five-man committee. After Raymond Moley and Will H. Hays, an ex–national chairman, finally persuaded him against a group directorate, Willkie chose House Republican leader Joseph W. Martin as the new national chairman and campaign manager. It was a poor choice. Martin was a favorite of congressional Republicans, but he had little rapport with state and local party workers, and he was too busy with his Congressional duties to handle the job effectively. From the outset he was plagued by a serious rift between party regulars and the amateurs who surrounded Willkie, particularly Oren Root and Russell Davenport. "Living on top of a powder keg," was the way Martin described his new job, and although he kept on friendly terms with Willkie, he was never able to unify his campaign. Instead, the Willkie forces divided into three autonomous branches: the National Committee, headed by Martin; Democrats for Willkie, led by former Under Secretary of the Treasury John W. Hanes; and the Willkie for President clubs under Oren Root. The only man Willkie allowed to supervise this unwieldy machinery was Russell Davenport, an idealist with strong convictions but no practical experience in national politics.[2]

Awkward as this setup was, it did reflect Willkie's fundamental campaign strategy. Realizing that the Republicans were the minority party, he set out to win over the majority of independents and enough dissident Democrats to erode Roosevelt's normal margin of victory. Confident that the rank-and-file Republicans would vote for him, he felt he could ignore the regular leadership and instead woo anti-third-term Democrats and independents by playing down his party affiliation. A steady stream of Democratic defections throughout the summer, capped by Al Smith's announcement of support for Willkie, seemed to confirm the wisdom of his approach.

Foreign policy played a crucial role in Willkie's calculations. Many voters opposed Roosevelt for domestic reasons, but they supported his policy of aid to the Allies short of war. Though there were isolationists in both parties, most were Republicans, and Willkie reasoned that they would vote for him rather than Roosevelt, regardless of his stand on the war during the campaign. In early August, Willkie summoned William Allen White, leader of the interventionist Committee to Defend America, to a two-day meeting in Colorado Springs, where

Willkie had gone to prepare for the election. The two men went over a draft of Willkie's acceptance speech which he planned to give in mid-August, and agreed that he would make an unequivocal declaration of aid to the Allies in order to reassure interventionists who opposed FDR's bid for a third term. "Every recent major election has been determined by the independent voters," Willkie informed the press after his meeting with White. "I believe that this election will likewise be determined." Amateur though he was, Willkie had plotted out a shrewd course for his campaign that promised to test Roosevelt's political skill to the utmost.[3]

The President was equally aware of the importance of foreign policy to the election. In early August, Lowell Mellett, director of the Office of Government Reports, sent him a copy of a confidential poll which the Gallup organization had prepared for two Princeton professors. The results revealed dangerous crosscurrents in public attitudes toward the war. Although 59 percent of those questioned felt the United States should give priority to keeping out of the war, nearly three-quarters wanted to increase the level of aid to England. Almost half believed that England would win the war, but 69 percent thought that a German victory would endanger American security. Thus the poll indicated that Americans recognized the stake the United States had in the European conflict but still wanted to avoid direct involvement. Their presidential preferences were equally contradictory. Slightly more of them favored Willkie than Roosevelt, but when asked which candidate could "handle our country's foreign affairs better," they preferred Roosevelt by more than two to one. FDR, who told Mellett he found the poll "extremely interesting," must have realized how delicate his position was. The people clearly trusted his experience in foreign policy and approved his program of aid to the Allies, but they were also likely to desert him quickly if he flouted their strong desire to stay out of the war.[4]

Roosevelt, who would have preferred inaction, faced two critical foreign policy decisions in the summer of 1940. The first was conscription. A bipartisan group led by Republican Grenville Clark had been pressing for a selective service system since the German blitz. In June, Senator Edward R. Burke, an anti-New Deal Democrat, and Representative James Wadsworth, a New York Republican, introduced a bill proposing the registration of all men between the ages of 18 and 64 and the drafting of 400,000 single men between 21 and 30 by October 1, 1940. Roosevelt had casually spoken out in favor of the principle of "universal Government service" in a June press conference, but he tried to avoid any comment when reporters pressed him about the Burke-Wadsworth bill. Finally, on August 2, while still declining to comment on specific legislation, he allowed the press to quote him as saying, "I am in favor of a selective training bill and I consider it essential to adequate national defense." He refused further comment while Congress debated the conscription issue, but he was fully alive to its explosive political potential. Roosevelt agreed with a Tennessee politician who warned that passage of selective service might cost the Democrats the election, but he added that world conditions required him to "move for the preservation of American liberties and not just drift with what may or may not be a political doubt of the moment." [5]

The second issue, a British request for American destroyers that dated back to mid-May, was even trickier. Despite personal pleas from Winston Churchill and even from King George VI, Roosevelt had postponed consideration on grounds that Congress would never accept such a flagrantly unneutral act. Meanwhile, ardent interventionists had come up with the idea of swapping the destroyers to England in return for naval and air bases on British territory in the Western Hemisphere. Aware that Roosevelt was unlikely to accept this idea without some indication that Willkie would not make it a campaign issue, Archibald MacLeish, Librarian of Congress and occasional FDR speech-writer, volunteered to sound out the Republican candidate through Russell Davenport. Willkie replied that he could not make any such agreement since he did not have access to all the pertinent information about the transaction. Despite this rebuff, on August 2 Roosevelt decided to go ahead with plans for a destroyers-for-bases swap, and called on William Allen White to persuade Willkie to request that Republicans in Congress support the necessary legislation.[6]

White cut short a vacation in the Rockies to be briefed on the proposed destroyer deal by Cordell Hull, Henry Stimson, and Frank Knox in Washington; then he went to Colorado Springs to convince Willkie. Joseph Martin, already disturbed by the GOP candidate's tendency to speak out on all issues, advised him not to commit himself on any major foreign policy question. Willkie called conservative columnist Arthur Krock, who had broken the story of MacLeish's approach to Willkie. Krock reinforced Martin's advice, saying, "Whatever your viewpoint may be, do not in any way take a public position for or against the transfer." Accordingly, Willkie released a statement on August 9 saying he did not consider it "appropriate" to comment on "specific executive or legislative proposals" and reserving "an unhampered right of public discussion" on all Roosevelt's foreign policy moves. Two days later, a disappointed White sent a telegram to FDR telling him that it was not as bad as it seemed. "I know there is not two bits difference between you on the issue pending," White asserted. "But I can't guarantee either of you to the other." [7]

Pushed hard by interventionists, Roosevelt on August 14 decided to go ahead with the destroyer transfer. Interpreting White's telegram as indicating that Willkie was unlikely to "give much trouble" on this transaction, the President told Hull to proceed with the negotiations with England, thus bypassing Congress. Two days later, the *New York Times* published a front-page story speculating on a trade of destroyers for bases, and although Roosevelt admitted the government was discussing the acquisition of British territory for naval and air bases, he denied that it was linked to the transfer of destroyers. Roosevelt maintained this position throughout August, as negotiations for the eventual destroyers-for-bases deal continued, but undoubtedly he was delighted when a Gallup poll taken on August 17 showed that 62 percent of the people approved the idea of "selling fifty of our destroyers to England." Though he had originally wanted Willkie's prior endorsement, he could now look forward to offering the destroyer deal to a receptive American public as his own bold act of leadership.[8]

I

In mid-August, Wendell Willkie was putting the finishing touches on the acceptance speech which Russell Davenport had drafted for him. Returning to the old custom which FDR had upset in 1932 when he flew to the Democratic convention to accept in person, Willkie wanted the formal ceremonies to take place at Elwood, the small Indiana town where he had spent his boyhood. Homer Capehart, the phonograph manufacturer and Indiana political leader, made the arrangements for a political extravaganza, spending $40,000 to transform a park on the edge of Elwood into an open-air amphitheater. The bewildered townspeople watched in amazement as 65 special trains, 1,200 buses, and tens of thousands of automobiles brought more than 200,000 people to Elwood for the largest political rally in American history.[9]

Willkie left Colorado Springs on August 15 as the European war burst out again with the start of the Battle of Britain. On August 11, German planes began heavy raids over the channel ports and airfields in the south of England. The raids increased in intensity for the next few days as the RAF tried heroically to meet the Nazi aerial challenge. The *New York*

Times voiced the sentiments of millions of Americans when it declared, "This is not only Britain's hour of peril. It is our own. It is civilization's. It is humanity's." The American people, their emotions already committed, waited to hear Willkie's views on selective service, on the proposed destroyer transfer, and above all on Roosevelt's policy toward England—all aid short of war.[10]

In blazing midsummer heat on the morning of August 17, Willkie drove to Elwood from his family's home in Rushville. Joseph W. Martin, on hand to make the formal offer of candidacy to Willkie on behalf of the party, saw the text of the speech only a few minutes in advance and was appalled to find that it was double-spaced in small type which would be hard for Willkie to read as he spoke. The huge crowd, already restive in the heat and the overtaxed facilities of Elwood, grew quiet as Willkie mounted the wooden platform to accept the nomination and to share with them and a nationwide radio audience his thoughts on the grave world crisis.[11]

From the outset, Willkie repudiated isolationism and identified himself with the victims of aggression in Europe. He ended the suspense about his views on the draft by endorsing "some form of selective service," although like Roosevelt he refused to back the Burke-Wadsworth bill specifically. He avoided any direct comment on the sale of destroyers, but he implied his approval when he stated that the loss of the British fleet would be "a calamity for us" and would leave America "exposed to attack." Then, forthrightly and without equivocation, he aligned himself behind Roosevelt's twin policies of a strong national defense and aid to those fighting against aggressors, short of direct American involvement. "As an American citizen," Willkie declared, "I am glad to pledge my wholehearted support to the President in whatever action he may take in accordance with these principles." Having affirmed the goals Roosevelt sought, Willkie went on to criticize his methods, condemning FDR for "inflammatory statements and manufactured panics" and for a consistent failure "to take the American people into his confidence." Willkie promised that if he were elected, he would be more candid with the American people and less belligerent toward foreign governments.[12]

Willkie's speech disappointed his listeners who came to Elwood to hear a partisan political appeal, for instead they received a high-toned lecture. Lacking his usual buoyancy and exuberance, Willkie read the address in a flat voice that failed to arouse his audience. Only near the end, when he challenged FDR to a series of debates and promised "to outdistance Hitler in any contest he chooses in 1940 or after," did the crowd give him a sustained cheer.[13]

The national reaction, however, was much more encouraging. Interventionists, ignoring Willkie's criticisms of Roosevelt, praised him for endorsing the main features of the administration's foreign policy. "He has placed national interests above politics in this crisis," wrote Raymond Clapper. *Life* called it "a courageous speech," while the *New York Times* said Willkie demonstrated that he possessed "a true understanding of the tremendous forces which are now changing the world's history." Isolationists played up the passages critical of Roosevelt's methods, and kept silent about Willkie's refusal to make foreign policy a campaign issue. Nearly all observers agreed that his endorsement of conscription insured the passage of the Burke-Wadsworth bill. Secretary of War Henry Stimson privately called this part of the speech "a godsend" and praised Willkie for his "able and courageous" address.[14]

Though Roosevelt must have been pleased to have Willkie endorse his policy of aid to England, he carefully refrained from commenting on the speech. He was meeting with Canadian Prime Minister Mackenzie King in Ogdensburg, New York, when Willkie spoke, and he heard only part of the address. Later he told a diplomat, with a chuckle, that it was only an accident of timing that his meeting with the Canadian leader had stolen the headlines from Willkie. "He said that there were times when it was wiser and more effective not to campaign," the diplomat recorded in his diary, "and this was one of them." When reporters pressed the President for a public comment, he declined, saying only that he was too busy conducting the nation's affairs to take up Willkie's offer for a series of debates.[15]

Roosevelt asked Harold L. Ickes, his aggressive Secretary of the Interior, to give the official reply to Willkie's speech. In a nationwide radio address on August 19, Ickes delivered a scathing denunciation of Willkie, accusing him of "demagogy" and ridiculing him with the classic line, "Willkie, the simple barefoot Wall Street lawyer." Ickes did thank the GOP candidate for endorsing selective service and aid to England, but he focused his attention on the passages critical of FDR's leadership, claiming that Willkie "felt compelled to toss a sop to the bitter anti-Roosevelt isolationists." Above all, Ickes defended the President as "the world's symbol of fearless support of democratic principles, the emblem of the world's faith in freedom." And then, having put Roosevelt on the side of the angels, Ickes accused Willkie of being the candidate of the isolationists. "The Republican party in 1940," he concluded, "contains the equivalent of England's and France's pro-Nazi Munich appeasers of 1938—the men with the black umbrellas." [16]

Ten days later, Henry Wallace pressed home the appeasement charge in his own acceptance speech in Des Moines. Instead of dwelling on the farm issue, as most commentators expected, Wallace focused on the war, claiming that Hitler wanted to see FDR defeated. Praising Roosevelt as "the symbol of democracy" to people around the world, Wallace charged that every sign of opposition to him at home led to "rejoicing in Berlin." "I do not wish to imply that the Republican leaders are willfully or consciously giving aid and comfort to Hitler," the vice-presidential candidate hastened to add, "But I do want to emphasize that replacement of Roosevelt, even if it were by the most patriotic leadership that could be found, would cause Hitler to rejoice. I do not believe that the American people will turn their backs on the man that Hitler wants to see defeated." [17]

"A grand speech and splendidly given," Roosevelt telegraphed Wallace. Few others agreed. The *New York Times* was appalled by Wallace's "reckless" and "irresponsible" charges. "If this says anything," the *Times* commented, "it says that a vote for Mr. Willkie is a vote for Hitler." *Newsweek* made a similar comment, noting that Wallace had mentioned FDR twenty-eight times, Hitler twenty-three times, "and Willkie not once." Willkie refused to get involved in the public controversy, contenting himself with the remark that Wallace was "100 percent wrong." [18]

The Ickes and Wallace speeches indicated that Roosevelt planned to exploit the war crisis for political purposes in the forthcoming campaign. Pressed by a reporter about Wallace's implication that the Republicans were the party of appeasement, FDR answered, "It speaks for itself excellently—as I said in my telegram to him." In private, to David Lilienthal, he defended the speech, saying, "You can't say that everyone who is opposed to Roosevelt is pro-Nazi, but you *can* say with truth that everyone who is pro-Hitler in this country is also pro-Willkie." When Mayor Kelly of Chicago warned Roosevelt of the risk in this tactic, pointing out that isolationists "represent a substantial segment of voters," the President agreed that "it is necessary for us to talk quietly but effectively with appeasers and semi-appeasers," but he continued to allow Wallace to hammer away at the Republicans on the war issue. Realizing, as Willkie did, that the isolationists were likely to vote Republican anyway, he saw nothing to lose and much to gain by playing up to the interventionist sentiment, which was at its height during the Battle of Britain.[19]

These tactics created a difficult problem for Willkie. He had tried to remove foreign policy from the campaign by endorsing the administration's efforts to aid England. Instead of thanks, he had found himself labeled the appeasers' candidate and lumped with the isolationists. The fact that he was now endorsed by the more extreme antiwar forces, including the German-American Bund and Father Coughlin, the Detroit radio priest, added greatly to his embarrassment. Desperately, Willkie tried to fight back by disowning this unwanted support. "I am not interested in the support of anybody who stands for any form of prejudice as to anybody's race or religion or who is in support of any foreign economic or political philosophy in this country." Despite this statement, right-wing agitators continued to speak out for Willkie, and the German embassy, working behind the scenes, financed an extensive propaganda campaign in his behalf.[20]

Willkie faced an insoluble dilemma. The only easy way out would have been to reverse himself on aid to the Allies, take a frankly isolationist stand as many old guard leaders advised, and challenge Roosevelt directly on the issue of peace or war. Willkie's genuine sympathy for England made this course unacceptable to him at this point in the campaign. He chose to stand by his acceptance speech, unable to fight back effectively against FDR's sly tactics. One Republican summed up the situation aptly when he commented that Roosevelt was running against Adolf Hitler "with Willkie a poor third." [21]

Meanwhile, the negotiations for the destroyers-for-bases deal proceeded in great secrecy. Cordell Hull and Frank Knox met with British Ambassador Lord Lothian and made rapid progress until August 25, when Lothian reported that Churchill wanted to give the bases to the United States instead of swapping them for the destroyers. Hull carefully explained that Roosevelt had to justify the transfer of the destroyers to the British as a bargain in order to satisfy Congress and public opinion. Hull and Lothian finally worked out a compromise under which six bases would be regarded as payment for the ships and two would be free gifts. Roosevelt continued to worry about the political implications of this transaction, agreeing with Governor Herbert Lehman of New York, who warned him that he would get his head "knocked off." FDR told his secretary that Congress would "raise hell about this," but he went ahead and gave his approval on September 1.[22]

Cordell Hull and Lord Lothian carried out the formal transaction in an exchange of notes on September 2. The United States gave Britain fifty World War I vintage destroyers that had recently been reactivated in return for ninety-nine-year leases on base sites in six British territories in the Western Hemisphere, and a pledge by Churchill that in case of a German victory the British fleet would not be scuttled or surrendered. Two additional bases, on Newfoundland and Bermuda, were to be considered gifts, as Roosevelt put it, "generously given and gladly received." [23]

The President was returning from the dedication of the Great Smoky Mountains National Park on September 3 when he made the destroyer deal public. Calling reporters into his car, he coyly told them a big story was about to break in Washington, and then he began reading them his message informing Congress of the trade. Roosevelt stressed the vital importance of the bases for national security, telling Congress that it was "the most important action in the reinforcement of our national defense that has been taken since the Louisiana Purchase." In his impromptu press conference, he also compared his decision to bypass Congress with Jefferson's handling of Louisiana, saying that he had gone back 137 years for a historical precedent. "Personally," he told the press, "I think it is a damned good trade." [24]

The isolationist outcry was even greater than Roosevelt had anticipated. Republican senators denounced it as a "dictatorial step" and "an act of war," and John T. Flynn called for Roosevelt's impeachment. Although most critics focused on the means Roosevelt had employed, Joseph Pulitzer, Jr., publisher of the *St. Louis Post-Dispatch,* attacked the transaction itself. Calling Roosevelt "America's first dictator," Pulitzer charged that "If this secretly negotiated deal goes through, the fat is in the fire and we all may as well get ready for a full-dress participation in the European war." Antiwar groups reprinted Pulitzer's editorial in full-page advertisements in papers across the nation.[25]

Willkie reacted more cautiously at first. Indicating indirectly his approval of the trade, he expressed regret that Roosevelt had bypassed Congress and had kept the public in the dark. "The people have a right to know of such important commitments prior to and not after being made," he said on September 3. When Republican isolationists began to complain that he was too soft on FDR, Willkie changed his position. On September 5, he warned that the destroyer deal created a dangerous precedent and might lead Roosevelt toward bolder steps. "If he is reelected," Willkie commented, "he may trade away the Philippines without consulting Congress." The next day, Willkie went all out to denounce the destroyer deal as "the most arbitrary and dictatorial action ever taken by any President in the history of the United States." [26]

Willkie had seriously miscalculated national sentiment. Though the isolationists protested, the American people seemed quite pleased with the destroyer deal. Public opinion polls showed that six out of ten voters backed Roosevelt's action, and a survey of the nation's press revealed overwhelming editorial support. *Newsweek*'s captions on the story were typical: "Swap of Destroyers for Bases Makes U.S. Dream Come True; Nation's Eastern Flank Thus Made Almost Impregnable; General Public Thrilled." Most Americans, alarmed by the Battle of Britain and the real possibility of a German victory, were delighted that Roosevelt had protected the nation by acquiring key bases and a pledge that the British fleet would fight on in the New World. "That it likewise benefited Britain was, if not coincidental, at least secondary," commented *Newsweek*. Democratic orators were quick to take advantage of the public response to the destroyer deal. Thus Senator Robert Wagner, campaigning in Maine, called it "one of the great achievements of all time," citing it as "the direct result of the foresight, courage, and experience in national defense of President Roosevelt." [27]

The destroyers-for-bases trade capped a successful effort by the President to regain the lead over Willkie before the fall campaign began. A Gallup poll taken in late August showed FDR now ahead of Willkie in electoral votes, and the September *Fortune* poll revealed that the President was leading his Republican challenger 53.2 percent to 35.6 percent, with 10.8 percent undecided. In early September, Lowell Mellett again passed on the results of a secret Gallup poll that showed "a slow but steady shift" in Roosevelt's favor. This survey revealed a "decided shift" in favor of more aid to England, while a published Gallup poll taken about the same time showed that if Germany defeated England, the voters preferred Roosevelt to Willkie, 58 percent to 42 percent.[28]

Many political observers noted the slump in Willkie's support, and most attributed it to the renewal of the war crisis and Roosevelt's shrewd handling of foreign policy. David Lilienthal commented on the lift the destroyer deal gave Roosevelt's prospects, noting in his diary, "at the moment, it looks good for 'our side.' " Harold Ickes was so encouraged that he urged Roosevelt to play up foreign policy in the campaign, claiming that a nervous public wanted an experienced leader at the helm. Noting that the upswing in FDR's fortunes coincided with the Battle of Britain, Ickes observed, "the President's chances seem to be the greater the deeper the danger in which England finds itself." If Ickes was right, the outcome of the election would be determined as much by what happened in the skies over Britain and in the mind of Adolf Hitler as by the words and deeds of Willkie and Roosevelt.[29]

II

In mid-September, Wendell Willkie set out to regain the initiative from FDR by launching an intensive whistle-stop campaign through the West. Eager to bring his case to the people, Willkie ignored the party leaders who wanted him to conduct an orthodox political swing by concentrating on backing local GOP candidates and addressing himself primarily to Republican audiences. Although he permitted Representative Charles Halleck and John Hollister, Senator Taft's former law partner, to accompany him, Willkie continued to rely on Russell Davenport, Oren Root, and Lem Jones, a public relations expert, for advice. At first, he had planned to write all his own speeches, but finally he had been persuaded to assemble a team of ghostwriters led by Elliott V. Bell, former financial reporter for the *New York Times* and speech-writer for Dewey. The political advisers and writers, who included Raymond Leslie Buell, a foreign affairs specialist with interventionist sympathies, rode in "the squirrel cage" which separated the seventy-five reporters traveling in the front cars from Willkie, who worked alone in a magnificent mahogany-paneled private car at the end of the train.

For seven weeks, Willkie roamed the nation, traveling more than 17,000 miles through 30 states, giving 38 prepared speeches and more than 500 extemporaneous ones. He attracted large, enthusiastic crowds, and frequently stirred them with his raucous, aggressive speeches and his occasional touches of idealism. He was at his best with small groups where he could bring the full force of his personality to bear on individuals; he was least effective on the radio, where his high voice sounded shrill in contrast to FDR's reassuring baritone. Despite his great reserves of energy, Willkie grew exhausted from the hectic pace as he spent forty-two of the next fifty-one days on the campaign train. His temper grew short, and he increasingly alienated party leaders as he refused to meet with local dignitaries or accept the advice of professionals. Halleck left the train in disgust after three weeks, complaining that Davenport was the only person Willkie would listen to. But reporters continued to be taken with Willkie's magnetic charm, and they gave him an exceptionally good press, playing down the tensions on the train and portraying Willkie as leading a gallant crusade for new national leadership.[30]

Chicago was the first stop. Over a million people turned out to hear Willkie deliver a series of sharp attacks on FDR's foreign policy. He won the greatest applause when he said, "And I promise that, when I am President, I shall not send one American boy into the shambles of a European war." The next day, traveling south across Illinois, Willkie swung over to the other extreme to accuse Roosevelt of selling out the democracies in the 1930's with a policy of appeasement. Using material supplied by Arthur Krock and Raymond Leslie Buell, Willkie cited the Munich pact to charge that Roosevelt, "the great appeaser," had "telephoned Hitler and Mussolini and urged them to sell Czechoslovakia down the river." When reporters questioned him about this accusation, Willkie backed down slightly, telling an audience at Peoria that the President had urged England and France to attend the Munich conference, "where they sacrificed Czechoslovakia." At the same time, Willkie continued to pledge "not to send American boys into the shambles of a European war," and added, in an obvious appeal for isolationist support, "If you elect my opponent you will have no such guarantee." Near the end of the day, with his advisers in turmoil over the conflicting charges and his voice barely audible from two days of shouting at the crowds, Willkie canceled four scheduled stops and sped on to Kansas City to prepare for a major address at Coffeyville, Kansas.[31]

The first two days of campaigning had proved to be a chastening experience for Willkie. Although he felt that Wallace's and Ickes' use of the appeasement theme had justified his attack on Roosevelt, the nation's press condemned him, and Secretary of State Hull issued a stinging rebuke. Buell, ill with pneumonia, left the train at St. Louis, to be replaced by Brooks Emeny, a more cautious foreign policy expert. Willkie, recovering his voice with the assistance of a throat specialist flown in from Hollywood, dropped the Munich line from his whistle-stop talks. When he spoke at Coffeyville, he stuck to domestic issues, condemning Roosevelt for weakening democracy by excessive reliance on big government. "A man who cannot save democracy in peace," Willkie warned, "cannot save it in crisis." [32]

On the West Coast, Willkie continued to straddle the war issue. In Los Angeles, he focused again on the New Deal, but delivered a sharp dig by comparing the Democratic platform's promise to stay out of war with Roosevelt's 1932 pledge to reduce the cost of government spending. "I hope and pray that he remembers the pledge of the 1940 platform better than he did the one of 1932. If he doesn't, you better get ready to get on the transports." In San Francisco the next day, Willkie took the opposite tack in his first major address on foreign policy. He began by restating the appeasement line in modified form, leaving out the Munich charge but accusing FDR of contributing to the weakness of the European democracies with unwise economic policies which "opened the way to the aggressive designs of Hitler." But then he identified himself clearly and openly with England, declaring, "We must send, and we must keep sending, aid to Britain, our first line of defense and our only remaining friend. We must aid her to the limit of prudence and effectiveness." [33]

Willkie's belated call for help to England came as the Battle of Britain reached its peak. Shifting from the early attacks on channel ports and airfields in the south of England, the Luftwaffe had begun massive raids on London designed to terrorize the British into submission. The American people, stirred by the gallant stand of the RAF and the English nation, became increasingly interventionist in sentiment. As a result, Willkie's first probing attacks on FDR's foreign policy backfired, contributing to a sharp decline in his popularity. In a Gallup poll taken on September 19, Roosevelt was leading in 38 states with 453 electoral votes, compared to Willkie's 10 states and 78 electoral votes. Roosevelt was now the choice of 56 percent of the electorate, and Willkie had fallen to a low of 38 percent, with only 6 percent undecided. Though some Republicans thought Gallup's figures must be mistaken (and some Democrats feared a deliberate distortion designed to make them overconfident), Senator Vandenberg decided that Willkie's cause was hopeless. He told his son, "We ought to do everything possible to save Michigan's Republican representation anyway." [34]

While Willkie struggled to master the techniques of campaigning, FDR stayed in Washington to guide national policy during the war crisis. He took occasional nonpolitical trips to visit defense plants as part of his preparedness program, and in mid-September he signed the draft bill which Congress had finally enacted despite significant Republican opposition. "He doesn't have to say a word about the campaign to make it patent that he is appealing to the voters every day by his constant and at times dramatic dealings with matters of foreign relations and national defense," commented Turner Catledge. "Who can think of strictly domestic issues with bombs raining in Piccadilly Circus . . . ?" Pointing out that newspapers relegated news of Willkie's campaign to the inside pages, *Time* complained that the headlines "were split between Franklin Roosevelt and the war." [35]

Roosevelt's one venture into active campaigning at this time came on September 11 when he addressed the Teamsters Union convention in Constitution Hall. Though most of the nationally broadcast speech dealt with domestic issues, FDR used this forum to assert his support for the antiwar pledge in the Democratic platform, repeating its firm ban on the use of American armed forces in foreign lands except in case of attack, and then commenting, "I hate war, now more than ever. I have one supreme determination—to do all that I can to keep war away from these shores for all time." Evidently the President decided that after the destroyer deal he needed to reassure the people and guard against a Republican assault on him as a warmonger. Yet five days later, when he issued the call for all men between 21 and 36 to register for the draft in October, Roosevelt avoided any further concessions to isolationist sentiment by stressing the need to be strong and on guard against "the philosophy of force now rampant in the world." "May we all strengthen our resolve to hold high the torch of freedom in this darkening world," he asked the nation, "so that our children and their children may not be robbed of their rightful inheritance." [36]

The President let Henry Wallace bear the brunt of campaigning throughout September. Concentrating on the farm states of the Middle and Far West, Wallace spoke in many of the cities Willkie visited as he traveled more than seven thousand miles in the first seventeen days. Reiterating the appeasement theme he had set forth in his acceptance speech, Wallace kept charging that Hitler wanted Roosevelt to lose the election. He was careful to admit that Willkie was not an appeaser or an admirer of the German dictator. "I'll say, too," Wallace conceded, "that every Republican is not an appeaser. But you can be sure that every Nazi, every Hitlerite, and every appeaser is a Republican." Accompanied only by a two-man staff, Wallace proved to be an unexpectedly tough political fighter who stuck doggedly to "this campaign to keep Hitler out of the White House," as Hugh Johnson put it.[37]

It soon became clear that the attempt to label Willkie and the Republicans as appeasers was a major part of Roosevelt's reelection strategy. On September 30, Governor Herbert Lehman of New York, the highest ranking Jewish officeholder in the country, told his party's state convention that "nothing that could happen in the United States could give Hitler, Mussolini, Stalin and the Government of Japan more satisfaction than the defeat of the man who typifies to the whole world the kind of free, humane government which dictators despise— Franklin D. Roosevelt." The *New York Times* labeled Lehman's speech "reckless" and observed, "If this says anything, it says that a vote for Mr. Willkie is a vote for Hitler." Lehman never retracted his remarks, however, and less scrupulous Democrats published a pamphlet which stressed Willkie's German ancestry to suggest that he was soft on fascism.[38]

On October 4, the President himself injected the appeasement issue into the campaign in an indirect fashion during the course of his morning press conference. When a friendly reporter asked him if he thought Germany and Italy wanted to see him defeated, Roosevelt responded by reading a *New York Times* dispatch by Herbert Matthews from Rome. Commenting on the forthcoming meeting of Hitler and Mussolini at the Brenner Pass, Matthews wrote, "the Axis is out to defeat President Roosevelt . . . because of the President's foreign policy and because of everything for which he stands in the eyes of the Italians and Germany." Roosevelt refused to comment on the story, just chuckling when a reporter quipped, "Pretty good ad, isn't it?" When several journalists pressed him, he simply said, "I am just quoting the press at you," as the reporters laughed.[39]

Though some interventionist commentators felt that Roosevelt was guilty of exploiting the appeasement theme, most defended his tactics on the grounds that the European dictators did indeed want to see him defeated. On October 9, Dorothy Thompson, who admired both candidates, finally announced her decision to support the President, citing his superior knowledge and experience in world affairs. Five days later, she shocked her Republican readers by charging that there was not "the slightest shadow of a doubt" that the Axis powers wanted Roosevelt defeated, and were doing everything possible to help Willkie win. Freda Kirchwey took a similar position in the *Nation,* writing that pro-Axis groups in the United States were rallying behind the Republican candidate without his knowledge. "Poor Willkie," she commented, "is fighting for election on a non-appeasement program with pro-appeasement backing against the man who is actually carrying out a non-appeasement policy." [40]

Roosevelt undoubtedly gained by lumping Willkie with the dictators. Any losses of those offended by such blatant tactics were more than offset by gains among Jewish, Polish, and Scandinavian voters who were already inclined to favor the more interventionist candidate. Even those without ethnic biases were likely to agree that Roosevelt stood as a greater symbol of resistance to totalitarianism than Willkie, who was relatively unknown outside the United States. Moreover, this interventionist appeal was unlikely to offend isolationists, who for the most part shared the national distaste for Hitler, disagreeing only on how to respond to him. Thus, by encouraging his subordinates to portray the election as one in which Roosevelt was running against Hitler, the President capitalized on the war issue in a dramatic and highly effective way.

III

In late September, the war took a new and startling turn when Hitler announced that he had signed the Tripartite Pact linking Germany and Italy in Europe with Japan in Asia. Although the published terms indicated it was defensive in nature, the new alliance threatened the United States with an eventual two-ocean war against the Axis powers. Roosevelt responded by extending to Japan the controls on exports which he had imposed in July to cover all scrap iron as well as high-octane gasoline. At the same time, he announced that aid to England would be increased, not lessened, in the face of this new threat to American security. Though Hull and Henry Wallace issued public statements playing down the Tripartite Pact, saying that it only formalized an existing relationship, it seems likely that Hitler had taken this step, as historian Saul Friedlander has argued, "to influence the American electorate and contribute to Roosevelt's defeat with this new demonstration of German power." [41]

Whatever Hitler's motives, the German-Japanese alliance intensified the threat to American security and marked a setback for Roosevelt's foreign policy. The President's critics were quick to argue that FDR had unnecessarily driven the Japanese into Hitler's arms. "[T]his alliance creates a situation of grave danger to the United States," commented the isolationist *Christian Century*. "President Roosevelt's attempts to intervene in Europe and Asia 'by measures short of war' have now left this country squarely in the middle of a possible conflict upon both our ocean fronts at once." Arthur Krock took a similar position in urging Willkie to make the Tripartite Pact a campaign issue, while interventionist journals, equally sensitive to the political impact of the new alliance, begged Willkie to stand behind the President. [42]

The Republican candidate was not in a mood to be cooperative. He deeply resented the implication that he was the appeasers' candidate, and he denounced Lehman's September 30 speech as "false, malicious and subversive." Although he had abandoned the war issue for the past two weeks, except to reply to attacks, his popularity continued to sag: the Gallup poll showed him leading in only five states with thirty-two electoral votes by early October. Despite the failure of his earlier efforts to exploit foreign policy issues, and despite his own deeply held convictions, he decided that since his opponent was playing politics with the war he must do likewise. [43]

Willkie spoke out on the Tripartite Pact for the first time in a Cleveland speech on October 2. Claiming that the alliance proved that the dictators "are thinking of the United States in terms of war, in terms of our participation in some bloody conflict of the future," he promised he would do all he could to keep the nation out of such a war. He went on to accuse the New Dealers of failing to prepare the nation for the present danger, but he was careful to reiterate his continued support for the policy of aid to England. By maintaining British resistance and building up America's defenses, he argued, he could offer the nation the protection that Roosevelt had failed to provide.[44]

The following week, as he began his first campaign swing into the East, Willkie became bolder. In New Jersey he charged Roosevelt with edging the United States toward war as well as dragging "the wars of Europe and Asia into American politics." Invading New York City, hostile territory for a Republican in 1940, Willkie implied that Roosevelt had made secret commitments that might lead to war. "Are there any international understandings to put America into the war that we citizens do not know about?" Willkie asked. Near the end of a talk at a Bronx high school, he turned to the audience and asked, "Is there anyone here who really thinks that the President is sincerely trying to keep us out of war?" In New England he kept repeating his question to the President about secret commitments, saying that the people had a right to know "if there are any secret treaties . . . which might involve us in war." In Boston, at the climax of this trip, Willkie again denounced Roosevelt for suggesting that the dictators wanted a Republican to win and then gave an unqualified antiwar pledge: "To begin with, we shall not undertake to fight anybody else's war. Our boys shall stay out of European wars." [45]

Roosevelt ignored this fresh attack on his foreign policy as he prepared a major Columbus Day address which he planned to deliver to the nation from Dayton, Ohio. Although the main theme would be international affairs, Democratic politicians put great pressure on him to include a kind word for Italian-Americans on a holiday that held special meaning for them. Ever since his stab-in-the-back reference to Italy in the Charlottesville speech, Americans of Italian ancestry had been angry at Roosevelt, and many were threatening to bolt the Democratic party in November. Italians were particularly sensitive to "an association with a stiletto or a knife," one Connecticut congressman told Roosevelt in pleading for a retraction, while a New York Congressional candidate warned Democratic National Chairman Flynn that the Italians were "off the reservation" this year. The Italian vote was particularly crucial in New York State, and Roosevelt was undoubtedly relieved when Mayor Fiorello LaGuardia of New York, an independent, endorsed him in September, saying, "I prefer Roosevelt with his known faults to Mr. Willkie with his unknown virtues." To help ease the situation further, Roosevelt agreed to send a Columbus Day greeting to Generoso Pope, publisher of the leading Italian-language newspaper in New York, which was read to a gathering of 1,800 prominent Italian-Americans, and to begin his Dayton speech with a flattering reference to the contributions of Italians to American history.[46]

The President started out for Dayton on October 11, stopping off in Pittsburgh and Akron to meet with local Democratic leaders. The huge crowds along the way belied the supposedly nonpolitical nature of the trip. The State Department had provided a routine draft for the speech, which was to inaugurate a new short-wave radio station beamed at Latin America. Robert Sherwood, the playwright whose strong interventionist sympathies had led him to become a speechwriter for FDR, argued with presidential aide Harry Hopkins for a strong speech that would clearly reject isolationism. When Hopkins told him that in Roosevelt's mind "there is absolutely nothing important in the world today but to beat Hitler," Sherwood and Sam Rosenman transformed the bland State Department draft into a bold and hard-hitting defense of the policy of all-out aid to the Allies.

"The people of the United States, the people of all the Americas, reject the doctrine of appeasement," Roosevelt declared in his address. "They recognize it for what it is—a major weapon of the aggressor nations." Stressing his determination to defend the entire Western Hemisphere, the President asserted "the right to the peaceful use of the Atlantic and Pacific oceans." He praised the British for their gallant stand against "the forces of evil" and restated his basic policy: "We will continue to help those who resist aggression, and who now hold the aggressors far from our shores." [47]

The Dayton speech, unlike the address to the Teamsters a month before, contained no reference to the antiwar platform pledge. Interventionists were delighted. *Time,* usually critical of FDR, praised the speech for its "lofty, sermon-like quality," while David Lilienthal wrote in his diary, "I thought it was tremendous, bold, unafraid, touching in its reference to Britain, and good politics as well." [48] The Dayton speech seemed to indicate that Roosevelt was through hedging against isolationism and was now ready to challenge Willkie's emerging antiwar tactics with a forthright reassertion of all-out aid to those fighting the Axis powers.

IV

"In the final analysis, I think the election may turn at the last moment on the war psychology," Arthur Vandenberg wrote to a despairing Republican friend. The polls seemed to bear him out. Gallup reported in early October that Roosevelt was now the choice of 56 percent of the voters, an all-time high, and commented that "a large part of Roosevelt's popularity is due solely to the fact that there is a war in Europe." Later in the month, Gallup asked voters whom they would favor if there were peace in Europe; a surprising 53 percent replied Willkie and only 47 percent Roosevelt. Noting that the war was particularly important to middle-income voters who had mixed feelings about the New Deal, Gallup stated, "The conclusion seems inescapable that if Roosevelt wins it will be because of the conflict abroad." [49]

A confidential report prepared for Willkie by a private research organization came to similar conclusions. Observing that national security was the "prime concern" of most Americans, the report stated, "The 'enemy-at-the-gates' psychology has given the Administration a new lease on its political life, and may result in a third term." But the authors also noted that a lull in the war would hurt Roosevelt politically by lessening the sense of crisis and enabling Willkie to exploit latent antiwar feelings. By mid-October, a prolonged pause in the fighting did take place. Although the German Luftwaffe continued its nightly bombings of London, the Nazi failure to drive the RAF from the skies had ended any possibility of a successful invasion. Hitler won headlines by his dramatic meeting with Mussolini at Brenner Pass, but he undertook no new military adventures. As 16 million American men prepared to register for the draft, it seemed expedient, as Vandenberg suggested, to appeal to "a vast underlying mass revulsion against the idea that America should be drawn into this war." Although his admirers later claimed that old guard professionals talked a desperate Willkie into a last-minute antiwar crusade, the candidate had toyed with this tactic from the outset, and probably needed no special urging to rely upon it at the climax of his campaign. Still stung by the appeasement charges, Willkie decided to do the only thing that seemed likely to rescue his candidacy: outbid Roosevelt for the peace vote.[50]

Willkie began the new tactic in a massive indoor rally at St. Louis, where he spoke on a nationwide radio hookup before 27,000 cheering admirers. At the outset he repeated the question he had asked Roosevelt rhetorically in New York City: "Has he entered into any secret pact or agreement with any foreign power which may involve us in war?" Mingling domestic with foreign themes, he went on to charge that the failure of the New Deal to pull the nation out of the depression had weakened the European democracies and had thus led to the present world crisis. Willkie then gave the pledge that brought the crowd to its feet: "We do not want to send our boys over there again. . . . And if you elect me President, we won't. But by the same token I believe if you reelect the third-term candidate, they will be sent." America could best contribute to the defeat of Hitler by producing more goods, he continued, not by sending armies overseas. "Production is the road to peace, and the only road to peace." [51]

In Chicago several lays later, Willkie told an equally large and enthusiastic audience that Roosevelt was not to be trusted on the issue of war or peace. "If his promise to keep our boys out of foreign wars is no better than his promise to balance the budget," he declared, "they're already almost on the transports." In a radio interview financed by the Republican National Committee, Willkie made the same point. "I have a real fear that this Administration is heading for war, and I am against our going to war and will do all that I can to avoid it," he affirmed. Asked later in the program how likely it was that those drafted would fight overseas, Willkie responded, "[M]y greatest effort will be to do all that is humanly possible to avoid war." [52]

While Willkie developed the antiwar theme in the midwest, his supporters pushed it hard in other parts of the nation. The two antagonists of 1928, Herbert Hoover and Al Smith, now united to warn that the New Deal was "trying to get us into war." The men Willkie had defeated in the spring, Taft and Dewey, joined in the effort, accusing Roosevelt of "furtive dealings" and of "doing nothing to avert a drift closer to war." Arthur Vandenberg, flattered when Willkie followed his advice, began making speeches for him in Michigan and Indiana. "I think we have them on the run," Willkie telegraphed Vandenberg on October 22. "God bless you and keep up the good work." [53]

Political observers began to notice a sharp surge for Willkie during the third week of October. "A subsurface, anti-war psychology seems to be taking hold generally and almost suddenly, right at the climax of the campaign," commented Turner Catledge. David Lilienthal noted in his diary that the Willkie campaign had come to life in mid-October, and "now presents a real threat." "That pounding away at fear in the minds of people naturally fearful, with all that is going on the world over, is bound to have an effect," Lilienthal concluded. The polls reflected the new Willkie momentum. The Republican candidate picked up one and a half points in the Gallup poll between October 6 and October 27, and made an even more impressive gain of 89 electoral votes in the same period. The gamblers' odds on a Willkie victory dropped from 12 to 5 to 7 to 5 as Gallup reported a Willkie surge "reminiscent of his dramatic gain on the eve of the Republican convention last summer." Roosevelt's percentage fell to 53 percent, a margin of only six points, by the end of the month. "The Republican candidate," Gallup declared, "is narrowing the contest to the point where he is now within easy striking distance of victory." [54]

Willkie's sudden resurgence led worried Democrats to urge Roosevelt to abandon his acceptance-speech pledge not to engage in active campaigning. Callers at the White House warned the President that Willkie had hit a sensitive public nerve with his antiwar theme. Professionals pointed out that the draft brought the issue home personally to millions of Americans, and they suggested that the President reassure mothers and fathers that their sons would not be sent into foreign wars. Mayor LaGuardia even urged the President to defer the first call for draftees "until after the election." Roosevelt refused to waver on selective service, defending the draft on registration day, October 16, as necessary in "preparation for total defense" to meet a threat which "has been imposed upon us from without." Thirteen days later, just before the election, the government issued a call for 800,000 men. Roosevelt presided at a brief ceremony at which Secretary of War Henry Stimson drew the first number from a large glass jar. Although FDR was careful to call the draft "a muster," to remind the people of the Minutemen at Concord and Lexington, he did not flinch from carrying through a step vital to national security despite the political risk involved. Noting that many people believed Roosevelt would delay acting until after the election, Stimson commented, "It was thus a brave decision on the part of the President to let it come now." [55]

Roosevelt proved more pliable on the question of campaigning, however. On October 17, Secretary of the Interior Harold Ickes held a long meeting with FDR, urging him to reply to Willkie and submitting two drafts for a public announcement of stepped-up activities. The next day, the President released a revised copy of one of the statements Ickes had prepared, telling reporters that he would give five political speeches within the next two weeks. He reminded reporters that in his acceptance speech he had said he would call attention to "deliberate or unwitting falsifications of fact," and he now felt it was time to go to the people to clear up Willkie's "misrepresentations." Carefully stressing his vital role in the continuing national emergency, he said he would limit his travels to areas within twelve hours of Washington, so that he could quickly return to make decisions. Privately, Roosevelt indicated that his return to the campaign trail was based more on anger at Willkie's warmongering charges than on fear of a Republican victory. "As far as Willkie was concerned," he permitted Lowell Mellett to tell Ickes, "all bets were off and . . . we could go after him with our bare hands." [56]

The President made his first avowed political speech of the campaign in Philadelphia on October 23. Huge crowds lined the streets as he drove through the city before going to Convention Hall, where Willkie had been nominated four months earlier, to address over 16,000 cheering admirers. Sticking to the announced theme of repudiating Republican falsehoods, FDR dealt first with Willkie's charge that he had made secret agreements that could lead to war. "I give to you and to the people of this country this most solemn assurance: There is no secret treaty, no secret obligation, no secret commitment, no secret understanding in any shape or form, direct or indirect, with any other Government, or any other nation in any part of the world, to involve this nation in any war or for any other purpose." Pleased with the huge cheer this all-embracing denial evoked, Roosevelt went on to domestic issues, but at the climax of his speech he returned to foreign policy to charge that Willkie's war warnings were designed "to strike terror into the hearts of our citizens." Claiming that his own sole objective in foreign policy was to keep the war away from the Americas, he repeated the Democratic platform's antiwar pledge. "It is for peace that I have labored," Roosevelt concluded, "and it is for peace that I shall labor all the days of my life." [57]

"The President was never in better form," commented a *New York Times* reporter. He had used his special mixture of irony, humor, and ridicule of his opponent to lift the crowd to a high pitch of enthusiasm and a standing ovation when he finished. "He was sarcastic, sly, arch, tough, ironic, intimate, confidential," *Time* noted. "He ad libbed, he laughed, rolled his head sidewise, lifted his eyes in mock horror. The audience ate it up." As the politicians had hoped, he did stress the peace issue and joined Willkie in ignoring the policy of all-out aid to England with its obvious risk of involvement. The Republicans had thus succeeded in forcing the President to qualify his foreign policy at the height of the campaign, but they failed to gain the political advantage they sought. FDR's personal involvement in the campaign rekindled the fervor he had stirred up in the past and invigorated the Democrats as the election approached.[58]

V

Isolationists rallied to Willkie's side as he raised the war issue. America First, the pressure group formed in response to the destroyer deal, avoided taking an official stand on the election, but its executive committee was almost unanimously for Willkie and the local chapters made no secret of their opposition to FDR. Their most effective speaker, Charles A. Lindbergh, delivered a ringing antiwar address at the height of the campaign. Though he mentioned no names, nearly all observers interpreted his remarks as aimed against FDR, especially his statement, "Above all, we must select leaders whose promise we can trust, who know where they are taking us, and who can tell us where we are going." Hugh Johnson, a member of the group's executive committee, was more outspoken. "We are hell bent for war," he informed those who were to be drafted. "The Third Term means war for all these boys." [59]

Many isolationists outside the ranks of America First announced their support for Willkie in October. The editors of the *Christian Century,* a Protestant journal, broke with tradition by endorsing the Republican candidate, who they felt genuinely wanted to stay out of war. "He has betrayed no messianic complex, no itch to solve the problems of Europe and Asia," they wrote of Willkie. Oswald Garrison Villard, who had quit the *Nation* over the war issue, came out reluctantly for Willkie, saying that if he were elected, "there will be at least a good fighting chance to stay out of it." More extreme isolationists called for a Republican victory on grounds that FDR was manufacturing a war scare. One pamphlet labeled Roosevelt the real threat to American freedom and called upon the people "to quarantine the aggressor in the White House." [60]

Democrats worried most about isolationist sentiment among Catholic voters, especially Irish-Americans whose traditional hatred of England made them critical of Roosevelt's policy. Catholic voters were an integral part of the New Deal coalition, and it came as a shock when Rev. James M. Gillis, editor of the *Catholic World,* told his readers that Roosevelt was too "inconsistent and unpredictable" to be trusted with the vital decision of war and peace. Asserting that the President's Dayton speech was a virtual challenge to the dictators, Gillis concluded, "We can stay out of war if on November 5th we vote Franklin D. Roosevelt out of office." The Jesuit journal *America* also opposed FDR's reelection; thus only the liberal Catholic periodical *Commonweal,* whose editors were divided, remained uncommitted. Though no more than a small percentage of Catholics were likely to heed the advice of editorial writers, their defection would hurt Roosevelt by cutting into a group that traditionally voted Democratic.[61]

The most dramatic isolationist bolt came on October 25 when John L. Lewis, head of the powerful CIO, delivered a nationwide radio address announcing his support for Willkie. In explaining his decision, Lewis stressed the war, accusing Roosevelt of moving the nation steadily toward involvement. "The President has said that he hates war and will work for peace, but his acts do not match his words," Lewis declared. Newspapers reported that Democrats-for-Willkie had financed Lewis' speech, but in fact James Rhodes Davis, a wealthy oil man with close ties to German agents, had bought the radio time. Hans Thomsen had been working since July to encourage Lewis' break with FDR. Although the labor leader was probably unaware of the German involvement, he had become a part of an extensive Nazi effort to influence the election outcome. The Lewis speech and a less successful attempt to publish a Polish document indicating FDR's plans for war led historian Alton Frye to conclude that the German efforts "constituted one of the most massive interferences in American domestic affairs in history."[62]

It is questionable whether the outpouring of the isolationist support in October really helped Willkie. Although the German activities did not become public, many Americans reacted unfavorably to the obviously vindictive nature of John L. Lewis' break with FDR. Most observers doubted that Lewis could carry the rank-and-file of labor with him. Indeed, the open support from isolationists may well have led many undecided Americans to vote for the President. The opponents of war were only a small minority, and their shrill charges and unfounded accusations had little appeal for more moderate citizens. The polls showed that by October nearly 60 percent of the people placed aid to Britain ahead of staying out of the war. Willkie could gain by a subtle appeal to avoid direct involvement, even among those who favored aid to England, but blatant isolationist backing could only hurt his cause.[63]

The Democrats responded to the isolationist support for Willkie by stepping up their attempt to portray the election as one of Roosevelt against Hitler. "President Roosevelt can defend himself on most of the issues but he cannot come out and say that the dictators are against him," one supporter advised Harry Hopkins. "Here is a job that *must* be done by a third party." There was no lack of volunteers for this assignment. Solicitor General Francis Biddle told a Harvard audience, "Of course, Hitler wants Roosevelt defeated." Chairman Ed Flynn charged that "Herr Hitler and the Axis generally are doing what they can to accomplish the defeat of President Roosevelt." Governor Lehman, in a speech Samuel Rosenman helped him revise, claimed that Willkie was under the influence of "the motley crowd of appeasers and extreme isolationists in and out of Congress who are the leaders of the Republican party." Harold Ickes accused the Germans of waging "a campaign to defeat Roosevelt, the experienced statesman who Nazis believe is capable of defending this country against the dictators." And Dorothy Thompson announced on a CBS broadcast three days before the election, "A vote for Wendell Willkie is a vote for fascism." At the same time, former Ambassador to Poland Anthony J. Drexel Biddle, Jr., and his wife spent forty-five days traveling to fifteen cities with large Polish populations to describe the German conquest of Poland while calling for FDR's reelection.[64]

It was still Henry Wallace, however, who bore the main brunt in denouncing Willkie as an appeaser. He shifted the point of his attack slightly in late October when he argued that it was the Republican candidate's lack of experience that endeared him to the dictators. Hitler, Wallace told a Philadelphia rally, "would rejoice to have in office a well-meaning but inexperienced man who cannot understand the Nazi plots." In contrast, the Axis leaders opposed FDR, Wallace asserted, "because he knows their tricks and because he is a man they cannot take in." The vice-presidential candidate saved his most demagogic charges for an American Labor party rally in Madison Square Garden on October 31. Referring to Willkie repeatedly as "the man Hitler wants elected President," Wallace told his supporters: "Millions of Americans know from personal observation the extent of Nazi propaganda and Nazi performance for the election of the Republican candidate. Regimented Nazi organizations are marching in the Republican parade." [65]

The Democrats may have gone too far in pushing the appeasement issue. One of Harry Hopkins' informants advised him to tone down Wallace's attacks, saying that they served "only to increase current isolationist midwestern apprehension that Democratic victory would tend to lead us toward war." The obvious British desire to see FDR defeat Willkie tended to reinforce this fear. "I know, at any rate, no Englishman who does not feel that your triumph will be our own," Harold Laski wrote Roosevelt on October 20, and the day before the election the *Daily Express* commented in London that "the best thing that could happen to Britain Tuesday is the reelection of our tried friend Roosevelt." The constant alignment of Willkie with the Axis implied that Roosevelt was wholeheartedly on the side of Britain, and while this was in accord with the prevailing national sympathies, it tended to confirm Willkie's claim that a third term for FDR meant war for the United States.[66]

As the campaign approached its climax, both sides tried to gain support by exploiting men closely associated with Roosevelt's foreign policy. Willkie made the first move when he announced in a Chicago speech on October 22: "To fill the post of Secretary of State, I shall choose the ablest man in the United States on foreign affairs. I shall choose him for his knowledge, his ability and his integrity and not for any other consideration." Reporters were quick to suggest that Willkie had Cordell Hull in mind. David Lawrence, writing his nationally syndicated column from the Republican campaign train, stated on October 24 that Willkie's close friends were certain that he planned to ask Hull to serve as his Secretary of State. Citing the precedent of Knox and Landon, Lawrence wrote, "There seems little doubt but that Mr. Hull would agree to serve." Two days later, radio broadcaster H. V. Kaltenborn reported the same news to his nationwide audience.[67]

Cordell Hull was furious. From the outset he had made it clear to both Democrats and Republicans that he did not wish to be involved in the campaign, believing that foreign policy should be above partisanship. As letters began coming in urging him to stay on if Willkie won, he was in a quandary. If he said no, then he would appear unpatriotic, declining to serve his country at a time of crisis, but if he answered affirmatively, he would aid Willkie's campaign. He went ahead with plans for a nonpartisan radio address on foreign policy which he gave on October 26, but he kept silent on the political issues. The Democratic National Committee became very concerned. James T. Mathews described the flood of letters coming in asking about Hull and told Chairman Flynn that the purpose of the Republican move was "to assure the people that foreign policy is no issue." Flynn sent the letters on to Hull with the suggestion that he make a second radio speech, this one avowedly political, in which the Secretary would endorse Roosevelt's bid for reelection.[68]

Hull, apparently still opposing a third term for FDR, ignored this proposal and instead issued a public statement in which he denounced the rumors that he would stay on as Secretary of State as "part of an electioneering situation," but he refrained from disclosing his future plans. Jerome Frank immediately complained to Harry Hopkins that Hull's statement was "too cryptic" and asked why the Secretary could not end the speculation by denouncing Willkie's attacks on the administration's foreign policy. Congressman Lyndon B. Johnson, directing the drive for a Democratic Congress, sent a memo to FDR urging him to have Hull deliver "a fighting speech on American foreign policy." At the same time, Hull learned from Hamilton Fish Armstrong, editor of *Foreign Affairs,* that Willkie was planning to offer him the position of Secretary of State in a dramatic election-eve broadcast.[69]

The Secretary decided he could no longer dodge the issue. Though he refused to speak at a party rally as Flynn wanted, he did deliver a radio broadcast to the nation on November 1, in which he came out clearly for Roosevelt's reelection. Rebutting Willkie's charges that the President was leading the nation into war, Hull declared: "The President's practical experience and his familiarity with the facts and problems of the international situation as they affect this country are at this moment an extraordinarily valuable asset. This is no time for the country to be making a change from experience to inexperience." These words effectively killed Willkie's indirect attempt to capitalize on the substantial, though probably overrated, public following of his opponent's Secretary of State. Once again, a Republican stratagem had backfired.[70]

In a parallel case, the President succeeded in winning the public support of Joseph P. Kennedy, his ambassador to England. Kennedy, a self-made millionaire who had supported FDR since 1932 and had served earlier as chairman of the Securities and Exchange Commission, became increasingly isolationist as he watched France fall and England come under the German aerial blitz. In late September, he reported that the English "are in a bad way," and urged Roosevelt not to enter the war to save them. Kennedy did not keep his views secret, and by October there were rumors that he planned to come back to the United States at the height of the campaign, resign his position in protest over FDR's interventionist policies, and announce for Willkie. When reporters asked him about this speculation in mid-October, FDR answered, "Joe's coming back early next week—coming back to report. Stories of resignation are not true." [71]

Despite this denial, Roosevelt was worried. Kennedy carried great weight with Irish-Americans, particularly in Boston, where there were already signs of isolationist defections. Moreover, the British had informed Harry Hopkins that Henry and Clare Booth Luce had persuaded Kennedy to give a speech upon his return announcing his repudiation of FDR. Taking no chances, Roosevelt had Sumner Welles send cables to Kennedy on board the Pan American clipper at Lisbon and Bermuda, asking him to come directly to the White House and not to talk to the press. Kennedy's wife, Rose, met him at LaGuardia airport and flew with him to Washington to have dinner with FDR. The President invited Senator James Byrnes, a Catholic by birth and an old friend of Kennedy's, Mrs. Byrnes, and Missy LeHand, Roosevelt's private secretary, to attend the dinner. Before the President came in, Byrnes asked the ambassador to give a political speech the following evening endorsing FDR, and Kennedy refused, saying that he had some things to get off his chest. After dinner, when the ladies left, Kennedy aired his grievances, which turned out to be personal rather than political. The ambassador complained about being bypassed on the destroyer deal, of being snubbed by the State Department, of not being kept informed of policy decisions. Roosevelt deftly soothed him, saying that others had the same complaint about the State Department and that when the election was over, he would conduct a thorough housecleaning. Kennedy's anger melted as Roosevelt cajoled him, and when the President asked him to make the radio speech, this time Kennedy agreed, saying, "All right, I will. But I will pay for it myself, show it to nobody in advance and say what I wish." [72]

The next evening, Kennedy gave one of the most effective speeches of the campaign. Though he admitted he differed with FDR on some points, he asserted, "Happily, on these great, momentous questions of foreign policy, trade, commerce and the future of the American way of life, I find little basis for disagreement with the President." Speaking from New York City on a network of 114 stations, Kennedy defended the policy of aid to England as giving the United States time to prepare its own defenses. He urged FDR's reelection, dismissing the claim that "the President of the United States is trying to involve this country in the world war." "Such a charge is false," Kennedy declared.

Roosevelt had dealt masterfully with a potentially dangerous situation. By preventing Kennedy from talking to the press when he arrived and then by carefully playing up to his bruised ego, the President had transformed a serious threat to his campaign into a great asset. The day after the election, Kennedy resigned his post, and a week later told reporter Louis Lyons that he would devote all his time and energy to a crusade to keep the United States out of the war. But in the last crucial week of the campaign, the Roosevelt magic kept him loyal.[73]

At the climax of the campaign, the war became the overriding issue. Citing the world crisis, Henry Luce declared in *Life,* "This is the most important American election since 1860." Anne O'Hare McCormick, the *New York Times* foreign correspondent, pointed out that the two candidates were referring to the conflict more and more as the campaigning reached its peak. The lull in Europe, which most observers felt helped Willkie, came to a sudden end in late October. Hitler stirred speculation of a new offensive designed to capture Gibraltar and gain control of the Mediterranean when he held dramatic meetings with Marshal Pétain on October 22 and with Generalissimo Franco at Hendaye in the Pyrenees the next day. Then, on October 28, Mussolini launched an unprovoked attack on Greece which most Americans assumed was the beginning of a new Axis effort to extend their domination of Europe. Actually, Hitler had tried to restrain Mussolini, asking him to wait until the American election was over, but the Italian dictator had plunged ahead in what proved to be an ill-fated adventure.[74]

As the war dominated the headlines again, Willkie continued to stress the peace theme. Whistle-stopping in the Middle West, he told his listeners that as President he would "so guide your affairs as to keep this great nation functioning and keep your boys from ever getting involved abroad." "They will never go to a foreign war under my direction," Willkie promised. Swinging into Maryland, Willkie kept reminding voters of the way FDR had violated his 1932 pledge to balance the budget and expressed doubt that he would honor the antiwar plank in the Democratic platform. "If he does not," Willkie warned, "some of these Maryland boys who are being called today in the draft will shortly be loading onto the transports."

Willkie made his most irresponsible accusation in a Baltimore speech on October 30. Though at the outset he advocated aid to Britain as a measure of self-defense, he placed emphasis on his desire for peace. "I have given you my pledge many times over: I will work for peace." Then, departing from his prepared text, he spoke directly to FDR, referring to him as "Mr. Third Term Candidate" and asking, "Are you kidding Joe Kennedy the same way you kidded Carter Glass?" Speaking to his audience again, Willkie delivered the clinching line. "On the basis of his past performances with pledges to the people," he shouted, "if you reelect him you may expect war in April, 1941." [75]

The charge hit home. Angry Democratic leaders urged FDR to "denounce in the strongest possible terms the contemptible political speech of Willkie" and "to smash and smash hard [the] Willkie charge [that] Roosevelt will take America to war by April." The Republican candidate probably regretted his own outburst. He was careful not to repeat the accusation in his remaining speeches, and a year later he rather sheepishly dismissed it as "campaign oratory." Indeed, he returned to domestic issues in his final speech in New York City, ignoring the war entirely. In a radio address on the afternoon before the election, aimed at the women of America, Willkie made his last antiwar plea. "I promise, as I have promised many times before, not to send your husbands, sons and brothers to death on a European or Asiatic battlefield." He made no reference to Roosevelt, simply asserting, "I will avoid bringing about a condition of affairs that will make a war necessary." [76]

Meanwhile Roosevelt prepared for his next two campaign speeches, in New York City on October 28 and in Boston on October 30. Advice continued to come in from local politicians. Mayor LaGuardia, who had mapped out the President's itinerary in New York City to avoid defense installations, urged FDR to refrain from making any reference to the draft, while a Long Island congressman told the President that if he would repeat his antiwar assurances, he could win over some

150,000 undecided voters in Queens County. Summarizing the flood of incoming telephone calls to the White House, Presidential aide Marvin MacIntyre reported to FDR that party leaders wanted him to "hammer away again on the peace issue." "According to these phone calls," MacIntyre said, "the consensus of opinion is that this fear of getting into war is having the most decisive effect on the still undecided voters." [77]

Roosevelt heeded this advice in his address to a packed Madison Square Garden audience. Referring to a triumphal fifty-eight-mile tour of the city on streets jammed with people eager to catch a glimpse of him, FDR began, "I've had a very happy day." But then he added that he was sad to learn from Secretary of State Hull that Italy had invaded Greece that afternoon. Carefully avoiding any assessment of blame, FDR commented, "I'm sure all of you too feel sorrow in your hearts because the Italian people and the Grecian people should be involved in conflict." Focusing on the preparedness effort, he blasted the Republicans for failing to vote for defense appropriations throughout the 1930's, delighting his audience by rhythmically singling out three GOP congressmen, "Martin, Barton, and Fish." Then, in an audacious display of political nerve, he took full credit for enactment of the neutrality legislation of the 1930's, laws he had actually fought hard to block in Congress. "Those were measures to keep us at peace," FDR boasted, "And through all the years since 1935, there has been no entanglement and there will be no entanglement." [78]

The crowd loved it, but the politicians were still not satisfied. Two days later, as Roosevelt traveled by train to Boston, telegrams continued to pour in, pleading with him to match Willkie's promise that the boys about to be drafted not be sent to fight and die overseas. When Ed Flynn repeated this request in an urgent message, an exasperated Roosevelt turned to Rosenman and Sherwood and asked how often he needed to make an antiwar pledge, saying he had done so several times already. "I know it, Mr. President, but they don't seem to have heard you the first time," Sherwood replied. "Evidently you've got to say it again—and again—and again." Reluctantly, the President gave in, telling Sherwood to work the desired promise into his Boston speech.

Roosevelt began his address that evening with a direct appeal to Irish-Americans by saying, "I have been glad to welcome back to our own shores that Boston boy, beloved by all of Boston, my ambassador to the Court of St. James, Joe Kennedy." The body of the speech dealt with the defense effort, and, at the urging of interventionist Cabinet members, FDR announced that he was approving a new British request for 12,000 additional American airplanes. But before he made this commitment of aid to England, he paused in a discussion of the draft and then read the words Sherwood had prepared on the train:

> And while I am talking to you mothers and fathers, I give you one more assurance.
>
> I have said this before, but I shall say it again and again and again:
>
> Your boys are not going to be sent into any foreign wars.

Though Roosevelt did add that the sole purpose of the draft was to "keep the threat of war far away from our shores," he deliberately left out the qualifying phrase he had insisted on for the Democratic platform, "except in case of attack." Rosenman had pointed out this omission to Roosevelt on board the train, but FDR had shrugged it off, saying, "Of course we'll fight if we're attacked. If somebody attacks us, then it isn't a foreign war, is it? Or do they want me to guarantee that our troops will be sent into battle only in the event of another Civil War?" [79]

"That hypocritical son of a bitch!" Willkie exclaimed. "This is going to beat me!" Willkie had little reason to complain about the Boston speech, since on the same day he had made his reckless charge that Roosevelt would have the nation at war by April. Neither man could take any pride in the way he exploited the peace issue at the climax of the campaign. Like Willkie, Roosevelt apparently regretted his statement, and in his final address at Cleveland, he took a much more idealistic position, saying that the United States must stay out of the war in order to pursue the American mission of being "a light of the world and a comfort to all people." [80]

Virtually all observers believed that the Republican surge that had begun in mid-October intensified during the last week of the campaign. "[A]s of Sunday, November 3, the trend was still continuing toward Willkie," George Gallup reported. His final poll showed FDR still in the lead, 52 percent to 48 percent, but he forecast "the closest election in twenty-four years." *Time* and *Newsweek* both called the election a toss-up. The *New York Times* put Roosevelt ahead with 231 electoral votes as against 111 for Willkie. Noting that the tide was still running strongly toward the Republicans, the *Times* said the election remained in doubt, since Willkie had a chance to win the remaining 189 electoral votes. Democrats were more optimistic, predicting publicly that FDR would receive at least 400 electoral votes and estimating privately as many as 500. Willkie remained "supremely confident that he could win by the very force of his personality," commented Marquis Childs. Joe Martin was much more skeptical. His confidential estimate was that at best Willkie could count on 246 electoral votes, with only an outside chance of carrying Michigan, Maryland, and New Jersey to give him the additional votes he needed. But when Willkie asked him about the prospects five days before the election, Martin stretched the truth and answered, "We've got a chance to win, Wendell." [81]

VIII

Roosevelt returned to his Hyde Park home on election day to cast his vote and await the verdict. He was less sure of victory than in past campaigns as he sat in the dining room tallying the votes as they came in over the radio and by special reports telephoned in to Harry Hopkins and Sam Rosenman. By ten o'clock his frown disappeared as the early returns indicated another sweeping victory. Shortly after midnight, he went out on to the porch to greet the neighbors who had come by to congratulate him, carrying homemade signs reading "Safe on Third" and "Keep the Fireside Chats Burning." Willkie listened to the results in the Commodore Hotel in New York City. Defying tradition to the end, he went to bed without sending the usual message conceding the election to his opponent. The next morning, he did release to the press a routine telegram of congratulations to FDR, and on November 11 he made up for his oversight in a radio broadcast in which he called upon his supporters to play the role of "loyal opposition" and support FDR's policy of all-out aid to Britain short of war.[82]

The day after the election it was clear that Roosevelt had won decisively. He carried 38 states with 449 electoral votes, compared to 10 with 82 votes for Willkie, and he received 55 percent of the popular vote. Both figures marked a decline over 1936, when FDR had gotten over 60 percent of the popular vote and had limited the Republicans to Maine and Vermont. In a record turnout, Willkie received 5.5 million more votes than Landon had in 1936. Yet it was still an impressive triumph for FDR. He had broken with the no-third-term tradition that went back to George Washington, and despite eight years of accumulated grievances, he had handily defeated an attractive Republican candidate.[83]

Joseph Martin attributed Willkie's defeat to the war in

Europe, saying that the Republican candidate did not have a chance "once France fell." Willkie's biographers have all agreed with Martin. "It was the grim battle in Europe," wrote Mary Dillon, "rather than the political contest in the United States which guided the American people to the decision that the Commander-in-Chief of the American Army and Navy, at this critical hour, should not be changed." Joseph Barnes, Ellsworth Barnard, and Donald Bruce Johnson all place similar weight on the war in explaining the outcome, stating that the voters preferred FDR's experience at a time of unprecedented national danger.[84]

This explanation is too simple. The war did have a significant impact on the election, but it alone did not determine the outcome. Samuel Lubell conducted a careful analysis of urban voting precincts to show that it was economic status which separated the Roosevelt from the Willkie voters. Noting that those who paid less than $40 a month in rent consistently voted for FDR, Lubell concluded, "The little fellow elected him, because there are more of the little fellow and because he believed Mr. Roosevelt to be his friend and protector." Other studies indicate that Willkie lost because Roosevelt swept the cities, gaining a majority in every urban center with a population above 400,000 except Cincinnati. Roosevelt won because he preserved the New Deal coalition intact: the solid South, the urban workers, the emerging Negroes, and even many of the poorer farmers remained loyal to the man they believed had brought the nation safely through the depression.[85]

In a sense, Roosevelt also won because Willkie lost. From the outset, the Republican candidate was hampered by a lack of experience in politics. His clumsy campaign organization, his reliance on amateurs when he desperately needed professionals to guide him, his naïve belief that energy and enthusiasm were more important than painstaking precinct work—all combined to weaken his challenge to FDR. Equally important, he failed to present clear-cut alternatives to Roosevelt's position on either domestic or foreign issues. Agreeing basically with the administration's aid-short-of-war policy, he also took a "me too" line on the New Deal, suggesting only that he could administer the regulatory machinery better than Roosevelt. The voters were thus faced with a choice between two personalities, one familiar and reassuring, the other attractive but erratic and unknown. Their decision was not surprising.[86]

The war, rather than ensuring Roosevelt's victory, may well have narrowed his margin. Nearly all commentators on the election have stressed shifts among ethnic groups due to foreign policy attitudes. Willkie benefited most by gaining a large number of German-American votes, especially in the Middle West. Lubell claims that German opposition to Roosevelt's interventionist policies enabled Willkie to carry five of his ten states. Many Irish-Americans defected from the Democrats, as party leaders had feared, but surprisingly the expected bolt by Italians did not occur. Soothed by FDR's friendly Columbus Day remarks and persuaded by men like Mayor LaGuardia, they voted Democratic. Only one Italian district in Brooklyn went for Willkie, reported New York's Lieutenant Governor Charles Poletti to Rosenman, commenting that "Americans of Italian extraction came through in fine style." At the same time, Roosevelt gained among Scandinavian, Polish, and Jewish voters, who bitterly opposed Hitler. Polish districts in Buffalo, normally expected to go Democratic by a 9–1 ratio, voted 25–1 for Roosevelt. Congressman Emanuel Celler told Roosevelt that most of the 180,000 new voters in Brooklyn were Jewish and "their favorable votes offset much of the hostile votes of the racial groups that were set against you." It is likely that the shifts among ethnic groups came close to canceling each other out, with probably a slight gain for the Republicans in the electoral outcome.[87]

The more important impact of the war came from Willkie's emphasis on the peace issue in the last three weeks of the campaign. He was floundering all through September and October, lacking any consistent theme and giving the impression of a man in over his head. But once he began suggesting that Roosevelt might be leading the nation into war, his campaign came to life. The polls reflected the steady inroads he made into Roosevelt's lead and the momentum he had built up by the end of October. Democratic leaders, as their telegrams to Roosevelt indicated, were fearful that Willkie had found the issue that would enable him to pull off a political miracle. Roosevelt himself was impressed enough to alter his campaign plans and take to the stump to out-promise Willkie on the peace issue. If the Republican candidate had adopted a moderately isolationist stance at the outset and played on the public's fear of war throughout the fall, he might have made the election race much closer, and conceivably could even have won. As it was, Willkie convinced enough voters that Roosevelt was leading the nation toward war to balance off those who backed the President as the experienced leader at a time of crisis.

The European antagonists reacted in expected fashion to the outcome of the election. "I feel as though we have won a victory comparable in magnitude to what we lost in the defeat of France. It is grand, grand, grand," wrote Englishman Harold Laski to the President. Churchill called the news of FDR's reelection a "message . . . of great encouragement and good cheer." The German Foreign Ministry instructed its missions overseas to treat the election result "with cool reserve," taking some satisfaction in the observation that Willkie had forced FDR "to stress the peaceful character of his foreign policy more than he originally wished to do." Hans Thomsen was careful to advise Berlin not to be misled by the political oratory. "As to the whole American people's determination to come to the aid of England with all means, there can be no doubt; this was clearly expressed in the course of the election campaign." [88]

At home, interventionists breathed a sigh of relief that the election was over. Cordell Hull issued a statement saying that the results gave "nationwide approval" to the policies the administration had been following. Those who had regretted Roosevelt's concessions to isolationist sentiment quickly dismissed his antiwar pledge, convinced that all along he was privately on their side. Freda Kirchwey assumed that both Willkie and Roosevelt were lying to the American people when they promised to keep the nation out of war. "I don't think the promise was ever wholly honest, if you will excuse my saying so," she wrote on election eve, adding that the two men "should have bravely warned the nation that war may be necessary." Historians William L. Langer and S. Everett Gleason, writing a decade later, agreed with Miss Kirchwey. "Was the survival of Great Britain vital to the security of the United States of America?" they asked. Feeling that it was, they criticized Roosevelt for failing to present this basic issue to the American people openly and candidly. [89]

Yet it is unfair to assume that Roosevelt saw things so clearly in the heat of the campaign. A man who had shared in the isolationist mood of the 1930's, he realized the genuine reluctance of the American people to become involved in the European conflict. He hoped that a policy of material aid would make it unnecessary to enter the war directly, though he must have realized it might ultimately become inescapable. He hated to give the ironclad assurances the politicians demanded, because he did feel committed by his campaign statements. "The dark cloud of rhetoric would linger on, blurring and confusing the issues," wrote Marquis Childs in 1942. "President Roosevelt took his campaign statements more seriously than his interventionist backers believed he would." [90] His promise not to enter the European war acted as a restraint for the next thirteen months, holding him back from the steps his more interventionist advisers kept insisting were needed to ensure Hitler's defeat. The campaign was over in November, but it continued to affect American foreign policy until the Japanese attack on Pearl Harbor finally thrust the nation into the war Roosevelt had promised to avoid.

1944

34567

"[M]y convictions regarding international cooperation and collective security for peace took firm form on the afternoon of the Pearl Harbor attack," confessed Arthur Vandenberg in 1949. "That day ended isolation for any realist." [1] Although Vandenberg's transition from isolationism to acceptance of an active world role for the United States was more gradual than he realized, his statement reflects the fundamental change in outlook that occurred in the United States during World War II. Convinced by the Japanese attack that the nation's security depended on a favorable balance of power abroad, the American people vowed that never again would they turn their backs on the world; this time they would see the task through to the end and create a new world organization to insure a lasting peace.

Recalling with shame their role in defeating Wilson's League of Nations, Republicans led the way in the new drive for world order. They took part in the activities of the many private groups that worked for a new international organization, and by the summer of 1942 the Gallup poll showed that fully 70 percent of the Republican voters surveyed wanted the United States to participate in a postwar world body. John

Foster Dulles, foreign policy adviser to Thomas Dewey, headed the Commission on a Just and Durable Peace, a Protestant postwar study group; while Harold Stassen, the young Minnesota governor, became one of the first to call for world federation as the only way to prevent future wars.

The most significant political development during the war was the gradual emergence of a bipartisan approach to postwar foreign policy. Cordell Hull made the initial move in the spring of 1942, when he asked senators Tom Connally, Democratic chairman of the Foreign Relations Committee, and Warren Austin, Vermont Republican, to join the State Department's Advisory Committee on Postwar Foreign Policy. Hull, who remembered the bitter partisanship that had destroyed Wilson's plans for peace, wanted to do everything possible to lift postwar planning out of the political arena. The glacial pace of administration efforts, however, led to a different form of bipartisan action. In March 1943, Republican senators Joseph Ball of Minnesota and Harold Burton of Ohio joined with Democrats Carl Hatch and Lister Hill to offer a Senate resolution calling for the immediate creation of a United Nations Organization as the nucleus of a postwar peace agency. In a bold move, they included a provision for establishing an international police force as part of the world body. The B_2H_2 resolution, as reporters quickly dubbed it, alarmed both administration leaders, who wanted to delay action until the war was nearly won, and also conservative Republicans like Vandenberg, who favored a more traditional form of world order.

Throughout the summer of 1943, senators Connally and Vandenberg, the ranking members of the Foreign Relations Committee, cooperated with the administration in bottling up the B_2H_2 resolution while public opinion built up behind it. In September, Republican leaders, realizing it was important for them to shed their prewar image of isolationism, met at a resort on Mackinac Island in Lake Michigan to hammer out a statement on postwar goals. Senator Vandenberg offered a vague draft on foreign policy which Warren Austin, backed by a number of Republican governors, forced him to strengthen. The final Mackinac Declaration called for "responsible participation by the United States in post-war cooperative organization among sovereign nations to prevent military aggression and to attain permanent peace with organized justice in a free world." When both isolationists and internationalists within the party endorsed this ambiguous statement, it became clear that despite the ponderous wording, the Mackinac Declaration signaled GOP willingness to join with the administration in working for a new League of Nations.

The growing bipartisan spirit was apparent when Congress reconvened in the fall of 1943. Republicans vied with Democrats to support a broadly worded resolution that representative William Fulbright had introduced in the spring, finally passing it by a vote of 360 to 29. In the Senate, Tom Connally offered an even vaguer resolution as a substitute for the B_2H_2 proposal and, despite backing from Vandenberg, ran into opposition from a bipartisan coalition of internationalists led by Joseph Ball, who insisted on a stronger statement. The two sides finally compromised by including a portion of the Moscow Declaration, which was signed by Cordell Hull in the Russian capital while the Senate debate took place and which called for creating, "at the earliest practical date, a general international organization, based on the principle of the sovereign equality of all peace-loving states." A few isolationists, led by Democrat Burton Wheeler, spoke out against the amended Connally resolution, but the great majority of Democrats and Republicans voted for it on November 5. Cordell Hull, flying back from his 26,000-mile journey, was delighted by this display of bipartisan support and quickly accepted an invitation to report directly to Congress on the Moscow conference. Given a standing ovation by the senators and representatives, Hull thanked them for their "vision and statesmanship" in passing the Fulbright and Connally resolutions and then painted a glowing picture of a postwar world in which "there will no longer be need for spheres of influence, for alliances, for balance of power." [2]

This bright outlook in foreign policy contrasted sharply with the wartime political fortunes of the Democrats. In 1942 the Republicans had won a sweeping victory in the Congressional elections, picking up forty-four seats in the House and gaining nine new senators. A sharp drop in voter turnout, caused by the dislocations of a mobile wartime population, reduced the normal Democratic margins, especially in the big cities, and enabled the Republicans to come within a few votes of gaining control of Congress. Southern Democrats joined with Republican conservatives to oppose the administration on a number of domestic measures; they watered down a bill for federal supervision of absentee voting by servicemen, and on a revenue measure they cut the Treasury's request for an additional $10.5 billion to $2 billion. FDR took up the challenge on the tax bill, sending it back to Congress with a stinging veto message listing "indefensible" special tax relief granted "not for the needy but for the greedy." Senate Majority Leader Alben Barkley resigned his post in protest over FDR's message, only to be unanimously reelected to the position by his fellow Democrats, and the Senate and the House then overrode the veto by huge majorities. "For the first time in the nation's history," historian Richard Polenberg comments, "Congress had passed a revenue law over a presidential veto." [3]

President Roosevelt blamed the Republicans, accusing them of "a campaign to sow discord among us" and claiming that there were "a very small number of people who would rather nail my hide to the barn door than win the war." Though many Democrats had joined in the Congressional rebellion against the President, they began to rally behind his leadership in an election year. They might disagree with his handling of domestic issues, but they shared the American people's nearly universal admiration for FDR's inspiring wartime leadership, and they viewed a fourth term as both necessary and desirable. Unlike 1940, there was no organized effort to deny Roosevelt the nomination, and the Gallup polls showed him as virtually the unanimous choice, favored by 89 percent of the Democrats surveyed, compared to 4 percent for Hull and 3 percent for Henry Wallace. "Except for the vice-presidency," commented *Time,* "the Democratic convention could be held by mail." Roosevelt kept silent about his plans, but he did nothing to discourage his supporters, thus confirming the growing belief that he would run again.[4]

The President's health created the only real doubts. Weakened by a bout with flu in January 1944, he complained of fatigue and recurring headaches all through the winter. Finally, in late March, he entered the Navy hospital at Bethesda for a checkup. The doctors found, in addition to bronchitis, that his blood pressure was 186/108 and his heart had become dangerously enlarged. His physicians immediately prescribed a less rigorous daily regime, with less work and more sleep, and a daily dose of digitalis; but incredibly no one informed the President that he had a serious heart condition. Told only that he needed to recuperate, Roosevelt willingly went to Hobcaw, Bernard Baruch's plantation in South Carolina, where he spent the next four weeks relaxing in the sun and recovering from the bronchitis. When he returned to Washington in early May, reporters noted that he looked well and rested, his face thinner but ruddy from the hours in the sun. Admiral Ross T. McIntyre, his personal physician, tried to dispel rumors that he was a dying man, saying, "I am perfectly satisfied with his physical condition." Reporters, used to seeing the President twice a week, realized for the first time how much FDR had aged, commenting that he now looked much older than his 62 years. Party leaders, however, accepted McIntyre's assessment and went ahead with plans to nominate Roosevelt for a fourth term.[5]

I

Heartened by their showing in the Congressional elections, Republicans looked forward eagerly to the 1944 campaign. Wendell Willkie was the most active GOP contender. Returning to his law practice in New York City after his 1940 defeat, Willkie had stayed in the spotlight with trips to England in 1941 and to Russia and China in 1942 on behalf of FDR. He reported on his second journey in *One World,* an eloquent book pleading the case of postwar world cooperation which became an instant best-seller in 1943. Yet as his fame grew, his standing within the party declined. Willkie continued to treat the party leaders with disdain, refusing to build a base within the Republican ranks. Instead, he acted as the party's conscience, attacking the old guard for their isolationist leanings and trying to reform the GOP along liberal, internationalist lines. Democrats and independents applauded, but most Republicans still viewed Willkie as an outsider who had led them to defeat.

Aware of his declining popularity, Willkie decided to challenge the party leaders by a vigorous primary campaign in the misguided belief that the rank-and-file were on his side. In mid-March he and his wife, accompanied by his public relations adviser, Lem Jones, and thirty-five reporters, invaded Wisconsin. Dynamic as always, Willkie toured all ten Congressional districts in quest of delegates. His charm won over many of the people who came into contact with him, but his campaign, planned and organized in New York, failed to include a single major state party leader. He spoke out frequently on foreign policy before audiences generally believed to be isolationist, and he gained grudging approval for his attacks on Roosevelt and for his promise to guide the party in the direction of international cooperation. Above all, he advocated American leadership in creating a new world organization that could "prevent future fires of war and capture future bandits before they destroy civilization." [6]

On April 4, the voters of Wisconsin repudiated Willkie, placing him last in the field of four Republican candidates and denying him a single delegate. As soon as he heard the news, Willkie withdrew from the race, attributing his defeat to the persistence of isolationism within the Republican party. Most commentators disagreed with Willkie's analysis, pointing out that his defeat was due more to grass-roots resentment of his attitude toward the party and to a poorly conceived and conducted primary effort. Many Republicans had been waiting patiently since 1940 to get their revenge on Willkie, the ex-Democrat who had stampeded the delegates at Philadelphia, and they rejoiced in his downfall. "It certainly served one good purpose—the elimination of Willkie once and for all," Robert Wood wrote to Vandenberg, who agreed, calling the Wisconsin results "spectacular." [7]

The victor in Wisconsin was Governor Thomas E. Dewey of New York, who led the popular balloting and gained 15 of the 22 delegates. Dewey had greatly strengthened his political position in 1942 in his second race for the New York governorship, winning by over half a million votes to become the first Republican governor since the 1920's. Having promised to serve out his four-year term in office, Dewey refrained from campaigning actively for the Republican presidential nomination, but by early 1944 he had become the front runner in the Gallup poll, the choice of 42 percent of Republican voters compared to 23 percent who favored Willkie. By his silence, Dewey was able to avoid taking stands on the issues, and although he was thought to be in favor of postwar international organization, he was able to attract support from all wings of the party. In Wisconsin, he relied upon prominent local leaders, including a number of prewar isolationists, to conduct his campaign. When he won so handily, *Newsweek* concluded that Wisconsin voters "had virtually chosen the next presidential nominee . . . three months in advance of the GOP national convention." [8]

In many ways Dewey was the very antithesis of Willkie. Cool and aloof, he lacked Willkie's warmth and personal charm. Associates commented on Dewey's super efficiency. He planned every move in advance, attended to the slightest detail, and insisted upon flawless execution. He had few friends, rarely seemed to relax or display a sense of humor, and appeared to be totally without ideology. He treated politics as a task to be mastered, with the presidency as the ultimate reward for a job well done. He expressed no passion, no strong convictions, no uplifting sense of mission beyond narrow personal fulfillment. Politicians, who missed the zest for the game and a sense of camaraderie, distrusted Dewey almost as much as they did Willkie. Seizing on his slight stature and neatly trimmed mustache, Alice Roosevelt Longworth had made the damning comment, "After all, how can you vote for a man who looks like the bridegroom on a wedding cake?" I. F. Stone compared him to an earlier Republican leader when he wrote, "Dewey is small stuff and cold fish, handsomer and physically robust but really a good deal like Coolidge, frugal spiritually, a man who does not give himself freely." [9]

Despite his handicaps, Dewey seemed certain to win the GOP nomination. Many Republicans who had backed him only to head off Willkie now found that it was too late to turn to another candidate. The two men actively seeking the nomination were John Bricker of Ohio and Harold Stassen. Bricker, the big, handsome, conservative governor of Ohio— "an honest Harding," as one wag put it—had the backing of Senator Robert Taft, who stood aside for him, but Bricker failed to convince even the old guard that he could govern the nation. Stassen, who had resigned as governor of Minnesota to enter the Navy, was viewed as the bright young man in the party, but Willkie supporters never forgave him for entering the Wisconsin primary and other Republicans considered him too liberal on both domestic and foreign issues.[10]

The only real threat to Dewey came from the dark-horse candidacy of General Douglas MacArthur, then commanding American forces fighting in the South Pacific. In 1943, Arthur Vandenberg had joined with publishers Frank Gannett and Roy Howard, former GOP Chairman John Hamilton, and General Robert E. Wood, Sears Roebuck executive and founder of America First, to draft MacArthur as the Republican candidate on the grounds that he was the only man with the stature necessary to defeat Roosevelt. Disregarding Vandenberg's advice, MacArthur's backers entered him in several primaries, including Wisconsin's, where he ran third to Dewey and Stassen. Vandenberg, sensing that MacArthur lacked broad popular appeal, shifted to Dewey, but Representative Arthur Lewis Miller of Nebraska created a sensation in mid-April by releasing the texts of two letters MacArthur had written him. The first, sent in 1943, referred to "our present chaos and confusion"; in the second, written in February 1944, MacArthur commented favorably on Miller's assertion that the New Dealers were establishing a monarchy in the United States and complained that not enough supplies were being sent to the Pacific. MacArthur quickly released a statement saying his letters were not intended for publication; then he commented that he was not a candidate, but added, "My sole ambition is to assist our country to win this vital struggle by the fulfillment of such duty as has been, or may be, assigned to me." When his eager supporters took this as a sign that he would accept a draft, MacArthur responded with a second statement on April 29. "I request that no action be taken that would link my name in any way with the nomination," MacArthur declared flatly. "I do not covet it, nor would I accept it." [11]

With the collapse of the MacArthur boomlet, Dewey had the Republican nomination locked up. Public opinion polls showed that by the end of April he was the choice of 55 percent of Republican voters. Although he trailed Roosevelt by ten percentage points in the Gallup poll, when people were asked to assume that the war would be over before the election in November, they favored Dewey over FDR, 58 to 42 percent.[12]

Dewey finally broke his long silence on foreign policy in a speech to a group of newspaper executives in New York City on April 27. Reading from a text prepared by John Foster Dulles, Dewey expressed his desire to "organize in cooperation with other nations a structure of peace backed by adequate force to prevent future wars." Warning that we must not repeat the tragic failure of Versailles, he called for close cooperation with Britain, China, and Russia after the war. Backing away from his prewar opposition to the Soviet Union, Dewey declared, "Russian affairs are in the hands of hardheaded, realistic leaders. That is nothing we should be afraid of provided we are equally realistic and devoted to our country." Though a few liberals chided Dewey for hopping aboard the bandwagon at so late a date, most internationalists were pleased with his views. Claiming that isolationism was now dead within the Republican party, *Time* asserted that Dewey's speech "removed the broad objective of U.S. foreign policy from 1944 campaign debate." [13]

II

The memory of the Senate's rejection of Woodrow Wilson's League of Nations haunted Cordell Hull. In preparing plans for the coming peace, he wanted to do everything possible to keep them out of politics in an election year. When he learned that Harry Hopkins was planning to write a magazine article touching on foreign policy, the Secretary protested to Roosevelt in late March, saying, "I was under the impression from some of our conversations that we were to make an earnest effort to deal, especially with postwar planning, on a non-partisan basis." The magazine article never appeared. A month later, Hull's close friend, Representative Albert Gore of Tennessee, told him that Paul Porter, publicity director of the Democratic National Committee, wanted Gore to challenge the Republicans on foreign policy, an issue which Porter thought was "the most important aspect of the coming campaign." Hull had one of his aides help Gore draft a reply in which he argued that the Democrats stood to gain politically from taking foreign policy out of the campaign. Warning that an attack on the Republicans as isolationists could lead to "disaster," Gore urged Porter to have the Democratic National Committee clear all statements on foreign policy with the State Department.[14]

Above all, Hull wanted to be certain that international organization did not become a partisan issue. State Department committees which had been working since 1942 completed a draft plan for a new world body in March. Before presenting this proposal to England, Russia, and China for their approval, Hull decided he would try to gain the prior assent of leading Democrats and Republicans in Congress. In late March, he asked Chairman Tom Connally to arrange for a small bipartisan delegation from the Senate Foreign Relations Committee to meet with him. Then, in a radio speech on April 9, the Secretary informed the nation of this plan to consult with Congress before undertaking negotiations with our allies on international organization. "Once before in our lifetime we fell into disunity and became ineffective in world affairs by reason of it," Hull reminded his listeners. "Should this happen again it will be a tragedy to you and to your children and to the world for generations." [15]

Connally appointed a Committee of Eight to meet with Hull—four Democrats led by Connally himself, three Republicans including Arthur Vandenberg, and Robert LaFollette, Jr., of Wisconsin, a Progressive and staunch isolationist. Vandenberg was careful to check with Robert Taft before accepting the assignment, and he followed the Ohio senator's advice in telling Connally that participation by Republicans in these talks did not bind them to support the administration's proposals. Vandenberg respected Hull and was willing to work with him in a bipartisan spirit, but he profoundly distrusted FDR. "I do not believe that Mr. Roosevelt's idea of 'protecting American interests' would square with mine for an instant," he told a friend who had written urging that Republicans back the President's peace plans. The Michigan senator thought Roosevelt was too soft toward the Russians, and he apparently hoped to take political advantage of this tendency. "When we actually get around to the November campaign," Vandenberg wrote, "it is my own opinion that Roosevelt foreign policies will actually contribute to our victory." [16]

Hull met with the Committee of Eight for the first time on April 25. He gave each senator a copy of the American draft plan, discussed it briefly, and then asked them to study it carefully. That evening Hull sent a telegram to Roosevelt, who was still resting in South Carolina. "The meeting was entirely informal," he reported. "They seemed intensely interested; only a few questions were asked. . . . The atmosphere was good at the end." [17]

A week later, the eight senators met again with Hull. To his delight, they expressed general agreement with the American plan, which called for an organization similar in many ways to the League of Nations, with a general assembly in which all members had an equal voice and a security council dominated by the United States, Russia, England, and China. Vandenberg, who had feared a more radical proposal along the lines of world federation, was greatly relieved. "This is anything but a wild-eyed internationalist dream of a world State," he wrote. "On the contrary, it is a frame-work (without passing on details) to which I can and do heartily subscribe." The only objection he raised dealt with timing. Vandenberg, backed by LaFollette, pointed out that the main task of the new body would be to supervise and enforce the postwar peace settlement. Until he knew the nature of the peace, he could not in good conscience endorse the world organization. "Otherwise," he told Hull, "we would be signing the most colossal 'blank check' in history." But under prodding from Hull, Vandenberg did admit that it was necessary to go ahead now with at least preliminary steps toward forming the world organization.[18]

The smooth course of these consultations hit a snag on May 17 when the Committee of Eight refused to send Hull a letter he asked for, endorsing the American plan and urging the State Department to open negotiations on it with other nations. Instead, the committee sent Hull a letter endorsing his plan to enter into negotiations but withholding full approval "until it may be put in final form and terms of peace are known." Hull was furious. He sent the letter back, and for the next week Senator Connally and Hull's aides tried to draft a compromise letter, only to have their efforts rejected by Vandenberg and LaFollette. Finally, Hull decided to dispense with formal Congressional approval. After meeting for a last time with the Committee of Eight on May 29, Hull called in the press and read a prepared statement. Describing the bipartisan consultations as "frank and fruitful," Hull announced that he was ready to proceed with "informal discussions" with England, Russia, and China on plans for a world organization.[19]

President Roosevelt, now back in Washington, was not surprised at the limited nature of Republican cooperation. In March, he had warned Hull that the GOP planned to make foreign affairs a campaign issue in 1944. Commenting on their refusal to endorse the plan, Roosevelt now told a leading internationalist, "it should be clear that the Republican leaders, not knowing how to cooperate with the Democrats, know even less how to cooperate with other nations." Convinced that his opponents were prepared to play politics with postwar planning, the President decided it was time to outflank them. Calling together an impromptu press conference on Memorial Day, Roosevelt for the first time gave reporters his ideas on the nature of a future world organization. Commenting that he had once campaigned for the League of Nations, he said that the times required a new approach to achieve the same objective—"the prevention, if we can humanly help it, of another World War." Then he carefully emphasized his belief that a new world body should be formed "without taking away the independence of the United States in any shape, manner or form, or destroying—what's the other word?—the *integrity* of the United States in any shape, manner or form." With this stress on retaining American sovereignty, Roosevelt ended any speculation on plans for a world federation and took a safe, middle-of-the-road position which the Republicans would find hard to attack.[20]

A week later, the long-awaited D-Day landings took place in Normandy, promising an end to the war in the near future. Cordell Hull wanted to go beyond FDR's tantalizingly brief preview of American plans for world organization in order to insure Republican approval at their upcoming convention. On June 15, the Secretary and his aides prepared a press release on the draft American plan and took it to FDR for his assent. Later that afternoon Stephen Early, the President's press secretary, handed out mimeographed copies of the statement, commenting to the handful of reporters in the White House lobby, "I think this is a pretty good story." [21]

The press release described the American plan for an organization consisting of a council, an assembly, and a world court without giving any specific details. Roosevelt and Hull disguised the fact that the Big Four would control the proposed body by possessing veto power, and they were purposefully vague on how the organization would keep the peace.

Their real intent became clear when they stated, "We are not thinking of a superstate with its own police forces and other paraphernalia." Aware of the public's desire for a new venture in international order, yet also knowing that the American people wanted to retain full national sovereignty, the administration, as *Time* put it, "was shrewdly working both sides of the street." When all but the most extreme internationalists and a few diehard isolationists praised the plan, Roosevelt proved he was still the master of political timing. "He has taken the wind out of the Republicans' sails about as completely as possible," concluded the *New Republic*. More important, at least for Cordell Hull, the President had virtually insured that the international organization would not become a partisan issue in the coming election.[22]

III

Three other foreign policy issues with political overtones emerged in the spring of 1944—Palestine, Poland, and Pearl Harbor. Palestine was the first to develop. In 1939, the British decided to hedge on the Balfour Declaration, their 1917 commitment to provide a homeland for Jews in Palestine. In the 1920's and 1930's, the movement of Jewish people into Palestine, then under British control, had led to fighting with the native Arab population. With World War II approaching, the British needed to placate the restive Arab peoples throughout the Middle East, so they issued a White Paper on May 17, 1939, which set a limit of 75,000 additional Jewish immigrants over the next five years. After April 1, 1944, no more Jews would be permitted to enter Palestine.[23]

As the White Paper deadline approached, sentiment began to build up in the United States to intervene on behalf of the Jews. Hitler's vicious persecution of European Jews had stimulated the Zionist movement in the United States during the war. In 1942, American Zionists had called a special meeting at the Biltmore Hotel in New York City and adopted a resolution calling for unlimited migration of Jews into Palestine and the establishment of a Jewish Commonwealth there after the war. Jewish leaders pushed hard to implement the Biltmore program, and in early 1944 they succeeded in getting bipartisan sponsorship for the introduction of a resolution in both the House and Senate calling for the United States to press for "free entry of Jews" into Palestine, "so that the Jewish people may ultimately reconstitute Palestine as a free and democratic Jewish Commonwealth." [24]

This resolution created a serious dilemma for the Roosevelt administration. In 1943, as part of an attempt to advance postwar American oil interests in Saudi Arabia, the President had promised King Ibn Saud that the American government would not allow the status of Palestine to be altered "without full consultation with both Arabs and Jews." If the President permitted Congress to enact the Zionist resolutions, he would clearly violate his promise to King Saud; yet if he blocked the measures in Congress, he risked alienating American Jews, who normally voted heavily for him.[25]

The State Department, vitally interested in maintaining the good will of the Arab leaders, wanted to oppose the resolutions, but Cordell Hull, aware of the political risks, hesitated. Secretary of War Henry L. Stimson spared Hull further agony. On February 7, he sent a letter to Chairman Connally of the Senate Foreign Relations Committee urging him to table the Senate resolution, which he termed "a matter of deep military concern to the War Department." Reflecting the anxiety of army leaders who feared that further immigration into Palestine might lead to fighting between Jews and Arabs, Stimson declared, "I believe therefore that our war effort would be seriously prejudiced." The President urged Stimson to make his letter public in order to placate Zionist opinion, but the Secretary of War refused, since he did not wish the War Department to become involved in a political controversy. Finally, Stimson permitted General George C. Marshall, the Army Chief of Staff, to appear before a secret session of the Senate Foreign Relations Committee on February 23. According to Senator Vandenberg, Marshall made an "utterly frank and blunt *confidential* statement" that so impressed the committee that they immediately tabled the resolution.[26]

A few days later, Rabbi Abba Hillel Silver, a prominent Zionist leader, called on Assistant Secretary of State Breckinridge Long to voice his "great consternation and bewilderment" at the sudden killing of the Palestine resolution. Hiding behind the war, Long told Silver, "It was a military decision pure and simple." The Rabbi was not convinced, pointing out that the Jewish people, who had supported FDR so loyally in the past, "would be disappointed when they discovered that under his Administration this difficulty had arisen." Silver finally suggested that the President at least issue a statement endorsing the Zionist cause, and when Long said he thought this would not be possible, Silver expressed, according to the harried Long, "resentment and a smoldering anger." [27]

Informed of the Zionist reaction, Roosevelt found a unique solution. On March 9, he met with Silver and Dr. Stephen S. Wise, another prominent rabbi, at the White House. When the meeting was over, the two Jewish leaders reported to newsmen that Roosevelt had told them he had never approved the British White Paper and authorized them to say: "The President is happy that the doors of Palestine are today open to Jewish refugees and that when future decisions are reached full justice will be done to those who seek a Jewish national home." Thus FDR cleverly endorsed the Zionist program without making any formal commitments. On March 17, when the House Foreign Affairs Committee threatened to act on the Palestine resolution, the administration finally made public Stimson's letter stating that its passage "at this time would be prejudicial to the successful prosecution of the war." When reporters asked Roosevelt how he could tell Zionists he favored open immigration into Palestine in light of the Army's opposition, the President dismissed the apparent conflict, saying that the military were concerned with the immediate wartime situation, while he was looking ahead to the future.[28]

Republicans were furious as they realized they had been outmaneuvered by Roosevelt. "Frankly we do not relish the position into which we were put when the full Committee's recent forthright acquiescence in State Department recommendations, for the common good, was speedily followed by Presidential statements which all but nullified our actions," complained Vandenberg to Chairman Connally. All that the Republicans could do, however, was include a plank in their platform promising free immigration and a democratic commonwealth for Jews in Palestine and condemning "the failure of the President" to force the British to live up to the Balfour Declaration. The Democrats responded by endorsing the same two Zionist objectives in their platform. When the Arab nations protested against these pledges, Cordell Hull told FDR, "In view of the strategic importance to us of the Near East, I believe that it would be advisable for leaders of both parties to refrain from making statements on Palestine during the campaign." But it was unlikely that either Roosevelt or the Republican candidate would be able to heed this advice and still capture the Jewish vote.[29]

The Democrats faced an even more delicate problem with Poland. When Germany invaded Poland in September 1939 to begin World War II, Russia moved in from the east to reclaim a large slice of territory that she had lost after World War I. Hitler's attack on Russia in 1941 brought the Soviets into the war against the Axis, and immediately raised a serious boundary issue. The Polish government in exile, with headquarters in London, claimed the prewar boundary, far to the east, while the Russians insisted on retaining the Polish territory they had occupied in 1939. The fact that the Soviet claim approximated a line drawn in 1919 at the Paris Peace Conference by

Lord Curzon, a British diplomat, strengthened the Russian case, but the London Polish government stubbornly refused to concede. Matters grew worse in 1943 when the Soviets broke off relations with the London Poles, after the exile government asked for an international investigation of a German charge that the Russians had slaughtered thousands of Polish officers in Katyn Forest. Then in early 1944, as the Russian army drove the retreating Germans back toward Poland, the Soviets announced the formation of a rival Polish government composed almost entirely of Communists. Thus not only the territory but the future government of Poland was now at stake.[30]

President Roosevelt was fully aware of the political implications of the Polish issue. There were more than six million Polish-American voters in the United States, and although they normally voted Democratic, their strong emotional commitment to Poland's future could well cause them to defect. When Roosevelt met with Stalin and Churchill at Teheran in November 1943 in the first wartime summit conference, he tried to avoid taking part in the discussions on Poland, which Harry Hopkins told Anthony Eden were "political dynamite" in the United States. Churchill finally agreed to a compromise with Stalin whereby, in return for accepting the Curzon line, Poland would be compensated with German territory in the west. Meeting later with Stalin, Roosevelt tacitly accepted this agreement; but he informed the Soviet leader "that he could not publicly take part in any such arrangement at the present time," reminding him that there were "six to seven million Americans of Polish extraction, and as a practical man, he did not wish to lose their vote." In the months following Teheran, the State Department adhered carefully to Roosevelt's position, refusing to participate in efforts to settle the boundary dispute but ready to use its "good offices" to reestablish diplomatic relations between the London Poles and the Soviet Union.[31]

The Republicans realized the possibilities open to them. In late April, a prominent Detroit party leader wrote to Senator Vandenberg pointing out how important the Polish vote was in Michigan and several other states. He urged the Senator to press for a plank favorable to Poland in the Republican platform, saying it might "have considerable effect on the outcome in November." Vandenberg agreed that "Polish voters will be more responsive to us this Fall than in many previous years," but he shied away from a platform pledge. He feared that such a blatant vote-getting tactic would backfire, and he did not want the Republicans to "*promise* anything which we cannot *perform*." Instead, he advised letting the facts speak for themselves and "let nature take its course" as Polish Americans watched the Soviets swallow up Poland.[32]

Meanwhile, Americans of Polish ancestry began to take action themselves. A small group, led by CIO official Leo Krzycki, formed the Kosciusko League in Detroit in February, and began a campaign stressing friendship with the Soviet Union. The great majority of Poles, however, sided with the London government. In March, prominent Polish Americans, including Charles Rozmarek of Chicago and Frank Januszewski, publisher of a Polish-language newspaper in Detroit, began making plans to convene an American Polish Congress in Buffalo on May 28. Working through existing Polish fraternal and social groups, coordinating committees arranged for the election of delegates to the Buffalo Congress, which was designed to bring pressure for support of the London Polish government and influence the party conventions. David Niles, a White House aide, went to Detroit to interview the organizers of the Congress in mid-May and reported to Roosevelt that they displayed "a terrific resentment against the Administration, which will eventually crystallize in some unfriendly form." "The main aim of this Congress," Niles told FDR, "is to save Poland from a new partition." [33]

Over three thousand delegates came to Buffalo to attend

the three-day congress, the largest and most representative gathering of Polish-Americans ever held. Conducting all their sessions in Polish, the delegates quickly adopted a constitution and formed a permanent organization to work for "the sovereignty of Poland and the integrity of her boundaries." They elected Rozmarek their president and then approved a memorandum to Roosevelt urging him to back the London Polish government and to refuse to accept any territorial changes brought about by the use of force. Although the congress refrained from making any direct political threats, it was clear that Polish Americans were warning the administration that their votes could no longer be taken for granted.[34]

Roosevelt responded by inviting Stanislaw Mikolajczyk, the Prime Minister of the Polish government in exile, to meet with him in Washington in early June. Mikolajczyk, who had requested a meeting several times before and had been rebuffed, agreed to rather humiliating conditions: he was to "refrain from any public discussion of the Polish question" and not to attend any public gatherings dealing with Poland. On June 7, the day after the Normandy landings, he arrived in Washington and had dinner with Roosevelt in the White House. In the course of four long conversations over the next week, the President told him that he had not approved of the Curzon line at Teheran (which at best was stretching the truth) and offered him "the moral support" of the American government in reaching a solution with the Soviets. When a puzzled Mikolajczyk asked a State Department official exactly what "moral support" entailed, Hull made it clear that it meant nothing more than "our tender of good offices." The President finally suggested that Mikolajczyk fly to Moscow to try to reach agreement directly with Stalin, promising to send the Russian leader a message endorsing such a journey.

After his final talk with Roosevelt, Mikolajczyk met with the press and told reporters that while no agreement had been reached on the boundary issue, he had come away convinced that "Poland can count on the support and real friendship of the United States." This statement eased the anxiety felt by Polish Americans and thus improved FDR's standing with them. But the President had not resolved the Polish issue, which was bound to become more intense as Russian armies moved in to "liberate" the country. He was still caught between the necessity of maintaining good relations with the Soviet Union and the need to placate Polish voters in an election year.[35]

The third foreign policy issue was domestic in origin. In early 1942, President Roosevelt had asked Supreme Court Justice Owen J. Roberts to head a secret investigation of the Pearl Harbor attack. The Roberts Report placed the primary responsibility on the two service commanders in Hawaii, Admiral William Kimmel and General Walter Short, and recommended that they be court-martialed. The War and Navy departments, however, opposed any public trials which might reveal military secrets to the enemy in wartime, and therefore, in December 1943, Congress passed special legislation extending the statute of limitations for Kimmel and Short to June 1944. As the new deadline approached, a debate developed in Congress over resolutions to postpone the courts-martial for another year.

In the Senate, Republicans suggested that the administration wanted to avoid public discussion of Pearl Harbor in an election year. Robert Taft read from an Arthur Krock column calling for a public inquiry to deal with the many unanswered questions about the tragedy. "In general, what is the share the Washington Administration should have in culpability for the success of the Japanese attacks?" Krock pointedly asked. The Democratic leadership quickly beat back this partisan challenge and passed a resolution extending the statute of limitations for twelve months.[36]

Republicans were much stronger in the House, and when the Senate resolution came up for debate, they proposed limiting the extension to only three months, which would force courts-martial before the election in November. "There has already been too much delay and shadow-boxing by the administration in order to avoid telling the whole truth to the American people," charged Representative Hamilton Fish, who promised a full public investigation when the Republicans gained office. Other congressmen hammered away at the idea that the administration had something to hide, demanding that the people be told the facts before the election. Dismissing the Roberts Report as a whitewash, an Illinois Republican asserted that "the responsibility for the Pearl Harbor disaster rests basically on the heads of government at Washington who failed to give adequate warnings to the officers in the Pacific." Despite spirited Democratic rebuttals—most notably by Emanuel Celler of New York, who claimed that public courts-martial would add "grist to Goebbels' mill and would give aid and comfort to Emperor Hirohito"—the House rejected the Senate resolution and enacted its own measure, providing for the Short and Kimmel courts-martial within three months.[37]

The issue then went to a conference committee, which finally arranged a compromise. The time limit was extended for six months, which would take it beyond the election in November, but the resolution directed the secretaries of War and Navy to conduct prompt investigations of the Pearl Harbor attack. Republicans in the House tried to block the conference report, but it passed on a roll-call vote, 213–141. In an unusual step, Roosevelt issued a statement reporting that secretaries Stimson and Knox had recommended that he veto the resolution on the grounds that the required investigations "would give publicity to matters which national security requires still to be withheld from the enemy." But the President then said that he would sign the measure, since he was confident that Congress would not insist on proceedings which "would interrupt or interfere with the war effort." Republicans realized this meant that there would be at best only a perfunctory inquiry, but they were still content. They had raised a potentially embarrassing issue which they could exploit more fully in the fall.[38]

IV

The question of American participation in a new world organization was uppermost in the minds of Republicans as they prepared for their convention. Senator Vandenberg once again took the lead, preparing a one-page draft foreign policy plank based on the Mackinac Declaration and sending it to Thomas E. Dewey in late March for his approval. While Dewey studied it, Senator Warren Austin revised Vandenberg's draft along internationalist lines by including specific provisions for a world organization with the power to enforce peace. In mid-May, Austin and Vandenberg reached agreement on a compromise text which called for American participation in a "postwar cooperative organization among sovereign nations" with the power to use "peace forces to repel or to prevent military aggression." Though Austin's phrase "peace forces" seemed quite ambiguous, Governor Dewey, his foreign policy adviser John Foster Dulles, and Robert Taft, speaking for Bricker, all approved the new draft.[39]

Wendell Willkie threatened the developing Republican consensus on international organization in mid-June when he published a series of newspaper articles outlining his ideas for the party platform. In the last piece, Willkie made an eloquent plea for a postwar policy of international cooperation. He stressed the need for equality between all states, large and small, and urged the immediate creation of a United Nations Council during the war as a first step toward the future world body. Above all, he insisted that the platform be "clear and unambiguous in its attitude toward sovereignty." Criticizing those who stressed national integrity, Willkie pleaded for a platform that would permit genuine cooperation by surrendering part of the nation's power to the international organization. It should emphasize that our sovereignty is not something to be hoarded," Willkie wrote, "but something to be used." [40]

A week before the Republican convention opened in Chicago, senators Vandenberg and Austin presented their draft foreign policy plank to the platform committee, chaired by Robert Taft. Isolationists within the party voiced no objection, but a small group, led by Senator Joseph Ball of Minnesota and Governor Walter Edge of New Jersey, protested that it did not go far enough toward insuring American participation in an effective world organization to keep the peace. They criticized the inclusion of a sentence denouncing the concept of a world state, and they wanted the platform to spell out concretely the nature of the "peace forces" that would be used to prevent aggression. Governor Edge warned against using "rubber words," while Russell Davenport, Willkie's adviser in 1940, announced, "I demand of my party a platform without a single hedge, without a single quaver, on the issue of America's role in the world." Willkie himself, obtaining a draft of the platform from Arthur Krock, on the eve of the convention released a statement critical of the vague wording. Reminding the GOP of the need to avoid repeating its experience in 1920 under Harding, Willkie asserted, "We cannot afford in 1944 to be ambiguous." [41]

Ignoring these criticisms, the Republican leadership moved quickly to accept the Vandenberg-Austin plank. Ball and Edge dropped their threats to take the issue to the convention floor when they realized the delegates were more likely to modify the draft along isolationist rather than internationalist lines. On the second day of the convention, Senator Taft read the platform and then gaveled it through a lightly attended session in just twenty seconds. The foreign policy plank promised a peace "based on justice and security," to be achieved "through organized world cooperation and not by joining a World State." Then it went on to call for American membership in an international organization of "sovereign nations" which would use "peace forces to prevent or repel military aggression." Though a few partisan Democrats attacked the GOP platform as a "straddle" designed to "woo both isolationists and internationalists," most commentators pointed out that the Republicans had taken a position squarely in line with the announced administration plans for world order. "There is no issue here between Republicans and Democrats," concluded the *New York Times*.[42]

The mood of bipartisan cooperation on foreign policy pervaded the brief and rather listless GOP convention. In his keynote address, Governor Earl Warren of California avoided any partisan attacks in calling for "effective cooperation with all the peace-loving nations of the world." Representative Clare Booth Luce, wife of the magazine publisher, struck the only discordant note when she accused Roosevelt of having led the United States into World War II. Referring to those who died in the war as "G. I. Jims," she reminded the delegates of the many times that the President had promised to keep the nation at peace. ". . . [T]hese promises, which were given by a Government that was elected again and again and again because it made them, lie quite as dead as young Jim now. Jim was the heroic heir of the unheroic Roosevelt Decade: a decade of confusion and conflict that ended in war." Though the delegates gave her a standing ovation, other speakers carefully avoided the warmongering charge that had proved ineffective in the 1940 campaign.[43]

On the second day, as the balloting began, the slight suspense over the choice of the nominee quickly disappeared when Governor Bricker removed himself from contention and Senator Ball withdrew Stassen's name. Joe Martin, once again presiding, maneuvered successfully to keep MacArthur's name from being placed in nomination, but a maverick delegate from Wisconsin managed to cast a single ballot for the General as the convention nominated Dewey by a vote of 1056 to 1. After Earl Warren declined the second spot on the ticket, Dewey chose John Bricker, who received the unanimous support of the delegates. Then the New York governor, pointedly departing from Willkie's tactics, delivered his acceptance speech at the final convention session. He promised not to bring the conduct of the war into the campaign, but offered new and fresh leadership on the home front, claiming that the Roosevelt administration was composed of tired old men. Dewey renewed his earlier commitment to international organization, rejecting both those who favored isolationism and those who wished "to renounce all sovereignty and join a super-state." Warning that achieving a decent peace would be a difficult job, he concluded, "This is no task to be entrusted to stubborn men, grown old and tired and quarrelsome in office. We learned that in 1919." [44]

Whatever hope internationalists had that the Republicans would take an advanced stand on world organization died with Dewey's nomination. In the next few days, he cleared most of the remaining Willkie men out of the Republican hierarchy, making Herbert Brownell, a New York lawyer and political adviser, the new national chairman. When reporters asked him if he favored an international police force, Dewey shot back, "If you mean American boys serving in a permanent army under some unseen figure functioning as an international police chief, I believe that is out." Aware of the tension between isolationists and internationalists within the party, Dewey took refuge on the same safe middle ground that Roosevelt already occupied. Unlike Willkie, this cool and methodical man was not going to engage in any emotional, quixotic crusades. Instead, Dewey would probe for politically vulnerable spots, such as the President's age and growing fatigue, in an effort to win an election that even Republican partisans felt was a long shot. [45]

V

The Democratic convention proved to be an even more cut-and-dried affair. On July 11, ten days after Dewey's nomination, Roosevelt ended the speculation about a fourth term. Replying to a letter from Democratic National Chairman Robert Hannegan, informing him that a majority of the delegates favored his renomination, the President announced, "If the Convention should . . . nominate me for the Presidency, I shall accept. If the people elect me, I will serve." He did so reluctantly, saying that he preferred to retire to Hyde Park but that "as a good soldier" he would continue to serve his nation, adding that he did not plan to campaign in the usual partisan sense. Though nearly all observers had anticipated his decision, it relieved his supporters. "I know what that means to the world," commented Samuel Rosenman to Robert Sherwood in London, "and how you will be affected when you read the flash." [46]

At the President's insistence, Rosenman drafted a very brief, 600-word platform. The foreign policy plank, which was shown to the State Department only at the last minute, contained a pledge to establish "an international organization based on the principle of the sovereign equality of all peace-loving states." On the crucial issue of enforcement, the plank called simply for giving the world body the "power to employ armed forces when necessary to prevent aggression," without suggesting any specific way to fulfill this responsibility. Though a few internationalists called for a more forthright statement, the convention quickly adopted the platform after voting down an amendment by a Texas delegate proposing an international air force to keep the peace. The Democrats, like the Republicans, wanted to appeal to the broad public demand for a postwar international organization without committing themselves on details.[47]

Although Roosevelt's nomination was a foregone conclusion, the Democrats used the convention to strike back at the Republicans. Keynote speaker Robert S. Kerr, governor of Oklahoma, answered Clare Booth Luce by charging that the Republicans had "sabotaged" the peace after World War I and had opposed every step Roosevelt took in the 1930's to prepare the nation for another war. Following Harold Ickes's advice, Kerr ridiculed Dewey's reference to "tired old men" by pointing out that nearly all the war leaders, including Churchill, Stalin, General Marshall, and Admiral King, were older than FDR. Turning age into an asset, he asked Dewey what experience he had to qualify him for "the most difficult and important responsibilities and duties ever placed upon the shoulders of any American." In their speeches in behalf of Roosevelt's nomination, Senator Alben Barkley and Vice-President Henry Wallace picked up the theme of mature leadership and pushed it hard. Barkley praised Roosevelt extravagantly for his "touch at the pilot's wheel" that promised to guide the nation safely "through the treacherous waters of international controversy and intrigue," while Wallace declared flatly, "Roosevelt is the only person in the United States who can meet on even terms the other great leaders in discussions of war and peace." [48]

The delegates quickly nominated Roosevelt for a fourth term, with only a scattering of southerners voting for Senator Harry Byrd. But the convention nearly blew apart over the vice-presidential nomination. Throughout the spring, party leaders had been telling Roosevelt that Henry Wallace was a serious liability. Big-city bosses distrusted him as an idealist and reformer; the South viewed him as a dangerous radical. Robert Hannegan finally persuaded FDR to drop him as a running mate, but the President, noted for his inability to break with close associates, led Wallace to believe he still wanted him. FDR also encouraged the candidacy of James Byrnes, the former senator and Supreme Court justice who served as economic coordinator during the war. Since neither labor nor the urban bosses could accept Byrnes, Hannegan had finally prevailed on Roosevelt to write a letter endorsing both Justice William O. Douglas and Senator Harry S. Truman for the job. Truman, who had a New Deal voting record and was on good terms with all elements within the party, was Hannegan's choice, and he used the President's letter to win over other party leaders at Chicago, notably labor men who still preferred Wallace. Truman, who came to the convention to work for Byrnes, did not seek the nomination, but when he was told FDR had chosen him personally, he agreed to run. The convention, however, proved surprisingly loyal to Wallace, and on the first ballot the Vice-President led Truman by more than one hundred votes. On the second ballot, the delegates fell into line and chose Truman by a commanding majority.[49]

The struggle over the vice-presidency highlighted the unspoken concern of virtually all Democrats—the President's health. Although the party leaders did not know of Roosevelt's heart condition, they realized it was unlikely he would live another four years. They considered Wallace too controversial and too volatile, and yet in picking Truman they chose a man who was relatively obscure and apparently without presidential stature. But they felt comfortable with Truman, a professional politician who had always supported the party and who seemed easy to manipulate. On foreign policy, Truman, like Wallace, was a strong internationalist. He had been active in the Senate group sponsoring the B_2H_2 resolution in 1943 and had taken a more advanced position than the platform on the issue of world organization. If anything did happen to Roosevelt, Truman could be counted on to carry through FDR's plans for peace.[50]

The President, who did not attend the convention, delivered his acceptance speech by radio from San Diego, where he had gone to begin a tour of Pacific bases. Commenting that "the isolationists and ostriches" who had opposed him in the past were becoming "extinct," he affirmed his own devotion to the creation of a new world order designed "to make another war impossible within the foreseeable future." Warning against turning over the worldwide responsibilities of the presidency "to inexperienced or immature hands," Roosevelt felt confident that the people would trust their future to "those who saw the danger from abroad, who met it head-on, and who now have seized the offensive and carried the war to its present state of success." [51]

The theme of mature leadership, already sounded at the convention, indicated that Roosevelt planned to stress his conduct of the war and his plans for peace in the fall campaign. With the fighting still raging in Europe and the Pacific, he clearly hoped to capitalize on his years of experience in dealing with world affairs. Yet his age might hurt him as well. In the pictures taken while he gave his acceptance speech, he looked ill, his face thin and haggard and his eyes lacking their usual luster. Though he had recovered from his spring illness, his heart remained enlarged and his blood pressure was still dangerously high. Unless FDR could display some of his old vitality, Dewey might well exploit his own youth and air of efficiency to convince the voters that he would be better equipped for the arduous task of negotiating a just and lasting peace.[52]

VI

With the political conventions safely over, Cordell Hull announced that the United States had invited representatives of Britain, China, and the Soviet Union to come to the United States in late August to draft a plan for a new world organization. The meeting would take place at Dumbarton Oaks, a magnificent Georgetown estate filled with medieval works of art. It was assumed that the conference would use the American draft plan as a starting point, but on August 15, a week before the session was due to open, the *New York Times* reported that the Russians had offered a counter plan which stressed control by the Big Four rather than giving all member nations an equal voice. Thomas Dewey reacted to this news by releasing a statement warning against a return to "the abyss of power politics." Affirming the rights of small nations in the proposed world body, Dewey declared, "The ideals for which we are fighting . . . must not be lost in a cynical peace by which any four powers dominate the earth by force." [53]

Fearful that international organization would now become a political issue, Cordell Hull immediately called a press conference. His voice quivering with emotion, the Secretary denied that the United States would create a world body without insuring equal rights for small nations. ". . . [T]he human race this hour, this day, this week, this year is confronted by the gravest crisis in all its experience," Hull declared in pleading for an end to partisan attacks on postwar planning. After more than an hour, a reporter asked him if he would be willing to meet with the Republican candidate to iron out their differences. "I would welcome such a conference with Governor Dewey," Hull quickly replied.[54]

The next day, Dewey announced that he favored the idea of bipartisan consultation and offered to send John Foster Dulles, his principal foreign policy adviser, to meet with Hull. When the Secretary accepted this arrangement, Dewey and Dulles held a press conference in Albany to stress to reporters that the proposed talks would deal only with international organization. Dulles explained that he and Dewey felt they had a duty to air all other foreign policy issues during the election in order to inform the American people. "This campaign," Dulles stated, "is one of the great educational opportunities that come to the American people. The only way in which a democracy makes up its mind, and makes up its mind in a way that it sticks, is by having these issues debated and discussed." [55]

Dulles set out for Washington after stopping off in New

York City for a conference with Wendell Willkie, who was carefully refusing to commit himself on the presidential contest. Arriving in the capital on August 23, Dulles met with senators Austin and Vandenberg before going to the State Department. For nearly three hours, Dulles and Hull exchanged views on a wide range of foreign policy issues. When the Secretary handed him a copy of the American draft plan, Dulles indicated that Dewey was willing to take the issue of international organization out of the coming campaign. But when Hull also suggested that such controversial subjects as wartime agreements with Russia and the fate of Poland be removed from politics, Dulles quickly disagreed. The session finally broke down in a long semantic struggle as Hull insisted on a nonpartisan agreement while Dulles countered with a demand for a bipartisan one. "The Secretary seemed to me very stubborn," Dulles later wrote. "Perhaps I seemed that way to him." [56]

The two men met the next day in a more cordial atmosphere. Dulles told Hull he approved the American draft plan, noting that there was ample protection for small nations. Hull then produced a statement for Dulles to sign that endorsed the American plan and promised not to make it a campaign issue. Dulles said he would be happy to sign as an individual but would have to consult with Governor Dewey before he could commit the candidate. The next morning Dulles returned with a revision of Hull's statement that incorporated Dewey's reservations, and after an hour the two men signed it. They then called in the press and read the text, which stated that Dewey agreed with Hull that the issue of international organization should be treated "as a nonpartisan subject which must be kept entirely out of politics." This arrangement, the statement continued, "did not preclude full public nonpartisan discussion of the means of attaining a lasting peace." In response to reporters' questions, Dulles made it clear that the understanding dealt only with international organization, commenting that "of course, all other aspects are not included in this agreement." [57]

Hull was delighted. All along, his great fear had been that his plans for international organization would become embroiled in the 1944 election. Recalling the way in which partisan considerations had doomed Wilson's League, he had worked steadily to prevent another such disaster. The bipartisan agreement with Dulles promised that the plans for world organization being discussed at Dumbarton Oaks would be protected from political criticism. Roosevelt apparently approved of the arrangement, but it is unlikely that he shared the Secretary's feeling of relief. FDR was always skeptical of Republican motives, and he knew from past experience how hard it was for candidates to restrict their statements in the heat of a campaign. Yet he allowed Hull to make the arrangement, probably because he recognized the value of GOP approval for his administration's postwar plans. The Republicans had acknowledged that Roosevelt was moving in the right direction on the issue of deepest concern to all Americans. [58]

Dewey realized the risk he was running, but he too acted with political calculation. The specter of Republican isolationism, going back to the defeat of the League and Harding's "return to normalcy," remained the party's most damaging legacy from the past. By affirming his commitment to the plans for world organization, Dewey hoped to brighten the GOP image and appeal to the strongly internationalist mood of the nation's voters in 1944. Equally important, the Republicans could now claim that it was not necessary for the nation to reelect FDR in order to insure American participation in a new international body. Yet at the same time Dewey was free to attack all other aspects of the administration's foreign policy, particularly Poland and future relations with the Soviet Union. With such tempting campaign targets, Dewey could easily afford to be cooperative in the sensitive area of international organization.[59]

"We have done something which is unique in American politics," Dulles commented. Although both sides acted out of short-run political considerations, they had taken a step which in the future would lead to broader areas of bipartisan cooperation in the formation and conduct of American diplomacy. In that sense, the Hull-Dulles agreement did constitute, as Dewey predicted, "a new attitude toward the problem of peace." But the two parties still had to prove that they could live up to their new commitment in the campaign that lay ahead.[60]

4567

In the summer of 1944, the course of the war appeared to hold the key to the presidential election. A month after D-Day, American armored forces led by General George Patton had broken out of Normandy, outflanking and then overcoming the stubborn German resistance. Allied armies liberated Paris on August 25, and by September they occupied all of France. Only a shortage of gasoline and ammunition held Eisenhower's forces back from a final assault on Germany. The war against the Japanese was going almost as well. General Douglas MacArthur had driven the enemy from New Guinea and was preparing for his promised return to the Philippines, while in the Central Pacific Admiral Chester Nimitz directed the successful conquest of Guam, Saipan, and Tinian in the Marianas, all within bombing range of Japan. Intense public interest in these stirring battles made politics seem quite secondary, creating, as Turner Catledge remarked, "as deep a sea of apathy as any crew of Presidential and Vice-Presidential candidates has been called upon to navigate in many years." [1]

Pollsters and political experts predicted a close race. The *Fortune* poll conducted by Elmo Roper showed FDR leading

Dewey 49 to 43 percent, with 8 percent undecided. Gallup indicated that in August the President was barely ahead in electoral votes, 286 to 245. A *Newsweek* board of political writers gave Roosevelt a slight edge, but noted that the trend was moving toward Dewey. Hadley Cantril, the Princeton expert who furnished the White House with confidential public opinion reports, warned the President's aides in early August that the election would be very close, though, he added, "neither Gallup nor I would as yet put any money on Dewey." In a published report, Cantril pointed out that the public overwhelmingly approved of Roosevelt's conduct of the war and preferred him to Dewey as the man to negotiate the terms of peace by a 3 to 1 margin. Nearly all the polls indicated, however, that if the war should end suddenly before the election, Roosevelt's vote would drop sharply and Dewey might be able to win. Most observers believed that the war would continue through November, and when voters were asked who they thought would win regardless of their own preference, two-thirds named Roosevelt and only 22 percent selected Dewey.[2]

Democratic strategists realized that the war was their greatest asset. Paul Porter, in charge of publicity for the National Committee, sent FDR a Walter Lippmann column in mid-July praising the President's leadership as Commander-in-Chief. "It should be used by many of our people over the air and in speeches," Porter urged, adding that Dewey had no knowledge or experience with high strategy. Hadley Cantril informed Samuel Rosenman in August that it was essential to point out to voters that peacemaking would last long after the war was over, and then advised, "Anything that can be done to maintain the sense of crisis with respect to the peace as well as the war would be most advantageous." The President's advisers worried most over the public apathy, remembering that a low turnout in 1942 had almost enabled the Republicans to gain control of Congress. They were also concerned with the President's lack of interest in campaigning. "His present attitude is to do practically nothing," Rosenman complained to Robert Sherwood.[3]

The President's aides need not have worried, for FDR realized that his continuing activities as wartime leader had greater political impact than partisan speeches. With his usual shrewd sense of timing, he embarked on a trip to Hawaii and the Aleutians at the conclusion of the Democratic convention. At Pearl Harbor, he met with Admiral Nimitz and General MacArthur to discuss future strategy in the Pacific, including the decision to invade the Philippines in the fall. Though the military discussions were secret, newspapers across the country carried front-page pictures of Roosevelt flanked by Nimitz and MacArthur, reinforcing the image of a President too busy conducting the war to bother with a political campaign.

Roosevelt reported to the nation on his trip from the deck of a destroyer in Bremerton, Washington, on August 12, and it was a disastrous experience. Wearing his heavy metal braces for the first time in over a year, Roosevelt stood unsteadily on the ship's sloping deck with a stiff wind ruffling his manuscript. He gave a rambling talk, speaking slowly and haltingly as agonizing pains enveloped his chest. His doctors, fearing a heart attack, found that he was suffering only from fatigue and the uncomfortable braces, but the nation's press began to speculate again about the state of his health. He seemed stronger and more like himself at a press conference held in Washington after his return, but reporters, noting he had lost weight and seemed very irritable, continued to wonder whether a young and energetic Dewey might not be a better man to lead the nation to victory and an enduring peace.[4]

I

Knowing that he faced an uphill struggle, Dewey spent the summer planning the fall campaign. His greatest concern was to avoid Willkie's errors. Rembering how the Republican candidate had alienated voters in 1940 by speaking out unnecessarily on controversial issues, Dewey kept silent throughout July and August. He worked in Albany to make sure that when the hectic barnstorming began in September he would be prepared. With characteristic attention to detail, he had a team of speech-writers, headed by Elliott Bell, preparing the major addresses he planned to give. They would hand him a draft, he would rework it, and then when it was in final form, Dewey would rehearse it carefully so that he knew within a minute how long it would take. He also invited party leaders to Albany, and, unlike Willkie, took their advice seriously—realizing that national elections were won state by state.[5]

In early September, Dewey announced that he would begin his active campaign with a three-week, 6,500-mile swing to the West Coast and back. Only a handful of people were present to see him off from Grand Central Station on September 7, but organization, not enthusiasm, proved to be the hallmark of the Dewey effort. Following his announced schedule precisely, he went from city to city without stopping for the usual back-platform, off-the-cuff talks along the way. He would travel by motorcade from the train to a downtown hotel, where he would meet with local party leaders, listening to their problems and patiently considering their recommendations. Then, after a brief press conference in which he usually managed to dodge the tough questions, Dewey would speak in the evening to a large audience, giving a prepared address that was carried on the radio so as to capitalize on his mellow speaking voice. Then, accompanied by Elliott Bell, Paul Lockwood, his private secretary, and Jim Hagerty, his press secretary, he would retire to the train and prepare for the next day's activities.[6]

Reporters found it incredibly tedious. There was no hand-shaking, no back-slapping, no display of warmth; there was never even a slip that revealed Dewey's humanness. Instead, as *Time* commented, the Dewey campaign moved with "almost metronomic precision." "The whole enterprise was a magnificent display of efficiency," wrote James A. Wechsler. "It was also monotonous, uninspired. It looked as if the GOP were engaged in a conspiracy to bore the electorate." Journalists began to let their contempt for Dewey color their dispatches. They stressed his short stature, pointing out that he insisted the lecterns for his speeches be exactly forty-two inches high and that Hagerty was instructed to remind the press that Dewey, at five-feet-eight, was taller than Stalin! They commented on his aloof, cold personality, and even mocked his rich baritone delivery, noting that he ran "the gamut of emotions from A to B" and possessed "all a speaker should have except warmth, humor and fellow feeling." With a touch of nostalgia, they yearned for the hectic, helter-skelter air of Willkie's crusade as they reported on Dewey's professional but drab performance.[7]

Not only did the Republicans face a serious problem with their candidate's image, but they lacked an outstanding issue. Roosevelt had monopolized the war, and the bipartisan agreement between Hull and Dulles excluded international organization from the campaign. And the voters seemed too preoccupied with the fighting to be interested in postwar domestic concerns. Finally the GOP hit upon a phrase that Roosevelt reportedly had uttered to Robert Hannegan in regard to the vice-presidential nomination, "Clear it with Sidney." According to Arthur Krock, Hannegan had told Democratic leaders at Chicago that FDR had ordered him to be sure that Sidney Hillman, prominent CIO leader and director of the Political Action Committee, a labor group trying to get out the vote for Roosevelt, approved of whoever was chosen to replace Wallace. Changing the phrase to "clear everything with Sidney," the Republican National Committee printed up thousands of pamphlets and sent out one-minute spot radio messages charging that Roosevelt was the captive of left-wing labor forces. Though Dewey was careful to avoid using this technique himself, he permitted his running mate, John Bricker, to cite the "clear everything with Sidney" line in his acceptance speech in early September. Bricker then went on to charge, "In that tense command the New Deal candidate delivered the Democratic party into the hands of Sidney Hillman, the radical leader of the Political Action Committee." As the campaign continued, Republican orators linked Hillman with Earl Browder, the Communist leader whom Roosevelt had released from prison, to suggest by innuendo that FDR was controlled by the Communists. This smear tactic reflected both a growing realization that the PAC was a powerful asset to Roosevelt and a desire to appeal to nativist, anti-Semitic, and anti-Communist sentiment.[8]

Dewey, meanwhile, stuck to the high ground in his speeches. Aware of strong internationalist feeling in the country, he realized he needed to clarify his own views and repudiate his past flirtations with isolationism, particularly after historian Gerald W. Johnson addressed an open letter to him in the *Atlantic Monthly* asking point-blank, "What do you, as a Presidential candidate, offer me, as a voter, that Harding did not offer in 1920?" Dewey gave his answer in Louisville in a nationally broadcast speech. In clear, forthright words, he endorsed the administration's plans for international organization, saying he favored "the use of force as well as the mobilization of international opinion or moral pressure" to restrain aggressors. At the same time, he appealed to supporters of Willkie and other internationalists by stressing again the importance of working with the small nations and not relying solely on "a few strong friends . . . to rule the world." Above all, he warned that Roosevelt alone could not make the peace. "No one man or two or three or four men can shape it," Dewey declared. "Some sixty nations all over the globe, great and small, must help to shape it, must believe in it, join it, and make it work over all these years to come."[9]

A chorus of praise greeted the Louisville speech as liberal

internationalists thanked Dewey for living up to the bipartisan agreement on world organization. He made no further mention of foreign policy as he traveled on to California. At Los Angeles, his address on domestic issues before a huge crowd of 90,000 at the Coliseum fell flat despite elaborate preparations by Cecil B. de Mille and David O. Selznick. In Portland, he referred briefly to the future peace, saying it "must not hang by the slender thread of personal acquaintance of any two or three men." As he returned to the East, he continued his precise campaign tactics without mentioning international issues again.[10]

Although Dewey conspicuously failed to generate excitement or bring out enthusiastic crowds, his first trip proved quite successful. *Newsweek* reported that Dewey had "scored marked gains in recent weeks and the re-election of President Roosevelt is now in doubt." The magazine's experts now gave FDR only 267 electoral votes, just one more than the number needed for victory. The estimate, based on trends within each state, reflected the effectiveness of Dewey's approach. Realizing that elections were won in the precincts and not in newspaper headlines, Dewey had carefully cultivated the local leaders who were responsible for delivering the votes in their areas. The private talks with the professionals, not the flat and routine public speeches, had boosted Dewey's chances and made him the most dangerous opponent Roosevelt had yet faced.[11]

II

While Dewey campaigned through the West, the President met with Winston Churchill at Quebec to make important wartime decisions. When Republicans claimed the Quebec Conference had been arranged to overshadow their candidate's activities, Churchill informed the press that he had insisted on meeting with FDR at this time because there were many pressing matters to be decided. For a week, the two leaders met in private, discussing military plans for the defeat of the Axis, signing a highly secret agreement on the future atomic bomb, and adopting the Morgenthau plan for the harsh treatment of postwar Germany. On September 16, they issued a communiqué announcing only that they had coordinated plans to end the war in Europe, which they said was "now approaching its final stages," and to transfer troops to defeat "the barbarians of the Pacific" as soon as Germany surrendered. In a press conference that followed, Churchill called FDR "my august friend" and suggested that their close personal relationship would facilitate the task of negotiating peace.[12]

The Democrats did all they could to advance the thesis that Roosevelt was indispensable for the achievement of a just and lasting peace. Harry Truman had revealed this basic campaign strategy in his acceptance speech, delivered August 31 in his birthplace, Lamar, Missouri. Though only 7,000 people were present, a radio audience of millions heard him extol Roosevelt for his experience, wisdom, and mature judgment in international affairs. He reminded his listeners of Republican isolationism after World War I and stressed FDR's years of close association with Churchill, Stalin, and Chiang Kai-shek. "Ask yourselves whether you would dare to entrust the negotiation of the peace of the world to those who are not familiar with world affairs," Truman concluded. "You can't afford to take a chance. You should endorse tried and experienced leadership—you should reelect Franklin D. Roosevelt President of the United States." [13]

Other prominent Democrats sounded the same theme. Josephus Daniels, the North Carolina politician who had served as Wilson's Secretary of the Navy, wrote to Cordell Hull asking him and Secretary of War Henry L. Stimson to tell the nation that "the only way to insure peace is to reelect Roosevelt." "If we are to win," Daniels added, "we must pull every string." Senator Robert Wagner apparently agreed; in a speech to the New York State CIO convention, he attacked Dewey's inexperience in foreign policy and then declared that the country could not leave the job of peace to "the isolationists and appeasers of 1940." The most effective statement came from Henry Wallace, who put aside his injured feelings and addressed a mass rally for Roosevelt in Madison Square Garden on September 21. The Republicans, he charged, could not be trusted with the peace. "In spite of everything Dewey has said, the isolationists are still going to vote Republican in 1944." Calling Dewey another Harding, he echoed Truman's claim that Roosevelt's intimate relationship with Churchill, Stalin, and Chiang insured "a lasting, liberal, democratic peace." "He has met them face to face," Wallace argued. "He knows their innermost reactions because he has been in continuous, almost daily contact with them for several years." [14]

Roosevelt's other major tactic was to woo the independents who were strongly in favor of international organization. The 10 million voters without party affiliation would decide the election, he told Robert Sherwood, and he planned to direct his campaign to win a substantial majority of them. Realizing that Wendell Willkie was the key to this crucial group, Roosevelt sent Samuel Rosenman to talk to him after hearing that Willkie had expressed interest in forming a new liberal party. Rosenman spent the evening of July 4 and much of the next day listening to complaints about the "reactionaries" within both parties and reported back to Roosevelt that Willkie would like to meet with the President after the election to talk about forming a new political coalition of progressives. FDR promptly asked Willkie to come to the White House for a private meeting to talk "about the future," promising not to raise anything relating to the "present campaign." When news of this invitation leaked to the press, Willkie feared that the President was trying to maneuver him into an endorsement, so he told

Roosevelt that he wanted to postpone the meeting until after the election. Aware that he had scared off his former rival, Roosevelt let the matter drop.[15]

In September, Willkie published a series of articles in *Collier's* urging both candidates to take a more advanced stand on international organization, but refusing to endorse either one. Later in the month, Willkie entered the hospital with a serious heart condition and died on October 8 without indicating how he had planned to vote. Partisans of both candidates claimed he would have supported their man, until his widow asked them to stop their speculations out of respect for her husband. Roosevelt may well have believed a report from Harry Hopkins that Willkie had informed Lord Beaverbrook, a member of Churchill's war cabinet, that he would declare for FDR in October. However, Roscoe Drummond, a Republican journalist who saw him only a week before his death, said Willkie remained uncertain till the end, telling Drummond, "Frankly, I cannot answer your ultimate question yet because I have not finally decided." But even though Willkie remained noncommittal, the fact that he refused to support Dewey gave Roosevelt an excellent chance of winning over many of his followers, Republicans as well as independents.[16]

Although Roosevelt helped shape the strategy, his basic lack of interest in the campaign worried his advisers. Robert Sherwood, returning from London, found him absorbed in the war and strangely reluctant to engage in the struggle for his reelection. Surprised by FDR's indifference, Sherwood was truly shocked by his appearance. The President had lost twenty pounds since May, partly because of the low-fat diet prescribed by his doctors and partly because of a lagging appetite. "His features had become sharpened and he looked somewhat haggard in place of his normal, robust appearance," commented his heart specialist, who was worried over the loss of weight and tried to get the President to eat more heartily. His blood pressure continued to rise, ranging from

180/100 to 240/130, but there were no more cardiac symptoms.[17]

Pressed by his advisers to enter into the campaign, FDR finally agreed to address the annual Teamsters convention banquet on September 21 in Washington. To Sherwood's delight, he began to take an interest in the speech, displaying his usual flashes of humor and zest for politics as he added some sharply barbed remarks to the drafts Rosenman and Sherwood prepared. Because of his weakened health, he spoke to the Teamsters sitting down, but from his opening sentence FDR proved that he still had the ability to hold an audience and win its roaring approval. Attacking the Republicans with a mixture of irony, sarcasm, and wit, the President provoked waves of laughter, especially when he mocked the GOP charge that he had sent a destroyer back to an Aleutian island to rescue his forgotten dog, Fala. Though he dwelt mainly on domestic themes, he reminded his audience of past Republican isolationism. "These peace-building tasks were faced once before, nearly a generation ago," he asserted. "They were botched by a Republican Administration. That must not happen again. We will not let it happen this time." [18]

The audience of more than a thousand rose to its feet to give the President a five-minute ovation. The nation's press was equally enthusiastic. The editors of the *New Republic* called it "one of the most effective political utterances of his whole career," while *Time* compared FDR to a piano virtuoso "playing a piece he has loved for years," who displays "a delicate fire, a perfection of timing and tone, and an assurance that no young player, no matter how gifted, can equal." Most important, Roosevelt had shown that he still possessed the vitality as well as the political skill demanded in a presidential election. Thus Arthur Krock, who disliked FDR intensely, admitted, "Mr. Roosevelt had swept away doubts of his physical capacity to carry on for another four years and had turned the Democratic campaign from defense to attack." [19]

The Teamsters speech had an electrifying effect, bringing a dull and apathetic campaign to life. Stung by FDR's charges, Dewey discarded the prepared text of a speech he planned to give in Oklahoma City and instead, for the first time, let fly directly at the President. Claiming that the Teamsters address was "a speech of mud-slinging, ridicule and wise-cracks," Dewey said it "plumbed the depths of demagogy." Then he accused the President of failing to prepare the nation for war, citing a report by General George Marshall that at the time of Pearl Harbor the army was only 25 percent ready for combat. Dewey denied Truman's claim that the President was "indispensable" in the making of peace, concluding that FDR was indispensable only to "the ill-assorted, power-hungry conglomeration of city bosses, Communists and career bureaucrats which now comprise the New Deal." [20]

For the next two weeks, the campaign took on an ugly aspect as Dewey hammered away at the Communist issue. When Earl Browder called upon his followers to vote for Roosevelt, Dewey charged that the Communist leader was directing FDR's "campaign for his fourth term." Dewey was careful not to attack the Soviet Union in his Red-baiting speeches, saying he was only concerned about the Communist influence at home. These charges worried Roosevelt, and finally, on October 5, he gave a fireside chat from the White House in which he accused the Republicans of using "the term 'Communism' loosely." "I have never sought," the President solemnly declared, "and I do not welcome the support of any person or group committed to Communism, or Fascism, or any other foreign ideology which would undermine the American system of government." [21]

Although Dewey forced FDR to take the defensive, the flurry of charges and countercharges created an aura of excitement and interest that greatly benefited the President. Democratic strategists feared apathy above all else, realizing that a low voter turnout would aid the Republicans, who could count on a solid core of GOP regulars. Many workers who had always supported Roosevelt had crossed state lines in taking war jobs, and unless they made a special effort to register, they could not vote. Sidney Hillman's Political Action Committee directed a massive registration drive among union members, but labor alone could not get all the potential Democratic voters to the polls. The Teamsters speech, touching off heated exchanges between Roosevelt and Dewey, provided the spark that FDR's advisers had sought in order to insure a lively campaign and a full turnout on election day.[22]

III

The tragic unfolding of events in Poland in the summer and fall of 1944 created a potentially explosive campaign issue. After his visit with FDR in June, Prime Minister Stanislaus Mikolajczyk had flown to Moscow to confer with Stalin. The Russian leader greeted him cordially, but insisted that he negotiate with the members of the Polish National Committee of Liberation, the puppet government the Soviets had established at Lublin in July when they began moving back into Polish territory. Mikolajczyk made no progress in his talks with the Lublin Poles. Then in August, as the Russian army approached the Vistula River, the Polish underground army in Warsaw began an armed uprising against the Nazi garrison. For two months the heroic Poles fought a savage battle against the superior German forces while the Russians remained stationary east of the Vistula. Despite appeals from Churchill and Roosevelt, Stalin refused to aid the Warsaw rebels, who finally surrendered in early October. They had lost nearly 300,000 in the futile struggle, which aroused world sympathy and made American Poles more sensitive than ever to the plight of Poland.[23]

Realizing that the Soviet Union would determine the final settlement, Mikolajczyk returned to Moscow in October when he learned that Churchill had gone there to confer with Stalin. On October 13, the British and Russian leaders permitted Mikolajczyk to join their discussion on Poland, with American Ambassador Averell Harriman sitting in to keep Roosevelt informed. When the boundary issue came up, Russian Foreign Minister Vyacheslav Molotov turned to the Polish leader and bluntly told him that at Teheran Roosevelt and Churchill had accepted the Curzon line. This statement contradicted Roosevelt's assertion in June that he had not agreed to the Curzon line, but when Mikolajczyk questioned the point, Molotov looked directly at Churchill, who nodded and said, "I confirm this." Three days later, Mikolajczyk sent his foreign minister to register a protest with Harriman. The American ambassador listened politely, said that it was his understanding that the President had not agreed to the Curzon line, but then pleaded with the Poles not to press the point, "as it would only raise further issues publicly which would lead to difficulties adverse to Polish interests." [24]

Though Harriman used polite diplomatic language, what he and other Democrats feared was the possible effect of the boundary question on the election. Observers noted in September that Polish voters, who normally went Democratic by about 9 to 1, were reluctant to commit themselves. Apprehensive about the future of Poland, they preferred to wait and see what policy the administration would follow. With more than 100,000 Polish voters in seven key industrial states, Democratic politicians began to grow very nervous. Senator O'Mahoney called the White House after conferring with party leaders in Chicago to report that "there are a lot of Poles in Illinois and Ohio" who were "emotionally disturbed." Frank Nurczyk, a leader of the Polish-American Businessmen's Association, wrote FDR in mid-September to warn about the apathy among Polish-American voters in Chicago. "Will you kindly talk to your friends, Messrs. Winston Churchill and Joseph Stalin, and really do somethin [sic] substantial, and soon, for those poor suffering Polish souls in Poland?" he pleaded to FDR. "We have here at least 300,000 Polish votes." [25]

Politicians realized that the American Polish Congress, the group organized in May, could influence Polish voting behavior most effectively. Attorney General Francis Biddle urged Roosevelt to receive a delegation from the Congress on October 11, the anniversary of the death of General Pulaski, the Revolutionary war hero. National Chairman Robert Hannegan reported to a White House aide that Mayor Ed Kelly of Chicago felt that this meeting was "absolutely imperative," while Senator Ed Guffey called it "urgent," saying, "It will help us greatly in Pennsylvania." Roosevelt finally agreed to meet with a delegation led by Charles Rozmarek to receive the memorial on Poland they had adopted in May. For nearly an hour, FDR talked with the Polish Americans, assuring them of his interest but avoiding any specific commitments. We are all agreed, the President said at the end of the interview, that "Poland must be reconstituted as a great nation." Then he allowed photographers to take a picture of the delegation shaking hands with him in front of a large map of Poland on which the prewar boundaries, extending far to the east into territory now held by Russia, were marked in heavy ink. In the remaining weeks of the campaign, Democrats arranged for the publication of this photograph in Polish-language papers across the nation, leading many to believe that the President backed the London government in rejecting the Curzon line. [26]

Republicans also tried to exploit the Polish issue, but with relatively little success. Governor Dewey did attend a Pulaski Day parade in New York City. After watching 45,000 Polish Americans march by, he declared his support for the "reestablishment of Poland as an independent and sovereign nation," adding that "American citizens of Polish descent would do well to do everything in their power to bring discussions of Poland's fate from the dark to the light." In a speech to the

New York Herald Tribune forum in mid-October, Dewey openly accused the President of engaging in secret diplomacy with Stalin on Poland. "As a result," he charged, "Mr. Roosevelt has not yet even secured Russian recognition of those whom we consider to be the true Government of Poland." A prominent Polish publisher wrote to Dewey praising him for the "irrefutable logic" of this speech and urging him to hammer away at the administration so that "a powerful campaign weapon can be forged, a magnet that might draw millions of Polish-Americans to our colors." But Dewey, following the advice of Arthur Vandenberg, made no further references to Poland in his campaign speeches, never even mentioning the crucial boundary question. Apparently fearful of disturbing wartime relations with the Soviet Union, Dewey refused to exploit the Polish issue.[27]

President Roosevelt, however, continued to worry. When the Soviet press attacked Dewey for supporting the "adventurist ambitions" of the London Poles in his Pulaski Day address, FDR arranged for Joseph Davies, former ambassador to Russia who had close ties with the Kremlin, to send a message to Stalin asking him to "pipe down" about the American election lest the GOP capitalize on Soviet interference. On October 20, Davies asked Stalin to keep the Russian press from commenting on Dewey's statements, pointing out that such comments "would be directed to arouse resentment among certain of our people, who otherwise would be favorable." Roosevelt wrote Davies on October 24 to thank him for this message, which the Russians heeded.[28]

The only remaining danger lay with Mikolajczyk, who could create a sensation by announcing that the President had secretly accepted the Curzon line. On October 27, the Polish prime minister sent a desperate telegram to Roosevelt, stating that he was under intense pressure from the British and the Russians to give way on the boundary issue. Mikolajczyk told FDR he still believed the President's assurances that he had not accepted the Curzon line, despite Molotov's statement, and he begged him to intervene with Stalin on behalf of a more favorable territorial settlement. Roosevelt temporized, telling Mikolajczyk the next day that he would take the matter under "personal consideration." "I expect to send you another message soon," the President added.[29]

That same day, October 28, the President traveled to Chicago to campaign in the Middle West. Charles Rozmarek, the chairman of the Polish-American Congress, met privately with him on board the train to urge him to take a tougher stand on Poland with the Soviets, suggesting that he threaten to cut off all lend-lease aid. Roosevelt replied that he could not jeopardize the war effort. "The President let it be understood," Rozmarek wrote later, "that once Hitler was defeated, he would know how to handle Stalin." FDR used all his persuasive powers to convince Rozmarek that he would stand behind Poland in the coming peace. Then Rozmarek, beaming with confidence, repeated these assurances to the press and declared, "Because I am convinced of his sincerity, I shall vote for him on November 7 for President of the United States." [30]

Rozmarek's endorsement, carried prominently in Polish-language newspapers, helped hold the Polish vote solidly for Roosevelt. Mikolajczyk kept his silence about FDR's agreement on the Curzon line, and when the President finally answered his urgent plea on November 17, he politely but firmly told the Polish Prime Minister that he would have to accept whatever arrangement the Russians would grant. Roosevelt's double-dealing on the Curzon line leaked out to the Polish community after the election, but it was too late to affect the results. When an irate Senator Vandenberg wrote to Republican publisher Frank Januszewski asking why "an overwhelming majority of Polish-Americans" had voted for FDR in light of his attitude toward Poland, Januszewski replied, "the majority of the Polish-American organizations deliberately refrained from injecting Poland's case into our election politics." Bemoaning the failure of the GOP to arouse Polish support, the publisher concluded, "Our party blundered this time." [31]

IV

Roosevelt also shrewdly manipulated two other ethnic groups during the campaign—Jews and Italians. The Palestine issue had lain dormant since Congress tabled the resolutions calling for unlimited immigration and a future Jewish commonwealth. On October 11, Rabbi Stephen Wise visited FDR at the White House, and when he left he told reporters that the President planned to endorse the Democratic platform plank on Palestine in a message to a forthcoming convention of the Zionist Organization of America. In an effort to beat Roosevelt to the punch, Dewey met with Rabbi Abba Hillel Silver on October 12 and released his own statement. "I am for the re-constitution of Palestine as a free and democratic Jewish commonwealth," Dewey declared, adding that he also favored unrestricted migration into Palestine after the war. Three days later, Senator Robert Wagner delivered the President's message to the convention. Repeating the Democratic platform's commitment to "a free and democratic commonwealth" in Palestine, Roosevelt then promised, "if re-elected I shall help to bring about its realization." Zionist leaders were quick to hail FDR's message as "the strongest and most unequivocal" ever made by an American president on Palestine.[32]

At the same time, the administration took one additional step to sway Jewish voters. On October 15, Chairman Sol Bloom of the House Foreign Affairs Committee made public the text of a new letter from Secretary of War Henry Stimson. Commenting on his earlier opposition to passage of the Palestine resolution, Stimson now wrote, "In my judgment, political considerations now outweigh the military, and the issue should be determined upon the political rather than the military basis." Zionists felt this meant that the United States was likely to intervene on their behalf with Great Britain, but the State Department immediately protested, reminding the President that he had promised King Saud not to act on Palestine without consulting the Arabs. Worried over the possible loss of political influence and oil concessions in the Middle East after the election, the administration again postponed action on the Palestine resolutions. Republicans felt that the President had outmaneuvered them. Dewey claimed that he received only one Jewish vote of every twenty in New York City, while Arthur Vandenberg protested, "The Zionists' trouble is that Roosevelt has been 'playing politics' with them." In reality, both parties had been playing politics with the Jewish vote, but the Democrats were more adroit at the game.[33]

Roosevelt proved equally adept at courting Italian Americans. After Pearl Harbor, Italy had been at war with the United States until a group led by Marshal Bagdolio ousted Mussolini and signed a surrender agreement in September 1943. Italy then became a battleground as American and British forces slowly fought their way to Rome, which fell in June 1944. The fighting continued to disrupt the Italian economy, already severely strained by the war. FDR discussed the plight of Italy with Churchill at the Quebec conference, and on September 26 Roosevelt announced plans to extend generous economic aid for Italian relief and to discuss resumption of normal diplomatic relations.[34]

The announcement of aid to Italy and the possibility of diplomatic recognition pleased Democratic leaders who were concerned about the Italian vote. On October 9, Dewey made an overt bid for support by insisting that Italy be considered "a friend and ally" against Nazi Germany. Roosevelt replied three days later in accepting a Columbus Day award from the Italian-American Labor Council in New York City. Stating that the Italian people had suffered for twenty years under the yoke of Mussolini, the President declared, "The American Army—including thousands of Americans of Italian descent —entered Italy not as conquerors but as liberators." He described Italy as among "the great peace-loving Nations of the world," and promised that when the fighting was over "the Italian people will be free to work out their own destiny, under a government of their own choosing." On October 26, the administration announced that the United States had appointed an ambassador in Rome and thus was resuming normal diplomatic relations with Italy. Roosevelt's generous policy, together with frequent public appearances through the northeast by Mayor LaGuardia of New York City, helped the Democrats retain their normal heavy majority among Italian voters.[35]

V

Pearl Harbor threatened to emerge as a prominent issue throughout the fall. In September, as both the Navy and War departments were conducting the required investigations of the Japanese attack, Republican congressmen kept up a steady call for a public inquiry prior to election day. Disguising their accusations in the form of questions, the GOP legislators asked if it were true that on the preceding day Roosevelt had received word of the coming assault. "The primary responsibility for the Pearl Harbor catastrophe was in Washington and not in the Pacific," declared Representative Ralph E. Church of Illinois. On September 18, Republican Representative Forest A. Harness of Indiana introduced a resolution calling for a House committee to conduct a special study of the disaster and report back within thirty days. Representative Hugh Scott of Pennsylvania endorsed this move, saying, "the Pearl Harbor tragedy has reached the proportions of a national scandal." [36]

Although observers predicted that Dewey would make

Pearl Harbor a major campaign issue from the outset, he consistently refrained from mentioning it. Instead, he permitted his supporters to develop the charge, in much the same way that FDR always allowed others to make the unsavory accusations. On September 20, John Bricker called for a prompt court-martial for Admiral Kimmel and General Short, charging that the Roosevelt administration was withholding facts on "the disgraceful Pearl Harbor episode." Clare Booth Luce hit out several times in October, rebutting Roosevelt's claim to greatness as a commander-in-chief by asserting that a great leader would have avoided the disaster at Pearl Harbor. "[H]e is the only American President who ever lied us into a war because he did not have the courage to lead us into it," she told a Chicago audience. "Thus, in the end, the shame of Pearl Harbor was Mr. Roosevelt's shame." Near the end of the campaign, Representative Melvin Maas, a Minnesota Republican, asserted that the President was suppressing the report of the Navy's recent investigation because it revealed that "the President and high officials had word of the Pearl Harbor attack plans six hours in advance and sent no warning." Secretary of the Navy James Forrestal, who had succeeded the late Frank Knox earlier in the year, then took the responsibility for withholding the report, announcing that it contained secret information that "would cause exceptionally grave damage to the nation." [37]

In late October, Harry Hopkins discovered why the President insisted on maintaining secrecy on Pearl Harbor despite the charges of political censorship. In the spring of 1941, naval intelligence had broken the Japanese diplomatic codes and was able to read the dispatches passing between Tokyo and Japanese diplomats in Washington. The armed forces relied heavily on this breakthrough during the war, and any public investigation of Pearl Harbor was bound to disclose this information to the Japanese and lead them to change their codes. In the early stages of the campaign, a high-ranking officer had informed Governor Dewey of the code-breaking, and the Republican candidate seriously considered revealing that FDR had received a direct warning of the Japanese attack on Pearl Harbor. General George Marshall learned of this possibility and, without consulting the President, wrote a personal letter to Dewey, warning him that disclosure of the code-breaking would have a "calamitous" effect on the war effort and asking him to remain silent. When Hopkins told Roosevelt of this incident, the President remarked that "he felt confident that Governor Dewey would not, for political purposes, give secret and vital information to the enemy." "My opponent," he added, "must be pretty desperate if he is even thinking of using material like this which would be bound to react against him." [38]

Dewey followed his patriotic impulses and never mentioned the breaking of the code. Despite Roosevelt's casual dismissal of this episode, General Marshall did the President a great favor. Pearl Harbor was a major political liability which the Republicans could have exploited to much greater advantage than they did. Subsequent Congressional investigations of Pearl Harbor proved that millions of Americans were ready to believe that President Roosevelt deliberately exposed the fleet to Japanese attack in order to enter the war via a Pacific back door. Stories of early sightings of Japanese planes and submarines near the Hawaiian Islands in early December 1941 were already circulating widely by the time of the campaign. A dramatic revelation that Roosevelt was reading secret Japanese messages and still was unprepared for the attack on Pearl Harbor might have had a devastating impact on the election.

VI

The foreign policy issue that came to dominate the campaign dealt with the future, not the past. On October 9, the administration released the proposals that the United States, the Soviet Union, England, and China had agreed upon at Dumbarton Oaks. They called for the creation of a world organization along lines similar to the League of Nations, with an assembly of all member states, an eleven-seat security council on which the four founders and France would have permanent representation, and an international court of justice. On the crucial question of preventing aggression, the Dumbarton Oaks Proposals suggested the creation of a military staff committee to direct and administer armed forces provided by the member nations under special agreements with the security council. Praising the negotiators for accomplishing so much in "so short a time," President Roosevelt told the nation that "the task of planning the great design of security and peace has been well begun." In keeping with the bipartisan agreement reached in August between Dulles and Hull, Dewey immediately voiced his approval, saying he was "very happy over the result" of the Dumbarton Oaks Conference.

Observers were quick to note that there were two vital omissions from the preliminary agreement on world organization. The Dumbarton Oaks Proposals made no mention of voting procedure on the security council, leaving the issue of a great power veto unresolved. In fact, the veto had been a stumbling block; nearly everyone agreed it was necessary, but when the negotiators differed over its scope, they decided to let Churchill, Roosevelt, and Stalin settle it at a future summit conference. The other question left hanging was domestic in nature: who would have the power to commit the use of American troops against an aggressor? The administration wanted the American representative to the security council, who would follow the instructions of the President, to be endowed with this authority, claiming that crisis situations required prompt action. Arthur Vandenberg and several other Republican senators disagreed. They pointed to the constitutional requirement that Congress declare war, insisting that the President must secure congressional consent on each occasion before allowing American forces to be used for collective security. Cordell Hull, fearing that this difference of opinion would jeopardize his bipartisan arrangement with Dulles, finally prevailed upon the Republican senators to agree to postpone settlement of this dispute until after the United States joined the world organization.[39]

It proved impossible, however, to keep such a vital issue out of the campaign. "How much of its war-making power would Congress be willing to surrender?" *Life* asked pointedly. Senator Joseph Ball was deeply troubled by the same question. As one of the leading Republican internationalists, Ball had called upon his party to purge itself of its former isolationism, announcing in late September that he would not campaign for Dewey until the candidate clarified his views on the plans for peace. With the death of Wendell Willkie on October 8, Ball emerged as the logical spokesman for his followers. Determined to force the two candidates to take forthright stands during the campaign, Ball released a public statement on October 12 asking Dewey and Roosevelt three questions about the future international organization. The first two were routine, but the third was crucial. "Should the vote of the United States' representative on the United Nations security council commit an agreed upon quota of our military forces to action ordered by the council to maintain peace," asked Ball, "without requiring further congressional approval?" In essence, the Minnesota senator was trying to force Roosevelt and Dewey to deal with the question which went to the very heart of collective security and national sovereignty.[40]

The senator's challenge stirred up great interest in the White House. Ball had told Ben Cohen, one of the President's aides, what he planned to do on October 10 at Willkie's funeral. Cohen helped persuade speech-writer Samuel Rosenman to advise Roosevelt to give an affirmative answer to Ball's third question before Dewey delivered his foreign policy speech at the *Herald Tribune* forum on October 18. Paul Porter, publicity director for the Democratic National Committee, gave the same advice after talking to Russell Davenport, Willkie's 1940 campaign manager who was now heading up the Committee of Independent Republicans for Roosevelt. Unless FDR advocated giving the security council representative "real power," Davenport warned, "independents everywhere are going to construe the Administration attitude toward international organization as purely political and no better than Tom Dewey's." In a separate memo to Harry Hopkins, Davenport reiterated that Roosevelt's stand on this issue "will be critical for the independent vote, especially that portion which was closest to Wendell Willkie." Fearing that Dewey would answer Ball's question affirmatively on October 18, the President's advisers recommended that he make his reply public in a letter to the Senator on October 17.[41]

Roosevelt refused to be stampeded, however. He first asked Acting Secretary of State Edward Stettinius to give him the views of the State Department. On October 13, Stettinius reported that "there seems to be no essential difference between the position taken by the Administration and that advocated by Senator Ball." On Sunday, October 15, the President invited Ball to the White House, apparently hoping to win his endorsement without having to make his answer public, but the senator refused to give in so easily. The President then told Ball he would reply in the course of a major address on international affairs in New York City on October 21. Rejecting the advice of his aides, he decided to give Dewey the chance to speak out first and then adjust his comments accordingly.[42]

The President made a shrewd gamble. In the course of his remarks to the *Herald Tribune* forum on October 18, Dewey gave clear answers to Ball's first two questions, but he dodged the third one. "The world organization must be enabled, through the use of force, when necessary, to prevent or repel military aggression," was all he would say on the issue of implementing collective security. Three days later, after an exhausting tour of rain-swept New York City designed to curb rumors of his failing health, the President addressed a dinner meeting of the Foreign Policy Association. Asserting that the security council "must have the power to act quickly and decisively to keep the peace by force," Roosevelt compared the problem to a policeman in a small town. The policeman could not do his job if, when he caught a criminal breaking into a house, he had to go to the town council and request a warrant before he could arrest the thief. "So to my simple mind," the President concluded, "it is clear that, if the world organization is to have any reality at all, our American representative must be endowed in advance by the people themselves, by constitutional means through their representatives in Congress, with authority to act." [43]

The next morning, Ball told reporters that he found FDR's words satisfactory, dismissing as unimportant the qualification about "constitutional means." The senator formally endorsed President Roosevelt in the course of a speech in Baltimore on October 24. Pointing out that Dewey had failed to clarify his position, Ball said that if Congress retained the right to decide on each occasion whether to supply troops for collective security, the world organization "will be simply a debating society, without power to act, and future aggressors will sneer at it just as Hitler sneered at the League of Nations." Republicans were quick to play down Ball's defection, calling him "an insignificant voice." In one sense, they were right. Ball was not a powerful man in the party, and it was doubtful whether he could even control the outcome of the election in his own state of Minnesota. But these GOP commentators failed to realize that Ball had inherited Willkie's mantle among liberal Republicans and independents. "We honor Senator Ball for his stand," commented the editors of the *Nation*. "And it will spur to action the thousands of independent voters who owe allegiance to neither party but who want President Roosevelt to carry back with him an overwhelming mandate for continued leadership in world affairs." [44]

Dewey recognized his mistake and tried belatedly to undo it. Changing the focus of an announced speech in Minneapolis from the farm problem to world affairs, he dealt at length with Ball's key question in the senator's home state. He expressed his determination to lead America into a world organization if he were elected. But if this body were to be effective, he said, the American representative must not be forced to consult with Congress each time he made a decision. "Obviously Congress has the constitutional power to determine what quota of force it will make available, and what discretion it will give to our representative to use that force," Dewey asserted. "I have not the slightest doubt that a Congress which is working in partnership with the President will achieve the result we all consider essential and grant adequate power for swift action to the American representative." [45]

Dewey's statement was as advanced as Roosevelt's, containing only the qualification that the arrangement for granting power to the American delegate be done by constitutional means. Yet it came too late. If Dewey had said this on October 18, he might well have gained Ball's endorsement and forced FDR into taking a "me too" position. Internationalist voters would then have faced a difficult choice. But by ducking Ball's challenge and letting the President speak out first, Dewey gave his statement an air of expediency, a grudging concession forced out of a reluctant candidate.

During the last week of the campaign, Republicans added to this impression by running a full-page ad in the *New York Times,* in which they charged that Roosevelt wanted "a blank cheque to control our world relations without Congress." Such a course, they warned, would lead to American troops spending "the next twenty years rotating as members of an international army available at an instant's notice for every conceivable armed conflict." Then Robert Moses, who had written the ad for the Republican National Committee, charged that in raising this issue the President had violated the arrangement Hull had negotiated with Dulles. "Why did he break this agreement?" Moses asked. Dewey apparently shared this feeling; three years later he told James Forrestal that he was "very cynical about entering into 'gentlemen's agreements' after his experience in the 1944 campaign." [46]

The charge was understandable, but it was less than fair to Roosevelt. The President had not raised the issue initially, and he gave Dewey the first opportunity to deal with it. Once the Republican candidate missed his chance, then Roosevelt exploited the opening and achieved a handsome political breakthrough. In the week following his Foreign Policy Association address, virtually every important spokesman for liberal internationalism endorsed his candidacy. The *Nation* and the *New Republic,* skeptical over his conservative turn on domestic issues, found his statement on international organization sufficient ground for approving a fourth term. Walter Lippmann, who had backed Willkie in 1940, came out against the Republican candidate on October 21. "I cannot feel that Governor Dewey can be trusted now with responsibility in foreign affairs," Lippmann wrote. "He has so much to learn." The *New York Times,* which had opposed the third term, was even more reluctant, but the editors finally announced for Roosevelt, saying that his leadership "might easily prove in itself to be one of the most important cohesive forces binding together a new world organization in its first experimental years." Arthur Hays Sulzberger, publisher of the *Times,* had explained to David Lilienthal in late September why his paper was likely to endorse FDR: "We can survive another four years of bad management on the home front but we can't survive another war." [47]

Senator Ball, motivated solely by a desire to advance the cause of peace, had enabled Roosevelt to make political capital out of an issue which Cordell Hull thought he had safely placed beyond the reach of partisan politics. Through adroit but quite scrupulous maneuvering, the President had found a way to reach the independent voters he still felt would decide the election.

VII

"[T]he whole strategy of the Dewey campaign has been to soft-pedal questions of foreign policy so as not to renew the old cleavage between Western 'isolationists' and Eastern 'interventionists,' " commented Arthur Vandenberg. The debate over international organization forced Dewey to depart from this plan and deal with the future peace in late October. He did so reluctantly, because he knew that FDR was most vulnerable on domestic issues, but he realized, as the *New York Times* noted, that foreign policy "is where the deep American interest really lies." Citing the public's desire for a world without war, the *Times* concluded, "The vital issue all along has been which candidate and which party can be relied upon more safely to win us such a peace." [48]

In the October 18 speech to the *New York Herald Tribune* Forum, Dewey launched his first all-out attack on FDR's foreign policy. Carefully excepting Cordell Hull's and the State Department's efforts at international organization, Dewey accused Roosevelt of conducting "personal, secret diplomacy" which undermined the future peace. In addition to Poland, he criticized FDR's handling of relations with Italy, France, and Rumania, and in his sharpest comments condemned the Morgenthau Plan for harsh postwar treatment of Germany. Claiming that Goebbels was already using this plan to intensify fanatical German resistance, Dewey charged, "We are paying in blood for our failure to have ready an intelligent program for dealing with invaded Germany." He accused Roosevelt of making deals without consulting the State Department and without informing the American people. "The result is that no one knows what our foreign policy is with respect to Poland, France, Germany, Rumania or other countries of Europe. We have no hint of what commitments we have made." [49]

Ignoring the charge of secret diplomacy, Roosevelt in his Foreign Policy Association speech countered with a slashing attack on Republican isolationism. Ranging back to the defeat of the League in 1919, the President accused the GOP of scuttling the Navy, raising tariffs, opposing the World Court, voting against Selective Service, and ignoring the Nazi threat in the 1930's. Commenting on GOP charges that he had failed to prepare the nation for war, Roosevelt remarked, "These same voices were not so very audible five years ago— or even four years ago—giving warning of the grave peril which we then faced." The President cited the list of Republican isolationists who would dominate the Congress if their party gained a majority: Hiram Johnson of California, Gerald Nye of North Dakota, and of course Martin and Barton and Fish. "Can anyone really suppose that these isolationists have changed their minds about world affairs?" an incredulous FDR asked his audience. He concluded with a plea for international cooperation. "We either work with the other great Nations, or we might some day have to fight them. And I am against that." [50]

Democrats were jubilant over FDR's assault on GOP isolationism. "Shouldn't Dewey's feet be kept to the fire on the issues of foreign policy?" Oscar Cox asked Hopkins. "That's where he is weakest." Harold Ickes, Robert Hannegan, and Senator Claude Pepper of Florida eagerly responded. They called the Republicans "false prophets" and "false patriots," accused Dewey of being "an isolationist at heart," and demanded that he disavow the support of the Chicago *Tribune* and America First leader Gerald L. K. Smith. Henry Wallace again made the most extreme charges. Claiming that Dewey's advocacy of international cooperation "smacks of death-bed repentance," he told an Iowa audience that "those appeasers, isolationists, and America-Firsters who fought Willkie to the death are able to swallow Dewey and Bricker without gagging." Vice-presidential candidate Truman made the isolationist issue the central theme of his campaign. He termed Dewey another Harding as he urged voters not to make the same mistake they had made in 1920. In a Minneapolis speech on October 23, he challenged Dewey to repudiate eight prewar isolationist senators who were running for reelection in 1944, including Robert Taft and Arthur Vandenberg. When Dewey failed to do so, Truman kept up a steady drumbeat, asking the Republican candidate every day how he could achieve a lasting peace as the leader of an isolationist party.[51]

Driven to the defensive, Dewey searched for a way to escape the isolationist label. John Foster Dulles, his chief foreign policy adviser, had tried out a possible tactic in early October when he replied to a Republican internationalist who had asked if Dewey would be able to secure Senate approval for American participation in a world organization. Dulles said that he had consulted GOP members of the Foreign Relations Committee, and that they had promised "to back up a Republican President." But, he added, he was skeptical whether they would cooperate with FDR "in view of the very bad relations which exist between him and both houses of Congress." When both Arthur Krock and the editors of *Life,* his strongest supporters in the national media, urged Dewey to capitalize on his ability to get along with a conservative Congressional coalition, Dewey adopted this line in his Minneapolis speech on October 24. Citing FDR's stormy relations with the House and Senate, he declared, "It is unmistakably clear that our future demands that we have a new Chief Executive who can and will work with the new Republican Congress beginning next January 20." He read telegrams from six Congressional leaders who pledged to support Dewey as President in carrying forward plans for international cooperation, then warned: "Only with the unity now demonstrated by the telegrams I have read to you tonight . . . can we achieve the kind of action necessary to preserve peace." [52]

"Political blackmail!" cried the *Nation*. T.R.B. accused the Republicans of saying, "Elect our man and we'll work for world peace; otherwise—watch out." Roosevelt made the same point, calling Dewey's threat "a deliberate and indefensible effort" to place political advantage ahead of the national interest. "I do not think that the American people will take kindly to this policy of 'Vote my way or I won't play.' " [53]

The President's comment seemed a little sanctimonious in light of Democratic attempts to smear Dewey as an isolationist, but he was undoubtedly right about the public reaction. It was poor politics to threaten the electorate on the sensitive issue of peace. The party's isolationist heritage was one of Dewey's greatest handicaps, and he could not suddenly transform it into an asset by claiming that only a Republican President could get a peace treaty through the Senate. Yet once Dewey had permitted Roosevelt to preempt the internationalist position, he could not afford to repudiate his isolationist supporters. Thus he was caught neatly in a trap, and his efforts to free himself only made things worse.

VIII

Despite his inept handling of foreign policy issues, Dewey gradually narrowed Roosevelt's lead. Pollsters differed on how far the President was ahead, ranging from 51 to 53.5 percent in their estimates of the popular vote, but they all perceived a Republican trend in October. FDR's conduct of the war and his role as peacemaker continued to be his greatest assets. When Gallup asked voters which candidate was "likely to do the best job of dealing with foreign nations and preventing future wars," 51 percent replied Roosevelt and only 30 percent chose Dewey. Thirty-eight of the fifty political writers polled by *Newsweek* thought that the war and international affairs gave FDR his main advantage with voters. Yet even so, the *Newsweek* experts saw the election as virtually even in terms of the electoral vote, giving Dewey 232, Roosevelt 230, and saying the rest could go either way. Gallup gave FDR a slight edge in the Electoral College, but not a majority. *Time* reported that the *Fortune* poll showed that "a Republican tide is running," and claimed that if the war in Europe ended suddenly, Dewey would win with ease. Even Hadley Cantril forecast an election so close that the independent vote would decide the outcome.[54]

Just as in 1940, Democratic politicians became nervous and urged the President to engage in active campaigning. Roosevelt, who had felt from the outset that the election would be extremely close, announced on October 19 that he would give a series of speeches at the height of the campaign. At the same time, he did everything possible to stress his role as Commander-in-Chief. When General MacArthur's forces landed in the Philippines on October 20, he called a special press conference to make the announcement, saying, "We promised to return; we *have* returned." In his Philadelphia speech a week later, he talked about the battle of Leyte Gulf, in which the American Navy scored a decisive victory over the Japanese. Chiding the Republicans for accusing him of failing to prepare the nation for war, he pointed out that all the battleships and aircraft carriers in Admiral Halsey's fleet had been authorized by the Roosevelt administration prior to Pearl Harbor. In Chicago, 110,000 people filled Soldier Field to hear the President speak from his car, with at least 150,000 more outside the gates listening over loudspeakers. There, though he focused on domestic issues, he carefully worked in a reference to the fact that the isolationist Chicago *Tribune* was supporting Dewey. Then, pleading the need to return to Washington to direct the war effort, he canceled plans to speak in Detroit and Cleveland. Still, reporters estimated that more than a million people had seen the President in person during this two-day tour of six states with 120 electoral votes.[55]

Back at the White House, Roosevelt spoke to the nation by radio on November 2. He again played up his war duties, but he also talked about the coming peace. Noting that he had met not only with Churchill and Stalin but with the leaders of small nations, such as Beneš of Czechoslovakia and Mikolajczyk of Poland, he stated, "It is only through an understanding acquired by years of consultation that one can get a viewpoint of their problems and their innate yearnings for freedom." The world was looking to the United States for leadership, he added. "It would be a sorry and cynical thing to betray this hope for the sake of partisan advantage, and a tragic thing to shatter it because of the failure of vision." [56]

Two days later, the President traveled to Boston to give his last public campaign speech. Stopping off at Springfield, Massachusetts, he recalled his 1940 promise not to send American boys into foreign wars. "Our pledge was kept," he declared. "We fought when we were attacked—obviously, rightly." Before a partisan crowd of 45,000 in Fenway Park, the President again referred to the controversial statement he had made four years before. Saying that any good American would have responded to the Japanese attack as his administration did, Roosevelt brought the audience to its feet by asserting, "As for myself, under the same circumstances, I would choose to do the same thing—again and again and again." On election eve, the President spoke once more by radio to the people. Avoiding any partisan appeal, he called simply for victory in the war and a lasting peace, closing with a prayer for those fighting and dying overseas.[57]

There was no way Dewey could match the President's appeal. He avoided foreign policy issues until his final speech, delivered in Madison Square Garden on November 4. Then he hammered away again on the theme of secret diplomacy, citing the Morgenthau Plan as a prime example. News of this secret arrangement to crush Germany had leaked out after the Quebec conference, Dewey asserted, enabling Nazi propagandists to exploit it. "That was as good as ten fresh German divisions," he claimed, charging that "the blood of our fighting men is paying for this improvised meddling." Then Dewey pleaded for a just peace. "It can never be the product of secret agreements worked out in secret conferences between two or three rulers," Dewey contended. "A world organization for peace can only be built by a President and a Congress— Republicans and Democrats alike—working in harmony and in mutual respect. To achieve that harmony," Dewey concluded, "we must have a new Chief Executive." [58]

Dewey's eloquent plea was lost in a last-minute Democratic blitz. Using virtually every prominent diplomat and politician associated with foreign policy, the President's aides tried to leave the impression that Roosevelt was indispensable both to the winning of the war and the making of peace. Ambassadors Averell Harriman and John Winant were called home from Moscow and London to testify that Roosevelt alone had the confidence of our Allies. In a huge "Everybody for Roosevelt" rally in New York City, Mayor LaGuardia, Senator Robert Wagner, and Harold Ickes called Dewey "an obvious second-rater" who would jeopardize our future relations with the Soviet Union. By contrast Roosevelt was a peacemaker "whose courage in righteous causes is a household word among the nations." The President even asked Cordell Hull to give a radio address, despite the fact that the Secretary had become so disenchanted with Roosevelt's conduct of diplomacy that he had handed in his resignation, to be effective after the election. Too ill to make a speech, Hull finally released a statement praising FDR as a "far-sighted" leader who had the experience and wisdom to guide mankind through "the gravest crisis in all its experience." In Independence, Harry Truman ended his campaign by referring again to the past. "History gives us the answer to Harding's promises," he declared. "His failure is the reason our boys are now dying again on the battlefields of the world." James Byrnes went even further, asserting that Germany and Japan were watching the election with great anticipation. "And you and I know the defeat of Roosevelt would revive their fading hopes, stiffen their opposition, and delay the end of the war." In other words, a vote for Dewey was a vote for Hitler and Hirohito.[59]

IX

"I think we stand a fifty-fifty chance of winning," wrote Arthur Vandenberg to a friend a week before the election. "Thus, the fate of America for the next ten generations hangs by a slender thread." As usual, the Michigan senator was exaggerating, but the outcome was almost as close as he predicted. FDR won his fourth term by a margin of 3.6 million votes, the smallest for any victorious candidate since 1916. To Roosevelt's surprise, Dewey had run a strong campaign, well organized, thoughtful, and shrewd. Nevertheless, the President had still won 53.4 percent of the popular vote and had carried 36 states to Dewey's 12, amassing a commanding majority in the Electoral College.[60]

The Political Action Committee contributed powerfully to Roosevelt's triumph. The registration drive that Sidney Hillman directed led to a much larger voter turnout than the experts had expected—47 million Americans went to the polls, just two million less than in 1940. Most of the dropoff came in the South, where Roosevelt received 1.4 million fewer votes. But in urban areas, the PAC helped deliver the usual overwhelming New Deal majorities. Roosevelt gained 60.7 percent of the vote in cities with populations exceeding 100,-000; in seven key states, he carried metropolitan areas by large enough majorities to offset Republican domination of towns and rural regions. World issues probably had less impact on this urban vote than the economic and social gains that city dwellers had experienced in Roosevelt's first three terms.[61]

Most observers, however, attributed FDR's victory to the war and the hopes for peace. "Franklin D. Roosevelt had been re-elected in a war year as a war President who could promise the country victory in the war and, on the basis of victory, a lasting peace," commented the editors of the *New York Times*. Arthur Krock believed that the people chose Roosevelt again because they were unwilling to change the Commander-in-Chief at the height of the war; few voters, apparently, had accepted the GOP slogan: "End the war quicker with Dewey and Bricker." *Time* and *Newsweek* stressed the coming peace settlement in explaining Roosevelt's reelection, saying that the people expressed "a vote of confidence" in "America's most skilled negotiator." [62]

There was virtually unanimous agreement that the outcome signified the triumph of internationalism and ensured American participation in the future United Nations. "The election returns have announced to the world that 1944 is not 1920," the *Nation* asserted, while *Newsweek* declared that "the nation cast its vote for global stature this week." America's allies, who had observed a self-imposed silence during the campaign, now greeted FDR's victory with great enthusiasm. "The cheers could be heard around the world," noted *Time,* pointing out that foreigners interpreted the election as "an endorsement of the working partnership of Stalin, Churchill, Roosevelt, and Chiang Kai-shek, both in war and peace—and a promise that this time the U.S. would not withdraw." Even the Russians, who had privately expressed doubts about the Republicans, saying they "remembered with some apprehension the Hoover administration," hailed Roosevelt's victory as contributing to continued Soviet-American cooperation.[63]

"The clearest lesson of the 1944 election," commented the editors of *Life,* "was that isolationism is political poison." Dewey's great mistake, they argued, was his failure to take up Ball's challenge and appeal to the crucial independent voters.

The Congressional results bore out this analysis and proved how shrewd the Democrats were in pinning the isolationist tag on their opponents. The Republicans, who had been gaining steadily in Congress since 1934, lost twenty-two seats in the House and added only one in the Senate. Moreover, those who lost were the diehard isolationists whom Truman had called on Dewey to repudiate, such as Gerald Nye of North Dakota and Hamilton Fish of New York as well as Democrats Bennett Clark of Missouri and Cotton Ed Smith of South Carolina. At the same time, outspoken internationalists who supported Roosevelt, like Claude Pepper and Robert Wagner, won easily and the Senate gained such strong advocates of international cooperation as Democrat William Fulbright and Republicans Wayne Morse and Leverett Saltonstall. "The mandate of the polls was clearly for full collaboration . . . in meeting the problems of world security," concluded the *New York Times*.[64]

The voters' firm rejection of isolationism also ensured the continuation of the bipartisan tradition begun by Hull and Dulles. Although Dewey was miffed at the way FDR had exploited Ball's challenge on international organization, other Republican leaders were quick to assure the Roosevelt administration of their future cooperation. Vandenberg wrote to Hull a few days after the election urging him not to resign and assuring the Secretary he had the confidence of the Senate, of America, and of the world. Although Hull did retire after the election, Edward Stettinius, the new Secretary of State, immediately invited John Foster Dulles to Washington to consult as a Republican on the plans for the future world organization. Dulles was happy to participate in this continuing bipartisan effort. "Throughout the campaign," he wrote to Roosevelt on November 10, "my principal concern was that nothing should occur to jeopardize, through partisan division, the plans for permanent peace which were being evolved at the Dumbarton Oaks Conference." Over the next few months, Vandenberg and Dulles made good their pledges, participating in the San Francisco Conference which founded the United Nations and then playing important roles in the ultimate Senate ratification of the Charter. The election of 1944 was thus a victory for bipartisanship; it spared the nation a repetition of the political bickering that had blocked American entry into Wilson's League of Nations.[65]

1948

"I have been disturbed about the trend of international affairs since the end of the war," Secretary of Commerce Henry Wallace wrote to President Truman on July 23, 1946, "and I am even more troubled by the apparently growing feeling of people that another war is coming and the only way that we can head it off is to arm ourselves to the teeth." [1] These words by the former Vice-President indicate how the onset of the Cold War had destroyed the fine hopes that World War II would lead to a new era of lasting peace. The tensions with the Soviet Union over Poland, which lay submerged during the 1944 campaign, came to the surface in the spring of 1945. At Yalta in February, Roosevelt made extensive concessions in an effort to prevent a split with the Russians, but by April even FDR had become pessimistic over the future. When FDR died suddenly, an inexperienced and unprepared Harry S. Truman was elevated to the presidency at the crucial time of transition from war to peace. Influenced by tough-minded advisers who had chafed at FDR's conciliatory policies, Truman took a hard line toward the Soviets. He tried to block Communist control in Poland, abruptly cut off lend-lease in May (though he restored it until Japan was defeated), and procrastinated on a Russian request for a billion-dollar loan to finance postwar reconstruction. In his only face-to-face meeting with Stalin at Potsdam in July, Truman, bolstered by his knowledge of the successful atomic detonation at Alamogordo, took an even firmer position on Germany and Eastern Europe. Yet the tougher Truman's line, the more intransigent the Russians, who interpreted the changed American policy as proof of a capitalist plan to encircle and destroy the Soviet Union.

The atomic bombs dropped on Hiroshima and Nagasaki in August ended World War II and intensified Russian fears of American power. Secretary of War Henry L. Stimson, supported by Henry Wallace, urged Truman to make a dramatic offer to the Soviets to give up our atomic monopoly, but the President moved much more cautiously on this vital issue. In November, he joined with the British and Canadian prime ministers to call for international control of atomic energy through the new United Nations. For the next several months, Dean Acheson and David E. Lilienthal worked on a plan for nuclear disarmament that Bernard M. Baruch took over and modified before presenting to the United Nations Atomic Energy Commission on June 14, 1946. Baruch insisted that the procedures be exempt from the veto, a feature the Russians were certain to resist. The gravest weakness of the Baruch Plan, however, was the American insistence on proceeding by carefully defined stages, beginning with the creation of a new international atomic agency with an extensive system of inspection and control. Only when this agency was formed, and an inspection system was in operation, would the United States turn over its nuclear technology and surrender its atomic bombs. The Russians, claiming Baruch wanted inspection rather than disarmament, countered with an equally unacceptable plan that called for the outlawing of atomic weapons and the immediate destruction of the American stockpile.[2]

The deadlock that developed over nuclear disarmament

triggered Wallace's long letter to Truman on July 23, 1946. Claiming that the Baruch Plan reflected a fundamental distrust of the Soviet Union, Wallace pleaded for a new effort to "clear away the fog of political misunderstanding." Arguing that a tough line only increased the Russians' feeling of fear and insecurity which lay behind their bluster, Wallace urged Truman to adopt a softer attitude toward the Soviet Union, designed to restore the friendly wartime relationship. When Truman politely rejected Wallace's advice, the Secretary of Commerce brought the issue into the open in a political speech in New York City in September 1946. Claiming that Truman had read and approved his remarks, Wallace accused the British of fomenting quarrels between the United States and Russia, and called for a new policy that included accepting Soviet domination of Eastern Europe. Truman, who had casually glanced at Wallace's speech in advance without reading it, tried to deny his approval, hoping the whole affair would quiet down. But when parts of Wallace's July 23 letter appeared in the press, the President published the full text. Under intense pressure from Secretary of State James F. Byrnes and Bernard Baruch, Truman finally decided that he would have to fire Wallace. On September 20, the President announced Wallace's resignation as Secretary of Commerce.[3]

Wallace was the last of the New Dealers in the Truman administration. Frances Perkins, Henry Morgenthau, Jr., and Harold Ickes had all left the Cabinet earlier, and it seemed likely that Truman would be unable to prevent the breakup of the Roosevelt coalition of liberal intellectuals, labor, and the South. In the Congressional elections in November, Republicans played on the growing split in Democratic ranks and the frustrations with problems of demobilization and reconversion, and gained control of both houses of Congress for the first time since 1928. In December, left-wing intellectuals and labor leaders formed the Progressive Citizens of America (PCA) and began booming Wallace as the only authentic voice of liberal protest. Many former New Dealers, repelled by the pro-Soviet cast of the PCA, came together in January 1947 to found the Americans for Democratic Action (ADA). Led by such prominent figures as Eleanor Roosevelt, Reinhold Niebuhr, and Chester Bowles, the ADA pressed vigorously for liberal reform at home and opposition to Soviet expansion abroad.[4]

The split in liberal ranks came just as the developing Cold War reached its full maturity. In March 1947, responding to a forthcoming British withdrawal from the Eastern Mediterranean, President Truman outlined a bold program of economic and military aid to Greece and Turkey. Urged by Senator Arthur Vandenberg to "scare hell out of the American people," the President justified his proposals by sketching out a struggle between the forces of good and evil and promising that the United States would "support free peoples who are resisting attempted subjugation by armed minorities or by outside pressures." The global anti-Communist implications of the Truman Doctrine bothered many liberals as well as conservatives like Senator Robert Taft, who feared that the United States would have to become policeman of the world. Wallace led the assault. In an extensive speaking trip in the spring of 1947, he denounced the Truman Doctrine as "a curious mixture of power politics and international carpetbagging," warning that in enforcing it, "America will become the most hated nation in the world." [5]

When Secretary of State George C. Marshall, who replaced James Byrnes in January, announced a sweeping plan for the economic recovery of Europe in a Harvard commencement speech in June, Wallace leaped to the attack. He accused the United States of bypassing the United Nations in an effort to build up an anti-Soviet bloc in Western Europe. Other liberals, however, saw in the Marshall Plan a positive, constructive proposal to rescue Europe from economic stagnation, and they rallied, along with the anti-Communist ADA, to the defense of the Truman administration. When Truman vetoed the Taft-Hartley bill, he ensured the support of labor leaders, who had always viewed Wallace with skeptical eyes as a dreamy, unreliable idealist. Thus, by the end of 1947, Wallace had lost the support of much of the liberal constituency and found himself surrounded more and more by Communists and fellow travelers who were out to use him for their own purposes.[6]

Undaunted, Wallace announced his candidacy as a third-party candidate for the presidency on December 29, 1947. On a nationwide radio broadcast, he stressed foreign policy, speaking as the self-proclaimed peace candidate who would fight "the bipartisan reactionary war policy which is dividing the world into two armed camps." He declared that he was assembling a "Gideon's army, small in number, powerful in conviction," and he concluded, "By God's grace, the people's peace will usher in the century of the common man." He quickly won the endorsement of the Progressive Citizens of America and went ahead with plans for what he termed "the new party." In a book entitled *Toward World Peace,* published in early 1948, Wallace set forth his program, which dealt mainly with the Cold War. He accused the Truman administration of being dominated by Wall Street and the military. The first thing he would do if elected, he said, would be to meet personally with Stalin and work out a sphere-of-influence deal that would end the tensions between the two super powers. His other major proposal was to create a UN Reconstruction Fund financed by all the nations of the world to achieve the economic recovery of Europe and Asia from the devastation of World War II. Offering this fund as an alternative to the Marshall Plan, he proposed that the United States pledge at least five billion dollars a year for this purpose.[7]

The Democrats took Wallace's challenge seriously. In June 1947, when Wallace had attracted large crowds with his denunciation of the Truman Doctrine, Gael Sullivan of the Democratic National Committee warned presidential aide Clark M. Clifford that "Wallace had captured the imagination of a strong segment of the American public." He was "hotter than a busted blowtorch," Sullivan reported, despite his "fuzzy thinking," and thus would be "a major consideration in 1948!" "Action should be taken either to (1) appease Wallace or (2) pull the rug on him." [8]

Clifford favored the second alternative. In a forty-three-page memorandum to President Truman on November 19, he outlined a comprehensive plan for the 1948 campaign, based upon moving to the left on domestic issues to preempt potential Wallace support. Assuming that the South would stay loyal to the party, Clifford recommended a vigorous appeal to the groups that made up the bulk of the old New Deal coalition —farmers, workers, and ethnic minorities, particularly Negroes and Jews. At the same time, he urged a vigorous attack on Wallace, who, Clifford claimed, was a real threat with a large and enthusiastic national following. The way to blunt his appeal, Clifford stated, was "to identify him and isolate him in the public mind with the Communists." But he was quick to add that only the liberal and progressive Democrats should attack Wallace; they were the only ones likely to reach his followers.

Although Clifford focused on domestic issues, he did not neglect the influence of foreign policy on the campaign. Recognizing that the Cold War was a major national concern, he argued that it could not be kept out of the election under a bipartisan agreement, and that in fact the "battle with the Kremlin" could be turned to the administration's advantage. "The nation is already united behind the President on this issue," Clifford observed. "The worse matters get, up to a fairly certain point—real danger of imminent war—the more is there a sense of crisis. In times of crisis the American citizen tends to back up his President." To exploit this advantage,

Clifford recommended making the Marshall Plan one of six major campaign issues. He also urged the President to identify himself personally with the conduct of foreign policy, making the major pronouncements on diplomacy and assuming the role of Commander-in-Chief whenever feasible. Urging that his proposals be acted on immediately, he closed by warning that the coming election would be "a tough, bitterly fought struggle." [9]

Truman accepted Clifford's campaign plan, though he was reluctant to attack Wallace, who he felt was "an honest man and a faithful public servant." He finally rationalized his tactics by viewing Wallace as an innocent dupe of the Communists. "I had learned that the Russians understood only force," Truman wrote in his *Memoirs*. "Wallace did not think this was true, but he did not have the experience with the Soviets that had been mine." Thus when Wallace announced his candidacy, Truman permitted the Democratic National Committee to release a statement that charged, "A vote for Wallace . . . is a vote for things for which Stalin, Molotov and Vishinsky stand." For the next few months, Jack Redding, the publicity director of the Democratic party, "pinned Red labels" on Wallace and his followers. "Through every avenue," Redding wrote, "we were pointing out that Wallace and his third party were following the Kremlin line slavishly." [10]

At first it seemed that these smear tactics might backfire. A Gallup poll asking voters to name the man they favored for President showed 10 percent for Wallace, compared to 17 percent for Truman. State surveys showed that the third-party candidate was capable of winning from 10 to 15 percent of the vote in New York and Massachusetts, enough to enable the Republicans to capture these traditionally Democratic strongholds in November. Optimistic Wallace supporters talked of winning 10 million votes, a fifth of the national electorate and more than enough to deny Truman reelection. Letters coming into the White House reflected the deep emotion that Wallace stirred up. "I shall vote for Henry Wallace because you have betrayed everything that Roosevelt stood for," a West Coast resident told Truman. "I think your Truman Doctrine killed the UN." [11]

A special election in a Bronx Congressional district in mid-February revealed how dangerous the Wallace movement had become to the Democratic party. Leo Isacson, a member of the American Labor Party and a Wallace backer, defeated the Democratic candidate by a two-to-one margin in a district normally controlled by boss Ed Flynn's Bronx machine. Political commentators quickly pointed out the significance of this, claiming that Wallace was likely to poll enough votes in the large industrial states to insure a Republican victory. It would be a "miracle," *Newsweek* commented, if Truman carried New York in the fall. "It looks as if Ed Flynn was not quite so strong in his Bronx District as he informed me he is," Truman commented wistfully to Bernard Baruch. But he had not given up hope. "If we can get the crackpots on one side of the fence, and the fellows who want to look backward on the other," he told Baruch, "honest people ought to be able to do something about the situation in the world and in this country."

The Isacson victory actually was a fluke which did not reflect Wallace's true appeal. The district was 55 percent Jewish, and the vote was a protest against Truman's wavering Palestine policy. Isacson had played up to Zionist feelings throughout the campaign, and even Wallace, in speaking for his candidate, had charged that "Truman talks like a Jew and acts like an Arab." The people of the Bronx were far less concerned with the Marshall Plan than with the fate of the Jews in Palestine, and they elected Isacson to make their concern felt in Washington. Thus the Congressional election served as a warning to Truman that Palestine would rival the Cold War as an election issue in 1948.[12]

I

The fate of Palestine became a major international issue after World War II. Those Jews who survived Adolf Hitler's concentration camps demanded the right to go to Palestine, where the Arab population bitterly resisted further Jewish immigration. The British, caught in the middle as the rulers of Palestine, tried to regulate the flow of immigrants and maintain order amid growing violence. President Truman, sympathetic to the plight of the Jews as a result of their wartime persecution, supported the recommendation of an Anglo-American Commission which called for the admission of 100,000 Jews into Palestine in 1946. Truman remained neutral on a second recommendation by the commission to establish a federal state in Palestine with Jewish and Arab components. In the spring of 1947, the British submitted the Palestine issue to the United Nations, which appointed a special committee to find a solution.

In September, the committee reported back to the General Assembly. The majority submitted a plan for the partition of Palestine into separate Jewish and Arab states, while the minority favored a federal solution. With the issue now before the General Assembly, President Truman was put under intense pressure. Zionists argued for accepting the partition plan, contending that this would fulfill at last the Balfour commitment for a Jewish homeland. Public opinion in the United States ran strongly in favor of the Zionists, and Truman complained to Senator Wagner that the pressure from Jews was "extensive and continuous." Yet inside the administration, the State Department and the Pentagon defended the interests of the Arab states, with Secretary of Defense James V. Forrestal serving as the leading spokesman. Supported by State Department officers, Forrestal warned against alienating the Arabs in the midst of the Cold War with Russia, and argued that at the current rate of consumption the United States would soon need to tap the rich Middle Eastern oil reserves. Despite these pleas, Truman instructed the delegation to the UN to announce American support for the partition plan on October 11, and in the succeeding weeks White House aides played an active role in lining up the necessary two-thirds vote in the General Assembly. Finally, on November 29, the United Nations accepted the partition arrangement by a wide margin, 33 to 13.[13]

Zionist gratitude for Truman's action was quickly cut short by the administration's subsequent actions. When the Arabs threatened to use force to resist partition, the British washed their hands of the problem by refusing to execute the UN decision. Instead, London announced that all British troops would leave Palestine by May 15. Hoping to prevent excessive violence, the United States joined with the United Nations in imposing an arms embargo on Palestine; this infuriated Zionists, who claimed that the British were supplying the Arabs with weapons to kill defenseless Jews. More important, President Truman told reporters in January that while he stood behind the partition arrangement, he opposed the use of American troops to carry it out. In February, when the General Assembly passed the partition issue on to the Security Council, Warren Austin, the American delegate, made it clear that while the United States still supported partition in principle, it did not favor the use of force to achieve this goal.[14]

It was this vacillating stand on partition that infuriated American Jews and led those in the Bronx to elect Leo Isacson. In his memorandum to Truman in November, Clark Clifford had recognized the explosive nature of the Palestine issue, but he had advised against dealing with it "on the basis of political expediency." "In the long run," he advised, "there is likely to be greater gain if the Palestine problem is approached on the basis of reaching decisions founded upon intrinsic

.

merit." Forrestal was even more worried about the political implications of the problem, fearing that Truman would give in to Zionist pressure to retain the Jewish vote. When Postmaster General Robert Hannegan alluded to the fact that wealthy Jews were waiting for Truman to clarify his stand on Palestine before contributing to the Democratic party in 1948, Forrestal urged that the Democrats seek a bipartisan agreement with the Republicans to take the issue out of politics. Party Chairman J. Howard McGrath refused, pointing out that Jewish votes were critical in several pivotal states and that Jews made substantial contributions to the party's treasury. Truman did allow the Secretary of Defense to approach the Republicans about a bipartisan agreement, but when he mentioned his idea to Senator Vandenberg and Governor Dewey, both men scoffed. Dewey approved in principle but said the Democrats would never give up the advantage of the Jewish vote, while Vandenberg claimed that since the Democrats had already played politics with Palestine, the Republicans felt "they were entitled to make similar use of the issue." Forrestal finally gave up when he realized his party would never surrender an issue on which it hoped to win so many votes.[15]

By February, however, Truman may have wished he had followed Forrestal's suggestion. Zionists kept up a steady round of criticism for Truman's failure to lift the arms embargo and to advocate the use of force to achieve partition. "The policy on which we seem now to have embarked is a rank betrayal of the declared policy of this country," *Nation*'s editor Freda Kirchwey telegraphed Truman and McGrath on February 25 in response to Austin's speech. "It is appeasement in its worst form." Calling upon the Democratic leaders to carry out the partition policy, she warned, "There is a tremendous revolt brewing among all sections of the American people in the face of what they believe to be an unwarranted betrayal." [16]

The Zionist outcry hit home to McGrath. He was already deeply worried about defections from other elements within the Democratic party. On February 20, a group of fifty-two southern congressmen had adopted a resolution condemning a vigorous civil rights program that Truman had released earlier in the month. Talk of a southern bolt from the party now began to be heard. Then on February 21, the ADA, meeting in convention in Philadelphia, failed to give Truman the expected endorsement for reelection. Instead, the liberals criticized his failure to repeal the arms embargo on Palestine and announced that they would postpone any endorsement of candidates until after the party conventions in the summer. Rumors now spread that even the big-city bosses were dissatisfied with Truman and were willing to dump him for either General Dwight D. Eisenhower or Justice William O. Douglas. Truman's stock was never lower. " [O]nly a political miracle or extraordinary stupidity on the part of the Republicans can save the Democratic party, after 16 years in power, from a debacle in November," concluded *Time*. [17]

Chairman McGrath hurried to consult with Truman in early March when the President returned from a brief vacation in Key West. Truman, who had already decided to run for a term in his own right but planned to keep this decision quiet, finally agreed to let McGrath announce his candidacy. But when the chairman also asked him to change his position on Palestine, the President quickly set him straight. "The Palestine issue will be handled here," Truman declared. "And there'll be no politics involved." Emerging from this conference, McGrath announced that if the party nominated him, Truman would accept and run. Reporters, realizing that the President had been forced to declare his candidacy early, felt that he had only a fighting chance to be renominated and virtually no hope of winning in November. [18]

II

Events abroad came to Truman's rescue just when his political fortunes were at their lowest. On February 17 a grave crisis developed in Czechoslovakia when moderate and rightist members of the coalition government headed by Communist Clement Gottwald handed in their resignations to President Eduard Beneš in protest over reorganization of the security police. After a week's hesitation, and apparently pressured by the Soviet Union, Beneš accepted the resignations and permitted Gottwald to form a new government, which was under unquestioned Communist control. The new regime proceeded to transform Czechoslovakia into a totalitarian society, liquidating Foreign Minister Jan Masaryk, the leading Czech advocate of democracy, in a fall from a window which was passed off to the outside world as suicide.[19]

The United States reacted strongly to the Czech coup. The government joined with England and France on February 26 to label the cabinet change "a crisis artificially and deliberately instigated" in order to achieve "a disguised dictatorship." For most Americans, it was Munich all over again. Recalling the way in which Germany had taken over Czechoslovakia in 1939 after forcing England and France to abandon the country, commentators warned that the pattern of piecemeal aggression Hitler had used in the 1930's was repeating itself. *Newsweek* spoke of the tragic death of a Wilsonian republic, and then quoted testimony given by Secretary of Commerce W. Averell Harriman in January to a Congressional committee: "There are aggressive forces in the world coming from the Soviet Union which are just as destructive in their effect on the world and our own way of life as Hitler was, and I think are a greater menace than Hitler was." The implication was clear —the United States must act forcefully to halt the Russian aggression before it swept over all Western Europe in the Nazi pattern of the 1930's.[20]

By early March, a full-scale war scare had developed. On March 5, General Lucius D. Clay, the American military governor in Germany, sent a telegram stating that his earlier belief that war with Russia was unlikely had changed in the past few weeks as a result of "a subtle change in Soviet attitude." He now felt that war might come "with dramatic suddenness." Former Secretary of State James Byrnes warned that hostilities might break out within "four or five weeks from now," while a *Newsweek* man-on-the-street survey revealed a growing sentiment for a preventive atomic strike against the Soviet Union. On March 10, the day of Masaryk's death, a reporter asked Secretary of State George Marshall about the growing talk of war. To the surprise of newsmen, Marshall, instead of denying these reports, spoke of the "reign of terror in Czechoslovakia" and concluded, "the situation is very, very serious." The next day, in a speech before the Federal Council of Churches, Marshall called for calm and sound judgment while acknowledging, "The world is in the midst of a great crisis inflamed by propaganda, misunderstanding, anger and fear." [21]

The sense of crisis speeded Congressional action on the Marshall Plan. On March 1, Vandenberg presented the final version of the European Recovery Program to the Senate before packed galleries. In a long, impassioned speech, the Republican senator asked his colleagues to act quickly, warning that the nations of Europe needed reassurance in the face of the mounting Soviet threat. Though Henry Wallace called the Marshall Plan a "blueprint for war" and "a colossal hoax" on the American people, the senators were much more impressed by the Czech coup and the sense of urgency it imparted. After less than two weeks of debate, they passed the European Recovery Program by the lopsided margin of 69 to 17.[22]

Wallace was also out of step in his reaction to the events in Czechoslovakia. In a Minneapolis speech on February 27, he passed the coup off as an inevitable Russian response to our containment policy. Stating that the men in Moscow would be "utter morons" if they failed to match the American "get tough" policy by getting even tougher themselves, Wallace declared that "the Czechoslovakian story will repeat itself so long as our gun and dollar policies in Greece, in China and elsewhere on Russia's doorstep are continued." Two weeks later, after Masaryk's death, Wallace astonished many of his supporters by telling reporters that plans for a right-wing coup in Czechoslovakia involving American Ambassador Laurence S. Steinhardt had precipitated the Communist takeover of that country. When pressed by the newsmen, Wallace refused to give any supporting details, nor did he substantiate his parting remark to the effect that Masaryk had committed suicide because he had cancer.[23]

Meanwhile, President Truman remained silent. In a press conference on March 11, he denied persistent reports that he was planning a personal meeting with Stalin, and he withheld comment on questions about the Czech coup and Secretary Marshall's remark about a serious world crisis. Then the President heightened the tension by announcing plans to address a special joint session of Congress on March 17 on the foreign situation. As he prepared for the major speech, the CIA submitted a forecast stating that while war was not likely within sixty days, the intelligence services could not extend this prediction beyond that two-month period. The press was equally nervous. On March 16, Secretary of Defense Forrestal wrote in his diary, "Papers this morning full of rumors and portents of war." The same day, Truman wrote to Eleanor Roosevelt, explaining how his efforts to carry on FDR's policy of friendship toward Russia had been frustrated. "We have been blocked at every point by the Russians. . . . I shall go to the Congress tomorrow and state the facts." [24]

When Truman mounted the rostrum the next day, a "sense of urgency" that had not been felt since "the desperate days of 1939" gripped the nation. In a grim monotone, Truman leveled his indictment against the Soviet Union. Labeling Russia the chief threat to world peace, he accused the Soviets of destroying "the independence and democratic character of a whole series of nations in Eastern and Central Europe." "It is this ruthless course of action," he continued, "and the clear design to extend it to the remaining free nations of Europe, that have brought about the critical situation in Europe today." Praising plans of the Western European nations to join together in their common defense, Truman promised them military aid. Then he called upon the House to speed passage of the European Recovery Program and asked Congress to enact a permanent program of universal military training and to reinstitute selective service to meet the existing critical manpower shortage in the armed forces. Finally, in an effort to moderate the belligerent tone of his remarks, Truman closed with an expression of willingness to enter into negotiations with Russia to preserve the peace.[25]

In the course of this speech, Truman briefly alluded to the bipartisan nature of his foreign policy. The world situation, he asserted, was too critical to permit "any party struggles to weaken our influence for maintaining the peace." Yet the speech had an undeniable political impact. Though some liberals found it too militant, most commentators felt that Truman had given expression to the prevailing public desire for a firm policy toward the Soviet Union, with a few calling for even harsher measures toward Russia. Whether consciously or not, Truman was following the advice Clifford had given him in November for capitalizing on the conflict with the Kremlin. His bold speech made it clear that the President, not Secretary Marshall, was directing American foreign policy, and his call for action on the European Recovery Program was in line with Clifford's advice to make the Marshall Plan a key campaign issue.[26]

Truman's follow-up to his Congressional speech suggests that he was fully alive to the political implications of the international crisis. He flew to New York City later that same day, and in the evening addressed a St. Patrick's Day dinner audience composed largely of politicians. He began by repeating his charges against Russia and his call for legislative action on the Marshall Plan, UMT and the draft, and then turned his attention to his left-wing critics. Referring obliquely to Henry Wallace, Truman warned, "We must not fall victim to the insidious propaganda that peace can be obtained solely by wanting peace." Then he proceeded with a frontal assault: "I do not want and I will not accept the political support of Henry Wallace and his Communists. If joining them or permitting them to join me is the price of victory, I recommend defeat." As he noted later in his diary, he had spent the evening "reading Henry Wallace out of the Democratic Party." The final step in the Clifford strategy, hanging the Red label on Wallace and thereby enhancing Truman's appeal to all anti-Communists, had been carried out by the President personally.[27]

Truman's speeches on March 17 marked the climax of the war scare. Reassured by his tough rhetoric, the American people gradually relaxed, though continued signs of Soviet hostility, most notably in interruptions in rail traffic to Berlin which began on March 31, kept the Cold War at a tense level throughout the spring. The House passed the European Recovery Program in early April, and though Congress balked at universal military training, it did vote in June to resume selective service.

The crisis had enabled Truman to make a remarkable political recovery. The sense of foreign danger, as Clifford predicted, led the people to rally behind their President. Though big-city bosses, disaffected southerners, and restless liberals still searched for a more attractive candidate, Truman's assertion of firm presidential leadership in foreign policy made him the man to beat for the nomination. Above all, he had met and overcome the challenge posed by Henry Wallace. By becoming the nation's leading Cold Warrior, Truman had transformed Wallace into a lightning rod to ward off Republican charges of softness toward Communism, the precise role that Clifford had cast him in.[28]

III

Palestine proved to be a much greater political challenge for Truman than the Cold War. All during the March crisis his advisers continued to disagree over the proper American course. Clark Clifford, sensitive to the Jewish vote, sent memorandums to the President urging him to put pressure on both the British and the Arabs to agree to partition before the May 15 deadline. Clifford also recommended lifting the arms embargo so that the Jews would have weapons to defend themselves, claiming that there was no need to fear Arab reprisals. The Arab states needed the dollars they received from oil sales, he argued, concluding, "Their need of the United States is greater than our need of them." Forrestal disagreed strongly. He had the Joint Chiefs of Staff send Truman a series of memos stressing the importance of Middle Eastern petroleum to American national security. State Department experts, led by Loy Henderson, chief of the Near Eastern Division, and Dean Rusk, in charge of United Nations affairs, backed up the military, warning that a pro-Zionist policy would drive the Arab nations into the waiting arms of the Soviet Union.[29]

Truman grew weary of the controversy. "So much lobbying and outside interference has been going on in this question that it is almost impossible to get a fairminded approach to the subject," he told a St. Louis Zionist. His temper short, he finally refused to see any more American Jews and even turned down the request of Dr. Chaim Weizmann, the leader of the Zionist movement, for a personal interview. Undaunted, Weizmann contacted Eddie Jacobson, a World War I pal of Truman's and his partner in an ill-fated business venture in the 1920's. Jacobson saw Truman on March 13 to request an appointment for Weizmann, and though at first Truman said "he didn't want to discuss Palestine or the Jews or the Arabs or the British," he finally relented, telling Jacobson, "You win, you bald-headed . . . I will see him." On March 18, Weizmann slipped into the White House through the seldom-used east gate and met privately with Truman for three-quarters of an hour. The Zionist leader did most of the talking, with Truman nodding sympathetically but refusing to make any firm commitments. The President did assure Weizmann, however, that he would continue to support the UN policy of partition.[30]

The next day, Warren Austin stunned the Zionists by telling the Security Council that the United States now favored a temporary trusteeship in Palestine. Austin explained that unless action were taken immediately, a civil war would break out in Palestine when the British withdrew on May 15. Therefore, the United States wanted the General Assembly to meet and draw up plans for the United Nations to take over responsibility for maintaining order. "Such a United Nations trusteeship would, of course, be without prejudice to the character of the eventual political settlement, which we hope can be achieved without long delay." Despite this qualification, American Jews interpreted Austin's statement as a "betrayal" and "shocking reversal" of American policy, while an Arab League spokesman gleefully described it as "wonderful." [31]

Truman was furious. He told Admiral Leahy, his military adviser, that this change had been made "without obtaining his permission and without his knowledge." He ordered Clifford to find out what had happened, pointing out that just the day before he had assured Weizmann that he would stick to the partition formula. Clifford discovered that on March 8 Truman had approved an early draft of Austin's speech, but that the State Department officials had not bothered to get a final okay from the President. Truman then called Secretary of State Marshall, who was on a trip to California. Marshall immediately agreed that his department was at fault and said he would take full responsibility for the change in policy.[32]

The next day, March 20, Marshall held a press conference in San Francisco. Stating that the President had approved the trusteeship statement on his personal recommendation, the Secretary called it "the wisest course to follow." He said a trusteeship would avert "chaos and widespread disorder" that otherwise would follow the British withdrawal. Then, alluding to the Cold War, he said, "The interest of the United States in a peaceful settlement in Palestine arises . . . out of vital elements of our national security." After returning to Washington, Marshall stressed the same Cold War rationale in telling the Senate Foreign Relations Committee that the partition policy would have led inevitably to the entry of Russian troops into the strategic Middle East.[33]

Marshall's explanations helped reduce the public outcry, but Truman still faced a very difficult decision. Zionist pressure continued without letup, as Democratic politicians warned that the "Jewish people feel they have been betrayed." The President's aides, led by Clark Clifford and David Niles, urged him to reassure American Jews by lifting the arms embargo. On March 24, Truman met with a group of State Department officials and White House assistants to discuss this proposal. When Clifford put the case for removing the arms embargo, Secretary Marshall replied that the State Department was working on plans for a truce to prevent open hostilities between Jews and Arabs in Palestine. A sudden influx of arms from the United States would destroy this move for peace. Reluctantly, the President agreed to give the State Department time to secure the desired truce.[34]

Truman made his first public comment on the new Palestine policy in a press conference on March 25. Reading a prepared statement, the President stated that "it has become clear that the partition plan cannot be carried out at this time by peaceful means." He cited the likelihood of violence in May unless a UN trusteeship was established, and he stressed that this temporary move did not prejudice partition as a long-run solution. For the present, however, he said the United States would "lend every appropriate assistance to the United Nations in preventing bloodshed and in reaching a peaceful settlement." When reporters repeatedly asked him if American troops would take part in the trusteeship arrangement, Truman tried to duck, finally saying, "We will cross that bridge when we come to it." [35]

"It took the British 25 years to sell us out," commented Chaim Weizmann; "the Americans have done it in 2½ months." The Zionist leader's bitterness was understandable, if overstated. On March 20, Truman had asked Samuel Rosenman, FDR's old speech-writer, to explain to him the foul-up within the administration. Weizmann accepted this explanation, telling Eddie Jacobson that the President did not know of Austin's speech when he talked to him on March 18. "Don't forget for a single moment that Harry S. Truman is the most powerful single man in the world," Weizmann reminded Jacobson. "You have a job to do: so keep the White House doors open." [36]

Other Zionists could not be placated so easily. Bernard Baruch told Austin that "our weather-vaning attitude" on Palestine troubled him deeply. "First we ask the world to follow us and then we want to change." Some Jews charged that Truman showed that he placed a greater value on oil than on human lives, which led Clark Clifford to comment that "every Jew thought that Truman was a no-good." Even those outside the Zionist movement regretted the reversal in policy. "There are few Americans who will be able to regard the action of their government without a sinking of the heart," observed the *New York Herald Tribune*. Caught between the conflicting claims of Cold War strategy and political expediency, Truman had tried to act in a statesmanlike manner and ended up with a hesitant and indecisive policy that alienated everyone. *Time* summed up the prevailing judgment: "Harry Truman's comic opera performance had done little credit to the greatest power in the world." [37]

IV

The Republicans looked forward to the 1948 election with mounting enthusiasm. They viewed their triumph in Congress in 1946 as a bright omen for the future. Wallace's defection, the growing southern revolt within the Democratic party, and Truman's inept handling of Palestine all fed the GOP's hopes for victory in November. For the first time in twenty years, Franklin D. Roosevelt would not be on the ballot; instead, the candidate would probably be Harry Truman, whose standing in the Gallup poll sank to an all-time low of 32 percent in the early spring. Yet despite these encouraging prospects, the Republicans faced two difficult decisions—what stand to take on foreign policy and which of the many contenders to select as the party's nominee. [38]

The coming of the Cold War had muted but not ended the tension between isolationist and internationalist Republicans. Those who had opposed entry into World War II, like Senator Robert Taft and Kenneth S. Wherry, now called themselves nationalists. Although they opposed the Soviet Union, they displayed great skepticism of activist foreign policies, especially those requiring the expenditure of large sums of American money. The majority of Republicans, however, followed the leadership of Arthur Vandenberg, who came to symbolize the bipartisan tradition. Building on his wartime cooperation in creating the United Nations, Vandenberg worked closely with the administration in securing Congressional support for the Truman Doctrine and played the leading role in passage of the Marshall Plan. Warning that it would be "political suicide on a national scale" to make foreign policy a partisan issue, he had prevailed upon Republicans to avoid international questions in the 1946 Congressional elections. "Politics are important," he told a close friend, "but *peace* is *indispensable*." [39]

In 1948, a number of Republicans began to question the wisdom of this viewpoint. Senator Taft fought hard to limit the scale of the Marshall Plan, saying "I do not believe that America can save the world with money." He finally voted for the European Recovery Program, but a dozen Republicans opposed its final passage. More important, the sense of crisis with Russia led to increasing calls for the GOP to take a tougher line than the Democrats on the Cold War. In a Lincoln Day address in Boston, Thomas E. Dewey embraced the containment measures but then attacked the Truman administration for following "policies which resulted in surrendering 200,000,000 people in middle Europe into the clutches of Soviet Russia and are rapidly delivering the 400,000,000 people of China into the same hands." Representatives Charles Kersten of Wisconsin and Richard M. Nixon of California introduced a resolution in Congress during the March war crisis calling for a "solemn warning to the conspiracy in the Politburo" that the United States was prepared to fight to halt further Soviet aggression. And Senator Styles Bridges of New Hampshire, a prewar Republican isolationist, replied angrily to Truman's March 17 speech on the Russian danger by claiming "he waited too long to speak out and . . . he did not go far enough." Bridges accused the Democrats of appeasing the Russians "by throwing them chunks of territory and the freedoms of innocent populations" at Teheran, Yalta, and Potsdam. Truman's "indecisive and vacillating foreign policy," he argued, ". . . has jeopardized the military and political position of our country." [40]

Vandenberg became the focus of GOP complaints against continued cooperation with the Democrats. Joseph Pugh, Republican leader in Pennsylvania, complained that under Vandenberg "the so-called bipartisan foreign policy had evolved into a one-man foreign policy so far as Republicans were concerned." A Michigan constituent wrote to Vandenberg: "At present the voters have but the choice of Mr. Wallace's wishful thinking, and Mr. Truman's honest blunders. But the American people, and for that matter the poor tormented peoples of the world, deserve better than that." Vandenberg hastened to assure her that Republicans should not rubber-stamp all Democratic measures. "I think I should say," the senator answered, "that the overriding impulse of 'bipartisan foreign policy' is that *all* questions dealing with foreign policy should be considered and settled on an *unpartisan* basis which is completely divorced from partisan considerations." In the coming campaign, the Republicans would have to decide whether or not they wished to continue Vandenberg's idealistic course.[41]

The choice of a candidate seemed even more bewildering to the GOP. After twenty years of defeat, they wanted a man who could not only lead them to victory but establish an enduring Republican majority. Many were tempted to go beyond the party's ranks to draft General Dwight D. Eisenhower, the Supreme Commander in Europe during World War II who was presently serving as Army Chief of Staff. No one knew Ike's politics, but a Gallup poll in December 1947 showed him leading all the presidential contenders, and as a result both parties wooed him. In late 1947, President Truman even sent Secretary of the Army Kenneth C. Royall to make a startling proposition: should Eisenhower accept Democratic nomination, Truman would step aside, and even run as the vice-presidential candidate if Ike so desired.[42] Eisenhower politely rejected this secret offer, and in January 1948 he also rebuffed Republican overtures, releasing a public letter to a New Hampshire publisher asking that his name not be entered in that state's primary. Calling his decision "definite and positive," Ike declared, "I could not accept the nomination even under the remote circumstance that it were tendered me." [43]

Eisenhower's withdrawal left Thomas Dewey as the GOP front-runner. Although after his defeat by FDR Dewey had told Arthur Vandenberg that he was "not going to be one of these unhappy men who yearned for the Presidency and whose failure to get it scarred their lives," he announced his candidacy early in 1948. As usual, Dewey took a very cautious stance and refused to state his views on any controversial issues, leading a journalist to "wonder whether a man who follows such an opportunistic course is qualified to be President." Senator Robert Taft also sought the nomination, and although he took firm public positions, he preferred to work behind the scenes, courting support from state and local GOP chieftains. Vandenberg continued to be mentioned as a dark horse; he refused to campaign, but he acknowledged that he would run if the party selected him. In Tokyo, General Douglas MacArthur, now in charge of Japanese occupation policies, announced that he would accept "any public duty to which I might be called by the American people" and permitted a group of backers to enter his name in the Wisconsin primary.[44]

By March, Harold Stassen, the former boy governor of Minnesota, had become Dewey's chief rival. He had been campaigning for the nomination since 1946, stressing international cooperation through the UN, and with Ike's refusal to run, he seemed to be the man most likely to appeal to the independents and Democrats who had followed Wendell Willkie in the past. With Warren Burger directing his campaign, the forty-one-year-old Stassen stumped Wisconsin, a state most commentators had conceded to MacArthur, who was being boosted as "the one American who knows how to deal with Stalin." Stassen's vigorous campaigning finally forced Dewey to come to Wisconsin in the last days before the primary. To the experts' surprise, Stassen won a smashing victory, gaining nineteen convention delegates to eight for MacArthur and none for Dewey, who ran a poor third. When Stassen repeated his triumph the following week in Nebraska, MacArthur dropped out of the race and Dewey realized that he faced a major challenge for the nomination.[45]

The showdown came in Oregon in mid-May. Departing from his aloof stance, Dewey toured the state for three weeks, shaking hands, putting on Indian headdresses, and flooding the radio with spot commercials. Although foreign policy was not a major issue between the two candidates, Dewey lashed out at the administration, accusing Truman of wavering between appeasement and bluster and promising that if elected he would "wage peace with all of the energy and determination and force with which we waged war." When Stassen advocated outlawing the Communist party, Dewey took up his challenge in a statewide radio debate. Comparing the Communists to "worms," Dewey asserted, "I want to keep them above ground, where we can see them and lick them as we have in New York." On May 18, Dewey won a narrow victory that ended Stassen's chances and left the New York governor as the leading contender but no longer the certain candidate. Dewey had made many enemies within the party, noted Arthur Krock, who predicted an open convention which would nominate a dark horse like California's Earl Warren or Senator Arthur Vandenberg.[46]

The emphasis on foreign policy brought on by the Czech crisis and passage of the Marshall Plan boosted Vandenberg's chances. "The international crisis is so great and some of the aspirants for the Presidency so unequal to the task," wrote former Willkie backer Oren Root, Jr., to Vandenberg on April 23, "that I feel the Convention must eventually turn to you." Novelist Sinclair Lewis told Vandenberg a few days later that he thought Vandenberg would be the next President, and such influential GOP internationalists as Pennsylvania Governor James Duff and Massachusetts Senator Henry Cabot Lodge announced their support of him.[47]

An initiative by the Truman administration helped keep the

spotlight on Vandenberg's contributions to American foreign policy. When Britain, France, Belgium, Holland, and Luxemburg signed the Brussels Pact for mutual security in March, the President authorized Under Secretary of State Robert A. Lovett, a Republican, to approach Vandenberg about possible American participation in a broader plan for European defense. The Michigan Senator was receptive, and in May he introduced a Senate resolution that promised continued support for the United Nations and encouraged further regional efforts at collective security under the UN charter. The press was quick to point out that the real purpose of the Vandenberg resolution was to achieve "the alignment of the U.S. with Europe, for the first time in its peacetime history, for mutual defense." On May 22, Vandenberg succeeded in winning unanimous approval for his measure from the Senate Foreign Relations Committee.

The Vandenberg resolution placed Republican isolationists in a difficult position. They opposed the idea of American involvement in a European defense arrangement, yet they hesitated to attack their party's leading foreign policy spokesman. Taft, Wherry, and Bridges kept silent as Vandenberg argued that his measure "encourages individual and collective self-defense against armed aggression," but GOP Senator George Malone of Nevada spoke out. The Vandenberg resolution, he charged, would "make the Rhine the frontier of the United States" and would lead to "the encirclement of Russia." To Malone's embarrassment, the only voices supporting him were those of Glen Taylor of Idaho, a Wallace backer, and left-wing Democrat Claude Pepper of Florida, who claimed that the resolution would lead to "a military commitment to western Europe comparable to the economic commitment in the Marshall Plan." Malone joined the other isolationist Republicans in abstaining on the final vote as the Senate passed the resolution easily, 64 to 4, on June 11. Only two GOP Senators opposed the measure, which *Newsweek* claimed marked "the complete abandonment of the whole concept of isolationism." Thus, just two weeks before the Republican convention, Vandenberg established himself as Dewey's chief rival by gaining national headlines for a major foreign policy achievement.[48]

V

"The disintegration of the Democratic party . . . reached the point of almost complete demolition last week," commented *Newsweek* on April 5. The debacle began on March 26 when Franklin D. Roosevelt, Jr., the late President's son, issued a public call for General Eisenhower to accept a draft as the Democratic nominee. Learning of this move beforehand, Secretary of Defense Forrestal talked to Eisenhower, who immediately called Roosevelt and asked him to reconsider. The General said his January letter still reflected his feelings and that it would be dangerous to question Truman's leadership at such a critical time in the Cold War. Unmoved, FDR, Jr., released his statement; then Leon Henderson, ADA chairman, called a special meeting of the group's national board to discuss a "draft Eisenhower" movement. Southern Democrats, still smoldering over civil rights, joined in the cry to dump Truman, and several prominent Jews, led by Chicago boss Jacob Arvey, announced for Eisenhower in protest over Truman's Palestine policy. Even the *New Republic,* the liberal journal that had flirted with Wallace before rejecting him, indirectly boosted the Ike bandwagon by proclaiming, "We'll admit that any Stop Truman move looks good to us." [49]

When the ADA board met in Pittsburgh on April 12, the members quickly endorsed Eisenhower and Justice William O. Douglas as the ideal ticket. The anti-Truman movement continued to grow as the Gallup poll revealed in mid-April that every major Republican candidate except Taft led the President in trial ballots. *Newsweek* could find only six Democratic senators who favored the President's renomination, with thirteen opposed and twenty-six uncommitted.[50]

Yet despite the furor, Truman stood his ground and gradually regained control of the political situation. From the outset, he realized that his domination of the party machinery virtually assured him of nomination. His one great worry was Eisenhower, but in early April, the General told the President he had no intention of running. Truman praised Ike for his decision, saying politics could only tarnish his fine career as it had Grant's and encouraging the general to make another public statement reiterating his refusal to run. When Ike told reporters in mid-April that he still "meant every word" of his January letter, the Eisenhower boom began to flag, and with it any chance of jettisoning Truman. Ike was the cement that held together the loose coalition of southern Democrats, ADA liberals, and disgruntled Zionists; without him to rally around, the anti-Truman forces collapsed.[51]

Instead of discouraging Truman, the abortive revolt simply reinforced his determination to run for reelection. Telling reporters that opposition "doesn't disturb me," Truman confidently predicted on March 25, "The Democrats will win in November." "I have started measures for peace which I must see through," he told Arthur Krock. "I am not a quitter." [52]

The President began his political counterattack in a speech to the American Society of Newspaper Editors on April 17. After reading a prepared address in his flat monotone, Truman decided to make some additional remarks off the cuff to the nation's most influential journalists. Speaking with a rare animation and with growing force, he amazed the editors by giving a blunt summary of where we stood in the Cold War with Russia. "He spoke fluently, with deep feeling, almost passion, and courageously," commented David Lilienthal. "The important point was that he took the editors quite by surprise, and by storm." Truman's aides, who for some time had been encouraging him to speak spontaneously, persuaded him that he had hit upon an effective speaking style which he could use to great political effect. Impressed by the ovation the editors gave him, Truman agreed to speak extemporaneously in the future, using only a few notes for guidance. As talk of a new Truman developed, the White House announced that the President would take a preconvention swing around the country in June on his way to the University of California in Berkeley, where he was to receive an honorary degree. By mid-May, the man the experts were ready to count out two months before was back on his feet and ready to fight.[53]

VI

As the May 15 deadline for British withdrawal approached, the Palestine issue absorbed Truman's attention. He clung to the trusteeship solution Warren Austin had proposed to the United Nations in March, and on April 20 he permitted Austin to declare American willingness to furnish troops to help keep order in Palestine under UN auspices. But by the end of April, trusteeship seemed an unworkable solution as the Jews in Palestine began taking control of the areas assigned to them in the original partition arrangement. Beating back Arab attacks, the Zionists seized the port of Haifa in late April and went ahead with plans to proclaim the existence of an independent Jewish state in May. Though American officials, led by Dean Rusk, tried hard to negotiate a truce as a first step toward trusteeship, the enmity between the Arabs and the Jews became too great an obstacle. By early May, it was apparent that *de facto* partition would occur when the British left.[54]

American Zionists mounted an intense campaign to persuade President Truman to recognize the new state of Israel at its birth. In April, a delegation from the United Committee to Save the Jewish State picketed the White House, the State Department, and the headquarters of the Democratic National

Committee; it then left Chairman McGrath a petition calling for recognition, an end to the arms embargo, and a large loan to the forthcoming nation of Israel. In early May, forty-three members of Congress, including Chet Holifield of California, Estes Kefauver of Tennessee, and John F. Kennedy of Massachusetts, sent the President a letter urging him to aid the Jews in Palestine. Zionist leaders announced plans for massive rallies in major American cities on Sunday evening, May 16, to celebrate the "liberation" of Palestine and to demand American recognition. Informing Truman of these plans, Chicago Democratic leader Jacob Arvey pleaded for recognition, saying, "Mr. President, such declaration, timely made, will turn millions to hail you as the champion of justice for the most sorely tried people on the face of the earth." [55]

Within the White House, Clark Clifford and David Niles advanced more pragmatic arguments. They pointed out that recognition was consistent with the original policy of partition, that a separate Jewish state was certain to emerge, and that it would be wise to act ahead of the Russians. "We must recognize inevitably," wrote Clifford on May 4. "Why not now?" Reminding Truman how he had alienated the Jews by his retreat from partition, his aides urged him to recognize the Jewish state as soon as it was proclaimed. "Such a statement will retrieve prestige that has been lost by the President, the U.S. Government and the U.N.," they contended. Finally, Clifford and Niles argued that recognition would prevent the Republicans from making Palestine an effective political issue. [56]

Impressed by these arguments, Truman called a conference at the White House on May 12 attended by Secretary of State Marshall, Under Secretary Robert Lovett, Clark Clifford, and David Niles. When Truman said he wished to recognize Palestine, Marshall and Lovett voiced strong objections, warning that it would antagonize the Arab nations. Clifford countered that Truman was already on record as in favor of an independent Jewish state, a development which was bound to occur regardless of American action. "Marshall's face flushed," Clifford recalled later, as the Secretary objected to discussing this issue with political aides like Clifford and Niles. "This is a serious matter of foreign policy determination," Marshall said, "and the question of politics and political opinion does not enter into it." Though Clifford resented Marshall's "righteous God-damned Baptist tone," he kept quiet as Truman agreed to withhold a decision on recognition for the time being.[57]

The next day, Chaim Weizmann, soon to become the first President of Israel, sent Truman a letter informing him that on May 15 the new Jewish state would come into existence. He expressed his hope that the United States would extend prompt recognition. "The world, I think, would regard it as especially appropriate that the greatest living democracy be the first to welcome the newest into the family of nations." Touched by this appeal, Truman began to reconsider his decision. At the same time, Under Secretary Lovett also had second thoughts, probably fearing that Russia would beat the United States to the punch by recognizing Israel immediately. On May 13 Lovett conferred all day with his staff and then met with Clifford for lunch on May 14 to report that the State Department now favored recognition but that Marshall insisted it be delayed several days to permit coordination with England and France. When Clifford informed Truman of this development, the President decided to act immediately. He instructed Clifford to find out the precise moment when the Jews planned to proclaim their independence, saying he planned to extend recognition simultaneously. Since there was no time to consult with the provisional government in Palestine, Clifford asked Eliahu Epstein, representative of the Jewish Agency in Washington, to write the official letter requesting recognition. Epstein, aided by Ben Cohen, former counselor of the State Department, drew up the letter and sent copies to Secretary of State Marshall and President Truman. Israel proclaimed its existence at midnight on May 15 (6 P.M. on May

14 in Washington), and eleven minutes later President Truman announced that the "United States recognizes the provisional government as the de facto authority of the new State of Israel." [58]

"Thanks and God bless you," Eddie Jacobson wired the President on May 14. Other Zionists were equally elated at Truman's action, but they were disappointed that he did not couple recognition with an end to the arms embargo and a large loan. Republican spokesmen reacted favorably, though with a noticeable lack of fervor. Senator Taft issued a statement endorsing recognition, while Arthur Vandenberg praised Truman's action as "a logical and proper step." The press viewed it as an obvious play for Jewish votes, but acknowledged that most Americans were sympathetic to the new state of Israel. The *New York Times* spoke disapprovingly of "another abrupt reversal of American policy in Palestine" while supporting the decision itself. *Newsweek* summed up the prevailing sentiment when it termed recognition the latest bit of Truman's "pretzel bending" on Palestine. Although the Soviet Union followed the U.S. example several days later, ardent Cold Warriors still feared that premature recognition had weakened America's position in the strategic Middle East. Former Secretary of State James Byrnes expressed his displeasure to Bernard Baruch, writing that "our wobbling on the question has done the United Nations untold harm." James Forrestal, who was not consulted, worried most over the effect on our relations with England. "[A]nything which drives a wedge between Great Britain and ourselves at this juncture," he told military commentator Hanson Baldwin, "might have the most tragic implications and consequences." [59]

As the furor over recognition died down, it became clear that Truman had not acted as precipitously as it appeared. Despite a personal visit from Chaim Weizmann on May 25, he continued to refuse to lift the arms embargo and to delay granting a loan to Israel. Instead, he threw American influence behind UN efforts to achieve a truce between the Jews and Arabs who were fighting to establish the actual lines of partition in Palestine. He recognized that in the Cold War the United States required a stable balance of power in the Middle East and he directed his policy toward achieving a peaceful solution to the Arab-Israeli conflict, winning temporary success when Count Folke Bernadotte, the UN mediator, arranged a four-week truce in mid-June. At the same time, Truman had been influenced by domestic political considerations. He could not ignore the significant Jewish vote, and when Clifford persuaded him that Israel would come into existence with or without the support of the United States, Truman realized that prompt recognition was the only way he could regain the favor of U.S. Zionists. In recognizing Israel, Truman acted out of broad consideration of worldwide American interests, in which domestic politics played an important but subsidiary role.[60]

VII

In the spring of 1948, the American people expressed greatest anxiety over the Cold War, not Palestine. When the Gallup poll asked a national sample in mid-April what they considered "the most important problem facing this country today," 65 percent replied preventing war and getting along with the Soviet Union, compared to 9 percent who cited domestic politics and 8 percent who mentioned inflation and the high cost of living. Polls taken earlier in the year indicated that a majority were dissatisfied with Truman's conduct of policy toward Russia, with 73 percent feeling that the United States was being "too soft" on the Soviets. Equally alarming to Truman's aides was Gallup's April report that a slight majority of people felt that the Republicans were better equipped to handle foreign policy issues than the Democrats. William Batt, who directed the Democratic National Committee's research bureau, told Clifford in early May that private polls indicated that 40 percent of the American people were critical of the administration's foreign policy, with 35 percent approving and 30 percent expressing no opinion. Batt attributed this lack of confidence to a growing fear of war and suggested that Truman make clear to the nation his determination to achieve peace. Another Gallup poll, taken on May 2, backed up Batt's analysis. Responding to a persistent rumor that Stalin wanted to meet with Truman to reduce Cold War tensions, the poll asked people how they felt about such a summit conference. Sixty-three percent replied they thought it would be "a good idea," 28 percent "a poor idea," and 9 percent gave no opinion. Thus it seemed that while the American people favored a hard line toward the Soviet Union, they still longed for a bold diplomatic move that would reduce the possibility of war.[61]

An inept American approach to the Russians in early May brought home to the Truman administration the contradictory state of public opinion. At the suggestion of "doves" within the State Department, notably George Kennan and Chip Bohlen, Truman approved a plan to have Walter Bedell Smith, Eisenhower's wartime chief of staff who was now serving as ambassador to Russia, inform the Kremlin that the United States did not intend to threaten the Soviet Union with its containment policies but instead was acting solely out of self-defense. At the same time, others within the administration, especially James Forrestal, thought it would be useful to remind the Russians that Henry Wallace spoke only for a tiny minority and that the United States was firmly committed to the defense of Western Europe. In other words, Ambassador Smith should make the Russians understand the true nature of American containment—a determined but limited effort to halt Soviet expansion without threatening Russian security.[62]

On May 4, Smith delivered this message orally to Vyacheslav M. Molotov, the Soviet foreign minister, and then, at Molotov's request, left behind a written copy. The last sentence, included in order to underline the peaceful intent of the American communication, said simply, "As far as the United States is concerned, the door is always wide open for full discussion and the composing of our differences." Five days later, Molotov called Smith back with his reply, which consisted of a long, rambling defense of Soviet postwar moves and ended up with a "hope for the possibility of finding the means to eliminate present disagreements and to establish between our countries good relations." Smith saw nothing unusual in these words, so he simply told Molotov that he would refer his message back to Washington, and then left Moscow for a brief vacation in Germany. When the ambassador arrived in Berlin on May 10, he was astonished to learn that the Soviets had published a carefully edited text of Smith's original note and Molotov's reply to make it appear that the United States had proposed bilateral peace negotiations which the Russians were generously accepting.[63]

"RUSSIANS ACCEPT A U.S. BID TO PARLEY ON DIFFERENCES," headlined the *New York Times* the next day. A brief peace euphoria swept over the nation as people naively assumed that the Cold War was suddenly about to end. Even Thomas Dewey, normally so circumspect, reacted to the report by telling an Oregon audience that it was "the best news since V-J Day if they mean it." "It encouraged that most attractive of all American illusions," wrote James Reston, that "there was some neat, quick way in which the Russian problem could be solved without danger or expense." The effect on our European allies, however, was just the opposite. The British and French, perhaps remembering their own roles at Munich, now feared that the United States and Russia were going to decide the fate of Europe behind their backs. A steady stream of European diplomats called on the State Department to register their governments' protests.[64]

The administration moved quickly to reassure its allies. On

May 11, Truman released a statement citing the original intent of Smith's message to the Russians and denied all talk of a new departure in American relations with the Soviet Union. Secretary Marshall was even more blunt in a press conference on May 12. "General Smith did not ask for any general discussion or negotiation," the Secretary declared. Pointing out that successful diplomatic talks required months of careful preparation, he called upon the Russians to show their good will by altering their rigid stand on such issues as Berlin, Korea, and an Austrian peace treaty. Then the United States would be willing to sit down for talks, but only if other nations were allowed to participate.[65]

Truman and Marshall effectively scotched the Soviet proposal for negotiation, but in the process they weakened the already shaky public confidence in their Cold War policies. The Russian ploy put the administration in a bad light with the American people, and the argument that it was a clever Soviet trick simply added to the growing lack of confidence in Truman's ability to conduct foreign policy. Either through clumsy diplomacy or through an unwillingness to negotiate, the Truman administration became the villain in the eyes of the American press. Herblock summed up the net effect most succinctly when he drew a cartoon of Truman at bat with the ball whizzing past him untouched as the umpire cried out, "Strike one." [66]

The only one who seemed to gain from the abortive Smith-Molotov exchange was Henry A. Wallace. Throughout the spring, he had engaged in a national speaking tour, but despite the use of evangelistic techniques, his crowds grew thinner and his support gradually melted away as he came to sound the Communist line more and more often. Earnest but dull on the platform, Wallace read the speeches prepared by left-wing writers "as if they were rare insights he had just acquired." His hair almost pure white, he took on the air of an injured martyr as he accused his nation of being "guilty of almost every charge we level at the Russians" and of pursuing an "utterly insane and suicidal foreign policy." He kept suggesting that all the next President needed do to end the Cold War was to meet with Stalin, appealing to the memory of FDR by claiming, "Roosevelt always said he could do business with Stalin." [67]

The Russian peace initiative thus came as a godsend to the Wallace movement. On May 11, at a mass rally in Madison Square Garden, Wallace capitalized on it by reading an open letter to Stalin. More moderate in tone than his earlier statements, the letter blamed the Cold War on both nations and then listed six issues, ranging from disarmament to a resumption of unrestricted trade, as the basis for new negotiations between the United States and Russia. In the last line of this appeal to the Russian dictator, Wallace stated, "There is no misunderstanding or difficulty between the United States of America and the Union of Soviet Socialist Republics which can be settled by force or fear and there is no difference which cannot be settled by peaceful, hopeful negotiation." In a public message a week later, Stalin accepted Wallace's call for discussions to end the Cold War. Praising the six-point agenda as a "good and fruitful" basis for negotiation, Stalin declared that "the co-existence of these systems and a peaceful settlement of differences between the U.S.S.R. and the United States are not only possible but also doubtlessly necessary in the interests of a general peace." [68]

A grateful Wallace said he was "overwhelmed" by Stalin's reply, but the Truman administration was something less than ecstatic. The State Department put out a formal statement on May 18 which called Stalin's letter "encouraging" but then went on to cite the many outstanding issues which the United States had tried unsuccessfully to settle with the Russians in the United Nations and the Council of Foreign Ministers Conferences. Once again the State Department reminded the American people that the United States could not engage in bilateral talks that excluded our allies, who had equally vital interests at stake. A week later, Secretary Marshall took an even cooler stand in a speech in Portland, Oregon. Warning the American people against being seduced by Soviet propaganda, he asked for continued support for the containment policies he and Truman had established. "I am absolutely certain," he declared, "that only such a firm and determined course can save the situation for the democracies." [69]

In California, Wallace struck back. "The policies of Truman, Vandenberg, Marshall, and Forrestal have stained the world with blood," he charged, adding that the administration was betraying the world's hopes for peace by turning down "an understanding with Russia." His fiery oratory drew big crowds and helped fill his nearly empty coffers, but Wallace's attempt to exploit the Soviet peace move also aroused the suspicions of many Americans. *Newsweek* commented on a growing belief that the Russians were dabbling in American domestic politics while Norman Thomas, the veteran Socialist candidate for President, called Wallace "the apologist for the slave state of Russia, and the preacher of peace by blind appeasement." Thus the letter to Stalin and the Soviet leader's reply created only a brief resurgence in the Wallace crusade. Yet Truman emerged from the episode with his stature diminished as millions of Americans regretted that the bright promise of peace had died so quickly. [70]

VIII

On June 3, a beaming Harry Truman, accompanied by forty-two reporters, boarded a sixteen-car train in Washington's Union Station to begin what he termed a "nonpolitical" trip around the country. The ostensible purpose was to receive an honorary degree and address commencement exercises at the University of California in Berkeley, but everyone realized that politics lay behind the journey. Truman wanted to build up grass-roots support before the Democratic convention met in July, and he wished to try out his new off-the-cuff speaking style under campaign conditions. His main target would be the Republican 80th Congress, which had opposed nearly all his domestic proposals. He planned to play down foreign policy in his attacks on the GOP, referring to events abroad only when dealing with the Wallace movement.[71]

Reporters found it difficult to account for Truman's air of confidence as he set out on this trip. Wearing a neatly pressed blue suit, he looked more "like a nice fellow with a face you might pass on Main Street in your home town than the President of the United States." Though he spoke extemporaneously from notes prepared by Clark Clifford and Sam Rosenman, FDR's old speech-writer, he failed to excite the curious crowds who gathered round the back platform at stops in the Middle West. In Omaha, poor advance planning led to a fiasco when he spoke to a pitifully small audience at the reunion of the 35th Division in the huge Ak-Sar-Ben auditorium. But as he moved into the Far West, he aroused his audiences with a series of increasingly sharp attacks on the Republican failure to act on conservation, farm policy, and price controls. "Give 'em hell, Harry," voices began to call out, and the President obliged. He left foreign policy alone, except for one costly slip in Eugene, Oregon. In an apparent effort to attract Wallace supporters, he talked of his efforts to achieve peace with Stalin at the Potsdam conference. "I got very well acquainted with Joe Stalin, and I like old Joe," Truman confided to the crowd. "He is a decent fellow. But Joe is a prisoner of the Politburo." This novel view of Stalin's personality and power shocked editorial writers and State Department officials alike, and though Truman was careful never to repeat it, Republicans filed it away for future use. Speaking off the cuff had its drawbacks as well as its advantages.[72]

While Truman traveled through the West, his aides worked feverishly on the Berkeley speech, which was intended to be a statesmanlike rebuttal to the Wallace charges on Russian relations. Chip Bohlen and George Kennan wrote the early drafts, and then Clifford and his assistant, George M. Elsey, wove in passages from Rosenman, Robert Sherwood, and lawyer Louis Nizer. Secretary Marshall and Under Secretary Robert Lovett vetoed some of the additions, and Truman finally approved the fifth of seven drafts. Up to the last minute the speech-writers kept searching for phrases that would "grab" the audience, with one suggesting slyly, "I don't want a Cold War, I want a hot peace." [73]

On June 12, Truman delivered his foreign policy address to an audience of 50,000 in Berkeley's Memorial Stadium. He began by reciting the many steps the United States had taken to achieve peace since World War II: demobilization of the armed forces, the Baruch Plan for control of atomic energy, more than $20 billion in foreign aid. The failure of these measures, he charged, "lies largely in the attitude of one nation—the Soviet Union." Accusing the Russians of waging "indirect aggression" in Europe since 1945, he delivered the punch line his advisers worked so long to perfect. "The cleavage that exists is not between the Soviet Union and the United States. It is between the Soviet Union and the rest of the world." He then went on to accuse the Russians of blocking all avenues to peace and said only a change in Russian behavior, not clever propaganda ploys, could lead to fruitful negotiations and an end to the Cold War. "We have sought to help free nations protect themselves against aggression," Truman concluded. "We are determined . . . to keep strong for the sake of peace." [74]

It was a very effective address. By avoiding the usual Cold War clichés, Truman had made the case for his containment policies on the high ground of national interest. Editorial writers seized on his assertion that the quarrel preventing real peace was between Russia and the world, and played up the contrast between this dignified defense of American foreign policy and his highly partisan rear-platform talks. *Time,* usually hostile to Truman, called it "one of the best speeches of his career, delivered with dignity, poise and eloquence." In this one appearance, he had gone a long way toward restoring public faith in his ability to conduct American foreign policy in the Cold War.[75]

The remainder of the trip took on a triumphal air. Nearly a million people turned out in Los Angeles, lining the streets between the railroad station and Truman's hotel. As he headed back to Washington, the President delighted audiences with a series of blazing attacks on the GOP Congress, claiming again and again that "the issue in this country is between special privilege and the people." He carefully avoided foreign policy in these attacks on Congress, however. "We are unanimously for the foreign policy of the United States," he told an audience at York, Pennsylvania. "[P]artisanship should stop at the water's edge; and it has stopped just there." [76]

On June 18, the President returned to the White House. He had traveled 9,500 miles in 15 days and given 73 speeches along the way. Truman was delighted with the people's response, and the once-skeptical reporters now began to speak of a "human Truman" who appealed to voters with "his fight and his folksiness." When Senator Taft complained that the President had been "blackguarding Congress at every whistle-stop," the alert Democratic National Committee arranged for the mayors of towns across the country where he had spoken to protest against their communities being dismissed as "whistle-stops." Some liberal editors were disturbed by Truman's earthy language and partisan tactics, but others shared the relief expressed by the *New Republic*'s TRB that "Truman has nailed the New Deal flag to his mast." [77]

Most important, Truman had proved that he could not be counted out. "He does not say he will win," an aide told reporters; "he only says he'll make a hell of a fight for it." Complacent Republicans who had thought their only problem in choosing a candidate was to decide who would be the next

President must have begun to develop second thoughts. In three months, from March to June, Truman had boxed off Wallace's threat from the left and had found a telling issue to use against the Republicans in the record of the 80th Congress; he had perfected a campaign technique that suited his down-to-earth personality and fitted in perfectly with Clifford's master plan of appealing to all the elements in the old New Deal coalition. He still faced a possible rebellion from the South and a continued liberal search for a more attractive candidate, but he had proved he was the man to beat within the Democratic party. Roger Sermon, the mayor of Independence, Missouri, and a veteran Truman watcher, summed it up best when he observed, "He can fall harder and bounce back further than any man I ever saw." [78]

67

The Republicans ignored Harry Truman's resurgence as they prepared for their convention in June. Convinced that their nominee would become the next President, they looked forward to the election with great optimism. A *Newsweek* survey of political experts bolstered this feeling, revealing that all fifty writers expected a GOP victory in November. Dewey remained the front-runner, with over three hundred delegates, followed by Taft and Stassen with approximately two hundred apiece. Vandenberg had few first-ballot commitments, but because he was nearly everyone's second choice, a slight majority of the experts predicted his nomination after a deadlock developed between Dewey, Taft, and Stassen.[1]

In the weeks before the convention opened, Vandenberg devoted himself to beating off a threatened isolationist rebellion against his bipartisan policy. On June 3, the House Appropriations Committee, led by Republican isolationist John Taber, voted to cut Marshall Plan funds by more than $1 billion for the first year. Two days later, the full House, with the approval of Speaker Joe Martin and Majority Leader Charles Halleck of Indiana, confirmed the cut and sent the reduced appropriation bill to the Senate. The Democrats, led by

J. Howard McGrath, immediately charged that the House had played "directly into the hands of the Communists" and claimed the reduction proved that isolationists still controlled the Republican party. Vandenberg responded by appearing before the Senate Appropriations Committee to plead for restoration of the billion dollars for the European Recovery Program. Stassen also testified in person, and Governor Dewey sent a telegram advocating a full appropriation for the Marshall Plan to maintain "the confidence of the peoples of the free world in our good faith and leadership." Senator Taft, who had earlier tried to make a similar cut, agreed to the full amount, and on June 12 the Senate Committee voted to restore all but a small fraction of the original funds. The matter then went to a conference committee where the Senate version prevailed, and on June 20, the day before the GOP convention opened, the House finally concurred by a vote of 318 to 62.[2]

Vandenberg won lavish praise in the press for his role in saving the Marshall Plan from isolationist attacks, but his action undoubtedly injured his chances for the nomination. By taking the lead in beating back the House challenge, he had antagonized GOP isolationists and jeopardized his status as a dark-horse candidate acceptable to all elements within the party. The Michigan senator, however, was more concerned with preserving bipartisanship than winning the nomination. "I considered it to be the dedication of my life," he wrote afterward of his bipartisan policy. "I thought it to be the greatest cause on earth." [3]

Senator Vandenberg also took the lead in shaping the Republican platform. In May he began exchanging ideas with John Foster Dulles, who was still serving as Dewey's foreign policy adviser. When Dulles sent him a long, platitudinous draft plank, Vandenberg said it had some "good stuff" in it and urged him to refine it some more. "I think we *must* set down in a few terse, cogent sentences precisely what the Re-

publican Party stands for in terms of international cooperation." Dulles responded with another general statement stressing the need to roll back the Iron Curtain and accusing the
Democrats of weakening national prestige by following policies that made the United States "appear uncertain, inefficient,
vacillating and unreliable." Vandenberg wove a few sentences
from the Dulles draft into a new statement of his own, which
he then submitted to the chairman of the Resolutions Committee, Senator Henry Cabot Lodge of Massachusetts. Lodge
and Vandenberg included some sentences on foreign aid for
GOP isolationists to attack, and then won quick approval for
their draft platform after they agreed to remove these passages.[4]

The final platform dealt very briefly with foreign policy.
The Republicans gave qualified support ("within the prudent
limits of our own economic welfare") to foreign aid, praised
"the sturdy progress toward unity in Western Europe," and
promised to "protect the future against the errors of the Democrat Administration, which has too often lacked clarity, com-
petence or consistency in our vital international relationships."
There was no attack on Democratic appeasement at Yalta or
Potsdam, however; instead, the GOP expressed pride in their
participation in "limited areas of foreign policy" and promised, "We shall invite the Minority Party to join us under the
next Republican Administration in stopping partisan politics
at the water's edge." Under strong Zionist pressure, the Resolutions Committee did beef up a vague Palestine plank. The
platform criticized the Democrats for "vacillation" and promised full recognition of Israel, favorable boundaries, and "aid
in developing its economy."[5]

" [We] have the best platform in many years," Vandenberg
exclaimed. The *New York Times* was almost as pleased, saying that the platform promised to "keep foreign policy out of
the campaign." The oratory at the convention confirmed the

prevailing belief that the isolationists within the party had been routed. Keynoter Dwight Green, governor of Illinois, endorsed the Marshall Plan, and even Herbert Hoover, in his traditional appearance, declared that "it is in our interest and above all in the interest of liberty throughout the world that we aid in giving strength and unity to the nations of western Europe." Only the irrepressible Clare Booth Luce attacked the Democrats on foreign policy. Recalling Truman's "I like Old Joe" gaffe, she told the delighted delegates, "Good Old Joe. Of course they liked him. Didn't they give him all Eastern Europe, Manchuria, the Kuriles, North China, coalitions in Poland, Yugoslavia and Czechoslovakia?" [6]

The critical issue remained the choice of a candidate. Vandenberg formally announced his willingness to run when he arrived in Philadelphia on the opening day of the convention, but his chances still depended on a deadlock. On the first ballot, Dewey made such a strong showing that only a deal between Taft and Stassen could stop him. Taft tried to win Stassen's support, promising him second place on the ticket, but when Stassen stubbornly declined, the Ohio senator withdrew from the race at the end of the second ballot. The GOP then nominated Dewey unanimously on the third ballot, amid mixed feelings. Vandenberg hid his disappointment by calling Dewey an "almost invincible" candidate, while Taft supporter Colonel Robert McCormick took some solace in the outcome, commenting, "Well, it might have been worse; it might have been Vandenberg." [7]

The next day Dewey removed any suspicion of lingering isolationism within the Republican party by rejecting Charles Halleck and choosing Earl Warren for his running mate. The California governor appealed strongly to GOP internationalists, who saw in Halleck a continuation of midwestern opposition to an active foreign policy. Warren's nomination, together with the appointment of Pennsylvania Congressman

Hugh Scott as national chairman, indicated that internationalists from the two coasts had now taken firm control of the party.

Above all, the Republicans emerged from their convention in a mood of supreme confidence. In his acceptance speech, Dewey avoided all controversial issues in an effort to stress party unity, as he encouraged Republicans to look forward to a sweeping victory in the fall. Vandenberg was already looking ahead to a bright future, telling a correspondent that with "Dewey in the White House and Dulles in the State Department . . . we could be sure of the right kind of a foreign policy for the next four (and probably eight) years." Ernest Lindley predicted certain defeat for Truman and the Democrats while *Time* concluded, "Barring a political miracle, it was the kind of ticket that could not fail to sweep the Republican Party back into power." Only Truman remained skeptical, writing in his diary that Dewey's nomination "will make the campaign easier—all he can do is make a 'warmed-over' approach to the situation with which the country is faced and I don't think the country is going to take a 'warmed-over' approach." [8]

I

On June 23, the day the Republicans nominated Dewey, the Russians cut all rail, truck, auto, and barge traffic to Berlin, thereby touching off the gravest crisis of the Cold War. The Soviet action came in response to Western plans to unify their occupation zones and permit the formation of an independent West German government. In early June, representatives of the United States, England, and France who had been meeting since February on the German problem announced agreement on plans for a sovereign German state. When the Western nations took the first step in this direction by instituting currency reforms in their three sectors of Germany, the Russians began gradually cutting off the city of Berlin by halting land transportation. The extension of the currency reform to the Western-controlled sections of Berlin on June 23 led the Soviets to make the blockade absolute. A city of nearly three million people was now cut off from all normal outlets to the West; the only communication was by air, as the Russians respected the flight corridors they had agreed to in 1945.[9]

The Soviet blockade posed a terrifying dilemma for President Truman. If the American troops tried to bring supplies into Berlin by force, the far larger Russian army could easily stop them. Yet if the President gave in to the military realities and withdrew from the city, he would undermine European confidence in the American commitment to halt Soviet expansion. Though time was of the essence, since Berlin had only a thirty-day supply of food on hand, the President refused to make a hasty decision. Keeping silent himself, he permitted General Lucius Clay, the American military governor in Germany, to announce, "They can't drive us out by an action short of war as far as we are concerned." Meanwhile, Secretary of Defense Forrestal met on Sunday afternoon, June 27, to canvass the situation with his advisers. The next day, when he began to weigh the advisability of staying on in Berlin, "the President interrupted to say that there was no discussion on that point, we were going to stay period." Although Admiral Leahy, Truman's personal military adviser, called the situation in Berlin "hopeless," the President approved plans to increase the small airlift of supplies to the city that was already under way and to prepare to shift two squadrons of B-29's (the plane that delivered atomic bombs was a B-29) to bases in Germany.

With the Democratic convention coming up in mid-July, Truman preferred to postpone any public action on the Berlin blockade. He continued to refrain from making any comments on it at news conferences; instead, he let General Marshall speak for the administration. On June 30, Marshall told reporters that the United States would not be driven out of Berlin, saying that the airlift was proving more effective than had been thought possible. On the same day, the administration made public the transfer of the atomic-bomb carrying planes to Germany in an attempt to impress the Russians and reassure the American people.[10]

The administration placed its main reliance on diplomacy. In early July the State Department, in cooperation with Senator Vandenberg, drafted a protest note it planned to send to Russia in concert with England and France. After toning down the language to placate the frightened European allies, the State Department sent the note on July 6, a week before the Democratic convention was due to open. In the note, the United States "categorically asserts that it is in occupation of its sector of Berlin with free access thereto as a matter of established right deriving from the defeat and surrender of Germany. . . . It further declares that it will not be induced by threats, pressures or other action to abandon these rights." This firm statement was coupled with a proposal to enter into negotiations to deal with both access rights and currency reform in Berlin. Despite this peaceful offer, most commentators realized that the United States and Russia were on a collision course. "Hold on to your seats, folks," wrote the *New Republic*'s TRB. "This is the showdown." [11]

II

At home, Truman faced a revived challenge from the dissidents within the party. The "Draft Ike" movement, which had collapsed in April, sprang back to life in June, despite the fact that Eisenhower gave it no encouragement. Taking office as president of Columbia University early in the month, the general tried to ignore the continued call for him to seek the Democratic nomination. Disaffected southern Democrats asked him "to lead the people of this Nation in their fight against communism, tyranny and slavery and to maintain the peoples of the world at peace." ADA leader Leon Henderson tried a shrewder appeal, meeting personally with Eisenhower and telling him that he was the only Democratic candidate who could keep Republican isolationists in line. Senator Claude Pepper of Florida became the most ardent wooer of Ike, even coming up with a song, "More Power to Eisenhower." The increasing pressure only convinced Ike that the presidency ought not "be a political plum which military officers should look forward to." On July 5, he finally broke his long silence by issuing a statement: "I will not, at this time, identify myself with any political party, and could not accept nomination for any public office or participate in a partisan political contest." Incredibly, Pepper and a few others still persisted in their draft movement. When Truman learned that they planned to place Eisenhower's name in nomination at the Democratic convention, the President worked through intermediaries to have Ike send a telegram to Pepper in which he stated, "No matter under what terms, conditions or premises a proposal might be couched, I would refuse to accept the nomination." Finally admitting defeat, Pepper read the telegram to the press on the Saturday before the convention opened, thus ending the abortive boom for Ike.[12]

Eisenhower's reluctance to run led other liberals to turn to William O. Douglas as a man who could revive the old New Deal coalition. Justice Douglas, off on a fishing trip in the Oregon wilderness, quickly punctured this movement by issuing the statement, "I am not a candidate, have never been a candidate, and don't plan to be a candidate." In sheer desperation, Senator Pepper offered himself as an alternative to Truman, but after this gesture conspicuously failed to attract any support, the Florida senator withdrew. With his challengers in disarray, Harry Truman had locked up the nomination before the convention opened.[13]

The drafting of the Democratic platform went much more smoothly, except for the troublesome Palestine issue. The

State Department proposed a vague plank that stressed cooperation with the United Nations in restoring peace between the Arabs and the Jews. Zionists and liberal politicians countered with demands for removing the arms embargo and extending *de jure* as well as *de facto* recognition to Israel. Truman permitted Clifford to draft a compromise plank which promised economic aid, favored revision of the arms embargo through the United Nations, and praised the President for recognizing Israel, but did not mention the Zionist request for *de jure* status. In the remaining foreign policy sections, the Democrats took full credit "for resisting Communist aggression" through the Truman Doctrine and the Marshall Plan, and criticized the Republicans for their "reluctance to provide funds to support . . . the greatest move for peace and recovery made since the end of World War II." This departure from bipartisanship alarmed many internationalists and led Governor Dewey to condemn the Democrats for their "extremely partisan and provocative assertions concerning foreign affairs." [14]

The major excitement at the convention dealt with civil rights, not foreign policy. A group of northern liberals led by Minneapolis Mayor Hubert H. Humphrey challenged the vague civil rights plank the administration favored, and won a floor fight to substitute much more specific wording. Some of the Alabama and all the Mississippi delegates walked out, but most southerners stayed on to vote for Georgia Senator Richard Russell, who lost to Truman on the first ballot, 263 to 947½. In an effort to reassure the South, Truman accepted Kentucky Senator Alben W. Barkley as his running mate, after Justice Douglas declined. The delegates, still in a restive mood, voted for Barkley but failed to show any great enthusiasm for the ticket. "We're Just Mild About Harry," read one sign, which seemed to reflect the prevailing feeling of defeatism. [15]

Truman brought the slumbering convention to life with an

aggressive acceptance speech delivered in his new impromptu style. Focusing his attack on the Republican legislative record, Truman ridiculed the GOP for its failure to pass his domestic program and then announced he was calling Congress back into special session so that the Republicans could make good on their glib platform promises before the campaign began. "In the space of 3,000 words Mr. Truman had given the Democratic Party its first real chance for hope in months," commented *Newsweek*. The slashing attack won widespread praise from Democratic politicians, who called it "superb." Yet Truman was careful to confine his assault to domestic issues. Claiming that "we have converted the greatest and best of the Republicans to our viewpoint" on foreign policy, Truman gave the GOP full credit for supporting the Marshall Plan and the Truman Doctrine. "As I have said time and time again, foreign policy should be the policy of the whole Nation and not the policy of one party or the other," Truman declared. "Partisanship should stop at the water's edge; and I shall continue to preach that through this whole campaign." [16]

III

Henry Wallace and his new Progressive party challenged Truman's attempt to bury foreign policy issues. Meeting in Philadelphia in late July, the leaders of the third-party movement singled out bipartisanship for their fiercest attacks. In the keynote speech, Charles P. Howard, a Des Moines lawyer, called the bipartisan containment policy "the brain child of banking house diplomats and banking house brass," and said the choice facing the nation was "Wallace or war." In a *New Republic* article published on the eve of the convention, Wallace charged that both political groups were "definitely war parties" and added, "Vandenberg and Dulles are every bit as much responsible for the Democratic foreign policy of cold war and rearmament as the Democrats themselves." Urging liberals to carry on FDR's fight for peace, he promised to end the Cold War by direct negotiation with Stalin.[17]

The Progressive platform, written by New Dealer Rexford Tugwell and Communist fellow traveler Lee Pressman, made foreign policy the central issue. Unlike the Democrats, the new party called for "the immediate de jure recognition of the State of Israel," together with a large loan and the lifting of the arms embargo. The major portion, however, dealt with the Cold War. "Three years after the end of the second world war, the drums are beating for a third," it began. Accusing the Truman administration of trying "to rebuild Nazi Germany as a war base" and supporting "corrupt, fascist governments in China, Greece, Turkey, and elsewhere," the Progressives claimed that there was no problem between Russia and the United States that could not be solved by peaceful negotiation. The one moment of real excitement came when a Vermont delegate proposed an amendment from the floor which read, "It is not our intention to give blanket endorsement to the foreign policy of any nation." Intended to rebut charges that Communists dictated the platform, the amendment met with a storm of protest, as delegates accused its sponsor of "Red-baiting." The convention rejected it by voice vote and thus confirmed the growing belief that the Communists had captured the Progressive party.[18]

Henry Wallace ignored the charges that he had become a Red dupe as he accepted the Progressive party nomination in a speech to 25,000 faithful followers in Shibe Park. Once again he attacked bipartisanship, claiming that any deal to take foreign policy out of the campaign was "an agreement which would doom the nation and the world." Saying that he alone stood for peace, he dismissed the Berlin crisis as the inevitable result of Truman's "get tough" policy toward Russia. "In all earnestness, I assure you that if I were president, there would be no crisis in Berlin today," Wallace declared, adding that in the present situation he favored withdrawal from the city.[19]

" [I]t is surprising and disturbing that no honest advocate of a radical, non-Communist program could be found among the assembled Gideonites," commented the editors of the *Nation*. More conservative journals simply concluded that the Communists controlled the Progressive party, a conclusion that won widespread support when the Communist party voted to back Wallace rather than field its own candidate in 1948. Such an explanation is too simple. Experienced Communists did indeed infiltrate the Progressive party leadership and exercise considerable influence, but the rank-and-file consisted of liberals, radicals, and pacifists who honestly believed that America, not Russia, was primarily responsible for the Cold War. Although their views happened to coincide with the Communist party line, they held them independently and deeply resented the charges that they were Red dupes. Nevertheless, the majority of the American people were ready to write off Henry Wallace and the Progressives as subversives, precisely as Clark Clifford had predicted in his campaign plan. As a result, the nation lost the opportunity for a genuine debate on the merits of the containment policy as hysterical cries of "Commie" and "Red" drowned out Wallace's quixotic crusade.[20]

IV

On July 14, the day Truman won renomination, the Soviets intensified the Berlin crisis by demanding four-power talks on the future of Germany before they would consider lifting the blockade. The United States responded the next day by announcing the transfer of sixty B-29 atomic bombers to bases in England. Though the Pentagon described the flight as "a routine training mission," more than 150 reporters and photographers were on hand in Britain to record the arrival of the B-29's. The sixty bombers, along with thirty more in Germany, could deliver atomic bombs to any Russian target west of the Urals. Newspapers referred openly to the American move as a warning to the Russians "that the United States was capable of resisting efforts to force the United States, Britain and France out of Berlin," while *Newsweek* commented grimly that if Russia contemplated war, she faced "not just defeat, not just destruction, but obliteration." [21]

A full-blown war scare quickly developed. Stocks broke sharply on Wall Street as informed sources said the chances of war had gone from 1 in 10 to 1 in 4. "Almost anything could touch off a fight and a fight that would mean war," Budget Director James Webb told David Lilienthal, chairman of the Atomic Energy Commission, who noted in his diary that the AEC was making war preparations. On July 19, General Clay sent an urgent cable from Berlin saying, "I feel that the world is now facing the most vital issue that has developed since Hitler placed his political aggression under way." Clay believed that the Russians were bluffing, and he recommended sending an armed convoy down the Autobahn to Berlin. Although this proposal remained secret, on July 17 General William Donovan, the wartime head of the OSS who was now in private life, told reporters in Berlin that he favored sending out a tank column as a reconnaissance in force to probe Soviet intentions. Pointing out that Donovan was close to Clay, reporters emphasized his forceful recommendations. "If the Russians are determined to have war," they quoted Donovan as saying, "we might as well have it here as 500 miles farther back." [22]

A worried President Truman met for several hours with his top diplomatic and military advisers on July 19. He reiterated his determination to stand firm in Berlin, but he was open to advice on how to implement this decision. When Secretary of State Marshall opposed the use of force, the President decided to call General Clay and his diplomatic adviser, Robert Murphy, to Washington for a conference. Republicans Arthur Vandenberg and John Foster Dulles, consulted by the State Department, urged a cautious policy, Vandenberg advising, "I hope we shall not resort to any sort of unilateral force which, in effect, *asks* for war." By the time Clay arrived in Washington on July 21, he had developed second thoughts on the armed convoy idea and now placed greater reliance on a stepped-up airlift. The Joint Chiefs of Staff provided the clinching arguments when they informed the President that the United States would need eighteen months to prepare for an all-out war with the Soviet Union. On July 22, Truman told a morning press conference that he thought the chances for peace were now "excellent," and then he met with Clay and Murphy at a session of the National Security Council. The President approved a twofold policy of supplying Berlin through an expanded airlift and making a new diplomatic overture to the Kremlin. The next day tension eased noticeably as General Clay, preparing to return to Germany, told reporters that he also believed there was "an excellent chance" for a peaceful settlement of the Berlin crisis.[23]

While the Truman administration wrestled with the blockade, Dewey and the Republicans debated over the stand they should take. At the close of the GOP convention, Dewey gave several indications that he planned to make foreign policy a major campaign issue. On June 25, he accused the Truman administration of failing to give adequate aid to Chiang Kaishek, who was in the midst of a civil war in China with Mao Tse-tung's Communists. A week later, Dewey called a special press conference in Albany to announce that he would draw a careful distinction between those Truman policies on which Republicans had been consulted and those on which they had been ignored. Classifying only the Marshall Plan and the United Nations in the first category, Dewey said he would attack the Democrats in the fall for their failures in Greece, China, and Palestine and for their appeasement of Russia at

Potsdam. Dewey had made clear, *Time* commented, that "Foreign policy . . . was going to be a major target in the campaign." [24]

Dewey's threat to overturn bipartisanship alarmed Arthur Vandenberg. The Michigan senator sent an urgent message to Dulles arguing that the bipartisan policy was politically advantageous, since it permitted Republicans to take credit for such positive steps as the Marshall Plan. While conceding that there were Democratic measures which deserved criticism, he warned against stirring up issues that might come back to haunt a future Republican administration. "Otherwise," he cautioned Dulles, "November will represent a pyrrhic victory." At the same time, Vandenberg urged the Truman administration to keep Dulles fully informed of current foreign policy developments in an effort to influence Dewey. Secretary of State Marshall heeded this advice, assigning Robert Lovett, a Republican, the task of briefing Dulles on the Berlin crisis. [25]

Speculation about Dewey's plans grew as the Republican candidate kept silent while the Berlin crisis escalated in mid-July. Arthur Krock suggested that Dewey might well blame the Democrats for the Berlin situation, since they had failed to negotiate for secure access rights at the Potsdam conference. On July 21, at the height of the crisis, Dewey met at his Pawling, New York, farm with Harold Stassen, and confined his comment on Berlin to the cryptic statement, "Our gravest concern is honorably to preserve and build and strengthen the peace of the world." The next day the governor's office announced that Dewey had asked Vandenberg and Dulles to come to Pawling on July 24 to advise him on the Berlin situation. While reporters tried to guess what the Republicans would do, Dewey held a surprise "non-political conference" with General Eisenhower on Berlin. The United States "must stand with absolute firmness in Berlin," the GOP candidate told reporters afterward, but then added that the nation should "neglect no avenues to a peaceful solution." [26]

On July 24, after spending most of the day with Dulles and Vandenberg, Dewey announced his decision. Although he faulted the Democrats for failing to negotiate "specific international agreements to define our rights in Berlin," he stated that time and usage had confirmed our presence there. "In Berlin," Dewey declared, "we must not surrender our rights under duress." Then he went beyond this endorsement of administration policy to announce his commitment to Vandenberg's concept of bipartisanship. "The present duty of Americans is not to be divided by past lapses but to unite to surmount present danger," Dewey stated. "We shall not allow domestic partisan irritations to divert us from this indispensable unity." Thus Dewey placed patriotism above party and renounced his earlier plan to make foreign policy a major campaign issue.[27]

"Peace is 'busting out all over' here this week-end," exclaimed James Reston on July 25. Dewey's declaration of bipartisanship coupled with Truman's decision to seek a peaceful solution in Berlin ended the ominous talk of war and allowed the American people to breathe easier. "The talk of thrusting an armed convoy through the Russian zone of Berlin, of facing the terrible issue of war now and not later," commented *Newsweek,* "died away like a distant flourish of drums." The crisis was far from over, but the administration, bolstered by firm Republican support, felt that it was once again in control of a dangerous world situation.[28]

Dewey's decision not to attack Truman's Berlin policy, made at the moment of gravest tension, had profound repercussions in the forthcoming campaign. The Republican candidate had given up a promising foreign policy issue on which the Democrats were extremely vulnerable as a result of their failure to secure access rights at Potsdam. Public opinion polls taken in the summer of 1948 showed that the American people still gave foreign policy issues a priority over domestic concerns, and that a slight majority felt that the Republicans were better equipped than the Democrats to handle the delicate international situation. Yet by accepting bipartisanship on Berlin, and at least by implication on other Cold War matters, Dewey lost the chance to exploit this favorable climate of opinion.[29]

The Berlin crisis was a godsend for the Democrats. The fear of war rallied the people around Truman's leadership; the President now monopolized public attention as the press focused on the various steps he took to defend the nation. The fresh evidence of Russian hostility further weakened the sagging Wallace crusade, as people felt that Soviet behavior confirmed Truman's "get tough" policy rather than Wallace's idea of direct negotiation with Stalin. Above all, the Republican commitment to bipartisanship fitted in perfectly with Clifford's master plan for the campaign. With the GOP following his lead in foreign affairs, Truman could deliver an all-out attack on the Republican 80th Congress on domestic issues. This artificial division between developments at home and abroad gave Truman a significant advantage in an election that now promised to be closer than anyone had thought possible in the spring.[30]

V

The emerging spirit of bipartisanship survived several jolts before the campaign began in September. The first came when Truman called Congress into special session and dared the Republicans to enact the liberal domestic measures they had advocated in their platform. After two weeks of acrimonious debate, the Republican-controlled Congress adjourned without passing a single significant piece of legislation. Truman immediately labeled the 80th Congress "the worst in history," to the intense anger of Senator Vandenberg. In a letter to Dulles on August 9, Vandenberg pointed out that the Republican leadership had cooperated magnificently with the Truman administration in enacting the Marshall Plan, supporting the Truman Doctrine, and approving nearly every treaty and foreign policy resolution submitted. "I think it is the most amazing record of constructive Congressional cooperation ever written in *any* Congress," he told Dulles, adding that the GOP could take pride in fostering a unity "which may well spell the difference between peace and war." Agreeing that it was "an amazing record," Dulles urged Vandenberg to "carry that record to the country" during the fall campaign.[31]

Other Republicans, however, wanted to respond to Truman's attack on Congress with an all-out assault on Democratic foreign policy failures. The Republican National Committee prepared a pamphlet entitled "Democratic Duplicity and Appeasement in Foreign Policy—1935–1947." Based on the memoirs of thirteen prominent Democrats, ranging from James Byrnes to William Bullitt, this campaign pamphlet accused FDR and Truman of appeasing first Germany and then Russia, "resulting in the terrible debacle of World War II and the near loss of the post-war peace." Although Congressional candidates were free to use this material, the National Committee withdrew its endorsement at the request of Dewey, who reaffirmed his commitment to bipartisanship. The Truman administration responded by continuing its policy of briefing Vandenberg and Dulles on current international developments and by inviting Dulles to serve as a member of the American delegation to the United Nations, which was due to convene in Paris in late September.[32]

The most serious threat to bipartisanship occurred on August 17, when Governor Dewey released a statement to the press urging that former Italian colonies in Africa be restored to Italy under a UN trusteeship. The peace treaty with Italy, signed by the United States, Great Britain, France, and the Soviet Union in September 1947, left the fate of the colonies, which included Libya, Eritrea, and Italian Somaliland, to subsequent negotiation and ultimate resolution by the United Nations if the Big Four failed to agree. The Western nations wanted to continue their occupation of these territories, particularly Libya in the sensitive area of the Eastern Mediterranean, while the Soviet Union pressed for a United Nations trusteeship which would give them some voice in the final disposition of the colonies. Italian-Americans urged that the colonies be restored to Italy as soon as possible, and they applied pressure on both Democrats and Republicans to endorse this solution. Disregarding the advice of John Foster Dulles, who counseled against making the Italian colonies a partisan issue, Dewey decided to speak out after a conference in Albany with an Italian-American delegation headed by State Industrial Commissioner Edward Corsi. "The Communist menace will receive another setback," Dewey declared, "if the Italian people are now given an ample opportunity to take part in the future development of the resources of these African areas." [33]

Democratic politicians immediately branded Dewey's statement as a blatant attempt to play politics with a foreign policy issue. Democratic National Chairman J. Howard McGrath tried to fend off the pressure from prominent Italians in the party who warned that Dewey was making serious inroads into the normally Democratic Italian vote. Jack Redding, publicity director for the National Committee, urged Truman to take issue with Dewey openly, and when the President declined, Redding spoke to Under Secretary of State Robert Lovett. Although Lovett refused to issue a public statement, he told Redding that the United States opposed the return of the colonies to Italy, particularly since they would be a financial drain on a country the United States was already subsidizing heavily. Redding then quietly informed *New York Times* correspondent Clayton Knowles of the State Department's position, and the next day a front-page story appeared describing the administration's anger at Dewey for making a political issue out of the delicate question of the Italian colonies. When reporters asked Truman about the *Times* account at a press conference on August 19, the President seized the opportunity to chastise Dewey for meddling in foreign policy for partisan advantage. The fate of the colonies, Truman told the newsmen, "is a United Nations and a four-power treaty proposition, and cannot very well be handled politically in the United States." [34]

Although Dewey replied through a spokesman that he felt he had a duty to state his views on world affairs "fully and frankly," he let the issue drop when he met with criticism on all sides. The Ethiopian government asked the Republican candidate "why the economy of the aggressor enemy should be rehabilitated at the expense of the victim ally," while the *New York Times* warned, "This is no time for an appeal to particular and narrow interests." The strongest criticism came from Vandenberg, who telephoned Dulles to express his fear that Dewey had sabotaged the bipartisan policy. In a letter on August 20, Dulles tried to explain the pressures on a candidate running for office, but promised that he and Dewey would be "more careful in the future" and try to keep the candidate's public statements "within the spirit of your wise counsel." Vandenberg refused to be mollified, replying that the question of the Italian colonies was *"sheer dynamite."* Pointing out that the United States was engaged in a "life-and-death struggle with Soviet conspiracy and intrigue," Vandenberg declared, "I do *not* believe that our campaign discussion of foreign problems should announce *any* decisions . . . respecting specific subjects which are involved in current international negotiation." [35]

After this brief flare-up, the issue of the Italian colonies faded out of politics. In September, the Big Four failed to reach agreement on their fate at a Council of Foreign Ministers session, and the issue finally went to the United Nations. Its chief impact was to discourage Dewey from making any future deviations from bipartisanship. Dulles informed Robert Lovett on August 20 that he had persuaded Governor Dewey to keep his statement on the Italian colonies deliberately vague, despite intense pressure from domestic political advisers for a more specific commitment. "I hoped that this would not disrupt unity with respect to the critical and vital issues, particularly involving current issues with the Soviet Union," Dulles added. Lovett accepted his account of the episode and promised to continue consulting with Dulles and Vandenberg. At the same time, Vandenberg kept pressing party leaders to place national unity before partisan advantage, claiming such a tactic was expedient as well as patriotic. By stressing the Republicans' role in framing the containment policy, he told GOP National Chairman Hugh Scott, they could prevent the Democrats from taking full credit for halting Soviet expansion. "From the standpoint of sheer politics, I respectfully submit that we can *prove* from the *record* that Republicans can be *wholly* trusted with these foreign policy responsibilities," Vandenberg wrote to Dulles. "I respectfully submit that our only political danger is to UNPROVE it." With his two foreign policy advisers so adamant, Dewey was unlikely to make any more partisan sallies into international affairs.[36]

VI

Throughout the month of August, the Truman administration engaged in a major diplomatic effort to lift the Berlin blockade. The American ambassador to Russia, Walter Bedell Smith, met with Stalin on the evening of August 2, accompanied by the British and French representatives in Moscow. In a conference that lasted for more than two hours, Stalin outlined a promising solution to the Berlin crisis, offering to lift the blockade in return for acceptance of Russian currency throughout the city. When Smith tried to work out the details of such a settlement, however, Foreign Minister Molotov insisted that in addition the U.S. agree to postpone indefinitely the plans for an independent West German government. As

Truman's advisers feared, the Soviets were using the blockade as a pretext to prevent the emergence of a sovereign West Germany.[37]

The United States responded to Russian intransigence with a variety of military and diplomatic measures. The Air Force expanded the airlift, stripping planes from other parts of the world to carry on round-the-clock flights into Tempelhof airfield. By mid-August, Allied planes were bringing in more than 4,000 tons of supplies to the beleaguered city each day. At the same time, the Strategic Air Command consolidated the 90 B-29's sent to Britain and Germany earlier in the summer at Burtonwood Air Base in England. Twenty-five hundred maintenance technicians transformed the old World War II field into a modern facility capable of unleashing a devastating atomic assault on the Soviet Union. Finally, on August 23, Ambassador Smith, frustrated by Molotov's tactics, held a second conference with Stalin. After several more meetings, Smith appeared to have scored a significant breakthrough. Dropping the crucial issue of West German independence, Stalin agreed to lift the blockade in return for the extension of Russian currency into all sectors of Berlin, coupled with a new attempt at four-power government for the entire city. Smith agreed to let the Western and Soviet officials in Berlin work out the precise details of this settlement.[38]

Truman was delighted that his mixture of firmness and wlllingness to negotiate was finally paying off. His political advisers wanted him to take full political advantage of the pending settlement. William Batt, director of research for the Democratic National Committee, urged the White House to make sure that President Truman personally released the news that the blockade was over. Batt even drafted a speech in which Truman would inform the American people of his triumphant diplomacy and conclude by stating, in words reminiscent of Neville Chamberlain after Munich, "our goal must be—not peace in our time—but peace for all time." [39]

Although hints of a peaceful solution appeared in the press throughout the first week of September, with the *New York Times* predicting that the blockade would be lifted by September 15, the Berlin negotiations gradually broke down as the Russians kept bringing up new points to block a final agreement. On September 5, Secretary of Defense Forrestal reported in his diary that the Berlin situation was "deteriorating" when the Russians threatened to violate the air corridors to the city. Two days later, a mob drove the Berlin assembly from the City Hall in the Soviet sector, and when West Berliners held a mammoth rally in the British zone to protest this move, Russian soldiers fired on the crowd. Once again fear of war swept over the United States as the expected peaceful settlement disintegrated.[40]

"U.S.-Russian relations had never been as taut," reported *Time*. Truman called a special meeting of the National Security Council on September 7. George Marshall and Robert Lovett painted a bleak picture of the Berlin talks; the group agreed to make one more approach to the Russians and, if that did not work, to consider taking Berlin to the UN Security Council as an issue threatening world peace. Secretary Marshall told a press conference that the United States intended to stand firmly in the city, and labor leader David Dubinsky reported that Truman had said, "We will not go out of Berlin." On September 9, the National Security Council decided to increase the airlift to 5,000 tons of supplies a day, enough to supply the city with food and fuel in the coming winter months, and agreed to take the Berlin issue to the Security Council when the UN convened in Paris at the end of the month.[41]

As the crisis reached its new peak, Republicans once again rallied behind the administration. Vandenberg and Dulles met for two hours with Thomas Dewey in New York City on September 10, after which the senator told the press that Dewey stood squarely behind Truman's Berlin policy. "Regardless of political differences at home," Vandenberg declared, "we are serving notice on the world that America is united to protect American rights everywhere." He went on to warn foreign countries not to be misled by heated campaign oratory. "We shall be in internal controversy regarding many phases of foreign policy," Vandenberg explained. "But we shall not be in controversy over the basic fact that America is united against aggression and against the foes of freedom." [42]

Though undoubtedly Truman was relieved by the Republican commitment to bipartisanship, the crisis weighed heavily on his mind. Secretary of Defense Forrestal pressed him hard on the crucial issue of whether he was prepared to use the atomic bomb in case of war with Russia. "The President said that he prayed that he would never have to make such a decision," Forrestal wrote in his diary on September 10, "but that if it became necessary, no one need have a misgiving but what he would do so." James Webb, the director of the Budget, reported Forrestal's urgings to Atomic Energy Commission Chairman David Lilienthal, and said that "anything" might happen over Berlin. "The President has always been optimistic about peace," Lilienthal quoted Webb as saying. "But he is blue now, mighty blue. It is very hard on him, coming right now particularly." Truman himself revealed how pessimistic he had become in a diary entry on September 13. "Have [had] a terrific day," he commented, mentioning briefings on atomic targets in Russia. "I have a terrible feeling afterward that we are very close to war. I hope not." [43]

The possibility of atomic war thus cast an ominous shadow over the coming election. Though Truman still hoped that an expanded airlift and a new round of negotiations at the UN Security Council level could preserve peace in Berlin, he knew that if the Russians tried to block the air corridors and thus isolate the city, he would have to begin World War III. Given the lack of available conventional forces and Forrestal's relentless pressure within the Cabinet, such a step meant an atomic strike against the Soviet Union. His aides might continue to view the Berlin crisis as a fortuitous event which defused Republican criticism of Truman's foreign policy and rallied support behind a discredited administration, but for the President such political gains could hardly offset the knowledge that the world was poised on the brink of the most terrible conflict in history. The Russian challenge in Berlin, far more than Dewey's campaign at home, must have occupied his thoughts as he set out to win an election the experts claimed was already beyond his reach.

7

Harry Truman faced problems at home nearly as grave as those abroad as he began campaigning for reelection. Disaffected southerners, led by South Carolina Governor J. Strom Thurmond, had met in Birmingham, Alabama, right after the Democratic convention to form the States Rights party. Although such prominent southern Democrats as Georgia's Richard Russell and Virginia's Harry Byrd stayed away, six thousand cheering Dixiecrats, as they called themselves, nominated Thurmond for the presidency and chose Mississippi Governor Fielding Wright as his running mate. Reacting solely to the Democratic party's strong civil rights plank, the Dixiecrats ignored the Cold War and foreign policy in pleading for continued racial segregation in the South, without federal interference. The southerners knew they could not win, but they hoped to take enough votes away from Truman to insure his defeat and thus command future respect for their views within the Democratic party.[1]

Hearings held before an obscure Senate subcommittee during the special session of Congress created an even greater threat to Truman's political fortunes. On July 30, Elizabeth T. Bentley, a mousy-looking government employee, testified that a number of high officials in the Truman administration were Communist spies; a few days later journalist Whittaker Chambers made the still more sensational disclosure that Alger Hiss, former State Department officer and president of the prestigious Carnegie Endowment for International Peace, had passed government secrets to the Soviets in the 1930's. Truman tried to dismiss the spy charges in a news conference on August 5, repeating a reporter's phrase that they were just "a red herring" and allowing the press to quote this remark. The American people, already deeply concerned over the Soviet threat as a result of Truman's containment rhetoric, took the spy charges far more seriously, viewing them as revealing a new front in the already dangerous Cold War. Politicians were quick to realize the potential of this new issue. Sam Rayburn told a reporter confidentially, "There is political dynamite in this Communist investigation . . . it creates just one impression, that is that the government is full of Communists handing out information to spies for transmission direct to Moscow." *Newsweek* put it more succinctly when it called the Congressional probe "the hottest story since the Teapot Dome scandal." [2]

The postconvention polls revealed how slim Truman's chances appeared to be. Gallup found that Dewey enjoyed a substantial lead, with 53 percent of those expressing opinions favoring him, compared to 41 percent for Truman and 6 percent for Wallace. Nearly all the political columnists conceded the election to Dewey before the campaign even began. The most startling forecast came from Elmo Roper, whose *Fortune* polls had been the most accurate in predicting the outcome in 1940 and 1944. Reporting in early September that Dewey was leading Truman by 44 percent to 31 percent, Roper said only a "political convulsion" could save the President from certain defeat. "My whole inclination," Roper confessed, "is to predict the election of Thomas E. Dewey by a heavy margin and devote my time and efforts to other things." [3]

Despite this gloomy outlook, Truman refused to concede the possibility of defeat. Instead, he spent most of August preparing for an intensive national campaign, relying on the help of such seasoned professionals as J. Howard McGrath, Under Secretary of the Interior Oscar Chapman, and Federal Security Administrator Oscar Ewing, as well as White House aides Clark Clifford and Charles Murphy. This group agreed that Truman should conduct his campaign along the lines of his June speaking tour, relying on extemporaneous talks from brief notes that would enable him to appeal directly to the people. Only major policy statements and speeches dealing with foreign affairs would be prepared in advance by a small staff in Washington, which included David D. Lloyd, George M. Elsey, David Bell, and A. Z. Carr.[4]

"The campaign was built on one issue—the interests of the people, as represented by the Democrats, against the special interests as represented by the Republicans and the record of the Eightieth Congress," Truman wrote in his *Memoirs*. "I staked the race for the presidency on that one issue." Truman exaggerated slightly. In a detailed memorandum to the President on August 17, Clifford set forth the campaign plan, which followed closely his November 1947 outline. The Democrats would hammer away at liberal domestic issues in order to rally the support of all elements of the New Deal and appeal to the independent voters who held the balance of power. But at the same time, Clifford urged Truman to stress foreign affairs "by showing the policy of the Truman Administration has kept the nation on a road leading to peace, not to war." The President should take full credit for the Truman Doctrine and the Marshall Plan and seize any opportunity that developed to advocate a peaceful settlement of the Cold War with Russia. In advocating reform at home and peace abroad, Clifford suggested that Truman concentrate on seventeen states where the outcome was marginal in 1944, proposing three long tours of the Middle West, Far West, and Northeast.[5]

After a brief trip to Detroit to deliver the traditional Labor Day address in Cadillac Square, Truman began his first long campaign tour on September 17. Secretary of State George Marshall was one of the handful who came down to Union Station to wish the President well on his swing to the West Coast and back. "I'm going to give 'em hell," Truman told reporters, and in speech after speech across the Middle West he blasted the 80th Congress, accusing the Republicans of serving the special interests and ignoring the people. Along the way, he made only glancing references to foreign policy, but each time he did so he carefully stressed his efforts for peace and praised the Republicans for their cooperation. He avoided any direct references to the still-critical Berlin blockade, although in a preface to his farm-policy speech in Dexter, Iowa, he did mention his determination to stand firm and adopt a reasonable attitude toward "a very disturbing international situation." "It is the policy of this Government to continue working for peace with every instrument at our command," Truman affirmed. When he arrived in California, he developed his peace theme more often, in an effort to appeal to the many Wallace supporters in the state. In a major address in Los Angeles, he heeded the advice of his aides not to make a martyr of Wallace by branding him a Communist. Instead, Truman claimed that he could work much more effectively to resolve the Cold War than the third-party candidate. "We have worked for peace in a difficult international situation," he declared, "and we shall continue with all our strength to work for peace." [6]

As Truman left the West Coast, his associates were discouraged. The crowds were small and the party nearly ran out of money to pay for the return trip; only last-minute fund raising by the governor of Oklahoma enabled the President to continue. Then in Texas larger crowds began to appear, giving Truman and his associates a second wind after they had been ready, as Clifford told David Lilienthal, "to crawl into a hole and die." At Uvalde, Truman met with John Nance Garner, FDR's first Vice-President, and then traveled to San Antonio, where he again dwelt at length on his desire to end the Cold War. "And what we are trying to do is sell the world on the idea that peace is the best policy. . . . That is much more important than whether I am President of the United States." The warm applause that greeted this statement led Truman to use it again and again as a sure crowd pleaser. After a conference with Walter Bedell Smith, who flew in from Europe to report on the Berlin crisis, Truman went to Oklahoma City, where he planned to give his first campaign radio broadcast on the sensitive issue of Communism in government.[7]

Truman's advisers, particularly those responsible for foreign affairs, urged him not to associate the containment policy with the Communist problem at home. The President disregarded this advice. Denying that the threat of Communism was internal, Truman declared that "the greatest danger has been that communism might blot out the light of freedom in so much of the rest of the world that the strength of its onslaught against our liberties would be greatly multiplied." Only the Truman Doctrine and the Marshall Plan had saved the world from the spreading Soviet aggression. "It is a plain and unanswerable fact that all these great programs were conceived and sponsored by the Truman Administration," the President concluded.[8]

On October 2, two weeks after his departure, a smiling Harry Truman arrived back in Washington. Encouraged by the growing enthusiasm of his audiences on the return trip, he remained confident that he could overcome Dewey's lead and win reelection. Strong support from organized labor, who resisted Wallace's lure, gave him some basis for his optimism; and though the pollsters continued to predict a Dewey victory, reporters noticed the warm response Truman had evoked from the people. Clifford's shrewd tactic of claiming full political credit for the bipartisan policy of containment while lambasting the Republicans on domestic issues was beginning to pay off. Above all, Truman's reiteration of his desire for peace in the midst of the ominous Berlin crisis soothed a worried public and greatly enhanced the President's appeal.[9]

I

While Truman toured the West, the attention of most Americans was riveted on Paris, where the third annual meeting of the United Nations opened on September 21 at the elegant Palais de Chaillot, a white, crescent-shaped building on a slope overlooking the Seine. Secretary of State Marshall headed the bipartisan American delegation, which included Republicans Warren Austin and John Foster Dulles as well as Democrat Eleanor Roosevelt. As he left Washington on September 19, Marshall underlined the tension over Berlin, describing the world situation as "unusually critical." In his opening address to the UN, he was equally grim. Warning the Russians not to mistake patience for weakness, the Secretary told the world body, "We will under no circumstances barter away the rights and freedoms of other peoples." [10]

Behind the scenes a vigorous debate was taking place over the proper course for the West to follow. England and France wanted to resume direct negotiations with the Soviet Union, hoping that they could work out a face-saving accommodation with Foreign Minister Molotov in Paris. Marshall and his State Department advisers, Chip Bohlen and Dean Rusk, preferred to take the issue directly to the UN Security Council and charge the Soviets with threatening world peace. Inside the American delegation, Dulles argued against Marshall's course, claiming that it would lead to a Soviet veto and thus reveal the inability of the UN to settle big-power disputes.

Dulles, certain that the Republicans would win the coming election, did not want Dewey to be confronted with an impossible choice when he took office. "My concern," he cabled the candidate from Paris, "has been that there should not be started a chain of events which might face you with necessity of going to war to vindicate Security Council decision or having to show such weakness as would itself invite further Soviet aggression." [11]

Secretary Marshall, backed by President Truman, won the debate. On September 26, the United States, Great Britain, and France announced that they would ask the Security Council to act on the threat to world peace created by the "illegal and coercive" Soviet blockade of Berlin. Reporters pointed out to the American people the seriousness of this step, stating that while it might rally world opinion behind the West, it could only lead to a Soviet veto and an even more serious clash of national interest. Truman withheld any comment on the move, but Thomas Dewey, campaigning in California, immediately issued a statement supporting the administration. Stating that Dulles had kept him informed daily on the worsening Berlin situation, Dewey declared, "This is too sober a moment in our history for threats or recriminations. . . . I call upon our own people and men and women of every land . . . to make it clear beyond misunderstanding that we stand together to strengthen the hands of those who speak and work for us and for the cause of peace in Paris." Dulles, loyally disguising his own doubts, defended the decision to take Berlin before the Security Council. "Whatever may be the risks to the United Nations, if indeed there are such risks," he asserted, "efforts to maintain peace and justice are paramount." [12]

Once again talk of war spread through the pages of American newspapers and magazines. While experts voiced their belief that the Soviets did not want war over Berlin, they admitted that neither side could back down now without suffering a great loss of prestige. *Time* concluded a two-page article entitled, "How Close Is War?" with the cautious estimate, "War this year is a real possibility, but is not probable." General Eisenhower, the nation's best-known military leader, was much more pessimistic. "The news over the weekend was completely depressing," he wrote to James Forrestal on September 27. "Frankly, the prospects look darker to me this Monday morning than they have yet," Ike continued, stating that he feared war was very likely. "I pray that you, with your closer view, seem to see some light in what I think a very dark sky." [13]

For Governor Dewey, the deepening Berlin crisis confirmed a prior decision to try to keep his campaign above the usual partisan level. Persuaded by the polls and by the unanimous judgment of his political advisers that he was certain to win the election, Dewey felt he should avoid saying anything in the heat of the campaign that would embarrass him later as President. Concerned by the threat of war, he believed his greatest contribution would be to stress national unity so as to demonstrate to the world, and above all to the Soviets, that regardless of domestic political squabbles, the American people spoke with one voice on the Cold War. He would conduct the usual speaking tour of the nation, but instead of flailing his opponent as he had Roosevelt in 1944, he would enunciate broad principles designed to uplift and reassure the people at a time of grave national danger. This strategy meant forgoing the Communist spy issue and avoiding any attack on Truman's foreign policy, even those portions, such as Palestine and China, on which Republicans had never been consulted and which were ripe for partisan criticism. [14]

Dewey approached the campaign with his usual efficiency. A staff of speech-writers under the direction of Elliot Bell, a veteran of the 1944 effort, prepared a series of speeches on all major topics. Allen Dulles headed up the foreign policy advisers, who included Gabriel Hauge, Christian Herter, and McGeorge Bundy. The State Department provided special facilities so that Dewey could communicate directly with John

Foster Dulles in Paris. Thus the governor received daily reports on the Berlin crisis from the man who was widely believed to be his choice for Secretary of State and who continually reinforced the decision to keep foreign policy out of the election.[15]

The Republican candidate began his formal campaign on September 19 when he set out for a tour of the West on the Dewey Victory Special, accompanied by a staff of forty-one and over a hundred newsmen. More relaxed than in 1944, Dewey made an effort to unbend with reporters so as to offset his reputation as a cool, aloof individual, but newsmen continued to quote with relish the familiar line, "You have to know Dewey to dislike him." The train moved with stopwatch precision, and mimeographed copies of all statements and speeches were ready for reporters hours in advance. Yet, as *Newsweek* noted, "they bristled with platitudes" and rarely displayed a spark of humor or wit. The team of speech-writers, including a specialist on "spiritual stuff," churned out turgid, committee prose reduced to the lowest common denominator of everyone's ideas. "The result was generality without even originality in expression," Raymond Moley commented. Moley put his finger on a still graver weakness when he pointed out Dewey's overreliance on "the rational and orderly in a field where reason and order have little authority." "An honest soul like Dewey's finds it hard to adapt itself to the habits of mystery, of subtle deception and ambiguity which are indigenous to politics," he noted. Unlike Harry Truman, Dewey had no feel for people, no sense that, at bottom, politics consists of emotion and human empathy, not facts and logic.[16]

The governor set the tone for his western tour in his first speech in Des Moines, Iowa. "[T]his campaign will not create division among our people," he declared. "Instead this campaign will unite us as we have never been united before. It will unite us so strongly that no force will again attack us and we will labor unceasingly and with unity to find common grounds of firm and peaceful agreement with all the nations of the earth." At Albuquerque two days later, he avoided any partisan criticism of Truman's foreign policy as he set forth a proposal for a Western European federation. In other speeches, he did refer to the issue of Communists in government by repeating a line which always won warm applause, "I suggest you elect an administration that simply won't appoint them in the first place." But he stopped short of accusing the Democrats of treason and he carefully separated his domestic criticism from the conduct of foreign policy. Calling upon members of both parties to support Secretary of State Marshall in Paris, Dewey told a San Francisco audience that "no good American will try to make political profit out of the sacrifices by our people in the cause of human freedom." [17]

Concerned by the pessimistic dispatches Dulles was sending him about the Berlin crisis, Dewey decided to speak out clearly on this issue. In Seattle, he warned the Russians that "no nation ever again can hope to profit from aggression." The next day he told a crowd in Missoula, Montana, that the American people stood "shoulder-to-shoulder" with their representatives in Paris. "We will not compromise our principles," he affirmed. "There is no peace in that and we will not endanger our freedom." In Great Falls the next day, he said the United States only wanted "peace with honor," and then added, "And let no dictator or trigger-happy militarist anywhere make any mistake about that purpose." Reporters noted that in contrast to Truman, who kept silent on Berlin, the Republican candidate spoke as if he were already elected, addressing his remarks not to the American electorate but to the men in the Kremlin. And indeed, those close to Dewey reported that he weighed his words with the Soviet leaders in mind, convinced, as he told Marquis Childs, that "the Politburo was only two votes away from war." [18]

Dewey's major foreign policy pronouncement came in a nationally televised speech from the Mormon Tabernacle in Salt Lake City on September 30. Speaking on the tenth anniversary of the Munich agreement, Dewey used the occasion to denounce isolationism and appeasement and to restate his support for the bipartisan containment policy. Several times he seemed to be on the brink of attacking the Truman record, but each time he drew back. Talking about postwar Russian expansion, he commented, "It wouldn't serve any useful purpose to recall tonight how the Soviet [Union] has conquered millions of people as a result of the failures of statesmanship." He alluded to the worsening plight of Chiang Kai-shek's Nationalists in the Chinese civil war, but he only hinted at Democratic responsibility when he promised "an end to the tragic neglect of our ancient friend and ally China." Instead of attacking the Truman administration, he ended the speech with a call to unity in the continuing struggle against the Soviet menace. "Our foreign policy in this troubled world can no longer be a passive, a dead—a negative thing," Dewey exhorted. "It must be a live and vital thing. We will wage peace, we will wage peace with all the vigor, and the imagination, and the skill and energy with which we waged war."

The eight thousand people crowded into the Tabernacle interrupted Dewey twenty-four times with bursts of applause, and at the end they stood up when Dewey asked the organist to play "America the Beautiful" and led the audience with his rich baritone voice. "It literally tore at you," reported one observer; ". . . it was terrific." Less emotional commentators were equally enthusiastic about his speech, praising Dewey for rising above partisanship at a time of such great international tension. "He seemed less like a candidate bidding for votes," *Time* observed, "and more like a statesman speaking not only for his party but for his country." [19]

Dewey's emphasis on bipartisanship came at a time when the Democrats appeared especially vulnerable to attack. In late August and early September, *Life* published a two-part article by William Bullitt entitled, "How We Won the War and Lost the Peace." Bullitt accused Roosevelt of disregarding expert advice, including his own, by gambling that he could charm Joseph Stalin into a policy of peaceful cooperation with the West. Rehashing the Teheran and Yalta conferences, the former diplomat accused FDR of appeasing the Soviet Union and charged that Truman had continued this disastrous policy until 1947, when he finally woke up to the nature of Soviet aggression. Comparing the Berlin crisis to the threat of Hitler in 1940, Bullitt concluded, "We face today a struggle not for security but for survival." At about the same time, Robert Sherwood's account of Roosevelt's and Hopkins' diplomacy at Yalta appeared in *Collier's,* with several damaging disclosures of what seemed by 1948 to be naïve faith in Soviet goodwill.[20]

Some Republicans began to attack the Democratic record in the Cold War. In a major speech in Detroit on September 7, Harold Stassen charged that "Potsdam was a colossal failure for the United States," as he pointed out that Republicans had not taken part in that important conference. House Majority Leader Charles Halleck, stung by Truman's attacks on the 80th Congress, accused the Democrats of failing to "slap down" the Russians during World War II when they were dependent on the United States for economic aid. The remarks of vice-presidential candidate Earl Warren were more surprising. Though Warren did occasionally echo Dewey's unity theme, he kept referring to the Truman administration's "secret deals" and "under-the-table diplomacy." "Our vacillation and appeasement at Yalta and Potsdam," he told a Polish audience in Buffalo, had led to the Iron Curtain being dropped in front of "our European friends." "Five years since Teheran and more than three years since Yalta and Potsdam, the American people still don't know what was decided at those conferences," Warren told representatives of twenty-six ethnic groups in Chicago. "All of it has been bad, bad for us and bad for our friends overseas." [21]

These partisan attacks remained the exception, however, as Dewey clung steadfastly to the bipartisan policy advocated by Dulles and Vandenberg. The Michigan senator was busy campaigning for his own reelection, but he did take time out for a nationally broadcast speech from Washington in early October. Using a text cleared by Dewey's advisers, Vandenberg made a remarkably low-key address in which he stressed the Republican contributions to the containment policy. The only passionate note came when he defended the 80th Congress from Truman's attack by claiming that it had the best record in foreign affairs of any Congress in history. He supported the administration's policy in Berlin and assured voters they could elect a Republican president "without affecting the continuity of our foreign policy." Dewey telephoned his congratulations, and then, to Vandenberg's amazement, Truman praised the speech, telling the senator he thought that preservation of the bipartisan foreign policy was more important than who won the election.[22]

On the day that Vandenberg spoke, Dewey held a three-and-a-half hour conference with John Foster Dulles, who flew back to give the Republican candidate a firsthand report on the Paris negotiations. Dulles painted a bleak picture of the Berlin situation and told Dewey that Europeans were heartened by his call for unity and his unwavering support for Truman's containment policy. In a press conference afterward, Dulles described the Berlin crisis as "much worse" and said relations with the Soviets were more tense "than at any time since the end of the war." "The whole situation is very delicate now," Dulles commented, "and I wouldn't want to do anything to rock the boat." [23]

This ominous assessment reinforced Dewey's determination to keep foreign policy out of the campaign. His advisers believed that bipartisanship was smart politics as well, gaining him the votes of independents alienated by Truman's "give 'em hell" tactics. On October 3, the *New York Times,* which had refused to endorse Dewey on foreign policy grounds in 1944, came out for his election, stating that "the bipartisan foreign policy would be in safe hands" in a Dewey administration. *Life* also backed him, commenting favorably on his admirable restraint in not blaming the Democrats for "the present Berlin crisis." Only the rabidly isolationist Chicago *Tribune* criticized Dewey for failing to present alternatives to Democratic foreign policies, but even so the editors endorsed him as "the least worst of the candidates." [24]

Dewey's bipartisan stand did not have any appreciable effect on the election forecasts. The pollsters continued to predict a landslide for the Republicans, and political experts prophesied that Dewey would receive at least 350 electoral votes compared to less than 100 for Truman. Encouraged by this rosy outlook, Dewey believed that his primary responsibility was to minimize partisan friction as he looked past election day to the burdens he would assume when he was inaugurated on January 20.[25]

II

Henry Wallace could not afford the luxury of looking ahead. Aware that his movement had sagged badly over the summer, he began campaigning on August 21 in a desperate effort to breathe new life into his candidacy. For the next ten weeks, he stumped the nation, traveling more than 25,000 miles as he sought to convince a hostile public that the bipartisan foreign policy risked an unnecessary war with the Soviet Union. Alone among the major party candidates, he ventured into the South, speaking out boldly for racial equality amid a barrage of eggs, tomatoes, and rocks from angry southern whites. He won widespread sympathy among liberals for his courage, but the Communist issue, inflamed by the Hiss case, continued to damage his credibility. In an effort to rebut the charges of being a Red dupe, he issued a statement disowning Communists who advocated violent change, but steadfastly refused to repudiate all others, telling astounded reporters, "There is as much variation in the beliefs of Communists as in the beliefs of Democrats and Republicans." [26]

He continued to attack both major parties on foreign affairs, referring repeatedly to containment as "the Truman-Dewey policy." When the Berlin crisis reached its climax in late September, Wallace charged that industrialists fomented "recurrent war scares" to seduce Congress into voting for vast defense appropriations. He called for a national fact-finding commission to study the Berlin situation, and demanded the withdrawal of all American occupation troops from Korea, Japan, and Germany. The only way to settle the Cold War, he kept asserting, was to deal directly with Moscow. "I ask now with all the urgency at my command," he pleaded in California on October 4, "that every American who hopes for peace demand of President Truman and the State Department that negotiations for the settlement of the dangerous controversies in Germany be resumed." [27]

Few Americans shared Wallace's faith in Russian goodwill. Militant liberals rejected his pleas as naïve, and Socialist Norman Thomas continued to accuse him of advocating appeasement of "the mightiest tyranny which has ever appeared on this earth." By October, political commentators began to scale down their estimate of the final Wallace vote from 5 million to 3 million at most, and probably less. His last remaining strongholds were California and New York; in these two key states he was heavily backed by Jewish voters, who were impressed by his forthright call for *de jure* recognition of Israel, and Negroes, attracted by his racial views. Yet even this support was jeopardized by the daily evidence of Russian intransigence in Berlin, which undercut his major contention that the United States, not the Soviet Union, was responsible for the Cold War.[28]

III

The Palestine issue flared up again in September. The truce that UN mediator Count Folke Bernadotte had arranged expired in July, but after a brief renewal of hostilities the Security Council succeeded in imposing a new cease-fire without a time limit. Meanwhile, the provisional government of Israel pressed hard to secure *de jure* recognition from the United States, a loan of $100 million, and American support for UN membership. Democratic politicians kept up a steady pressure on Truman, particularly after Henry Wallace released a statement on August 28 advocating full recognition and the granting of a large loan. Senatorial candidate Hubert Humphrey, CIO president Philip Murray, and the entire New York City Congressional delegation, led by Emanuel Celler, all urged Truman to implement the Democratic party platform pledges for assistance to Israel. The State Department, however, advised the President to remain silent, warning him that a public statement might jeopardize Bernadotte's continuing attempts to find a peaceful solution to the Jewish-Arab dispute.[29]

Zionists used every device they could to overcome the State Department's influence on Truman. Chaim Weizmann, who was recuperating from an eye operation in Switzerland, relied on Samuel Rosenman and Eddie Jacobson to bring Israel's case to Truman personally. On September 6, Weizmann wrote directly to the President to request immediate *de jure* recognition, and the next day Bartley Crum, a liberal New York publisher and ardent supporter of Israel, cabled Clifford after an interview with Weizmann in Geneva. Crum said the Zionist leader wanted Truman to grant full recognition before the United Nations met in Paris and "preferably before September

15." Clifford then drew up a draft memorandum to Secretary of State Marshall for Truman's signature. Restating the President's long desire to see an independent Jewish state flourish in Palestine, the memo instructed Marshall to authorize the pending loan, extend *de jure* recognition, and "take active steps to assist Israel in gaining admission to the United Nations." Despite the pleas of Party Chairman Howard McGrath, who claimed that "the President's sincere intentions have been sabotaged" by the State Department, Truman refused to sign Clifford's draft memo. Instead, he followed Marshall's advice and agreed to delay full recognition until after the elections in Israel, scheduled for early November, created a permanent government to succeed the provisional one established in May.[30]

The shocking assassination of Count Bernadotte by Jewish extremists on September 17 brought the Palestine issue to a new climax. Three days later, the United Nations released the text of the mediator's recommendations for a peaceful settlement. Bernadotte advised a supervised armistice and disarmament of both Jews and Arabs, measures for the return and compensation of Arab refugees and the internationalization of Jerusalem. The most controversial part of the Bernadotte plan dealt with boundaries. Departing from the original partition plan, the Swedish mediator had suggested that Israel be given western Galilee in return for the Negev, the large desert area in the south originally allocated to the Jews. Arab spokesmen immediately rejected the plan, since it recognized the legitimacy of Israel, and the Jews were equally opposed. Israeli leaders viewed the Negev, an area of nearly 4,000 square miles, as vital for the future growth of their tiny nation, and they vowed never to give it up.[31]

President Truman first learned of the Bernadotte plan on September 18, two days before it was released, when a courier delivered a copy to his campaign train in El Paso. Truman did not like the boundary changes, but he kept silent, and when the State Department sent him the text of a statement approving the Bernadotte plan on the morning of September 21, the President offered no objection. Accordingly, at four that afternoon in Paris, Secretary Marshall called in the press and told them, "The United States considers that the conclusions contained in the final report of Count Bernadotte offer a generally fair basis for settlement of the Palestine question." To the dismay of Zionists, he urged the Jews and Arabs to accept the recommendations "in their entirety," presumably including the surrender of the vital Negev. The next day British Foreign Secretary Bevin endorsed the Bernadotte report in the House of Commons, echoing Marshall's call for adoption "in its entirety." Angry Zionists immediately accused the State Department of a secret deal with the British, by which they recognized Israel in return for Arab retention of the Negev, and some even charged that American diplomats, not the Count, had written the Bernadotte report.[32]

The other members of the American delegation in Paris were furious with Marshall for his failure to consult with them before releasing his statement. Eleanor Roosevelt told Bernard Baruch that she had opposed the Bernadotte plan in delegation meetings, saying she thought the transfer of the Negev was "highly unfair," but that her objections made no difference. "We were simply handed a statement to read in the session after he had given it out to the press," she complained. John Foster Dulles had no strong opinions on the plan, but he too resented the way Marshall had issued his statement without prior notice. Dulles informed the Secretary that Palestine was "withdrawn" from the area of bipartisan cooperation, and he suggested to Dewey that the Republicans make this change public. "Governor Dewey does not believe that any public statement by either you or him would be wise at this time," Allen Dulles cabled back, explaining that Dewey was too busy campaigning in the West to give the delicate Palestine issue the careful consideration it deserved.[33]

The Democrats, however, began to panic as rumors spread that Dewey was preparing a statement challenging the Bernadotte report. "Like you and everyone else who is concerned about November 2nd," the Connecticut candidate for governor, Chester Bowles, wrote to Clark Clifford, "I am worried about the Jewish situation." Bowles wanted Truman to offset the effect of a possible Dewey statement by extending full recognition to Israel at the time of the Jewish New Year in early October. Other Democrats sent in equally urgent pleas, and on September 27 Chaim Weizmann sent a telegram to Eddie Jacobson urging him to persuade Truman to undo the damage Marshall had done. "Only intervention of your friend who has done so much for us can avert the worst dangers," Weizmann argued. Faced with this pressure, Truman finally permitted his staff to draw up a message to the Secretary on September 29. Informing Marshall that his statement endorsing the Bernadotte plan "requires clarification," the draft telegram stated that Truman would announce publicly on October 1 that he stood behind the Democratic platform, which supported the original partition boundaries for Israel, including the Negev.[34]

Truman never sent this telegram. His great respect for Marshall's judgment led him to wait until the Republicans raised the issue before he spoke out on Palestine. When Dewey released a routine message of greeting to Israel for the Jewish New Year on September 29 instead of the expected denunciation of the Bernadotte plan, Truman decided to withhold his own public statement pending Marshall's return for consultations in October. The President simply followed Dewey's lead and telegraphed Chaim Weizmann his "personal greetings and congratulations" on October 2. This New Year's message, drafted by Robert Lovett, made no mention of recognition, boundaries, or the Bernadotte report.[35]

Thus Truman continued to place the national interest above politics on the touchy Palestine issue. Subjected to intense pressure from Zionists as well as his own staff, he relied on Marshall's judgment, convinced that the Secretary of State viewed Israel in the broad international context his aides so clearly lacked. Yet there were limits to Truman's ability to withstand partisan considerations. As long as Dewey left the issue alone, the President was willing to remain silent. But if the Republicans exploited this delicate question, then Truman was prepared to respond with an open appeal to Jewish voters.

IV

In early October, the Berlin crisis seemed more menacing than ever. The Western request that the Security Council take up the issue marked the first time that three big powers had accused a fourth of creating a threat to world peace. Returning from his western tour, Truman resolved to take a dramatic step to break the impasse with the Soviet Union and avert the war that many were predicting. During the summer, he had considered sending General Eisenhower to Moscow to meet personally with Stalin in an effort to resolve the Berlin dispute. Truman had dropped that idea, but as the campaign began, two of his speech-writers, David Noyes and A. Z. Carr, revived it. Both men shared the growing fear of war, and both were fully aware of the political potential of the peace issue, particularly in enticing Wallace's supporters back to the Democratic party. The President himself found that his occasional campaign references to peace evoked the warmest and most sustained applause from his audiences. Thus when Carr and Noyes suggested that he reconsider sending Eisenhower on a goodwill mission to Moscow, he accepted the idea but insisted on asking Supreme Court Chief Justice Fred Vinson, his old Missouri friend, to undertake the journey.

The President explained what he had in mind to Vinson at a White House meeting on Sunday, October 3. The Chief Justice, who had had no diplomatic experience, at first declined, but when Truman made the request a command, Vinson reluctantly consented. In a briefing that evening, Truman explained that he neither expected nor wanted Vinson to negotiate on specific issues such as Berlin; all he hoped to do was clear the air of the doubt and suspicion that now clouded Soviet-American relations and threatened the world with a devastating war.

The next morning, October 4, Truman's press secretary asked the major networks for air time for a presidential speech the following evening, secretly telling the radio executives the President's topic. On Tuesday morning, October 5, Truman informed Under Secretary of State Robert Lovett of the proposed Vinson mission, and together the two men consulted with the Secretary of State in Paris via teletype. To Lovett's great relief, Marshall firmly opposed the plan, pointing out to Truman that such a unilateral approach to the Russians would antagonize our allies in Europe and undermine the Western alliance. Deeply disappointed, Truman accepted Marshall's arguments and agreed to defer the mission. That afternoon, October 5, the White House canceled the planned radio broadcast and announced that General Marshall was flying back to Washington to consult with the President over the coming weekend.[36]

David Noyes and A. Z. Carr shared Truman's feeling of disappointment. Though partly motivated by politics, they had come to believe that Vinson's mission might well mean the difference between peace and war. In the speech they had drafted, they underlined the ominous nature of the world crisis and stated that Vinson's task was to "discuss with Premier Stalin the possibility of taking specific and positive action to alleviate the mutual suspicion and fear which now block the road to peace." Stating that Vinson would deal with "the larger issue of the moral relationship between Soviet Russia and ourselves" rather than specific topics like Berlin, the speech concluded with the brave words, "We shall spare no effort to achieve the peace on which the entire destiny of the human race may depend." [37]

That evening a lonely Truman asked Senator Tom Connally, chairman of the Foreign Relations Committee, and Arthur Vandenberg to visit with him in the White House. Connally arrived first, and when Truman outlined the proposed Vinson mission to him, the Texas senator opposed it strongly. The President did not mention the trip to Vandenberg, but he startled both senators by asking casually what they thought about the idea of his telephoning Stalin in an effort to clear the air between the two nations. The senators raised a series of polite objections, focusing on the linguistic difficulties, and after an hour Truman dropped the idea. As the senators left, Vandenberg commented to Connally, "He must be feeling desperate about the campaign." [38]

The next day the President returned to the stump, touring the vote-rich states of the Northeast where Wallace still had some appeal. Everywhere he went, he emphasized his desire to avert a war with Russia. When a Philadelphia audience applauded enthusiastically his assertion that peace was "the goal of my public life," Truman brought down the house when he ad-libbed, "I wish for peace, I work for peace, and I pray for peace continually." In Pennsylvania, New Jersey, and upstate New York, he hammered away at the same theme, repeating again and again his favorite line, "I would rather have peace in the world than to be President of the United States," and each time the audience roared its approval. Sure that he had found the winning issue, Truman was preparing to give a major speech in Buffalo on October 8 when Chicago *Tribune* reporter Walter Trohan, using material supplied by radio executives, broke the story of the Vinson mission. By the next morning, newspapers around the nation carried front-page stories of the proposed trip, complete with speculation that General Marshall had threatened to resign if Truman went ahead with it.[39]

President Truman returned to Washington to meet Marshall when he stepped off the plane the morning of October 9. The President was gay and smiling, but reporters noted that the "tired, ashen-faced" Marshall looked grim. The two men met for most of the day, and then, late in the afternoon, Truman released a statement announcing the cancellation of the Vinson mission. "Secretary Marshall described to me the situation which we faced in Paris," the President stated, "and, in light of his report and the possibilities of misunderstanding to which any unilateral action, however desirable otherwise, could lead at present, I decided not to take this step." Then Marshall loyally stepped forward and declared that there was "no foundation" for rumors of a rift between him and the President. The next day the Secretary returned to Paris, after telling reporters that the nation was "completely united" on foreign policy and denying the rumors that he had threatened to resign.[40]

The press had a field day with the abortive Vinson mission. *Life* called it "Truman's Last Stand" and wrote it off as a political fiasco. Walter Lippmann thought it confirmed his belief that Truman was unfit to conduct American foreign policy; ". . . in plain words, Mr. Truman does not know how to be President," he commented. The *New York Times* thought the whole idea was "amazing" and said if it had come off, it "might well have wrecked the solidarity of the Western Powers," as well as "the whole painfully built-up bipartisan structure of our foreign policy." Even such friendly journals as the *Nation* and the *New Republic* could find little to say in Truman's defense, praising him only for good intentions. The sole endorsement came, predictably, from Henry Wallace, who claimed the State Department had "slapped down" the Vinson mission, thus proving to his satisfaction that "the real masters of our foreign policy" were "the big brass and the big gold." [41]

Republicans reacted much more gingerly to the episode. On

October 10, John Foster Dulles sent an urgent cable to Dewey, warning him that England and France were very upset at the idea of being bypassed. "From standpoint of bipartisan cooperation you may want to suggest necessity of unity behind Marshall," he advised. Dewey followed this suggestion in a brief statement he handed out to newsmen later that day in a hastily called Albany press conference. Speaking again more like the President than the challenger, Dewey said that the American people "wholeheartedly and vigorously support the labors of our bipartisan delegation at Paris" and assured the nations of the world that the U.S. "will firmly and unshakably uphold the United Nations and our friends of the free world in every step to build and preserve the peace." The Republican candidate studiously refrained from criticizing Truman in his public remarks, but off the record he told reporters that it was a "colossal blunder." The world was too close to war for him to attack Truman's policy publicly, he confided, saying, "I'd rather lose the election than add to the damage this country has already suffered from this unhappy incident." [42]

Actually, Dewey was trying to play the Vinson episode both ways. By taking the high ground, he hoped to underline his statesmanlike approach in contrast to Truman's bungling diplomacy. In his speeches for the next week he kept referring to the need for an administration that "knows where it is going" and "will unfailingly back up the work of its own representatives in the United Nations for peace." Some of his advisers wanted him to go beyond this subtle criticism and squeeze the full political value out of the President's inept handling of the Vinson affair. But Dewey, backed by Dulles and Vandenberg, felt that the world crisis was too serious to permit such tactics. Like Truman with Palestine, he preferred to place country above party, particularly when his election still seemed assured. [43]

Democrats generally took the advice of the *Nation: "The*

less said about the abandoned Vinson mission to Moscow, the better." Eleanor Roosevelt commented to Baruch that Truman's plan to send Vinson to Russia "was a stupid one at this particular time." The President disagreed. In a postmortem with his speech-writers, he nodded at their gloomy assessments of the affair, but then remarked, "I don't think it's that bad." He didn't explain his optimism, but presumably he felt from the crowd response to his speeches that there was a deep, underlying desire for peace. Even though he had been clumsy in appealing to this sentiment, he had succeeded in creating the impression that he cared deeply about the danger of war and was doing everything to spare the nation and the world that tragedy. Far from being a blunder, writes the chronicler of Wallace's movement, the Vinson mission was "one of the happiest accidents" of the Truman campaign. If Marshall had not vetoed the idea, it might have led to a futile meeting with Stalin; as it was, Truman won the peace vote without having to depart from his containment policy.[44]

In the following week Truman hit hard at the peace theme throughout the Middle West. Huge crowds came out in Ohio to hear him recite his administration's effort to avoid war while checking Soviet expansion. In St. Paul he challenged Dewey directly on the unity line, claiming that the Republicans were late-comers to the international bandwagon. "We did not have unity in foreign policy in 1940," he declared. "Even then, with half the world in flames, the Republican leaders were mainly isolationists." The American people, he argued, should think twice before voting for "recent converts" to the cause of world order. In these speeches, Truman avoided any mention of the Vinson mission, but in an address to the American Legion convention in Miami on October 18, the President faced the issue squarely. After listing his achievements in foreign policy, including the Marshall Plan, the Truman Doctrine, and the defense of West Germany, Truman explained that he had no hostile designs toward Russia. "We know that all the

259

world, and especially the continent of Europe, has nothing to gain from war and everything to lose." The only purpose he had in mind in sending Vinson to Russia, he explained, was "to ask Premier Stalin's cooperation in dispelling the present poisonous atmosphere of distrust which now surrounds the negotiations between the Western Powers and the Soviet Union." He had canceled the mission because Secretary Marshall feared it would disturb America's allies in Europe, but he would continue his search for appropriate ways to lessen world tension in the future. "I am working for peace," he concluded, "and I shall continue to work for peace." [45]

Skeptical reporters were impressed by the size and enthusiasm of Truman's audiences. Twenty-one thousand came out to hear him in St. Paul, compared to only seven thousand for Dewey later that week. Truman's own confidence grew as the people cheered his call for peace, and he was particularly pleased with the warm response he evoked from the Legionnaires in Miami. At the same time, old New Dealers, once cool to his candidacy, now began to rally to his support. Eleanor Roosevelt sent him a letter of endorsement from Paris, which his aides released in mid-October. A few days later, Americans for Democratic Action released a statement signed, as Harold Ickes put it, by "all of the prominent men and women associated with the Roosevelt administration." The ADA appeal called upon American liberals to support Truman and reject Henry Wallace. "A vote for the Progressive Party, whose foreign policy is an American carbon of Soviet policy, is a vote for the destruction of the anti-totalitarians of Europe," they declared. Truman, returning to Washington to prepare for the final campaign onslaught, felt that he had dealt the Wallace movement a crippling blow with his own peace offensive. [46]

Dewey ignored the upsurge for Truman as he toured the Middle West. "His rich, perfectly modulated baritone voice strokes an audience, fondles it, ravishes it," commented TRB in the *New Republic,* adding forlornly, "Dewey is going to be the next President and you might as well get used to him." When William Bullitt, a lifelong Democrat, announced for Dewey with a stinging attack on Truman for permitting Stalin "to dominate 130 million free Europeans," the Republican candidate echoed these charges in a major foreign policy speech in Louisville by accusing Truman of appeasing the Communists, "serving up diplomatic victories which only whetted the appetites of men whose appetites are world-wide." But then Dewey quickly retreated to the bipartisan line, claiming that he himself had originated the policy of removing foreign affairs from politics in 1944. Despite immediate corrections of the record by columnist James Reston and former Secretary of State Cordell Hull, Dewey renewed his claim in St. Paul, pointing out how he had patriotically refrained from revealing the breaking of the Japanese codes in the last election. On October 19, Dewey completed his midwest swing in Buffalo with a frank appeal to the Polish vote. In the last six years, he declared, Communism had swallowed up 200,000,000 people in Europe; only a Republican administration could "hold out hope to those who have been enslaved in recent years." [47]

Then, in an almost arrogant display of confidence, Dewey decided to take a week off from campaigning, to rest up in New York for the last few days of the race. The feeling of victory was so strong in Dewey's camp that a reporter blandly asked one of the governor's aides, "How long is Dewey going to tolerate Truman's interference in the government?" When California Senator William Knowland worried about "the letdown which has occurred in some places due to a feeling of over-confidence," Arthur Vandenberg assured him, "There seems to be no doubt of the presidential outcome." But a Gallup poll taken on October 20, the first in more than a month, revealed that Truman had sliced Dewey's lead in half. Now just 50 percent of the voters favored the GOP candidate, compared to 54 percent in early September. Truman jumped to 44 percent, a gain of four points, while Wallace dropped to 4 percent and Thurmond remained at 2 percent. Truman's whistle-stop campaigning, the sagging farm prices, and Dewey's failure to develop any significant issues all contributed to this Democratic surge, but the President's shrewd use of the peace issue was probably the major component. People who had been scared to death of an atomic war over Berlin breathed a sigh of relief as the President revealed his determination to avert a conflict without resorting to appeasement. A *Fortune* poll in September revealed that, by the wide margin of 49 percent to 30 percent, Americans preferred a President "especially good at handling international affairs and foreign relations" to one skilled in domestic matters. Despite his clumsiness in the Vinson episode, Truman's leadership in foreign policy—both in standing firm before Russian threats and in displaying his commitment to a peaceful solution—had impressed the American people and helped him close the gap on Dewey.[48]

V

A sudden renewal of the fighting in Palestine in mid-October thrust that troubled issue squarely into the presidential election. The Israelis began a major offensive in the Negev on October 15; in eight days, their army routed the Egyptian forces, driving them back into the narrow Gaza strip. At the same time, the General Assembly's Political Committee voted to postpone further consideration of the Bernadotte report, with its key proposal to give the Arabs the Negev, until after the American election.[49]

American Zionists, elated by the triumph in the Negev, stepped up their pressure on President Truman. Rabbi Stephen S. Wise sent the White House a fifteen-page memorandum urging *de jure* recognition of Israel. The American Zionist

Emergency Council published a full-page advertisement in the *New York Times* pointing out how the Bernadotte plan endorsed by Secretary Marshall differed on the boundaries in the original partition agreement approved by the UN. "Mr. Truman: Where Do *You* Stand on This Issue?" the ad bluntly asked. The situation was most critical in New York, where Wallace continued to appeal to Jewish voters with his forthright stand on Palestine. The New York City Congressional candidates kept trying to meet with the President to express their anxiety, but Truman repeatedly refused to see them. The White House staff was divided. Some feared that anything the President said on Israel would permit his opponents to attack him for a blatant political appeal; while others, notably David Niles, wanted him to declare that he would keep the Democratic party's pledges to "Americans of Jewish faith who have lived through the liquidation of six million of their fellow Jews." With characteristic stubbornness, Truman still refused to speak out on Palestine as long as Dewey remained silent. The one concession he made was to send a blunt telegram to Secretary Marshall on October 17: "I request that no statement be made or no action be taken on the subject of Palestine by any member of our delegation in Paris without obtaining specific authority from me and clearing the text of any statement." [50]

It was Dewey who finally made the first move. On Friday, October 22, he released a letter to Dean Alfange, chairman of the American Christian Palestine Committee, in which he reaffirmed his belief that the "Jewish people are entitled to a homeland in Palestine which would be politically and economically stable." Though he made no mention of the Bernadotte report, Dewey stated his support for the original UN partition arrangement, which awarded the Negev to Israel. Then, in a subtle dig at Truman, the Republican candidate concluded: "In my acceptance speech at Philadelphia, I pledged my wholehearted support of the Republican Platform and that included the Palestine Plank. My position today is the same." What was most surprising about the governor's statement was his failure to say what Zionists really wanted to hear—promises to lift the arms embargo, to grant loans to Israel, and above all to extend it full recognition. Dewey's advisers knew that Truman would respond ("We expect a blast of some kind from H.S.T.," Allen Dulles wired his brother in Paris), but they decided to stand pat with this simple restatement of the Republican platform plank.[51]

"I consider Dewey's action a serious error on his part and the best thing that has happened to us to date," an exuberant Clark Clifford told Truman. Clifford immediately contacted Robert Lovett and explained that the Republicans had impugned the President's integrity by suggesting that he had reneged on the Democratic platform commitment to Israel. Lovett agreed with this assessment, sending Marshall a cable stating that "Dewey has violated bi-partisan approach on Israel" and informing him that Truman felt compelled to issue a reply. Clifford then spent Saturday evening preparing a long statement, which Truman approved and released to the press on Sunday, October 24.[52]

"The Republican candidate for President has seen fit to release a statement with reference to Palestine," Truman began. Saying that he had hoped to keep foreign policy out of the campaign, the President declared that he had no choice but to reaffirm his support for the Democratic plank on Palestine. Then Truman proceeded to go beyond the party's position by promising to grant prompt financial aid to Israel and to extend *de jure* recognition as soon as a permanent government was elected. On the crucial boundary issue, Truman qualified Marshall's earlier endorsement of the Bernadotte plan by saying that the U.S. supported it only "as a basis of negotiation." The President continued to favor the original UN partition boundaries and believed "that modification should be made only if fully acceptable to the State of Israel." [53]

Truman followed up his statement, which Zionists greeted with great enthusiasm, with a direct appeal to Jewish voters in his principal New York City address, planned for Madison Square Garden on October 28. He asked Samuel Rosenman, FDR's speech-writer and an ardent Zionist, to draft the sections of his speech dealing with Palestine. After a tour of the city, Truman headed a torchlight parade to the Garden, where labor leader David Dubinsky was forced to fill the balconies with the bands and drill teams accompanying Truman to create the impression of a full house. Most of the talk dealt with domestic issues, but near the end, Truman turned his attention to "Palesteen." Asserting that he had avoided this issue until Dewey dragged it into the campaign, the President belied this claim by boasting of his support for partition and his prompt *de facto* recognition. Then Truman reached his climax: ". . . it is my desire to help build in Palestine a strong, prosperous, free, and independent democratic state," he declared. "It must be large enough, free enough and strong enough to make its people self-supporting and secure." [54]

"TRUMAN IN STRONGEST PLEA FOR ISRAEL," headlined the *New York Times* the next morning, pointing out that the President had repudiated Marshall's endorsement of the Bernadotte plan. The next day, Truman overrode his Secretary of State again by ordering him to withdraw American support for a British-Chinese resolution threatening military and economic sanctions against Israel unless it withdrew its troops from the Negev. Apparently Marshall, without consulting other members of the American delegation and in violation of Truman's October 17 telegram, had planned to support the move to force Israel to evacuate the disputed region. Truman refused to comment on this report to newsmen, and the American delegation in Paris remained silent, though one spokesman told an inquiring journalist, "Address all your questions to the White House." When the issue came up for a vote on October 29 in the Security Council, American delegate Warren

Austin supported a Canadian resolution to refer the whole issue to a subcommittee. Thus the administration succeeded in postponing any further action on Israel until after the election.[55]

Clark Clifford was undoubtedly right in calling Dewey's Palestine statement "a serious error." Given Truman's determination not to initiate discussion on Israel, it is likely that he would have remained silent despite the urgent pleas of Zionists. The President's press release and his Madison Square Garden speech gave the Democrats a fighting chance to carry New York, a state many had already conceded to Dewey. Yet even so, Truman had continued to act with caution, promising *de jure* recognition in the future but refusing to grant it immediately, as the Zionists wanted. It is indeed remarkable that such a partisan campaigner could be so restrained in appealing to this potentially crucial segment of the electorate.

VI

"The Presidential campaign was taking place in the midst of the greatest diplomatic crisis in American history," commented *Newsweek* on election eve. The tension over Berlin continued during October as the UN Security Council debated the Western motion to censure Russia for the blockade. Huge C-54 cargo planes carried an average of 5,000 tons of supplies to Berlin each day, despite the onset of bad weather. General Lucius Clay, home for a brief visit with officials in Washington, exuded confidence, telling reporters that the United States could supply the city by air throughout the coming winter, if necessary. In an effort to reinforce the bipartisan policy on Berlin, John Foster Dulles flew to Germany and met with Clay. On his return, he cabled Dewey, urging him to make a new statement supporting Truman's policy so that the Soviets "will not be misled into prolonging the Berlin blockade on the theory that result of election will bring about any weakening of U.S. determination." [56]

Hope for a peaceful settlement of the Berlin crisis soared briefly when six neutral nations sponsored a resolution calling upon the Russians to end the blockade without being censured, in return for new talks on the whole German problem. But on October 25, Andrei Vishinsky delivered a stinging veto to kill the compromise proposal, which was backed by every other member of the General Assembly except the Ukraine. Western diplomats then decided to let the matter rest while they waited for the outcome of the American election. [57]

Dulles had no doubts about who would win; he spent the week before the election preparing for a smooth transition. He accepted Dewey's suggestion that he stay in Paris rather than return home to vote, in order to symbolize the Republican concern for peace. He shared his brother's worry that "after November 2 it will be the tendency of both Truman and Marshall to dump the difficult and contentious questions in the Governor's lap," and he wrote a long memorandum to Dewey on how to avoid assuming responsibility before "your Administration" takes office. When Marshall told him "in utmost confidence" that he also was concerned about the transition period, Dulles sent a summary of the Secretary's views to Dewey by special courier. On October 30, Dulles cabled his last preelection dispatch from Paris; ". . . it is apparent," he told Dewey, "your election will bring to all our foreign friends new hope that United States power will be more effectively used for world peace." His only regret, he concluded, was "not to be with you on the day when what I have so ardently hoped for will, it seems, finally be realized." [58]

Observers at home seemed equally sure of the outcome. The final Gallup poll showed Dewey still with a commanding lead, 49.5 percent, to 44.5 percent for Truman, only a fraction off the October 20 finding. The Crossley poll had nearly identical figures; Roper had stopped taking samples in September, since he was certain Truman would lose. On October 25, reporting on a nationwide survey of political experts, the *New York Times* claimed that Dewey and Warren "appear certain to defeat" Truman and Barkley, winning at least 333 electoral votes to only 90 for the Democrats. In its last issue before the election, *Life* captioned a picture of Dewey, "THE NEXT PRESIDENT TRAVELS BY FERRY BOAT OVER THE BROAD WATERS OF SAN FRANCISCO BAY." Even many loyal Democrats despaired. Leslie Biffle, the secretary of the Senate, told James Forrestal on October 26 that Truman had made "very substantial gains" in the last two weeks, but the most Biffle would claim were possible victories in the Senate and House.[59]

Truman responded to these predictions with a furious last-minute drive in the big cities of the Middle West and Northeast. Beginning in Chicago, where Zionist donations enabled him to buy national radio time, the President hammered away on the peace theme. "I will never stop working for peace," he told a cheering audience as he reviewed the contributions of Woodrow Wilson and Franklin D. Roosevelt. Then, in a passage that several of his aides regretted, he lumped Dewey with Hitler, Mussolini, and Hirohito in decrying "the powerful reactionary forces which are silently undermining our democratic institutions." In Toledo the next day, he stressed the same theme, saying, "Peace is the most important question in the world today." At Boston on October 27, he recited his administration's record in checking Communist aggression in a strong appeal to the anti-Communist sympathies of the city's Irish voters. "The whole world knows of the success of this policy," he declared. "Now, the Communists will never forgive me for that." [60]

Truman made his most eloquent appeal to pacifist sentiment in his last eastern campaign speech on October 29 in Brooklyn, a Wallace stronghold. Defending the Vinson mission, he claimed it was the President's duty "to consider and study every possible approach to the heart and understanding of the Soviet leaders." "So long as I am President of the United States," he promised, "the door will not be closed to peace." He went on to accuse Dewey and the Republicans of being isolationists in disguise. "We must never withdraw to the Republican isolationism of the 1920's," he asserted. "If you do that, communism will become so powerful that the security of this Nation will be gravely endangered." He closed with words that seemed to echo Wallace. "Now, our foreign policy is a people's foreign policy. Its purpose is to win a people's peace."[61]

Stung by Truman's charges of dictatorship and isolation, Dewey briefly departed from his high ground to answer the President. "Millions upon millions of people have been delivered into Soviet slavery while our own administration has tried appeasement one day and blustered the next," he told a Chicago audience. In Cleveland, on October 28, he developed the theme of vacillation again. He reminded his listeners of Truman's Oregon statement that he "liked Old Joe," and then noted that one day the Truman administration "seemed to believe in appeasement and the next day it seemed to stand firm." The results, Dewey concluded, were disastrous. "In little more than three years the Soviet has extended its sway nearly halfway around the world and it now rules more than 500,000,000 human beings." The next day in Boston, Dewey again accused the Democrats of wavering "from appeasement to bluster and then back to appeasement and then back to bluster." But in his final campaign speech in New York's Madison Square Garden, the Republican candidate returned to his usual broad generalities, promising that if elected, "We will wage the peace patiently and firmly, with intense labor and a new devotion." The departure from bipartisanship was too brief and too late to make foreign policy a fundamental issue between the two parties.[62]

Henry Wallace remained the sole challenger of the containment policy, and by the end of October his influence had dropped sharply. He continued to wage a strenuous campaign, touring sixteen states in the North during the final two weeks, but the charge of Communist control limited his appeal to radicals and ardent Zionists, who admired his forthright support for Israel. On October 31, he spoke to over 100,000 people in rallies in Brooklyn, and then ended his campaign with a mass meeting in Madison Square Garden. Telling his supporters that their vote would "determine whether we have peace or war in 1949," Wallace claimed that his Progressive party had "stopped the cold war in its tracks" and had "gained time to re-form the forces of peace, here in the United States and in all the nations of the earth." But only the most diehard Progressives could believe that their naïve champion had changed American foreign policy. The real question was whether or not he had siphoned off enough votes in states like New York and California to insure Truman's defeat.[63]

VII

As American voters prepared to go to the polls, a major foreign policy setback occurred in China. The civil war that broke out in the summer of 1947 took a disastrous turn for Chiang Kai-shek's Nationalists as Communist armies won a series of victories in North China and Manchuria. "Not since the worst years of the Japanese war had China faced a prospect so bitter," commented *Time*. Dewey had referred to the Nationalist defeats on several occasions during the campaign, but in keeping with the bipartisan spirit, he did not accuse Truman of losing China to the Communists. Instead, he promised only that "we will renew and strengthen our ancient ties of friendship with this great wartime ally."

By late October, all eyes were on Mukden, where 40,000 beseiged Nationalist troops clung desperately to their last outpost in Manchuria. On October 30, three days before the election, the city fell. The next morning, the *New York Times* headline read, "MANCHURIA IS LOST BY CHIANG REGIME." Although the Generalissimo still had 1.5 million troops and control of Central and South China, experts forecast the downfall of his government, and even *Life,* strongly Nationalist in sympathy, saw the loss of Manchuria as "the beginning of the end of Chiang Kai-shek's China." The editors symbolized their belief that a Republican victory was the last chance for the Nationalists by printing a picture of Chinese children in Peking carrying banners reading, "Good luck Dewey." [64]

VIII

Truman's confidence in the voters never wavered. He spent election day in Independence, then went to a hotel in Excelsior Springs, twenty-two miles north of Kansas City, to wait for the returns. He retired around seven, but woke up several times in the night to check with his aides in Kansas City, who reported encouraging news from the Middle West to offset early losses to Dewey in the East. The next morning the outcome was still in doubt, but at ten-thirty, when Ohio finally went Democratic, Dewey sent his formal telegram of concession to Truman. That evening, the President told jubilant supporters at the Jackson County courthouse in Independence, "All my efforts will be devoted to the cause of peace in the world." Then he began a leisurely train trip east, with huge crowds along the way cheering the underdog who had confounded the experts. When he arrived in the capital, 750,000 people came to Union Station to give him what Admiral Leahy called "the greatest reception that I have seen in Washington." [65]

Although Truman received just under 50 percent of the popular vote, he defeated Dewey decisively by carrying twenty-eight states, mainly in the South and West. Thurmond carried four states in the deep South, but Wallace, who polled a disappointing 1.1 million votes, failed to gain a single electoral vote. Despite narrow victories in such major industrial states as New York, Michigan, and Pennsylvania, Dewey trailed Truman by more than 2 million votes in an unusually light election.[66]

The collapse of Henry Wallace's third-party movement spelled the difference for Truman in several key states, notably California, which the Democrats carried by only 18,000 votes. Wallace received over 500,000 votes in New York, nearly half his national total, enabling Dewey to win his home state by a scant 60,000 votes out of more than 6 million. But Michigan and Maryland were the only other states where the Wallace vote permitted Dewey to defeat Truman; in Ohio, Wallace got only 38,000 votes as the Democrats squeezed on to a 7,000-vote victory. The Berlin crisis, together with the charges of Communist control, blunted Wallace's appeal and prevented him from waging an effective national campaign. Samuel Lubell estimated that 75 percent of the Progressive vote was either Jewish or black. Thus the crusade to end the Cold War utterly failed; only Wallace's gallant stand for civil rights and his unequivocal support for Israel kept his candidacy alive.[67]

Not only did Truman win the presidency again, but his party captured both houses of Congress and regained control of a majority of the nation's statehouses. The all-out attack on the Republican 80th Congress apparently helped the entire ticket, as the Democrats gained nine seats in the Senate and nearly eighty in the House. Leo Isacson, the Wallace supporter who touched off the dump-Truman movement in February with his by-election victory in the Bronx, lost to a Democratic candidate, and in the Senate such prominent isolationists as Pappy O'Daniel of Texas and Wayland Brooks of Illinois went down to defeat.[68]

Bewildered Republicans were stunned by the outcome. Dewey attributed his defeat to overconfidence, claiming that many GOP voters had stayed away from the polls; but later analysis showed that a larger turnout would only have meant a greater victory for Truman. John Foster Dulles expressed his deep disappointment to Dewey, praising his dignified campaign and commenting, "I am rather frightened by the influences which prevented it from succeeding." Vandenberg was also disappointed, but he expressed his admiration for Truman's courage in beating the odds. "You've got to give the little man credit," Vandenberg told his staff. "He did it all by himself." Senator Taft, who harbored a deep resentment of Dewey, went even further, telling Truman that "neither he nor his wife were particularly disappointed in the result of the election." Other Republicans blamed the bipartisan policy for preventing the GOP from exploiting the weaknesses of the Truman administration in foreign policy. Senator Karl Mundt complained of the failure to focus attention on Yalta and Potsdam, and he was particularly critical of Dewey for refusing to capitalize on the Vinson mission. Allen Dulles agreed, telling James Forrestal that "the greatest mistake in Mr. Dewey's campaign strategy was the failure to attack the Democratic record more vigorously." Putting his finger on a central Republican misconception, Forrestal commented, "This stemmed from the failure to realize that they were the challenger and not the challenged." [69]

Foreign reactions ranged from unrestrained joy in Tel Aviv to deep gloom in China. Harry Truman wrote to Chaim Weizmann later in November to reiterate his intentions of carrying out his campaign promises on Israel; two months later, the State Department extended the long-awaited *de jure* recognition. In Nanking, the Nationalists realized that Dewey's defeat doomed their hopes for American intervention against the victorious Communist armies. The European response to Truman's reelection was mixed. Most spokesmen expressed their pleasure at the guarantee of continuity in American policy, but some worried that the President might decide to bypass

Western Europe with a new version of the Vinson mission. Truman relieved this anxiety at his first postelection press conference, telling reporters he did not intend to send any special missions to Moscow or to meet personally with Stalin. "I would be happy to see Stalin in Washington," he added in jest, "if he wants to come and see me." The Russians, who had been counting on a large Wallace vote, masked their disappointment by claiming that in defeating Dewey, the American voters were rejecting "a frankly reactionary and aggressive program" that could have led to war. *Pravda* took solace in calling the more than one million who supported Wallace, "the flower of the nation." [70]

At home, a great postmortem began as journalists and political observers tried to find out how they had been so mistaken as to predict a Republican victory. The *New Republic* best expressed the emerging consensus when it said, "Harry Truman won this election because Franklin Roosevelt had worked so well." Clifford's original concept of appealing to all elements in the New Deal coalition had proved the key to victory. Farmers, organized labor, ethnic minorities, and much of the South stayed loyal to the Democratic party despite the calls of Thurmond from the right and Wallace from the left. Most analysts stressed the crucial role of the farm vote, pointing out that sagging crop prices in the fall led to serious defections in such normally Republican states as Iowa and Wisconsin. These unexpected rural gains more than offset Democratic losses in the big cities.[71]

The role of ethnic groups is less clear. Wallace cut deeply into the normally Democratic Jewish and Negro vote, and resentment over the spread of Communism into Poland lowered the Democratic majorities in cities like Buffalo, Chicago, and Detroit with their large Polish populations. But on the other hand, Truman's fierce anti-Soviet stand won back many of the Catholic groups, notably the Irish and the Italians, who had been antagonized by Roosevelt's interventionism. The most significant shift took place among German Americans. Alienated by Roosevelt's pro-English policies, Americans of German descent had left the Democratic party in 1940 and 1944. But Truman's determined stand over Berlin won back their loyalties and their votes in 1948. "In view of the closeness of the 1948 election," claims Samuel Lubell, "the German-American swing can definitely be credited with giving Truman his margin of victory." [72]

Lubell probably placed too much emphasis on one ethnic group. Other explanations for the Democratic triumph included Dewey's failure to wage an effective campaign and Truman's lonely uphill struggle, "the gallant and almost single-handed scrap the President, himself, put up," as Forrestal described it. Yet this interpretation fails to account for the fact that Dewey ran well ahead of his party, while Truman consistently trailed the Democratic candidates for Congress. Truman did not win a lonely victory in 1948; he simply led a majority party back into office. [73]

The greatest asset that the Democrats possessed was their control of foreign policy during a time when the American people were obsessed with a sense of grave national peril. Much as Vandenberg hoped to have the credit for bipartisanship rub off on the Republicans who loyally supported it, the people identified the containment policy with the President and the Secretary of State. From the March crisis onward, Truman's popularity steadily increased, as he emerged in the public mind as the man who was leading the nation against the increasingly brutal and aggressive Soviet Union. The Berlin blockade, as much as the liberal domestic program or any one ethnic group, gave Truman a priceless political asset when day after day he stood firmly against the Communists abroad without involving the nation in war. "The country experienced a surge of pride, of which President Truman was the inevitable beneficiary," writes Cabell Phillips; ". . . the dramatic success of the Berlin airlift greatly enhanced Truman's image as a leader." Nor was this all unconscious on Truman's part. The President was fully alive to the political implications of the Berlin crisis, and he knew that the people above all wanted a peaceful solution. The proposed Vinson mission and the emphasis on peace during the final month of the campaign revealed that Truman was as skillful as FDR in manipulating foreign policy for partisan advantage.[74]

Above all, the election of 1948 marked the institutionalization of the Cold War. It had acquired legitimacy when the American people rejected Wallace's alternative approaches to the Soviet Union. This repudiation of Henry Wallace, accomplished both by Soviet aggressiveness in Czechoslovakia and Berlin and by Democratic Red-baiting, meant the end of meaningful dissent on foreign policy, as the two major parties imposed a Cold War consensus which was destined to prevail for nearly two decades. The supreme irony of Truman's give-'em-hell campaign in 1948 is that representatives of the same special interests he denounced on domestic issues were the men in charge of his foreign policy. Wall Street bankers and corporation lawyers such as Robert Lovett, James Forrestal, Averell Harriman, and John Foster Dulles continued to manage the bipartisan policy. Thus in 1948 the democratic process failed to offer the American voter choices and alternatives in the crucial area of foreign policy; all he could do was ratify the policy of containment or throw away his vote on the eccentric and unstable Henry Wallace.[75]

NOTES

List of Abbreviations Used

DDE   Dwight David Eisenhower
FDR   Franklin D. Roosevelt

Chapter 1

1. Bernard F. Donahoe, *Private Plans and Public Dangers* (Notre Dame, Ind., 1965), pp. 94–100.
2. *Ibid.*, pp. 113, 128–30.
3. James MacGregor Burns, *Roosevelt: The Lion and the Fox* (New York, 1956), pp. 411–12.
4. *Newsweek*, xv (January 15, 1940), 11; Kenneth G. Crawford, "War and the Election," *Nation*, CL (February 10, 1940), 162.
5. Donahoe, *Private Plans*, pp. 148–49; *Newsweek*, xv (April 1, 1940), 13; Fred L. Israel, ed., *The War Diary of Breckinridge Long* (Lincoln, Neb., 1966), pp. 79–80; Farley to Hull, May 6, 1940, Cordell Hull Papers, Library of Congress, Box 47; Hull to A. R. Keller, May 8, 1940, and Hull to W. T. Kennerly, May 29, 1940, Hull Papers, Box 47; *The Memoirs of Cordell Hull*, 2 vols. (New York, 1948), I, 859–60; Burns, *Roosevelt*, p. 414.
6. William L. Langer and S. Everett Gleason, *The Challenge to Isolation, 1937–1940* (New York, 1952), pp. 420–21.
7. Freda Kirchwey, "Can We Stay Neutral?" *Nation*, CL (April 20,

1940), 503–4; George Soule, "If Germany Wins," *New Republic,* CII (April 22, 1940), 425–26.

8. Langer and Gleason, *Challenge,* pp. 427–28; Roosevelt Press Conference 636A, April 18, 1940, Franklin D. Roosevelt Papers, Franklin D. Roosevelt Library, Hyde Park, PPF 1–P; Joseph Alsop and Robert Kintner, *American White Paper* (New York, 1940); *New Republic,* CII (May 6, 1940), 591; *ibid.* (May 13, 1940), 646–47; Israel, *Long Diary,* p. 91.

9. *Public Opinion Quarterly,* IV (September, 1940), 538–39; U.S. Department of State, *Documents on German Foreign Policy, 1918–1945* (Washington, 1956), Series D, IX, 206–7; *New York Times,* May 5, 1940.

10. Langer and Gleason, *Challenge,* pp. 446–50.

11. Roosevelt Press Conference 642, May 10, 1940, FDR Papers, PPF 1–P; *New York Times,* May 17, 1940; *Newsweek,* XV (May 27, 1940), 32–33.

12. Rexford G. Tugwell, "Must We Draft Roosevelt?" *New Republic,* CII (May 13, 1940), 630–33; *New York Times,* May 12, 1940; *Nation,* CL (June 22, 1940), 743–44, 752–54; *Time,* XXXV (May 27, 1940), 21, 22; Breckinridge Long diary, May 22, 1940, Breckinridge Long Papers, Library of Congress, Box 5.

13. *Nation,* CL (June 29, 1940), 782; *New Republic,* CII (May 27, 1940), 728; John T. Flynn, *Country Squire in the White House* (New York, 1940), pp. 99, 101, 103.

14. *New York Times,* May 26, 1940; *Public Opinion Quarterly,* IV (September 1940), 534, 540, 552.

15. Roosevelt Press Conference 645–A, May 23, 1940, FDR Papers, PPF 1–P.

16. *New Republic,* CII (May 20, 1940), 657.

17. *Newsweek,* XV (February 26, 1940), 13–14; John T. Flynn, "The Republican Campaign Huddle," *New Republic,* CII (April 8, 1940), 472.

18. *New Republic,* CII (April 22, 1940), 534; Robert E. Burke, "Election of 1940," in Arthur M. Schlesinger, Jr., and Fred L. Israel, eds., *History of American Presidential Elections, 1789–1968,* 4 vols. (New York, 1971), IV, 2923; *Newsweek,* XV (April 15, 1940), 15–16.

19. *Nation,* CL (February 24, 1940), 282; *ibid.* (March 16, 1940), 356–60.

20. *New York Times,* January 21 and March 30, 1940; *Newsweek,* XV (May 6, 1940), 28, 68.

21. *New York Times*, May 7, 12, and 28, 1940.

22. *Ibid.*, May 26, 1940; *Public Opinion Quarterly*, IV (September 1940), 537; *New Republic*, CII (April 29, 1940), 574.

23. *Nation*, CL (May 25, 1940), 649–52; *New York Times*, January 20 and May 21, 1940.

24. C. David Tompkins, *Senator Arthur H. Vandenberg: The Evolution of a Modern Republican, 1884–1945* (East Lansing, Mich., 1970), pp. 171–81; Howard C. Lawrence to Vandenberg, December 16, 1939, and Vandenberg to Lawrence, December 18, 1939, Arthur H. Vandenberg Papers, Clements Library, University of Michigan; *New York Times*, May 17, 1940; Vandenberg to Paul Rood, June 1, 1940, Vandenberg Papers.

25. Burke, "Election of 1940," p. 2925; Joseph Barnes, *Willkie* (New York, 1952), p. 161.

26. Mary Earhart Dillon, *Wendell Willkie: 1892–1944* (Philadelphia, 1952), pp. 124–27, 131–33; Donald Bruce Johnson, *The Republican Party and Wendell Willkie* (Urbana, Ill., 1960), pp. 61–66; *Newsweek*, XV (May 13, 1940), 31.

27. Wendell L. Willkie, "We, the People," *Fortune*, XXI (April 1940), 64–65, 173; Dillon, *Willkie*, p. 128; Barnes, *Willkie*, pp. 154–63.

28. *Newsweek*, XV (April 22, 1940), 28; *New York Times*, May 5, 16, and 29, 1940; *Time*, XXXV (May 20, 1940), 16–18.

29. *New York Times*, June 9, 1940; *Public Opinion Quarterly*, IV (September 1940), 537; Barnes, *Willkie*, p. 166; *Time*, XXXV (June 10, 1940), 20; William Allen White, "Wendell Willkie," *New Republic*, CII (June 17, 1940), 818–19.

30. Ellsworth Barnard, *Wendell Willkie: Fighter for Freedom* (Marquette, Mich., 1966), p. 162; *New York Times*, June 15, 16, and 19, 1940.

31. Langer and Gleason, *Challenge*, pp. 509–10; Grace Tully, *F.D.R., My Boss* (New York, 1949), p. 243.

32. Barnes, *Willkie*, p. 166; *New Republic*, CII (May 27, 1940), 712; Donald McCoy, *Landon of Kansas* (Lincoln, Neb., 1966), pp. 430–33; Roosevelt Press Conference 645, May 21, 1940, FDR Papers, PPF 1–P; *New York Times*, May 18, 20, 21, and 23, 1940; *Time*, XXXV (June 3, 1940), 12. In his memoirs, Joseph Martin states that Landon informed him FDR had offered him the post of Secretary of War and that Martin had advised him to decline it. Donald McCoy, who interviewed Landon at length, asserts that Roosevelt never offered the Kansan a Cabinet post. Joseph W. Martin, as told to Robert J. Donovan, *My First Fifty*

Years in Politics (New York, 1960), p. 152; McCoy, *Landon,* p. 434.

33. Samuel Rosenman, ed., *The Public Papers and Addresses of Franklin D. Roosevelt,* 13 vols. (New York, 1938–50), IX, 261–64; *New York Times,* June 11, 1940.

34. Max Freedman, ed., *Roosevelt and Frankfurter: Their Correspondence, 1928–1945* (Boston, 1967), p. 529; *Newsweek,* XV (June 17, 1940), 32–33; *New Republic,* CII (June 24, 1940), 856; *New York Times,* June 11 and 13, 1940.

35. U.S. Department of State, *Peace and War: United States Foreign Policy, 1931–1941* (Washington, 1943), p. 553; Long diary, June 16, 1940, Long Papers, Box 5.

36. Frank to Annie Knox, June 11 and 15, 1940, Frank Knox Papers, Library of Congress, Box 3; Elting E. Morison, *Turmoil and Tradition: A Study of the Life and Times of Henry L. Stimson* (Boston, 1960), pp. 398–99; Freedman, ed., *Roosevelt and Frankfurter,* pp. 524–25, 529; Henry L. Stimson and McGeorge Bundy, *On Active Service in Peace and War* (New York, 1948), pp. 323–24.

37. *New York Times,* June 21, 1940; *Newsweek,* XVI (July 1, 1940), 29; *New York Times,* July 5, 1940; *Congressional Record,* July 9, 1940, pp. 9341, 9411.

38. *Nation,* CL (June 29, 1940), 770; *New York Times,* June 22, 1940; Roosevelt Press Conference 654, June 21, 1940, FDR Papers, PPF 1–P.

39. *New York Times,* June 22 and 23, 1940; *Nation,* CL (June 22, 1940), 747–48; *Public Opinion Quarterly,* IV (September 1940), 537; *Newsweek,* XVI (July 1, 1940), 28.

40. Dillon, *Willkie,* p. 142; *New York Times,* June 23, 1940; Barnes, *Willkie,* pp. 179–84.

41. McCoy, *Landon,* pp. 439–42; *New York Times,* June 18, 19, 21, and 25, 1940; *Documents on German Foreign Policy,* Series D, IX, 550–51. Fish was apparently unaware of the Nazi support for his activities. Herbert S. Parmet and Marie B. Hecht, *Never Again: A President Runs for a Third Term* (New York, 1968), p. 139.

42. *New York Times,* June 22, 1940; *Vital Speeches,* VI (July 15, 1940), 578–83; Barnard, *Willkie,* p. 170; Warren Moscow, *Roosevelt and Willkie* (Englewood Cliffs, N.J., 1968), pp. 92–93.

43. *New York Times,* June 24, 25, and 26, 1940; *Newsweek,* XVI (July 8, 1940), 15; Johnson, *Republican Party and Willkie,* p. 86;

Charles A. Beard, *American Foreign Policy in the Making, 1932–1940* (New Haven, 1946), pp. 279–80; Moscow, *Roosevelt and Willkie*, p. 92.

44. Kirk H. Porter and Donald Bruce Johnson, eds., *National Party Platforms, 1840–1956* (Urbana, Ill., 1956), pp. 390–91.

45. *New York Times*, June 27, 1940; *Time*, xxxvi (July 1, 1940), 16–17; *ibid.* (July 8, 1940), 12; *Documents on German Foreign Policy*, Series D, x, 101–2.

46. *Vital Speeches*, vi (July 15, 1940), 586–89; Barnes, *Willkie*, pp. 179–86; Dillon, *Willkie*, pp. 155–74; Burke, "Election of 1940," p. 2930.

47. Robert Bendiner, "Grand Old Paradox," *Nation*, cli (July 6, 1940), 6–7; Johnson, *Republican Party and Willkie*, pp. 105–8; Barnard, *Willkie*, pp. 169–70; Dillon, *Willkie*, pp. 171–72; Martin, *First Fifty Years*, pp. 159–60.

48. *Newsweek*, xvi (July 8, 1940), 14; Barnes, *Willkie*, pp. 175–78; Bruce Bliven, "The Horse and Buggy Boys," *New Republic*, ciii (July 8, 1940), 50–51.

49. *Time*, xxxvi (July 8, 1940), 9–10; Frances Perkins, *The Roosevelt I Knew* (New York, 1946), p. 116; Robert E. Sherwood, *Roosevelt and Hopkins: An Intimate History* (New York, 1948), 174; *Time*, xxxvi (July 22, 1940), 12.

50. Donahoe, *Private Plans*, pp. 160–62; Samuel I. Rosenman, *Working with Roosevelt* (New York, 1952), p. 203; Harold L. Ickes, *The Secret Diary of Harold L. Ickes*, 3 vols. (New York, 1954), iii, 233; Freedman, *Roosevelt and Frankfurter*, pp. 531–35; Douglas to Roosevelt, July 2, 1940, Harry L. Hopkins Papers, Franklin D. Roosevelt Library, Confidential Political File, 1938–40.

51. James A. Farley, *Jim Farley's Story: The Roosevelt Years* (New York, 1948), p. 257; Tully, *F.D.R.*, p. 237; *New York Times*, July 8 and 9, 1940; Roosevelt Press Conference 660, July 12, 1940, FDR Papers, PPF 1–P.

52. Robert Bendiner, "Burton Wheeler," *Nation*, cl (April 27, 1940), 532–36; Hamilton Basso, "Burton the Bronc," *New Republic*, cii (April 22, 1940), 528–30; *Congressional Record*, June 12, 1940, pp. 8054–55.

53. *New York Times*, June 24, 25, and 29; July 1 and 3, 1940; Burton K. Wheeler and Paul F. Healy, *Yankee from the West* (Garden City, N.Y., 1962), pp. 18–21; *Newsweek*, xvi (July 15, 1940), 18.

54. Rosenman, ed., *Public Papers of FDR,* IX, 289; *New York Times,* July 11, 1940.

55. Rosenman, *Working with Roosevelt,* p. 211; James F. Byrnes, *All in One Lifetime* (New York, 1958), p. 121; undated drafts of foreign policy planks, Robert Wagner Papers, Georgetown University Library; 1940 election folder; *New York Times,* July 15 and 16, 1940.

56. Rosenman, *Working with Roosevelt,* p. 212; Byrnes, *One Lifetime,* pp. 121–22; Beard, *American Foreign Policy,* pp. 291–92; Hull, *Memoirs,* I, 862; Long diary, July 28, 1940, Long Papers, Box 5; Wheeler and Healy, *Yankee,* pp. 23–24; *New York Times,* July 17, 1940.

57. Porter and Johnson, eds., *Party Platforms,* pp. 381–83.

58. *New York Times,* July 18, 1940; Beard, *American Foreign Policy,* pp. 294–95; Marquis W. Childs, *I Write from Washington* (New York, 1942), p. 197; Robert Bendiner, "It Had to Be Roosevelt," *Nation,* CLI (July 27, 1940), 67–68.

59. Democratic National Committee, *The Democratic Book of 1940* (n.p., 1940), pp. 111–17; Burke, "Election of 1940," pp. 2934–35; *New York Times,* July 16, 17, and 18, 1940; *New Republic,* CIII (July 29, 1940), 137–39; *Time,* XXXVI (July 29, 1940), 9–12.

60. Burke, "Election of 1940," p. 2936; memorandum by Cordell Hull, July 16, 1940, Hull Papers, Box 47; Long diary, July 12, 1940, Long Papers, Box 5; Tully, *F.D.R.,* p. 239; Edward L. and Frederick H. Schapsmeier, *Henry A. Wallace of Iowa: The Agrarian Years, 1910–1940* (Ames, Ia., 1968), pp. 272–73.

61. Rosenman, ed., *Public Papers of FDR,* IX, 293–302; Rosenman, *Working with Roosevelt,* p. 220.

62. *Nation,* CLI (July 6, 1940), 3; *New York Times,* June 29 and July 28, 1940; *Newsweek,* XVI (July 8, 1940), 18; *Documents on German Foreign Policy,* Series D, X, 49.

63. David E. Lilienthal, *The Journals of David E. Lilienthal,* 4 vols. (New York, 1964–70), I, 185; Long diary, June 27, 1940, Long Papers, Box 5.

64. *New Republic,* CII (May 13, 1940), 639.

Chapter 2

1. Joseph Barnes, *Willkie* (New York, 1952), pp. 188–89; *New York Times,* August 4, 1940.

2. Raymond Moley, *27 Masters of Politics* (New York, 1949), pp. 49–50; Mary Earhart Dillon, *Wendell Willkie: 1892–1944* (Philadelphia, 1952), pp. 175–80, 184–85; Joseph W. Martin, as told to Robert J. Donovan, *My First Fifty Years in Politics* (New York, 1960), pp. 103–10; Henry O. Evjen, "The Willkie Campaign: An Unfortunate Chapter in Republican Leadership," *Journal of Politics,* XIV (May 1952), 244–47.

3. Dillon, *Willkie,* pp. 186–87; *New York Times,* July 3 and August 2, 1940; Walter Johnson, *William Allen White's America* (New York, 1947), p. 531.

4. Mellett to Roosevelt, August 7, 1940, and Roosevelt to Mellett, August 12, 1940, FDR Papers, PPF 4721.

5. *Newsweek,* XVI (August 5, 1940), 13; Roosevelt Press Conferences 653, 659, and 666, June 18, July 9, and August 2, 1940, FDR Papers, PPF 1–P; *New York Times,* August 3, 1940; Elliott Roosevelt, ed., *F.D.R.: His Personal Letters, 1928–1945,* 2 vols. (New York, 1950), II, 1058–59.

6. Mark Lincoln Chadwin, *The Hawks of World War II* (Chapel Hill, N.C., 1968), pp. 86–89; *New York Times,* August 1 and 2, 1940; Arthur Krock, *The Consent of the Governed and Other Deceits* (Boston, 1971), pp. 152–53; *Time,* XXXVI (August 12, 1940), 9; John Morton Blum, *From the Morgenthau Diaries,* 3 vols. (Boston, 1959–67), II, 178; Harold L. Ickes, *The Secret Diary of Harold L. Ickes,* 3 vols. (New York, 1954), III, 292–93; E. Roosevelt, ed., *F.D.R. Letters,* II, 1050–51.

7. Herbert S. Parmet and Marie B. Hecht, *Never Again: A President Runs for a Third Term* (New York, 1968), pp. 209–11; Martin, *First Fifty Years,* p. 110; Krock, *Consent,* p. 153; *New York Times,* August 10, 1940; Walter Johnson, *The Battle Against Isolation* (Chicago, 1944), pp. 128–29; White to Roosevelt, August 11, 1940, FDR Papers, PPF 1196.

8. Blum, *Morgenthau Diaries,* II, 180; *New York Times,* August 16, 1940; Roosevelt Press Conference 671, August 16, 1940, FDR Papers, PPF 1–P; *Public Opinion Quarterly,* IV (December 1940), 713.

9. Dillon, *Willkie,* p. 188; *Time,* XXXVI (August 26, 1940), 14–15; *Newsweek,* XVI (August 26, 1940), 11–12.

10. *New York Times,* August 12, 13, 14, 16, and 17, 1940.

11. Dillon, *Willkie,* p. 189; Martin, *First Fifty Years,* p. 112.

12. *Vital Speeches,* VI (September 1, 1940), 676–79.

13. Ellsworth Barnard, *Wendell Willkie: Fighter for Freedom* (Marquette, Mich., 1966), pp. 201–2; *Time,* xxxvi (August 26, 1940), 14; *Nation,* cli (August 24, 1940), 144.

14. *Time,* xxxvi (August 26, 1940), 15; *Life,* ix (September 2, 1940), 24; *New York Times,* August 18, 1940; *Newsweek,* xvi (August 26, 1940), 12; *New Republic,* ciii (August 26, 1940), 262; Nancy H. Hooker, ed., *The Moffat Papers* (Cambridge, Mass., 1956), p. 327.

15. Hooker, *Moffat Papers,* p. 325; Roosevelt Press Conference 673, August 20, 1940, FDR Papers, PPF 1–P.

16. *New York Times,* August 20, 1940.

17. *Ibid.,* August 30, 1940.

18. *Ibid.,* August 31, 1940; *Newsweek,* xvi (September 9, 1940), 15–16; *Time,* xxxvi (September 9, 1940), 13–14.

19. Roosevelt Press Conference 676, August 30, 1940, FDR Papers, PPF 1–P; David E. Lilienthal, *The Journals of David E. Lilienthal,* 4 vols. (New York, 1964–70), i, 210; Kelly to Roosevelt, August 20, 1940, and Roosevelt to Kelly, August 28, 1940, FDR Papers, PPF 3166; *New York Times,* September 4, 1940.

20. Barnes, *Willkie,* p. 223; *Nation,* cli (September 7, 1940), 194; *New York Times,* August 28, 1940; *New Republic,* ciii (September 9, 1940), 340; *Documents on German Foreign Policy,* Series D, x, 427–28, xi, 4.

21. *Time,* xxxvi (September 9, 1940), 15.

22. U.S. Department of State, *Foreign Relations of the United States, 1940* (Washington, 1958), iii, 70–71; memorandum of conversation with Lothian by Hull, August 25, 1940, Hull Papers, Box 58; memorandum by Hull, September 2, 1940, Hull Papers, Box 66; Frank to Annie Knox, August 28, 1940, Knox Papers, Box 3; Allan Nevins, *Herbert H. Lehman and His Era* (New York, 1963), p. 210; Tully, *FDR,* p. 244.

23. *Foreign Relations, 1940,* iii, 73–75; Rosenman, ed., *Public Papers of FDR,* ix, 391.

24. Roosevelt Press Conference 677, September 3, 1940, FDR Papers, PPF 1–P; Rosenman, ed., *Public Papers of FDR,* ix, 391.

25. *New York Times,* September 4, 1940; *Time,* xxxvi (September 16, 1940), 11–12, 70.

26. *New York Times,* September 4, 6, and 7, 1940; Barnard, *Willkie,* p. 229.

27. *New York Times,* September 6, 1940; *Time,* xxxvi (September

16, 1940), 72; *Newsweek,* xvi (September 16, 1940), 15–17; Wagner speech, September 6, 1940, Wagner Papers.

28. *New York Times,* August 25 and September 4, 1940; *Time,* xxxvi (September 23, 1940), 15–16; Mellett to Roosevelt, September 4, 1940, FDR Papers, PPF 4721.

29. Barnard, *Willkie,* pp. 227–28; *New Republic,* ciii (September 16, 1940), 372; Lilienthal, *Journals,* i, 212; Ickes, *Secret Diary,* iii, 312–13, 317.

30. *New York Times,* September 8, 1940; Dillon, *Willkie,* pp. 196–200, 206, 218–19; Barnes, *Willkie,* pp. 196–99; Marquis W. Childs, *I Write from Washington* (New York, 1942), pp. 203–5; *Newsweek,* xvi (September 23, 1940), 9; *Time,* xxxvi (October 7, 1940), 14–16; *ibid.* (November 4, 1940), 12–13.

31. Barnard, *Willkie,* pp. 231–33; *New York Times,* September 1, 14, and 15, 1940; *Newsweek,* xvi (September 23, 1940), 15–16.

32. *New York Times,* September 16 and 17, 1940; *New Republic,* ciii (September 23, 1940), 400; *Vital Speeches,* vi (October 1, 1940), 762.

33. Barnard, *Willkie,* pp. 243–44; *New York Times,* September 20 and 22, 1940; *Time,* xxxvi (September 30, 1940), 12–14.

34. *New York Times,* September 9, 11, 19, and 20, 1940; *Newsweek,* xvi (September 16, 1940), 22–23; Donald Bruce Johnson, *The Republican Party and Wendell Willkie* (Urbana, Ill., 1960), p. 142; Mellett to Roosevelt, September 30, 1940, FDR Papers, PPF 4721; Ickes, *Secret Diary,* iii, 331; Vandenberg to Arthur H. Vandenberg, Jr., September 20, 1940, Vandenberg Papers.

35. Rosenman, *Working with Roosevelt,* p. 222; *Time,* xxxvi (September 23, 1940), 19–20; *New York Times,* August 11 and September 22, 1940; *Time,* xxxvi (October 7, 1940), 13.

36. Rosenman, ed., *Public Papers of FDR,* ix, 415, 430–31; *Time,* xxxvi (September 23, 1940), 11–12.

37. Edward L. and Frederick H. Schapsmeier, *Henry A. Wallace of Iowa: The Agrarian Years, 1910–1940* (Ames, Ia., 1968), p. 277; Russell Lord, *The Wallaces of Iowa* (Boston, 1947), pp. 479–80; *New York Times,* September 10 and 21, 1940; *Newsweek,* xvi (September 23, 1940), 17; Hugh S. Johnson, "Heir Apparent," *Saturday Evening Post,* ccxiii (November 2, 1940), 18.

38. *New York Times,* October 1, 1940; Warren Moscow, *Roosevelt and Willkie* (Englewood Cliffs, N.J., 1968), p. 163; *Nation,* cli (October 19, 1940), 354; Parmet and Hecht, *Never Again,* p. 240.

39. *New York Times,* October 4, 5, and 6, 1940; Roosevelt Press Conference 686, October 4, 1940, FDR Papers, PPF 1–P.

40. *Washington Post,* October 9 and 14, 1940; *Time,* xxxvi (October 21, 1940), 19; Freda Kirchwey, "Pre-Mortem on Willkie," *Nation,* cli (October 12, 1940), 318.

41. *New York Times,* September 27, 28, and 29, 1940; *Newsweek,* xvi (October 7, 1940), 15–17; State Department, *Bulletin,* iii (September 28, 1940), 251; Saul Friedlander, *Prelude to Downfall: Hitler and the United States, 1939–1941* (New York, 1967), pp. 154–55.

42. *Christian Century,* lvii (October 9, 1940), 1238; *New York Times,* September 29, 1940; *Nation,* cli (October 5, 1940), 285.

43. *New York Times,* October 2, 1940; *Newsweek,* xvi (October 14, 1940), 17–18; *Time,* xxxvi (October 14, 1940), 26–28.

44. *New York Times,* October 3, 1940.

45. Barnard, *Willkie,* pp. 250–51; *New York Times,* October 8, 9, 10, and 12, 1940.

46. Louis L. Gerson, *The Hyphenate in Recent American Politics and Diplomacy* (Lawrence, Kans., 1964), pp. 124–25; James A. Shanley to Roosevelt, July 9, 1940, FDR Papers, PPF 6735; Beiter to Flynn, October 1, 1940, FDR Papers, PPF 2532; H. P. Koppleman to Henry Kannee, October 3, 1940, and Fred A. Ossanna to David Niles, October 10, 1940, FDR Papers, OF 233–A; *New York Times,* September 13 and October 13, 1940; Pope to Harry Hopkins, October 14, 1940, Harry Hopkins Papers, Box 91.

47. *New York Times,* October 12, 1940; Robert E. Sherwood, *Roosevelt and Hopkins: An Intimate History* (New York, 1948), p. 183; Rosenman, *Working with Roosevelt,* p. 233; Rosenman, ed., *Public Papers of FDR,* ix, 463–67.

48. *Time,* xxxvi (October 21, 1940), 15–16; Lilienthal, *Journals,* i, 219.

49. Vandenberg to John Blodgett, September 18, 1940, Vandenberg Papers; *Public Opinion Quarterly,* v (March 1941), 140; *New York Times,* October 11 and 23, 1940.

50. Parmet and Hecht, *Never Again,* p. 252; *New York Times,* October 15 and 19, 1940; *Newsweek,* xvi (October 14, 1940), 23; Barnes, *Willkie,* pp. 225–26; Johnson, *Republican Party and Willkie,* p. 148; Vandenberg to Blodgett, September 18, 1940, Vandenberg Papers.

51. *New York Times,* October 19, 1940; *Vital Speeches,* vii (November 1, 1940), 58–61; *Time,* xxxvi (October 28, 1940), 14.

52. *New York Times,* October 23, 1940.

53. *Ibid.,* October 24 and 25, 1940; *Newsweek,* XVI (October 21, 1940), 15; Willkie to Vandenberg, undated, Vandenberg Papers, Scrapbook 13.

54. *New York Times,* October 27, 1940; Lilienthal, *Journals,* I, 222, 226–27; *Time,* XXXVI (October 28, 1940), 12; *Newsweek,* XVI (October 28, 1940), 13–15; *New York Times,* October 30, 1940.

55. Sherwood, *Roosevelt and Hopkins,* p. 188; Ed Watson to Roosevelt, October 1, 1940, FDR Papers, PPF 1376; Rosenman, ed., *Public Papers of FDR,* IX, 473–74, 510–14; *Time,* XXXVI (November 11, 1940), 24; Henry L. Stimson and McGeorge Bundy, *On Active Service in Peace and War* (New York, 1948), p. 348.

56. Ickes, *Secret Diary,* III, 351–52; Ickes to Roosevelt, October 17, 1940, Hopkins Papers, Box 117; Roosevelt Press Conference 690, October 18, 1940, FDR Papers, PPF 1–P.

57. Rosenman, ed., *Public Papers of FDR,* IX, 485–95; *Time,* XXXVI (November 4, 1940), 11–12.

58. *New York Times,* October 24, 1940; *Time,* XXXVI (November 4, 1940), 12.

59. Wayne S. Cole, *America First: The Battle Against Intervention 1940–41* (Madison, Wis., 1953), pp. 167–70; *New York Times,* October 15, 1940; *Newsweek,* XVI (October 28, 1940), 17.

60. *Christian Century,* LVII (October 23, 1940), 1303–1304; *Nation,* CLI (November 2, 1940), 434; pamphlet, Claude Pepper Papers, Federal Records Center, Suitland, Md., Box 111.

61. *Catholic World,* CLII (November, 1940), 129–38; *New York Times,* October 23, 1940; Edward Skillin, Jr., "Catholic Press and the Election," *Commonweal,* XXXIII (November 1, 1940), 50–52; *Nation* CLI (November 2, 1940), 420.

62. *New York Times,* October 26, 1940; *Documents on German Foreign Policy,* Series D, X, 120–21; XI, 463–64; Parmet and Hecht, *Never Again,* pp. 233–34, 255; Ladislas Farago, *The Game of the Foxes* (New York, 1972), pp. 386–87; Alton Frye, *Nazi Germany and the American Hemisphere, 1933–1941* (New Haven, 1967), pp. 143–44, 150, 151.

63. *Newsweek,* XVI (November 4, 1940), 17–18; Hadley Cantril, Donald Rugg, and Frederick Williams, "America Faces the War: Shifts in Opinion," *Public Opinion Quarterly,* IV (December 1940), 651–56.

64. Nelson Poynter to Hopkins, October 22, 1940, Hopkins Papers, Box 92; *New York Times,* October 20, 23, and 31, November 2

and 3, 1940; Rosenman to Lehman, October 15, 1940, Samuel I. Rosenman Papers, Roosevelt Library, Box 28; Biddle to Roosevelt, November 13, 1940, FDR Papers, PSF Diplomatic Correspondence–Poland.

65. *New York Times,* October 26 and 27, November 1, 1940; Moscow, *Roosevelt and Willkie,* pp. 162–63.

66. "Spiv." to Hopkins, October 26, 1940, Hopkins Papers, Box 92; Laski to Roosevelt, October 20, 1940, FDR Papers, PSF Diplomatic Correspondence–Great Britain; *New York Times,* November 3, 1940.

67. *New York Times,* October 23, 1940; Mrs. E. Hammond to Hull, October 24, 1940, enclosing clipping from *San Francisco Chronicle,* October 24, 1940, Hull Papers, Box 48; Clyde O. Eastus to Stephen Early, October 28, 1940, FDR Papers, OF 20.

68. Hull, *Memoirs,* I, 863, 866; State Department, *Bulletin,* III (October 26, 1940), 331–36; Mathews to Flynn, October 28, 1940, Hull Papers, Box 48.

69. C. W. Gray to Mrs. E. Hammond, October 31, 1940, Hull Papers, Box 48; Frank to Hopkins, October 31, 1940, Hopkins Papers, Box 117; Johnson to Roosevelt, undated, Hopkins Papers, Box 91; Armstrong to Hull, October 30, 1940, Hull Papers, Box 48.

70. Hull, *Memoirs,* I, 867–68; *New York Times,* November 2, 1940.

71. *Foreign Relations, 1940,* III, 48–49; *New York Times,* October 8, 1940; *Time,* XXXVI (November 4, 1940), 19; Roosevelt Press Conference 689, October 15, 1940, FDR Papers, PPF 1–P.

72. Cyrus L. Sulzberger, *The Last of the Giants* (New York, 1970), p. 630; Watson to Roosevelt, October 25, 1940, FDR Papers, PSF Diplomatic Correspondence–Great Britain; James F. Byrnes, *All in One Lifetime* (New York, 1958), pp. 125–26; Arthur Krock, *Memoirs: Sixty Years on the Firing Line* (New York, 1968), pp. 335–36; Richard J. Whalen, *The Founding Father: The Story of Joseph P. Kennedy* (New York, 1964), pp. 329–32.

73. *New York Times,* October 30, 1940; Krock, *Memoirs,* p. 336; Freedman, *Roosevelt and Frankfurter,* pp. 533–39.

74. Henry Luce, "This Great Moment," *Life,* IX (October 21, 1940), 29–30; *New York Times,* October 19 and 28, 1940; *Newsweek,* XVI (November 4, 1940), 22–23; Saul Friedlander, *Prelude to Downfall: Hitler and the United States, 1939–1941* (New York, 1967), pp. 154–55.

75. *New York Times,* October 29, 30, and 31, 1940.

76. Adolph Sabath to Roosevelt, October 31, 1940, and Michael Musmanno to Hopkins, October 31, 1940, Hopkins Papers, Box 92; Barnard, *Willkie*, p. 288; *New York Times*, November 5, 1940.

77. LaGuardia to Flynn, October 25, 1940, FDR Papers, PPF 1376; William B. Barry to Roosevelt, October 24, 1940, Hopkins Papers, Box 117; undated memorandum, MacIntyre to Roosevelt, FDR Papers, PPF 1820.

78. *New York Times*, October 29, 1940; Rosenman, ed., *Public Papers of FDR*, IX, 499–510.

79. Sherwood, *Roosevelt and Hopkins*, p. 191; Rosenman, *Working with Roosevelt*, pp. 242–43; Blum, *Morgenthau Diaries*, II, 194–96; speech draft, October 30, 1940, Rosenman Papers, Box 2; Rosenman, ed., *Public Papers of FDR*, IX, 514–24.

80. Barnard, *Willkie*, p. 258; Rosenman, ed., *Public Papers of FDR*, IX, 544–53.

81. *New York Times*, November 3 and 4, 1940; *Time*, XXXVI (November 4, 1940), 19; *Newsweek*, XVI (November 4, 1940), 9; Long diary, November 3, 1940, Long Papers, Box 5; Howard O. Hunter to Hopkins, November 2, 1940, Hopkins Papers, Box 92; Childs, *I Write from Washington*, p. 207; Brien McMahon to MacIntyre, October 31, 1940, FDR Papers, OF 857; Martin, *First Fifty Years*, p. 119.

82. Tully, *FDR*, p. 240; Eleanor Roosevelt, *This I Remember* (New York, 1949), p. 221; *Time*, XXXVI (November 11, 1940); *New York Times*, November 12, 1940.

83. Johnson, *Republican Party and Willkie*, p. 160; Rosenman, *Working with Roosevelt*, p. 255.

84. Martin, *First Fifty Years*, p. 120; Dillon, *Willkie*, p. 7; Barnes, *Willkie*, pp. 222–24; Barnard, *Willkie*, p. 268; Johnson, *Republican Party and Willkie*, pp. 161–62.

85. Samuel Lubell, "Post-Mortem: Who Elected Roosevelt?" *Saturday Evening Post*, CCXIII (January 25, 1941), 9–11, 93; *Time*, XXXVI (November 18, 1940), 17; William Allen White, "Thoughts After the Election," *Yale Review*, XXX (Winter 1941), 217–27; *Newsweek*, XVI (November 11, 1940), 17.

86. *Nation*, CLI (November 9, 1940), 435–36; Dillon, *Willkie*, p. 224; Parmet and Hecht, *Never Again*, p. 278.

87. Samuel Lubell, *The Future of American Politics* (New York, 1952), pp. 132–33; Barnes, *Willkie*, p. 4; Moscow, *Roosevelt and Willkie*, pp. 195–97; Poletti to Rosenman, November 8 and 14, 1940, Rosenman Papers, Boxes 27 and 28; William E. Leuchten-

berg, *Franklin D. Roosevelt and the New Deal, 1932–1940* (New York, 1963), pp. 321–22; Celler to Roosevelt, November 13, 1940, FDR Papers, PPF 2748; James MacGregor Burns, *Roosevelt: The Lion and the Fox* (New York, 1956), pp. 454–55.

88. Laski to Roosevelt, November 6, 1940, FDR Papers, PPF 3014; *New York Times,* November 10, 1940; *Documents on German Foreign Policy,* Series D, xi, 476–77, 499.

89. State Department, *Bulletin,* iii (November 9, 1940), 407; Freda Kirchwey, "To the President Elect," *Nation,* cli (November 9, 1940), 437; William L. Langer and S. Everett Gleason, *The Undeclared War, 1940–1941* (New York, 1953), 201.

90. Childs, *I Write from Washington,* p. 213.

Chapter 3

1. Arthur H. Vandenberg, Jr., and Joe Alex Morris, eds., *The Private Papers of Senator Vandenberg* (Boston, 1952), p. 1.

2. Robert A. Divine, *Second Chance: The Triumph of Internationalism in America During World War II* (New York, 1967), *passim.*

3. Richard Polenberg, *War and Society: The United States, 1941–1945* (Philadelphia, 1972), pp. 187–89; James MacGregor Burns, *Roosevelt: The Soldier of Freedom, 1940–1945* (New York, 1970), pp. 434–36.

4. Roosevelt to Patrick H. Drewry, March 7, 1944, quoted in Polenberg, *War and Society,* p. 199; *Public Opinion Quarterly,* viii (Summer 1940), 278; *Time,* xliii (May 22, 1944), 18–19; *Newsweek,* xxiii (April 10, 1944), 27–28.

5. Burns, *Roosevelt: Soldier,* pp. 448–49; *Time,* xliii (May 15, 1944), 11; *ibid.* (May 22, 1944), 17.

6. Mary Earhart Dillon, *Wendell Willkie: 1892–1944* (Philadelphia, 1952), p. 329; *New York Times,* March 23 and 26, 1944; *Newsweek,* xxiii (April 3, 1944), 68; *ibid.* (April 17, 1944), 108.

7. *New York Times,* April 6 and 7, 1944; Donald Bruce Johnson, *The Republican Party and Wendell Willkie* (Urbana, Ill., 1960), pp. 282–83; *Time,* xliii (April 17, 1944), 18; Wood to Vandenberg, April 7, 1944, and Vandenberg to Wood, April 10, 1944, Vandenberg Papers.

8. *Newsweek,* xxxiii (April 17, 1944), 21–23; *Public Opinion Quarterly,* viii (Summer 1944), 277.

9. I. F. Stone, "Thomas E. Dewey," *Nation,* CLVIII (May 20, 1944), 586–88; Raymond Moley, *27 Masters of Politics* (New York, 1949), pp. 56–60; Robert Wood to Vandenberg, March 29, 1944, Vandenberg Papers; *New Republic,* CXI (July 31, 1944), 117.

10. *New York Times,* March 22, April 20 and 26, 1940; Eugene H. Roseboom, *A History of Presidential Elections: From George Washington to Richard M. Nixon* (New York, 1970), p. 481; Richard H. Rovere, "Stassen of Minnesota," *Nation,* CLVIII (June 3, 1944), 647–48.

11. C. David Tompkins, *Senator Arthur H. Vandenberg: The Evolution of a Modern Republican, 1884–1945* (East Lansing, Mich., 1970), pp. 233–34; Vandenberg to Wood, April 15, 1944, Vandenberg Papers; *New York Times,* April 14, 17, and 30, 1944; *Time,* XLIII (April 24, 1944), 18–19.

12. *Public Opinion Quarterly,* VIII (Summer 1944), 278.

13. *New York Times,* April 28, 1944; *Vital Speeches,* X (May 15, 1944), 450–52; *New Republic,* CX (May 8, 1944), 621–22; *Time,* XLIII (May 8, 1944), 15.

14. Cordell Hull, *The Memoirs of Cordell Hull,* 2 vols. (New York, 1948), II, 1656; Hull to Roosevelt, March 29, 1944, Hull Papers, Box 53; Porter to Gore, April 28, 1944, and Gore to Porter, May 2, 1944, Hull Papers, Box 65.

15. Hull, *Memoirs,* II, 1657; Harley A. Notter, *Postwar Foreign Policy Preparation, 1939–1945* (Washington, 1950), pp. 260–61; State Department, *Bulletin,* X (April 15, 1944), 335–42.

16. Tom Connally and Alfred Steinberg, *My Name Is Tom Connally* (New York, 1954), p. 265; Vandenberg, *Private Papers,* p. 94; Taft to Vandenberg, March 29, 1944, Vandenberg Papers; Vandenberg to Connally, April 4, 1944, Hull Papers, Box 53; Vandenberg to M. Shakespeare, March 18, 1944, Vandenberg Papers.

17. Hull, *Memoirs,* II, 1658–59; Hull to Roosevelt, April 25, 1944, Hull Papers, Box 53.

18. Vandenberg, *Private Papers,* pp. 95–97; Hull, *Memoirs,* II, 1660; Vandenberg to Hull, May 3, 1944, Hull Papers, Box 53.

19. Long diary, May 19, 22, 23, 27, and 29, 1944, Long Papers, Box 5; Vandenberg, *Private Papers,* pp. 99–104; Connally and Steinberg, *Connally,* pp. 266–67; Hull, *Memoirs,* II, 1667–69.

20. *Ibid.,* II, 1656; Roosevelt to Florence Harriman, June 12, 1944, Florence J. Harriman Papers, Library of Congress, Box 18; Samuel I. Rosenman, ed., *The Public Papers and Addresses of Franklin D. Roosevelt,* 13 vols. (New York, 1938–1950), XIII, 140–41.

21. Long diary, June 15, 1944, Long Papers, Box 5; *Time*, XLIII (June 26, 1944), 17.

22. *New York Times*, June 16 and 17, 1944; *Time*, XLIII (June 12, 1944), 12; *ibid.* (June 26, 1944), 18; *Nation*, CLVIII (June 24, 1944), 722; *New Republic*, CX (June 26, 1944), 835–36.

23. J. C. Hurewitz, *The Struggle for Palestine* (New York, 1950), pp. 101–2; Frank E. Manuel, *The Realities of American-Palestine Relations* (Washington, 1949), pp. 310–11.

24. Richard P. Stevens, *American Zionism and U.S. Foreign Policy, 1942–1947* (New York, 1962), pp. 4–5, 37–39; *Congressional Record*, January 31, 1944, p. 963.

25. *Foreign Relations, 1943*, IV, 790.

26. Hull, *Memoirs*, II, 1534–35; *Foreign Relations, 1944*, V, 563–64, 567–68; *New York Times*, March 5, 1944; Vandenberg to Philip Slomovitz, March 14, 1944, Vandenberg Papers.

27. Memorandum of conversation with Rabbi Silver by Breckinridge Long, February 24, 1944, Long Papers, Box 200.

28. *New York Times*, March 10 and 18, 1944; Stevens, *American Zionism*, pp. 47–49; Roosevelt Press Conference 945, March 28, 1944, FDR Papers, PPF 1–P.

29. Vandenberg to Connally, April 4, 1944, Vandenberg Papers; *New York Times*, March 29, 1944; Stevens, *American Zionism*, pp. 54–57; *Foreign Relations, 1944*, V, 606.

30. Gaddis Smith, *American Diplomacy During the Second World War, 1941–1945* (New York, 1965), pp. 69–71.

31. Anthony Eden, *The Reckoning* (Boston, 1965), p. 495; *Foreign Relations of the United States: The Conferences at Cairo and Tehran, 1943* (Washington, 1961), pp. 594, 599–600; *Foreign Relations, 1944*, III, 1267–68.

32. Milton Carmichael to Vandenberg, April 28, 1944, and Vandenberg to Carmichael, April 29, 1944, Vandenberg Papers.

33. Edward J. Rozek, *Allied Wartime Diplomacy: A Pattern in Poland* (New York, 1958), pp. 201–2; *Foreign Relations, 1944*, III, 1398–99; Eric Estorick, "Polish American Politics," *Nation*, CLVIII (May 20, 1944), 591–93; memorandum by David Niles, May 26, 1944, FDR Papers, PPF–Poland.

34. *New York Times*, May 28, 30, and 31, 1944; *Newsweek*, XXIII (June 12, 1944), 32–33.

35. *Foreign Relations, 1944*, III, 1280–81, 1283, 1285–89, IV, 874; Stanislaw Mikolajczyk, *The Rape of Poland: The Pattern of Soviet Aggression* (New York, 1948), pp. 56–61; Jan Ciechanowski, *De-*

feat in Victory (Garden City, N.Y., 1947), pp. 292–313; *New York Times,* June 15, 1944.

36. *Newsweek,* XXIII (April 24, 1944), 36; *New York Times,* May 31, 1944; *Congressional Record,* June 5, 1944, pp. 5281–87.

37. *Ibid.,* June 5, 1944, pp. 5341–54; *ibid.,* June 6, 1944, pp. 5403–15.

38. *Ibid.,* June 7, 1944, pp. 5456–57, 5474–76; *New York Times,* June 8, 1944; Rosenman, ed., *Public Papers of FDR,* XIII, 177–78; *Time,* XLIV (June 19, 1944), 21.

39. Vandenberg, *Private Papers,* p. 87; Vandenberg to Dewey, March 30, 1944, Dewey to Vandenberg, April 15, 1944, Austin to Vandenberg, May 5, 1944, Vandenberg to Austin, May 8, 1944, Vandenberg to Dulles, June 10 and 14, 1944, Vandenberg Papers.

40. *New York Times,* June 18, 1944.

41. *Ibid.,* June 21, 23, 24, 25, 26, and 27, 1944; Arthur Krock, *Memoirs: Sixty Years on the Firing Line* (New York, 1968), p. 196.

42. Kirk H. Porter and Donald Bruce Johnson, eds., *National Party Platforms, 1840–1956* (Urbana, Ill., 1956), pp. 407–8; *New York Times,* June 28, 1944; *Nation,* CLIX (July 8, 1944), 32–33.

43. *Vital Speeches,* X (July 15, 1944), 587, 588–92; *New York Times,* June 28, 1944.

44. Joseph W. Martin, as told to Robert J. Donovan, *My First Fifty Years in Politics* (New York, 1960), p. 162; *Newsweek,* XXIV (July 10, 1944), 35–38; *New York Times,* June 29, 1944; *Vital Speeches,* X (July 15, 1944), 578–80.

45. *New York Times,* June 30, July 1, 6, and 9, 1944; *New Republic,* CXI (July 10, 1944), 30–31, 43.

46. Rosenman, ed., *Public Papers of FDR,* XIII, 197–99; Rosenman to Sherwood, July 11, 1944, Rosenman Papers, Box 24.

47. *New York Times,* July 16, 20, and 21, 1944; Porter and Johnson, *National Party Platforms,* p. 403; Long diary, July 13, 15, and 25, 1944, Long Papers, Box 5.

48. *Vital Speeches,* X (August 1, 1944), 611–16, 628–31; *ibid.* (August 15, 1944), 650–51; Ickes to Roosevelt, July 3, 1944, FDR Papers, OF 3850.

49. *New York Times,* July 21, 1944; Rosenman, *Working with Roosevelt,* p. 439; Helen Fuller, "Throwing Wallace to the Wolves," *New Republic,* CXI (July 31, 1944), 121–22; Leon Friedman, "Election of 1944," in Arthur M. Schlesinger, Jr., and Fred L. Israel, eds., *History of American Presidential Elections, 1789–1968,* 4 vols. (New York, 1971), IV, 3024–28.

50. *Time,* xliv (July 24, 1944), 15–16; *New York Times,* July 10, 1944; Divine, *Second Chance,* p. 213.
51. Rosenman, ed., *Public Papers of FDR,* xiii, 201–6.
52. *Nation,* xxiv (July 31, 1944), 25; Howard G. Bruenn, M.D., "Clinical Notes on the Illness and Death of President Franklin D. Roosevelt," *Annals of Internal Medicine,* lxxii (April 1970), 584.
53. *New York Times,* July 18, August 2, 15, and 17, 1944; *Time,* liv (August 28, 1944), 13–14.
54. *New York Times,* August 18, 1944; Hull, *Memoirs,* ii, 1689.
55. John Foster Dulles, *War or Peace* (New York, 1950), pp. 123; *New York Times,* August 19 and 20, 1944.
56. Dulles, *War or Peace,* pp. 123–25; Hull, *Memoirs,* ii, 1690.
57. *Ibid.,* ii, 1691–93; Long diary, August 24 and 25, 1944, Long Papers, Box 5; *New York Times,* August 26, 1944.
58. Hull, *Memoirs,* ii, 1693.
59. Vandenberg diary, August 25, 1944, Vandenberg Papers.
60. *Time,* xliv (September 4, 1944), 22; State Department, *Bulletin,* xi (September 10, 1944), 255.

Chapter 4

1. *Time,* xliv (September 4, 1944), 17; *Newsweek,* xxiv (September 25, 1944), 38–41; *New York Times,* September 10, 1944.
2. *Time,* xliv (July 24, 1944), 17; *ibid.* (August 28, 1944), 15; *Newsweek,* xxiii (July 24, 1944), 42–43; Cantril to Samuel Rosenman and David Niles, August 3, 1944, Rosenman Papers, Box 10; Hadley Cantril, "The Issues—As Seen By the American People," *Public Opinion Quarterly,* viii (Fall 1944), 332–36; Louis H. Bean, "Who Will Win in November?" *New Republic,* cxi (September 25, 1944), 362; Raymond Moley, "The Political Consequences of Victory," *Newsweek,* xxiv (August 7, 1944), 100.
3. Porter to Roosevelt, July 17, 1944, FDR Papers, PPF 2037; Cantril to Rosenman, August 28, 1944, Rosenman Papers, Box 3; Rosenman to Sherwood, August 15, 1944, Rosenman Papers, Box 24.
4. *Time,* xliv (August 21, 1944), 21; *Newsweek,* xxiv (August 21, 1944), 42; Samuel Rosenman, ed., *The Public Papers and Addresses of Franklin D. Roosevelt,* 13 vols. (New York, 1938–1950), xiii, 227; Howard G. Bruenn, M.D., "Clinical Notes on the Illness and Death of President Franklin D. Roosevelt," *An-*

nals of *Internal Medicine*, LXXII (April 1970), 586; *Time*, XLIV (August 28, 1944), 16.

5. *Newsweek*, XXIV (July 17, 1944), 33; *Time*, XLIV (August 14, 1944), 20–21; *New York Times*, August 20, 1944.

6. *Time*, XLIV (September 18, 1944), 22; *ibid.* (September 25, 1944), 13; *ibid.* (October 23, 1944), 19–20; *Newsweek*, XXIV (September 11, 1944), 36.

7. *Time*, XLIV (October 30, 1944), 11; James A. Wechsler, "Bricker's Running Mate," *Nation*, CLIX (October 7, 1944), 398–99; *New Republic*, CXI (September 25, 1944), supplement on Dewey; *ibid.* (November 13, 1944), 624; Roger Butterfield, "Thomas E. Dewey," *Life*, XVII (October 9, 1944), 97.

8. *Nation*, CLIX (August 12, 1944), 171–72; *New York Times*, September 5, 10, 17 and October 24, 1944; *Vital Speeches*, X (September 15, 1944), 708; Richard Polenberg, *War and Society: The United States, 1941–1945* (Philadelphia, 1972), p. 208.

9. Gerald W. Johnson, "A Letter to the Honorable Thomas E. Dewey," *Atlantic Monthly*, CLXXIV (September 1944), 39; *New York Times*, September 9, 1944.

10. *Newsweek*, XXIV (September 18, 1944), 38–40; *New York Times*, September 9, 10, and 20, 1944; *New Republic*, CXI (September 18, 1944), 327; *Time*, XLIV (October 2, 1944), 23–24.

11. *Newsweek*, XXIV (September 18, 1944), 42.

12. *Time*, XLIV (September 25, 1944), 12; *New York Times*, September 10 and 17, 1944; *Life*, XVII (October 2, 1944), 34–35.

13. *New York Times*, September 1, 1944; *Newsweek*, XXIV (September 11, 1944), 40; *Vital Speeches*, X (September 15, 1944), 706–8.

14. Daniels to Hull, September 12, 1944, Hull Papers, Box 54; *New York Times*, September 8 and 22, 1944; *Vital Speeches*, X (October 1, 1944), 760–63.

15. Robert E. Sherwood, *Roosevelt and Hopkins: An Intimate History* (New York, 1948), pp. 822–23; memorandum of conversation with Willkie, July 4 and 5, 1944, Rosenman Papers, Box 24; Roosevelt to Willkie, July 13, 1944, FDR Papers, PPF 7023; *New York Times*, August 11 and 26, 1944.

16. Wendell Willkie, "Cowardice at Chicago," *Collier's*, CXIV (September 18, 1944), 11, 77–79; Donald Bruce Johnson, *The Republican Party and Wendell Willkie* (Urbana, Ill., 1960), pp. 305–6; *Time*, XLIV (October 30, 1944), 14; *New York Times*, October 10 and 13, 1944; memorandum by Hopkins, August 11, 1944, Hopkins Papers, Box 8.

17. Sherwood, *Roosevelt and Hopkins,* p. 820; Bruenn, "Clinical Notes," p. 587.
18. Sherwood, *Roosevelt and Hopkins,* p. 820; Samuel I. Rosenman, *Working with Roosevelt* (New York, 1952), pp. 473–74; Rosenman, ed., *Public Papers and Addresses of FDR,* XIII, 286–90.
19. *New Republic,* CXI (October 2, 1944), 413; *Time,* XLIV (October 2, 1944), 21–22; *New York Times,* September 24 and 26, 1944.
20. *New Republic,* CXI (October 9, 1944), 458; *New York Times,* September 26, 1944; *Vital Speeches,* X (October 1, 1944), 741–43.
21. *New York Times,* September 29 and October 8, 1944; *Time,* XLIV (October 9, 1944), 23; *ibid.* (October 16, 1944), 20–21; Rosenman, ed., *Public Papers of FDR,* XIII, 317–24.
22. *New Republic,* CXI (October 9, 1944), 458; Sherwood, *Roosevelt and Hopkins,* p. 822; *New York Times,* October 1, 1940; Polenberg, *War and Society,* pp. 203–7.
23. Heinz H. F. Eulau, "Poland and Russia," *New Republic,* CXI (August 7, 1944), 156–57; *Newsweek,* XXIV (August 14, 1944), 54; *New York Times,* September 17, October 1, 2, and 4, 1944; James MacGregor Burns, *Roosevelt: The Soldier of Freedom* (New York, 1970), pp. 534–35.
24. Edward J. Rozek, *Allied Wartime Diplomacy: A Pattern in Poland* (New York, 1958), pp. 274, 286; Stanislaw Mikolajczyk, *The Rape of Poland: The Pattern of Soviet Aggression* (New York, 1948), p. 96; *Foreign Relations, 1944,* III, 1323; *ibid., Yalta, 1945,* pp. 204–5.
25. James Loeb, Jr., "August Stock-Taking," *New Republic,* CXI (August 14, 1944), 178; *Nation,* CLIX (September 16, 1944), 323; undated record of telephone call to White House by Senator O'Mahoney, Rosenman Papers, Box 2; Nurczyk to Roosevelt, September 13, 1944, FDR Papers, OF 463–A, Box 4.
26. Biddle to Roosevelt, September 28 and October 7, 1944, Hannegan to Edwin Watson, October 7, 1944, Guffey to Roosevelt, October 7, 1944, FDR Papers, OF 463, Box 1; *New York Times,* October 12, 1944; Arthur Bliss Lane, *I Saw Poland Betrayed* (Indianapolis, 1948), p. 59.
27. *New York Times,* October 9 and 19, 1944; Frank Januszewski to Dewey, October 21, 1944, Vandenberg to Januszewski, October 31, 1944, Vandenberg Papers.
28. *New York Times,* October 16, 1944; Davies journal, October 14, 1944, and Davies to Molotov, October 20, 1944, Joseph E. Da-

vies Papers, Library of Congress, Box 15; Roosevelt to Davies, October 24, 1944, FDR Papers, PPF 1381.

29. *Foreign Relations, 1944,* III, 1329, 1330.

30. Lane, *Poland,* pp. 61–62; *New York Times,* October 29, 1944.

31. Jan Ciechanowski, *Defeat in Victory* (Garden City, N.Y., 1947), pp. 338–39, 352; Vandenberg to Januszewski, November 15, 1944, and Januszewski to Vandenberg, November 22, 1944, Vandenberg Papers.

32. *New York Times,* October 12, 13, and 16, 1944; Rosenman to David Niles, October 11, 1944, Rosenman Papers, Box 25; Frank E. Manuel, *The Realities of American-Palestine Relations* (Washington, 1949), p. 312.

33. *Foreign Relations, 1944,* V, 616–20, 624–26; J. C. Hurewitz, *The Struggle for Palestine* (New York, 1950), pp. 213–14; Vandenberg diary, December 1944, Vandenberg Papers.

34. Norman Kogan, *Italy and the Allies* (Cambridge, Mass., 1956), pp. 81–83; Cordell Hull, *The Memoirs of Cordell Hull,* 2 vols. (New York, 1948), II, 1566–67.

35. *New York Times,* October 13, 16, 18, 26, and 29, 1944; Robert Hurley to Harry Hopkins, October 27, 1944, Hopkins Papers, Box 8.

36. *Newsweek,* XXIV (September 4, 1944), 19; *Congressional Record,* September 7, 1944, pp. 7581, 7602–3; *ibid.,* September 18, 1944, pp. 7866, 7870.

37. *New York Times,* September 19 and 21, October 1, 14, 20, 21, 22, and 24, 1944; *Newsweek,* XXIV (October 23, 1944), 112; *Time,* XLIV (October 30, 1944), 16.

38. Undated memorandum by Hopkins, Hopkins Papers, Box 141; Sherwood, *Roosevelt and Hopkins,* p. 827.

39. Robert A. Divine, *Second Chance: The Triumph of Internationalism in America During World War II* (New York, 1967), pp. 220–28.

40. *Life,* XVII (October 23, 1944), 30–31; *Time,* XLIV (October 30, 1944), 15; *New York Times,* October 13, 1944.

41. Rosenman, *Working with Roosevelt,* p. 481; Cohen to Rosenman, undated, Rosenman Papers, Box 17; Rosenman to Roosevelt, October 14, 1944, FDR Papers, OF 4070; Porter to Rosenman, October 11, 1944, Rosenman Papers, Box 2; Davenport to Hopkins, undated, and Edward Pritchard to Rosenman, October 13, 1944, Rosenman Papers, Box 17.

42. Stettinius to Roosevelt, October 13, 1944, Rosenman Papers, Box

17; *Time,* XLIV (October 30, 1944), 15; speech draft, October 16, 1944, Long Papers, Box 153; Long diary, October 20, 1944, Long Papers, Box 5.

43. *New York Times,* October 19, 1944; Rosenman, *Working with Roosevelt,* pp. 482–85; Rosenman, ed., *Public Papers of FDR,* XIII, 350–51.

44. *New York Times,* October 23 and 24, 1944; *Christian Century,* LXI (November 1, 1944), 1243–44; Willard Shelton, "Wisconsin and Its Neighbors," *Nation,* CLIX (October 21, 1944), 463; *ibid.* (October 28, 1944), p. 503.

45. *New York Times,* October 24 and 25, 1944; *Vital Speeches,* XI (November 1, 1944), 39–40.

46. *Newsweek,* XXIV (November 6, 1944), 48; *New York Times,* November 3, 1944; Walter Millis and E. S. Duffield, eds., *The Forrestal Diaries* (New York, 1951), p. 348.

47. *Nation,* CLIX (October 28, 1944), 504; *New Republic,* CXI (November 6, 1944), 583; *Newsweek,* XXIV (October 30, 1944), 52; *New York Times,* October 16, 1944; David Lilienthal, *The Journals of David E. Lilienthal,* 4 vols. (New York, 1964–1970), I, 653.

48. Arthur Vandenberg, Jr., and Joe Alex Morris, eds., *The Private Papers of Senator Vandenberg* (Boston, 1952), pp. 123–24; *New York Times,* October 26, 1944.

49. *New York Times,* October 19, 1944.

50. Rosenman, ed., *Public Papers of FDR,* XIII, 342–54.

51. Cox to Hopkins, October 25, 1944, Hopkins Papers, Box 8; *New York Times,* October 9, 13, 17, 18, 21, 24, 26, and 28, 1944; Vandenberg to Pepper, October 23, 1944, and Pepper to Vandenberg, Nov. 17, 1944, Pepper Papers, Box 61.

52. *New York Times,* October 9 and 22, 1944; *Life,* XVII (October 30, 1944), 24; *Vital Speeches,* XI (November 1, 1944), 39–41.

53. *Nation,* CLIX (November 4, 1944), 548; *New Republic,* CXI (November 6, 1944), 594; Rosenman, ed., *Public Papers of FDR,* XIII, 365.

54. *New York Times,* November 5, 1944; *Public Opinion Quarterly,* VIII (Winter 1944–45), 570; *Life,* XVII (November 6, 1944), 23; *Newsweek,* XXIV (October 23, 1944) 42–46; *ibid.* (October 30, 1944), 24; *ibid.* (November 6, 1944), 46; *Time,* XLIV (October 23, 1944), 24; *ibid.* (October 30, 1944), 13.

55. *New York Times,* October 20 and 29, 1944; Sherwood, *Roosevelt and Hopkins,* p. 829; *Time,* XLIV (November 6, 1944), 17–18;

Newsweek, xxiv (November 13, 1944), 29; Rosenman, ed., *Public Papers of FDR*, xiii, 337–39, 358–59, 370.

56. *Ibid.*, 385–86.

57. *New York Times*, November 5, 1944; Rosenman, ed., *Public Papers of FDR*, xiii, 399, 410–12.

58. *New York Times*, November 5, 1944.

59. *Ibid.*, October 31, November 3, 4, and 5, 1944; Hull, *Memoirs*, ii, 1714–16; Hull statement, October 26, 1944, Hull Papers, Box 54.

60. Vandenberg to B. E. Hutchinson, October 28, 1944, Vandenberg Papers; Frances Perkins, *The Roosevelt I Knew* (New York, 1946), p. 119; *Time*, xliv (November 20, 1944), 20–21.

61. Polenberg, *War and Society*, pp. 212–13; *New York Times*, November 12, 1944; *Newsweek*, xxiv (November 20, 1944), 28.

62. *New York Times*, November 8, 1944; Eugene H. Roseboom, *A History of Presidential Elections: From George Washington to Richard M. Nixon* (New York, 1970), p. 490; *Time*, xliv (November 13, 1944), 21; *Newsweek*, xxiv (November 13, 1944), 8.

63. *Nation*, clix (November 11, 1944), 573; *Newsweek*, xxiv (November 13, 1944), 4; *Time*, xliv (November 13, 1944), 20–21; *New York Times*, November 9 and 12, 1944; *Foreign Relations, 1944*, iv, 974.

64. *Life*, xvii (November 20, 1944), 23, 28; *Nation*, clix (November 18, 1944), 604–5; *Atlantic Monthly*, clxxiv (December 1944), 21; *New York Times*, November 9 and 12, 1944.

65. Vandenberg to Hull, November 11, 1944, Hull Papers, Box 54; J. F. Dulles to Allan Dulles, December 20, 1944, John Foster Dulles Papers, Princeton University Library; Dulles to Roosevelt, November 10, 1944, FDR Papers, PPF 8988.

Chapter 5

1. Wallace to Truman, July 23, 1946, Clark M. Clifford Papers, Harry S Truman Library, Box 18.

2. Walter LaFeber, *America, Russia, and the Cold War, 1945–1971*, 2d ed. (New York, 1972), pp. 21, 34–36.

3. Wallace to Truman, July 23, 1946, Clifford Papers, Box 18; Edward L. and Frederick H. Schapsmeier, *Prophet in Politics: Henry A. Wallace and the War Years, 1940–1965* (Ames, Ia., 1970), pp. 146, 153–60; Jonathan Daniels, *The Man of Independence* (Philadelphia, 1950), pp. 312–16.

4. Karl M. Schmidt, *Henry A. Wallace: Quixotic Crusade, 1948* (Syracuse, 1960), pp. 25–27; Clifton Brock, *Americans for Democratic Action: Its Role in National Politics* (hereafter *ADA*) (Washington, 1962), pp. 51–53.

5. Stephen E. Ambrose, *Rise to Globalism: American Foreign Policy Since 1938* (Baltimore, 1971), pp. 146–52; Schmidt, *Wallace,* pp. 29–30; Irwin Ross, *The Loneliest Campaign: The Truman Victory of 1948* (New York, 1968), pp. 146–47.

6. Schmidt, *Wallace,* pp. 37–38; Alonzo L. Hamby, "Henry A. Wallace, the Liberals, and Soviet-American Relations," *Review of Politics,* xxx (April 1968), 153–69.

7. Schmidt, *Wallace,* p. 35; *Time,* li (January 5, 1948), 17; Henry A. Wallace, *Toward World Peace* (New York, 1948), pp. 37–39, 68–69.

8. Sullivan to Clifford, June 2, 1947, Clifford Papers, Box 18.

9. Clifford to Truman, November 19, 1947, Clifford Papers, Box 21.

10. Harry S Truman, *Memoirs,* 2 vols. (Garden City, N.Y., 1956), ii, 171–72, 185; Jack Redding, *Inside the Democratic Party* (Indianapolis, 1958), pp. 115, 143.

11. *Public Opinion Quarterly,* xii (Spring 1948), 166; *Time,* li (January 19, 1948), 20; Helen Fuller, "The New Party Meets," *New Republic,* cxviii (April 19, 1948), 15; Mrs. D. H. Powellson to Truman, January 13, 1948, Harry S Truman Papers, Truman Library, OF 1170.

12. *Nation,* clxvi (February 28, 1948), 229; *Newsweek,* xxxi (March 1, 1948), 15; Truman to Baruch, February 18, 1948, Bernard M. Baruch Papers, Princeton University Library, Box 82; *Time,* li (March 1, 1948), 13.

13. Truman, *Memoirs,* ii, 132–59; Daniels, *Man of Independence,* pp. 317–18; Herbert Feis, *The Birth of Israel* (New York, 1969), pp. 40–46; Truman to Wagner, October 1, 1947, Wagner Papers, Palestine file; John McCormack to Truman, September 24, 1947, Truman Papers, OF 204; Walter Millis and E. S. Duffield, eds., *The Forrestal Diaries* (New York, 1951), pp. 309, 323, 346.

14. Lillie Shultz, "Conspiracy Against Partition," *Nation,* clxvi (January 31, 1948), 119; Chaim Weizmann to Truman, December 9, 1947, Truman Papers, OF 204; *Public Papers of the Presidents of the United States: Harry S. Truman, 1948* (Washington, 1964), p. 101; *Time,* li (February 16, 1948), 24; State Department, *Bulletin,* xviii (March 7, 1948), 294–97.

15. Clifford to Truman, November 19, 1947, Clifford Papers, Box 21;

Millis and Duffield, eds., *Forrestal Diaries,* pp. 344–45, 347–48, 356–60, 364.

16. *Newsweek,* xxxi (March 8, 1948), 24; *Time,* li (March 8, 1948), 30; Matt Connelly to David Niles, February 18, 1948, Truman Papers, OF 204; Kirchwey to Truman, February 25, 1948, Truman Papers, OF 204; Kirchwey to McGrath, Feb. 25, 1948, J. Howard McGrath Papers, Truman Library, Box 63.

17. *Newsweek,* xxxi (March 1, 1948), 18; Dale Kramer, "Must It Be Truman?" *Nation,* clxvi (March 13, 1948), 295–96; *Time,* li (March 15, 1948), 26.

18. Redding, *Inside the Democratic Party,* p. 149; *Time,* li (March 15, 1948), 29; *Nation,* clxvi (March 20, 1948), 319.

19. John C. Campbell, *The United States in World Affairs, 1947–1948* (New York, 1948), pp. 488–92; Claire Sterling, *The Masaryk Case* (New York, 1970), pp. 341–49.

20. State Department, *Bulletin,* xviii (March 7, 1948), 304; *Time,* li (March 8, 1948), 19; *Newsweek,* xxxi (March 8, 1948), 17, 27.

21. Millis and Duffield, eds. *Forrestal Diaries,* p. 387; Lucius Clay, *Decision in Germany* (Garden City, N.Y., 1950), p. 354; *Time,* li (March 22, 1948), 19; *Newsweek,* xxxi (March 22, 1948), 23–24; State Department, *Bulletin,* xviii (March 21, 1948), 374–75, 381.

22. *Time,* li (March 8, 1948), 21–22; *Newsweek,* xxxi (March 15, 1948), 19; *ibid.* (March 22, 1948), 23.

23. Ross, *Loneliest Campaign,* p. 155; *Time,* li (March 29, 1948), 26; Curtis D. MacDougall, *Gideon's Army,* 3 vols. (New York, 1965), ii, 333–35.

24. *Public Papers of Presidents: Truman, 1948,* p. 179; Millis and Duffield, eds., *Forrestal Diaries,* pp. 394–95; William Hillman, *Mr. President* (New York, 1952), p. 52.

25. *Newsweek,* xxxi (March 29, 1948), 15; *Public Papers of Presidents: Truman, 1948,* pp. 183–86.

26. *Ibid.,* p. 186; Freda Kirchwey, "The President's Message," *Nation,* clxvi (March 27, 1948), 341; *Time,* li (March 29, 1948), 21; *Newsweek,* xxxi (March 29, 1948), 16; William Batt to Clifford, March 18, 1948, Clifford Papers, Box 20.

27. *Public Papers of the Presidents: Truman, 1948,* pp. 186–90; Hillman, *Mr. President,* p. 135.

28. *Newsweek,* xxxi (April 12, 1948), 32; *Time,* li (April 12, 1948), 19; *New York Times,* June 20, 1948; James A. Wechsler, *The Age of Suspicion* (New York, 1953), pp. 222–24; Schmidt, *Wallace,* pp. 73–74.

29. Clifford to Truman, March 6 and 8, 1948, Clifford Papers, Box 13; Forrestal to the Joint Chiefs of Staff, March 18, 1948, James Forrestal Papers, Princeton University Library, Box 94; Truman, *Memoirs,* II, 162.

30. Truman to M. J. Slonim, March 6, 1948, Truman Papers, OF 204; Eddie Jacobson to Josef Cohn, March 30, 1952, Truman Library; Daniels, *Man of Independence,* p. 318; Truman, *Memoirs,* II, 160–61.

31. State Department, *Bulletin,* XVIII (March 28, 1948), 407; *Newsweek,* XXXI (March 29, 1948), 26.

32. Leahy diary, March 20, 1948, William D. Leahy Papers, Library of Congress, Box 13; Daniels, *Man of Independence,* pp. 318–19; undated, handwritten memorandum, Clifford Papers, Box 13.

33. State Department, *Bulletin,* XVIII (March 28, 1948), 408; *Nation,* CLXVI (April 3, 1948), 365.

34. William Batt to McGrath, March 23, 1948, McGrath Papers, Box 63; Lester Hunt to Truman, March 23, 1948, Truman Papers, OF 204; memorandum of conference on Palestine by Clifford, March 24, 1948, Clifford Papers, Box 13.

35. *Public Papers of Presidents: Truman, 1948,* pp. 190–92.

36. *Time,* LI (April 5, 1948), 34; Jacobson to Cohn, March 30, 1952, Truman Library.

37. Baruch to Austin, April 5, 1948, Baruch Papers, Box 78; Ross, *Loneliest Campaign,* p. 72; Daniels, *Man of Independence,* p. 319; *Time,* LI (March 29, 1948), 22–23; *ibid.* (April 5, 1948), 19.

38. *Newsweek,* XXXI (May 3, 1948), 19.

39. H. Bradford Westerfield, *Foreign Policy and Party Politics: Pearl Harbor to Korea* (New Haven, 1955), pp. 297–98; Arthur Vandenberg, Jr., and Joe Alex Morris, eds., *The Private Papers of Senator Vandenberg* (Boston, 1952), pp. 311–12.

40. Henry W. Berger, "Senator Robert A. Taft Dissents from Military Escalation," in Thomas G. Paterson, ed., *Cold War Critics: Alternatives to American Foreign Policy in the Truman Years* (Chicago, 1971), pp. 180–82; *Newsweek,* XXXI (March 22, 1948), 23, 30; *Vital Speeches,* XIV (March 1, 1948), 294; *ibid.* (April 15, 1948), 391–94.

41. Forrestal to Robert Lovett, April 1, 1948, Forrestal Papers, Box 80; Mrs. Charles L. Stevenson to Vandenberg, March 31, 1948, and Vandenberg to Mrs. Stevenson, April 5, 1948, Vandenberg Papers.

42. *Public Opinion Quarterly,* XII (Spring 1948), 166; Cabell Phillips,

The Truman Presidency: The History of a Triumphant Succession
(New York, 1966), pp. 196–97; Arthur Krock, *Memoirs: Sixty
Years on the Firing Line* (New York, 1968), p. 243; C. L. Sulzberger, *A Long Row of Candles: Memoirs and Diaries,
1934–1954* (New York, 1969), p. 684.

43. Merlo J. Pusey, *Eisenhower the President* (New York, 1956), pp.
4–6; Millis and Duffield, eds., *Forrestal Diaries*, pp. 365–66;
Time, LI (February 2, 1948), 9.

44. Vandenberg diary, December 21, 1944, Vandenberg Papers; Robert G. Spivack, "Tactics of a Scared Candidate," *Nation*, CLXVI
(May 8, 1948), 498; *Time*, LI (January 19, 1948), 20; *ibid*. (February 23, 1948), 23; *ibid*. (March 22, 1948), 21.

45. *Newsweek*, XXXI (April 19, 1948), 27–28; Dale Kramer, "Progress
of a Prodigy," *New Republic*, CXVIII (April 19, 1948), 15; *Time*,
LI (April 26, 1948), 22–23.

46. Richard L. Neuberger, "Stassen vs. Dewey—Second Round," *Nation*, CLXVI (May 22, 1948), 567–68; *New York Times*, May 6
and 23, 1948; *Newsweek*, XXXI (May 31, 1948), 21–23; *Time*, LI
(May 31, 1948), 13.

47. Root to Vandenberg, April 23, 1948, and Lewis to Vandenberg,
May 2, 1948, Vandenberg Papers; *Time*, LI (May 24, 1948), 25.

48. Truman, *Memoirs*, II, 244–47; Westerfield, *Foreign Policy*, pp.
292–93; *Time*, LI (May 24, 1948), 24; *Congressional Record*,
June 11, 1948, pp. 7791–92, 7808–12, 7846; *New York Times*,
June 12, 1948; *Time*, LI (June 21, 1948), 19; *Newsweek*, XXXI
(June 21, 1948), 27.

49. *Newsweek*, XXXI (April 5, 1948), 19; Millis and Duffield, eds.,
Forrestal Diaries, pp. 404–405; Brock, *ADA*, pp. 90–92; *Nation*,
CLXVI (April 3, 1948), 367–68; *Time*, LI (April 5, 1948), 22–23;
New Republic, CXVIII (April 12, 1948), 5.

50. Brock, *ADA*, p. 91; *Time*, LI (April 19, 1948), 24; *Newsweek*,
XXXI (April 5, 1948), 19.

51. Truman, *Memoirs*, II, 185–87; *Newsweek*, XXXI (April 19, 1948),
31.

52. *Public Papers of Presidents: Truman, 1948*, p. 194; Krock, *Memoirs*, p. 241.

53. Daniels, *Man of Independence*, p. 348; Hillman, *Mr. President*, p.
135; David E. Lilienthal, *The Journals of David E. Lilienthal*, 4
vols. (New York, 1964–1970), II, 317; *New York Times*, May 9,
1948; *Time*, LI (May 3, 1948), 17–18.

54. State Department, *Bulletin*, XVIII (May 2, 1948), 572; *Newsweek*,

xxxi (May 3, 1948), 28; *ibid.* (May 10, 1948), 31–32; memorandum of conversation with Rusk by Clifford, May 8, 1948, Clifford Papers, Box 13.

55. Joseph Lawrence to McGrath, April 17, 1948, McGrath Papers, Box 63; Holifield to Truman, May 7, 1940, Truman Papers, OF 204; Arvey to Truman, May 12, 1948, Truman Papers, OF 204–D.

56. Handwritten memo by Clifford, May 4, 1948, Clifford Papers, Box 13; unsigned typed memorandum, May 9, 1948, Clifford Papers, Box 13; oral memoir by Kenneth M. Birkhead, Truman Library.

57. Daniels, *Man of Independence,* p. 319.

58. Weizmann to Truman, May 13, 1948, Truman Papers, OF 204–D; Daniels, *Man of Independence,* p. 320; Robert H. Ferrell, *George C. Marshall* (New York, 1966), p. 191; Truman, *Memoirs,* ii, 164; Eliahu Epstein to Moshe Shertok, May 14, 1948, Truman Papers, microfilm from Weizmann Archives in Israel, Box 1; Epstein to Truman, May 14, 1948, Truman Library, OF 204–D; *Public Papers of Presidents: Truman, 1948,* p. 258.

59. Jacobson to Truman, May 14, 1948, Truman Library, OF 204–D; Freda Kirchwey, "America and Israel," *Nation,* clxvi (May 22, 1948), 565; *New York Times,* May 15 and 16, 1948; *Time,* li (May 24, 1948), 24; *Newsweek,* xxxi (May 24, 1948), 21; Leahy diary, May 1948, Leahy Papers, Box 13; Forrestal to Baldwin, June 16, 1948, Forrestal Papers, Box 78; Byrnes to Baruch, May 24, 1948, Baruch Papers, Box 78.

60. *New York Times,* May 26, 1948; *Public Papers of Presidents: Truman, 1948,* pp. 279–81; *Time,* li (June 14, 1948), 30; Ferrell, *Marshall,* pp. 198–99.

61. *Public Opinion Quarterly,* xii (Spring 1948), 159; *ibid.* (Summer 1948), 354; *ibid.* (Fall 1948), 557, 559; Batt to Clifford, May 8, 1948, Clifford Papers, Box 20.

62. George F. Kennan, *Memoirs: 1925–1950* (Boston, 1967), p. 346; Millis and Duffield, eds., *Forrestal Diaries,* p. 424; Walter Bedell Smith, *My Three Years in Moscow* (Philadelphia, 1950), p. 158.

63. *Ibid.,* pp. 159–66; State Department, *Bulletin,* xviii (May 23, 1948), 679–82.

64. *New York Times,* May 11 and 12, 1948; *Time,* li (May 24, 1948), 23–24; *Newsweek,* xxxi (May 24, 1948), 21–22; Kennan, *Memoirs,* p. 347.

65. *Public Papers of Presidents: Truman, 1948*, p. 252; State Department, *Bulletin*, XVIII (May 23, 1948), 683–86.
66. *New Republic*, CXVIII (May 24, 1948), 6–7; *Nation*, CLXVI (May 29, 1948), 592–93; *New York Times*, May 13 and 16, 1948; Millis and Duffield, eds., *Forrestal Diaries*, p. 443; Kennan, *Memoirs*, p. 347.
67. *Time*, LI (April 19, 1948), 25; *ibid.* (May 10, 1948), 23–24; Wechsler, *Age of Suspicion*, p. 219.
68. MacDougall, *Gideon's Army*, II, 352–54; *New York Times*, May 12 and 18, 1948.
69. *New York Times*, May 18, 1948; State Department, *Bulletin*, XVIII (May 30, 1948), 705; *ibid.* (June 6, 1948), 744–46.
70. *Time*, LI (May 31, 1948), 16; MacDougall, *Gideon's Army*, II, 354; Schmidt, *Wallace*, p. 78; *Newsweek*, XXXI (May 31, 1948), 19; *New York Times*, May 10, 1948.
71. Truman, *Memoirs*, II, 178–79; *Newsweek*, XXXI (June 7, 1948), 19; *ibid.* (June 14, 1948), 23–24.
72. Norman Grieser, "Presidential Sales Trip," *New Republic*, CXVIII (June 21, 1948), 19–20; Phillips, *Truman Presidency*, pp. 214–15; *Public Papers of Presidents: Truman, 1948*, p. 329; Ross, *Loneliest Campaign*, p. 83.
73. Nizer to Clifford, June 5, 1948, Bohlen to Clifford, June 7, 1948, and Elsey to Clifford, June 11, 1948, Clifford Papers, Box 33; Kennan draft speech, undated, Elsey to Clifford, May 29, 1948, Bohlen draft speech, June 2, 1948, and Clifford to Elsey, June 11, 1948, George M. Elsey Papers, Truman Library, Box 7.
74. *Public Papers of Presidents: Truman, 1948*, pp. 336–40.
75. *New York Times*, June 13, 1948; *Newsweek*, XXXI (June 21, 1948), 24; *Time*, LI (June 21, 1948), 24.
76. *Ibid.*, 24; *Public Papers of Presidents; Truman, 1948*, pp. 357–78.
77. *Newsweek*, XXXI (June 28, 1948), 17; *Time*, LI (June 28, 1948), 13–14; *New York Times*, June 20, 1948; *Nation*, CLXVI (June 19, 1948), 673; *New Republic*, CXVIII (June 28, 1948), 4.
78. *Newsweek*, XXXI (June 7, 1948), 20; *ibid.* (June 28, 1948), 18.

Chapter 6

1. *Newsweek*, XXXI (June 7, 1948), 14; Robert Bendiner, "Putting Douglas on Ice," *Nation*, CLXVI (June 12, 1948), 650.
2. *New York Times*, June 4, 6, 8, 10, 13, and 20, 1948; *Time*, LI (June 21, 1948), 19; *Newsweek*, XXXI (June 21, 1948), 27.

3. *New York Times,* June 16, 1948; *Newsweek,* XXXI (June 14, 1948), 23, 29; Arthur H. Vandenberg, Jr., and Joe Alex Morris, eds., *The Private Papers of Senator Vandenberg* (Boston, 1952), p. 435.

4. *Ibid.,* pp. 427–29; Vandenberg to Dulles, May 14, June 2, June 4, and June 9, 1948, Vandenberg Papers; Dulles draft platform, June 8, 1948, Vandenberg Papers; *New York Times,* June 22, 1948.

5. Kirk H. Porter and Donald Bruce Johnson, eds., *National Party Platforms, 1840–1956* (Urbana, Ill., 1956), p. 453; David Niles to Matt Connelly, June 30, 1948, Samuel I. Rosenman Papers, Truman Library, Box 7.

6. Vandenberg to J. W. Kane, July 1, 1948, Vandenberg Papers; *New York Times,* June 23, 1948; *Time,* LI (June 28, 1948), 9–10; Irwin Ross, *The Loneliest Campaign: The Truman Victory of 1948* (New York, 1968), p. 97.

7. *New York Times,* June 22, 1948; Vandenberg to John Blodgett, July 6, 1948, Vandenberg Papers; *Newsweek,* XXXI (July 5, 1948), 16.

8. *New York Times,* June 27, 1948; Vandenberg to J. W. Kane, July 1, 1948, Vandenberg Papers; *Newsweek,* XXXI (July 5, 1948), 20, 26; *Time,* LI (July 5, 1948), 13; William Hillman, *Mr. President* (New York, 1952), p. 219.

9. *New York Times,* June 8, 17, 19, 20, 22, 23, 24, and 26, 1948; State Department, *Bulletin,* XVIII (June 20, 1948), 807–9; *ibid.* (June 27, 1948), 835–37.

10. *Newsweek,* XXXII (July 5, 1948), 30; Walter Millis and E. S. Duffield, eds., *The Forrestal Diaries* (New York, 1951), pp. 452–55; Leahy diary, June 29, 1948, Leahy Papers, Box 13; *New York Times,* July 1 and 2, 1948.

11. Vandenberg, *Secret Papers,* p. 453; *New York Times,* July 7 and 10, 1948; *Newsweek,* XXXII (July 19, 1948), 25; State Department, *Bulletin,* XIX (July 18, 1948), 85; *New Republic,* CXIX (July 19, 1948), 3.

12. *New York Times,* July 3, 6, and 10, 1948; Henderson to Baruch, undated, Baruch Papers, Box 79; Robert Staver to Pepper, undated, Pepper Papers, Box 109; Joseph Davies journal, May 17, 1948, Davies Papers, Box 25; Arthur Krock, *Memoirs: Sixty Years on the Firing Line* (New York, 1968), p. 243; Eisenhower to Pepper, July 8, 1948, Eisenhower Pre-Presidential Papers, Dwight D. Eisenhower Library, Box 85.

13. *Nation,* CLXVII (July 10, 1948), 34–36; *Newsweek,* XXXII (July 19, 1948), 15–17; *New York Times,* July 10, 1948.

14. *Ibid.,* July 10, 11, 12, 13, 14, and 15, 1948; State Department draft plank, undated, Clifford Papers, Box 20; Clifford draft plank, undated, Elsey Papers, Box 9; *Nation,* CLXVII (July 24, 1948), 85; Porter and Johnson, eds., *National Party Platforms,* pp. 430–36.

15. *Time,* LII (July 26, 1948), 12–14; Robert Bendiner, "Rout of the Bourbons," *Nation,* CLXVII (July 24, 1948), 91–93.

16. *Public Papers of Presidents: Truman, 1948,* pp. 406–10; *Newsweek,* XXXII (July 26, 1948); William Batt to Clifford, July 15, 1948, Clifford Papers, Box 20.

17. *New York Times,* July 24, 1948; Henry A. Wallace, "Farewell and Hail!" *New Republic,* CXIX (July 19, 1948), 14–18.

18. Porter and Johnson, eds., *National Party Platforms,* pp. 436–40; Karl M. Schmidt, *Henry A. Wallace: Quixotic Crusade, 1948* (Syracuse, N.Y., 1960), pp. 189–96; *Time,* LII (August 2, 1948), 12–13; Curtis D. MacDougall, *Gideon's Army* (New York, 1965), II, 571–76.

19. *New York Times,* July 25, 1948; *Vital Speeches,* XIV (August 1, 1948), 620–22.

20. *Nation,* CLXVII (July 31, 1948), 113; *New York Times,* July 26 and August 3, 1948; Ross, *Loneliest Campaign,* p. 161; Schmidt, *Wallace,* pp. 196–97.

21. *New York Times,* July 15, 16, and 18, 1948; *U.S. News and World Report,* XXV (July 30, 1948), 13–14; *Newsweek,* XXXII (July 19, 1948), 22; *ibid.* (July 26, 1948), 32.

22. *Ibid.* (July 26, 1948), 30; *Nation,* CLXVII (July 31, 1948), 116; David E. Lilienthal, *The Journals of David E. Lilienthal,* 4 vols. (New York, 1964–1970), II, 386, 388; Lucius Clay, *Decision in Germany* (Garden City, N.Y., 1950), p. 374; *New York Times,* July 18, 1948.

23. Hillman, *Mr. President,* p. 140; Millis and Duffield, eds., *Forrestal Diaries,* pp. 459–60; *U.S. News and World Report,* XXV (July 30, 1948), 64; Vandenberg to Lovett, July 19, 1948, Vandenberg Papers; Robert Murphy, *Diplomat Among Warriors* (Garden City, N.Y., 1964), p. 316; Clay, *Decision in Germany,* p. 368; Harry S Truman, *Memoirs,* 2 vols. (Garden City, N.Y., 1956), II, 123–24; *Public Papers of Presidents: Truman, 1948,* p. 412; *New York Times,* July 24, 1948.

24. *Ibid.*, June 26 and July 2, 1948; *Time,* LII (July 12, 1948), 14.

25. Vandenberg, *Private Papers,* pp. 446–47; Vandenberg to Dulles, July 2, 1948, Vandenberg Papers; John Foster Dulles, *War or Peace* (New York, 1950), pp. 130–31.

26. *New York Times,* July 8, 22, 23, and 24, 1948.

27. *Ibid.*, July 25, 1948; *Time,* LII (July 25, 1948), 9–10.

28. *New York Times,* July 25, 1948; *Newsweek,* XXXII (August 2, 1948), 26.

29. *Public Opinion Quarterly,* XII (Fall 1948), 558.

30. Schmidt, *Wallace,* p. 78; Jules Abels, *Out of the Jaws of Victory* (New York, 1959), pp. 153–55.

31. *New York Times,* August 8, 1948; Vandenberg to Dulles, August 9, and Dulles to Vandenberg, August 10, 1948, Vandenberg Papers.

32. *New York Times,* August 15 and September 5, 1948.

33. *Newsweek,* XXXII (August 30, 1948), 17; L. H. Pasqualicchio to McGrath, August 3, 1948, McGrath Papers, Box 65; McGrath to Truman, August 11, 1948, McGrath Papers, Box 62; oral memoir by Edward Corsi, Dulles Oral History Project; *New York Times,* August 18, 1948.

34. Luigi Criscuolo to McGrath, August 19, 1948, McGrath Papers, Box 62; Jack Redding, *Inside the Democratic Party* (Indianapolis, 1958), pp. 216–18; *New York Times,* August 19, 1948; *Public Papers of Presidents: Truman, 1948,* p. 178.

35. *New York Times,* August 20 and 21, 1948; Dulles to Vandenberg, August 20, and Vandenberg to Dulles, August 21, 1948, Vandenberg Papers.

36. *New York Times,* September 15, 1948; memorandum of conversation with Lovett by Dulles, August 20, 1948, Vandenberg Papers; Vandenberg to Scott, August 31, and Vandenberg to Dulles, August 21, 1948, Vandenberg Papers.

37. Walter Bedell Smith, *My Three Years in Moscow* (Philadelphia, 1950), pp. 242–45.

38. *New York Times,* August 6, 24, and 26, 1948; *Newsweek,* XXXII (September 20, 1948), 26; Smith, *Three Years in Moscow,* pp. 248–51.

39. Memorandum by Batt, August 30, 1948, and undated speech draft, Elsey Papers, Box 18.

40. *New York Times,* September 1, 4, 5, 8, and 10, 1948; Millis and Duffield, eds., *Forrestal Diaries,* pp. 480–81.

41. *Time,* LII (September 20, 1948), 23; Millis and Duffield, eds., *Forrestal Diaries,* pp. 483–84; *New York Times,* September 9 and 10, 1948; Truman, *Memoirs,* II, 128.
42. *New York Times,* September 11, 1948.
43. Millis and Duffield, eds., *Forrestal Diaries,* p. 486; Lilienthal, *Journals,* II, 406; Hillman, *Mr. President,* p. 141.

Chapter 7

1. *New York Times,* July 18, 1948; Kirk H. Porter and Donald Bruce Johnson, eds., *National Party Platforms, 1840–1956* (Urbana, Ill., 1956), pp. 466–68.
2. Cabell Phillips, *The Truman Presidency: The History of a Triumphant Succession* (New York, 1966), pp. 227–28; *Public Papers of Presidents: Truman, 1948,* pp. 432–33; Frank McNaughton to Don Bermingham, August 7, 1948, Frank McNaughton Papers, Truman Library, Box 14; *Newsweek,* XXXII (August 30, 1948), 15.
3. *Public Opinion Quarterly,* XII (Winter 1948–49), 767; *Time,* LII (September 13, 1948), 21.
4. Phillips, *Truman Presidency,* pp. 228–29; *New York Times,* August 1, 1948; *Newsweek,* XXXII (September 6, 1948), 9; David Lloyd to Wayne Grover, September 30, 1957, David D. Lloyd Papers, Truman Library, Box 25.
5. Harry S Truman, *Memoirs,* 2 vols. (Garden City, N.Y., 1956), II, 209; Clifford to Truman, August 17, 1948, Clifford Papers, Box 21.
6. *Newsweek,* XXXII (September 27, 1948), 17–18; *Public Papers of Presidents: Truman, 1948,* pp. 503, 542–43, 559; A. Z. Carr to Matthew Connelly, undated, Clifford Papers, Box 34.
7. Jack Redding, *Inside the Democratic Party* (Indianapolis, 1958), pp. 270–73; David E. Lilienthal, *The Journals of David E. Lilienthal,* 4 vols. (New York, 1964–1970), II, 413; *Newsweek,* XXXII (October 4, 1948), 21–22; *Public Papers of Presidents: Truman, 1948,* pp. 578–79.
8. Chip Bohlen to Robert Lovett, September 13, 1948, Clifford Papers, Box 34; *Public Papers of Presidents: Truman, 1948,* p. 610.
9. *New York Times,* October 3, 1948; *Time,* LII (September 6, 1948), 14; *ibid.* (September 27, 1948), 19.
10. *Newsweek,* XXXII (September 6, 1948), 26; State Department, *Bul-*

letin, XIX (September 12, 1948), 330; *New York Times,* September 20 and 24, 1948.

11. *Ibid.,* September 25 and 27, 1948; Dulles to Dewey, September 22 and 24, 1948, John Foster Dulles Papers, Princeton University Library, Box 141.

12. *New York Times,* September 27, 28, and 30, 1948.

13. *Newsweek,* XXXII (October 4, 1948), 26; *Time,* LII (October 4, 1948), 28–29; Eisenhower to Forrestal, September 27, 1948, Forrestal Papers, Box 79.

14. Irwin Ross, *The Loneliest Campaign: The Truman Victory of 1948* (New York, 1968), pp. 167–68; Jules Abels, *Out of the Jaws of Victory* (New York, 1959), pp. 160–62; oral memoir of Gabriel Hauge, Dulles Oral History Project.

15. Ross, *Loneliest Campaign,* p. 170; oral memoirs of Gabriel Hauge and Allen Dulles, Dulles Oral History Project; Albert Bender to Bernard Yarrow, September 21, 1948, Dulles Papers, Box 141.

16. Frank McNaughton to Don Bermingham, September 19, 1948, McNaughton Papers, Box 14; *Newsweek,* XXXII (October 4, 1948), 19; Raymond Moley, *27 Masters of Politics* (New York, 1949), pp. 58–64.

17. *Vital Speeches,* XIV (October 1, 1948), 741; *New York Times,* September 21, 23, 25, and 26, 1948; *Time,* LII (October 4, 1948), 20–21.

18. Frank McNaughton to David Halburd, September 30, 1948, McNaughton Papers, Box 14; *New York Times,* September 28, 29, and 30, 1948; Abels, *Jaws of Victory,* p. 188.

19. *New York Times,* October 1, 1948; Ross, *Loneliest Campaign,* pp. 206–7; Frank McNaughton to Don Bermingham, October 1, 1948, McNaughton Papers, Box 14; *Newsweek,* XXXII (October 11, 1948), 26–27, 35; *Time,* LII (October 11, 1948), 21–22.

20. William C. Bullitt, "How We Won the War and Lost the Peace," *Life,* XXV (August 30, 1948), 93–94; *ibid.* (September 6, 1948), 86, 100, 103; *Time,* LII (September 13, 1948), 25–26.

21. *New York Times,* September 8, 23, 26, and October 7, 1948; *Nation,* CLXVII (August 28, 1948), 220.

22. Vandenberg to Herbert Brownell, September 23, 1948, Vandenberg Papers; *New York Times,* October 5, 1948; Arthur Vandenberg, Jr., and Joe Alex Morris, eds., *The Private Papers of Senator Vandenberg* (Boston, 1952), pp. 450–52.

23. *New York Times,* October 6, 1948; Frank McNaughton memorandum, October 6, 1948, McNaughton Papers, Box 14.

24. *New York Times,* October 3, 4, and 6, 1948; *Life,* xxv (October 11, 1948), 36.
25. *Newsweek,* xxxii (October 11, 1948), 20; *Time,* lii (October 18, 1948), 25; *New York Times,* September 30, 1948.
26. *New York Times,* August 22, 1948; Karl M. Schmidt, *Henry A. Wallace: Quixotic Crusade, 1948* (Syracuse, N.Y., 1960), pp. 203–4; *Nation,* clxvii (September 4, 1948), 247–48; *Time,* lii (September 6, 1948), 19; *ibid.* (September 20, 1948), 27.
27. *New York Times,* September 18, 25, 27, 29, 30, and October 5, 1948.
28. *New Republic,* cxix (September 27, 1948), 32; *Vital Speeches,* xiv (October 1, 1948), 748–49; *Newsweek,* xxxii (September 13, 1948), 15; Schmidt, *Wallace,* pp. 221–23; Ross, *Loneliest Campaign,* pp. 227–28.
29. John C. Campbell, *The United States in World Affairs, 1948–1949* (New York, 1949), pp. 388–89; Eliahu Epstein to Robert Lovett, August 3, 1948, Clifford Papers, Box 13; Humphrey to Truman, August 6, 1948, and Murray to Truman, September 10, 1948, Truman Papers, OF 204–D; Celler to Truman, September 13, 1948, Truman Papers, OF 222–C; *New York Times,* August 11 and 28, 1948.
30. Weizmann to Truman, September 6, 1948, Truman Papers, OF 204–D; Crum to Clifford, September 7, 1948, and draft memorandum from Truman to Marshall, September 11, 1948, Clifford Papers, Box 13; McGrath to Truman, September 17, 1948, McGrath Papers, Box 65.
31. *New York Times,* September 18, 21, 23, 26, and October 4, 1948; I. F. Stone, "Secretary Marshall's Blunder," *New Republic,* cxix (October 18, 1948), 18–19.
32. Truman, *Memoirs,* ii, 166; unsigned handwritten memorandum, undated, Clifford Papers, Box 13; Lovett to Clifford, September 21, 1948, Clifford Papers, Box 14; State Department, *Bulletin,* xix (October 3, 1948), 436; *New York Times,* September 23, 1948; Freda Kirchwey, "Will Murder Pay Off?" *Nation,* clxvii (October 2, 1948), 360–61; McGrath to Harry Fisher, September 28, 1948, McGrath Papers, Box 65.
33. Eleanor Roosevelt to Baruch, October 14, 1948, Baruch Papers, Box 81; Dulles to Dewey, September 26 and 27, 1948, and Allen Dulles to J. F. Dulles, September 28, 1948, Dulles Papers, Box 141.
34. Donald Dawson to Clifford, undated, Clifford Papers, Box 14;

Bowles to Clifford, September 23, 1948, and Max Siskind to William Boyle, September 23, 1948, Clifford Papers, Box 14; Weizmann to Jacobson, September 27, 1948, Truman Papers, OF 204–D; draft message from Truman to Marshall, September 29, 1948, Clifford Papers, Box 13; Truman, *Memoirs*, II, 166.

35. *Ibid.*, II, 167; *New York Times*, September 30, 1948; Charles Murphy to Clifford, undated, Clifford Papers, Box 36; Clifford to Murphy, September 28, 1948, Clifford Papers, Box 13; *Public Papers of Presidents: Truman, 1948*, p. 223.

36. Albert Z. Carr, *Truman, Stalin and Peace* (Garden City, N.Y., 1950), pp. 106–18; Jonathan Daniels, *The Man of Independence* (Philadelphia, 1950), p. 361; Truman, *Memoirs*, II, 212–16; *New York Times*, October 6, 1948).

37. Jerry Hess oral memoir, Truman Library; draft speech, October 5, 1948, Charles Murphy Papers, Truman Library, Box 4.

38. Tom Connally and Alfred Steinberg, *My Name Is Tom Connally* (New York, 1954), p. 331; Vandenberg, *Private Papers*, pp. 457–58.

39. *Public Papers of Presidents: Truman, 1948*, pp. 679, 689, 698, 700; *Newsweek*, XXXII (October 18, 1948), 33; *New York Times*, October 9, 1948.

40. *Time*, LII (October 18, 1948), 24; *Public Papers of Presidents: Truman, 1948*, p. 724; State Department, *Bulletin*, XIX (October 17, 1948); *New York Times*, October 12, 1948.

41. *Life*, XXV (October 18, 1948), 42; *New York Herald Tribune*, October 12, 1948; *New York Times*, October 11 and 15, 1948; *Nation*, CLXVII (October 16, 1948), 413; *New Republic*, CXIX (October 18, 1948), 6.

42. Dulles to Dewey, October 10, 1948, Dulles Papers, Box 141; John Foster Dulles, *War or Peace* (New York, 1950), p. 135; *New York Times*, October 11, 1948; *New Republic*, CXIX (November 1, 1948), 3–4; Abels, *Jaws of Victory*, p. 203.

43. *New York Times*, October 12 and 17, 1948; *Newsweek*, XXXII (October 18, 1948), 32.

44. *Nation*, CLXVII (October 16, 1948), 413; Eleanor Roosevelt to Baruch, October 19, 1948, Baruch Papers, Box 81; Ross, *Loneliest Campaign*, p. 214; Curtis D. MacDougall, *Gideon's Army* (New York, 1965), III, 769.

45. *Public Papers of Presidents: Truman, 1948*, pp. 729, 730, 765–66, 771–72, 815–18.

46. *Newsweek*, XXXII (October 25, 1948), 27–28; *Time*, LII (October

25, 1948), 23–24; *ibid.* (November 1, 1948), 24; Ickes to Baruch, October 14, 1948, Baruch Papers, Box 79; Truman, *Memoirs,* II, 217–19.

47. *New Republic,* CXIX (October 25, 1948), 3; *New York Times,* October 13, 14, 16, 19, and 25, 1948.
48. *Newsweek,* XXXII (November 1, 1948), 19; *Time,* LII (October 25, 1948), 21–22; Knowland to Vandenberg, October 19, 1948, and Vandenberg to Knowland, October 21, 1948, Vandenberg Papers; *Public Opinion Quarterly,* XII (Winter 1948–49), 767, 771.
49. *New York Times,* October 17, 19, and 25, 1948; *Time,* LII (November 1, 1948), 37; *Newsweek,* XXXII (November 1, 1948), 33.
50. *New York Times,* October 18 and 20, 1948; Paul O'Dwyer to Truman, October 9, 1948, Truman Papers, OF 204–D; Niles memorandum, undated, Clifford Papers, Box 13; Niles to Clifford, October 21, 1948, and Truman to Marshall, October 17, 1948, Clifford Papers, Box 13.
51. *New York Times,* October 23, 1948; Allen Dulles to J. F. Dulles, October 22, 1948, Dulles Papers, Box 141.
52. Clifford to Truman, October 23, 1948, Clifford Papers, Box 13; *New York Times,* October 25, 1948.
53. *Public Papers of Presidents: Truman, 1948,* pp. 843–44.
54. Rabbi Silver to Truman, October 27, 1948, Truman Papers, OF 204; Rosenman to Truman, October 27, 1948, Clifford Papers, Box 36; Redding, *Inside the Democratic Party,* pp. 279–81; *Public Papers of Presidents: Truman, 1948,* p. 913.
55. *New York Times,* October 29, 30, and November 3, 1948; *Nation,* CLXVII (November 6, 1948), 511; *Time,* LII (November 8, 1948), 27.
56. *Newsweek,* XXXII (November 8, 1948), 21; *Time,* LII (November 1, 1948), 25; John Foster Dulles, *War or Peace* (New York, 1950), p. 134; Dulles to Dewey, October 21, 1948, Dulles Papers, Box 141.
57. *Time,* LII (October 25, 1948), 28; *Newsweek,* XXXII (November 1, 1948), 32–33; *New York Times,* October 22, 26, and 28, 1948.
58. Dewey to Dulles, October 22, 1948, Dulles to Dewey, October 22, 1948, Allen Dulles to J. F. Dulles, October 22, 1948; Dulles to Dewey, October 25, 1948, and Dulles to Dewey, October 30, 1948, Dulles Papers, Box 141.
59. *Public Opinion Quarterly,* XII (Winter 1948–49), 767; Ross, *Loneliest Campaign,* p. 240; *New York Times,* October 25, 1948; *Life,* XXV (November 1, 1948), 37; Millis and Duffield, eds., *Forrestal Diaries,* pp. 511–12.

60. *Newsweek,* XXXII (November 8, 1948), 23–24; Jay Franklin, "Inside Strategy of the Campaign," *Life,* XXV (November 15, 1948), 48; *Public Papers of Presidents: Truman, 1948,* pp. 848, 850, 859–60, 884–85.

61. *Ibid.,* pp. 925–30.

62. *New York Times,* October 27, 28, 29, and 31, 1948; H. Bradford Westerfield, *Foreign Policy and Party Politics: Pearl Harbor to Korea* (New Haven, 1955), pp. 322–23.

63. *Newsweek,* XXXII (November 1, 1948), 26; *New York Times,* October 27, 29, and November 1, 1948.

64. *Time,* LII (October 25, 1948), 30; *ibid.* (November 8, 1948), 32; *Newsweek,* XXXII (November 1, 1948), 34; *New York Times,* October 28, 30, 31, and November 1, 1948; *Life,* XXV (November 8, 1948), 35, 51.

65. *Newsweek,* XXXII (November 15, 1948), 23–24; *Time,* LII (November 8, 1948), 21–22; Leahy diary, November 5, 1948, Leahy Papers, Box 13.

66. Ross, *Loneliest Campaign,* p. 247.

67. *Time,* LII (November 15, 1948), 27; Westerfield, *Foreign Policy,* p. 315; Schmidt, *Wallace,* pp. 234–35; Samuel Lubell, *The Future of American Politics* (New York, 1952), p. 207.

68. *Time,* LII (November 8, 1948), 23–24; *Newsweek,* XXXII (November 8, 1948), 9.

69. *New York Times,* November 7, 1948; Helen Dinerman, "1948 Votes in the Making—A Preview," *Public Opinion Quarterly,* XII (Winter 1948–49), 585–98; Dulles to Dewey, November 3, 1948, Dulles Papers, Box 141; Vandenberg, *Private Papers,* p. 460; Abels, *Jaws of Victory,* p. 276; Millis and Duffield, eds., *Forrestal Diaries,* pp. 520, 535.

70. Truman, *Memoirs,* II, 169; Campbell, *U.S. in World Affairs, 1948–1949,* p. 401; *New York Times,* November 4 and 7, 1948; *New Republic,* CXIX (November 15, 1948), 10; *Newsweek,* XXXII (November 15, 1948), 43; *ibid.* (November 29, 1948), 20; *Public Papers of Presidents: Truman, 1948,* p. 944.

71. *New Republic,* CXIX (November 15, 1948), 6; *Time,* LII (November 15, 1948), 23–24; *Newsweek,* XXXII (November 8, 1948), 4–7; Ross, *Loneliest Campaign,* pp. 260–61.

72. Redding, *Inside the Democratic Party,* pp. 260–62; Samuel Lubell, "Who *Really* Elected Truman?" *Saturday Evening Post,* CCXXI (January 22, 1949), 15–17, 54–64; Lubell, *Future,* p. 134.

73. Abels, *Jaws of Victory,* p. 290, 301–2; Ross, *Loneliest Campaign,*

pp. 250–52; Forrestal to Herbert Bayard Swope, November 6, 1948, Forrestal Papers, Box 95; Richard S. Kirkendall, "Election of 1948," in Arthur M. Schlesinger, Jr., and Fred L. Israel, eds., *History of American Presidential Elections, 1789–1968,* 4 vols. (New York, 1971), 3143–44.

74. Phillips, *Truman Presidency,* p. 250.
75. Lawrence S. Wittner, *Rebels Against War: The American Peace Movement, 1941–1960* (New York, 1969), p. 198; Schmidt, *Wallace,* p. 251; Abels, *Jaws of Victory,* p. 195.

BIBLIOGRAPHY

Manuscript Collections

Baruch, Bernard M., Princeton University Library
Chapman, Oscar, Harry S. Truman Library
Clifford, Clark M., Harry S. Truman Library
Davies, Joseph E., Library of Congress
Dulles, John Foster, Princeton University Library
Eisenhower, Dwight D., Dwight D. Eisenhower Library
Elsey, George M., Harry S. Truman Library
Forrestal, James, Princeton University Library
Harriman, Florence, Library of Congress
Hopkins, Harry L., Franklin D. Roosevelt Library
Hull, Cordell, Library of Congress
Knox, Frank, Library of Congress
Leahy, William D., Library of Congress
Lloyd, David D., Harry S. Truman Library
Long, Breckinridge, Library of Congress
McGrath, J. Howard, Harry S. Truman Library
McNaughton, Frank, Harry S. Truman Library
Mitchell, Stephen A., Harry S. Truman Library
Murphy, Charles, Harry S. Truman Library
Pepper, Claude, Federal Records Center, Suitland, Maryland
Roosevelt, Franklin D., Franklin D. Roosevelt Library
Rosenman, Samuel I., Franklin D. Roosevelt Library
——————, Harry S. Truman Library

Truman, Harry S., Harry S. Truman Library
Vandenberg, Arthur H., William L. Clements Library, University of Michigan
Wagner, Robert, Georgetown University

Oral History Interviews

Dulles Oral History Collection, Princeton University Library

Edward Corsi	Henry Luce
Allen W. Dulles	William B. Macomber
Dwight D. Eisenhower	Thurston B. Morton
James C. Hagerty	Robert D. Murphy
Gabriel Hauge	Richard H. Rovere
Emmet John Hughes	Eustace Seligman

Truman Oral History Collection, Harry S. Truman Library

Kenneth M. Birkhead	Jerry Hess

Government Publications

Public Papers of the Presidents of the United States: Harry S. Truman. Eight volumes, Washington, 1961–1966.

U.S. Congress. *Congressional Record* (1940, 1944, 1948).

U.S. Department of State. *Bulletin* (1940–1948).

U.S. Department of State. *Documents on German Foreign Policy, 1918–1945.* Series D, Washington, 1956, IX, X, XI.

————. *Foreign Relations of the United States, 1940.* Washington, 1958, III.

————. *Foreign Relations of the United States, 1944.* Washington, 1965–66, III, IV.

————. *Foreign Relations of the United States: The Conferences at Cairo and Tehran, 1943.* Washington, 1961.

————. *Foreign Relations of the United States: The Conferences at Malta and Yalta, 1945.* Washington, 1945.

Newspapers and Periodicals

Atlantic Monthly (1944)
Catholic World (1940)
Christian Century (1940, 1944)
Commonweal (1940)
Life (1940–1948)

Nation (1940–1948)
New Republic (1940–1948)
Newsweek (1940–1948)
New York Times (1940–1948)
Public Opinion Quarterly (1940, 1948)
Saturday Evening Post (1940, 1948)
Time (1940–1948)
U.S. News and World Report (1948)
Vital Speeches (1940–1948)
Washington Post (1940)

Articles and Books

A. General

Ambrose, Stephen E. *Rise to Globalism: American Foreign Policy Since 1938.* Baltimore, 1971.

Campbell, Angus; Philip E. Converse; Warren E. Miller; and Donald E. Stokes. *The American Voter.* New York, 1960.

Campbell, Angus; Gerald Gurin; and Warren E. Miller. *The Voter Decides.* Evanston, Ill., 1954.

LaFeber, Walter. *America, Russia, and the Cold War, 1945–1971.* Second edition. New York, 1972.

Lilienthal, David E. *The Journals of David E. Lilienthal.* Four volumes. New York, 1964–1970.

Polsby, Nelson W., and **Aaron B. Wildavsky.** *Presidential Elections: Strategies of American Electoral Politics.* New York, 1964.

Porter, Kirk H., and **Donald Bruce Johnson, eds.** *National Party Platforms, 1840–1956.* Urbana, Ill., 1956.

Roseboom, Eugene H. *A History of Presidential Elections.* Third edition. New York, 1970.

Schlesinger, Arthur M., Jr., and **Fred L. Israel, eds.** *History of American Presidential Elections, 1789–1968.* Four volumes. New York, 1971.

Waltz, Kenneth N. "Electoral Punishment and Foreign Policy Crises." In James N. Rosenau, ed., *Domestic Sources of Foreign Policy.* New York, 1967.

B. Election of 1940

Barnard, Ellsworth. *Wendell Willkie: Fighter for Freedom.* Marquette, Mich., 1966.

Barnes, Joseph. *Willkie.* New York, 1952.

Beard, Charles A. *American Foreign Policy in the Making, 1932–1940.* New Haven, 1946.

Blum, John Morton. *From the Morgenthau Diaries: Years of Urgency, 1938–1941.* Boston, 1965.

Buell, Raymond Leslie. *Isolated America.* New York, 1940.

Burke, Robert E. "Election of 1940." In Arthur M. Schlesinger, Jr., and Fred L. Israel, *History of American Presidential Elections, 1789–1968.* Volume IV. New York, 1971.

Burns, James MacGregor. *Roosevelt: The Lion and the Fox.* New York, 1956.

Byrnes, James F. *All in One Lifetime.* New York, 1958.

Chadwin, Mark Lincoln. *The Hawks of World War II.* Chapel Hill, N.C., 1968.

Childs, Marquis W. *I Write from Washington.* New York, 1942.

Cohen, Warren I. *The American Revisionists: The Lessons of Intervention in World War I.* Chicago, 1966.

Cole, Wayne S. *America First: The Battle Against Intervention, 1940–1941.* Madison, Wis., 1953.

Democratic National Committee. *The Democratic Book of 1940.* N.p., 1940.

Dillon, Mary Earhart. *Wendell Willkie: 1892–1944.* Philadelphia, 1952.

Donahoe, Bernard F. *Private Plans and Public Dangers.* Notre Dame, Ind., 1965.

Evjen, Henry O. "The Willkie Campaign: An Unfortunate Chapter in Republican Leadership." *Journal of Politics,* xiv (May 1952), 241–56.

Farago, Ladislas. *The Game of the Foxes.* New York, 1972.

Farley, James A. *Jim Farley's Story: The Roosevelt Years.* New York, 1948.

Flynn, Edward J. *You're the Boss.* New York, 1947.

Flynn, John T. *Country Squire in the White House.* New York, 1940.

Freedman, Max, ed. *Roosevelt and Frankfurter: Their Correspondence, 1928–1945.* Boston, 1967.

Friedlander, Saul. *Prelude to Downfall: Hitler and the United States, 1939–1941.* New York, 1967.

Frye, Alton. *Nazi Germany and the American Hemisphere, 1933–1941.* New Haven, 1967.

The German White Paper. Foreword by C. Hartley Grattan. New York, 1940.

Gerson, Louis L. *The Hyphenate in Recent American Politics and Diplomacy.* Lawrence, Kans., 1964.

Gosnell, Harold F. *Champion Campaigner: Franklin D. Roosevelt.* New York, 1952.

Hooker, Nancy H., ed. *The Moffat Papers.* Cambridge, Mass., 1956.

Hull, Cordell. *The Memoirs of Cordell Hull.* Two volumes. New York, 1948.

Ickes, Harold L. *The Secret Diary of Harold L. Ickes.* Three volumes. New York, 1954.

Israel, Fred L., ed. *The War Diary of Breckinridge Long.* Lincoln, Neb., 1966.

Johnson, Donald Bruce. *The Republican Party and Wendell Willkie.* Urbana, Ill., 1960.

Johnson, Walter. *The Battle Against Isolation.* Chicago, 1944.

——. *William Allen White's America.* New York, 1947.

Krock, Arthur. *The Consent of the Governed and Other Deceits.* Boston, 1971.

——. *Memoirs: Sixty Years on the Firing Line.* New York, 1968.

Langer, William L., and Everett Gleason. *The Challenge to Isolation, 1937–1940.* New York, 1952.

——. *The Undeclared War, 1940–1941.* New York, 1953.

Lazarsfeld, Paul F.; Bernard Berelson; and Hazel Gaudet. *The People's Choice.* New York, 1944.

Leuchtenburg, William E. *Franklin D. Roosevelt and the New Deal, 1932–1940.* New York, 1963.

Lord, Russell. *The Wallaces of Iowa.* Boston, 1947.

McCoy, Donald. *Landon of Kansas.* Lincoln, Neb., 1966.

Martin, Joseph W., as told to Robert J. Donovan. *My First Fifty Years in Politics.* New York, 1960.

Matloff, Maurice, and Edwin M. Snell. *Strategic Planning for Coalition Warfare, 1941–1942.* Washington, 1953.

Michelson, Charles. *The Ghost Talks.* New York, 1944.

Moley, Raymond. *27 Masters of Politics.* New York, 1949.

Morison, Elting E. *Turmoil and Tradition: A Study of the Life and Times of Henry L. Stimson.* Boston, 1960.

Moscow, Warren. *Roosevelt and Willkie.* Englewood Cliffs, N.J., 1968.

Nevins, Allan. *Herbert H. Lehman and His Era.* New York, 1963.

Parmet, Herbert S., and Marie Hecht. *Never Again: A President Runs for a Third Term.* New York, 1968.

Perkins, Frances. *The Roosevelt I Knew*. New York, 1946.

Roosevelt, Eleanor. *This I Remember*. New York, 1949.

Roosevelt, Elliott, ed. *F.D.R.: His Personal Letters, 1928–1945*. Two volumes. New York, 1950.

Rosenman, Samuel. *Working with Roosevelt*. New York, 1952.

Rosenman, Samuel, ed. *The Public Papers and Addresses of Franklin D. Roosevelt*. Thirteen volumes. New York, 1938–1950.

Schapsmeier, Edward L. and **Frederick H.** *Henry A. Wallace of Iowa: The Agrarian Years, 1910–1940*. Ames, Ia., 1968.

Sherwood, Robert E. *Roosevelt and Hopkins: An Intimate History*. New York, 1948.

Stimson, Henry L. and **McGeorge Bundy.** *On Active Service in Peace and War*. New York, 1948.

Tugwell, Rexford G. *The Democratic Roosevelt*. Garden City, N.Y., 1957.

Tully, Grace. *F.D.R., My Boss*. New York, 1949.

Wallace, Henry A. *The American Choice*. New York, 1940.

Whalen, Richard J. *The Founding Father: The Story of Joseph P. Kennedy*. New York, 1964.

Wheeler, Burton K. and **Paul F. Healy.** *Yankee from the West*. Garden City, N.Y., 1962.

White, William Allen. "Thoughts After the Election." *Yale Review*, xx (Winter 1941), 217–27.

C. Election of 1944

Bruenn, Howard G., M.D. "Clinical Notes on the Illness and Death of President Franklin D. Roosevelt." *Annals of Internal Medicine*, LXXII (April 1970), 579–91.

Burns, James MacGregor. *Roosevelt: The Soldier of Freedom, 1940–1945*. New York, 1970.

Ciechanowski, Jan. *Defeat in Victory*. Garden City, N.Y., 1947.

Connally, Tom, and **Alfred Steinberg.** *My Name Is Tom Connally*. New York, 1954.

Divine, Robert A. *Second Chance: The Triumph of Internationalism in America During World War II*. New York, 1967.

Eden, Anthony. *The Reckoning*. Boston, 1965.

Friedman, Leon. "Election of 1944." In Arthur M. Schlesinger, Jr., and Fred L. Israel, eds., *History of American Presidential Elections, 1789–1968*. IV. New York, 1971.

Gerson, Louis L. *John Foster Dulles*. New York, 1967.

Hurewitz, J. C. *The Struggle for Palestine.* New York, 1950.

Johnson, Gerald W. "A Letter to the Honorable Thomas E. Dewey." *Atlantic Monthly,* CLXXIV (September 1944), 39–41.

Kogan, Norman. *Italy and the Allies.* Cambridge, Mass., 1956.

Lane, Arthur Bliss. *I Saw Poland Betrayed.* Indianapolis, 1948.

Manuel, Frank E. *The Realities of American-Palestine Relations.* Washington, 1949.

Mikolajczyk, Stanislaw. *The Rape of Poland: The Pattern of Soviet Aggression.* New York, 1948.

Notter, Harley A. *Postwar Foreign Policy Preparation, 1939–1945.* Washington, 1950.

Polenberg, Richard. *War and Society: The United States, 1941–1945.* Philadelphia, 1972.

Rozek, Edward J. *Allied Wartime Diplomacy: A Pattern in Poland.* New York, 1958.

Smith, Gaddis. *American Diplomacy During the Second World War, 1941–1945.* New York, 1965.

Stevens, Richard P. *American Zionism and U.S. Foreign Policy, 1942–1947.* New York, 1962.

Tompkins, C. David. *Senator Arthur H. Vandenberg: The Evolution of a Modern Republican, 1884–1945.* East Lansing, Mich., 1970.

Vandenberg, Arthur H., Jr., and **Joe Alex Morris, eds.** *The Private Papers of Senator Vandenberg.* Boston, 1952.

Willkie, Wendell. "Cowardice at Chicago." *Collier's,* CXIV (September 18, 1944), 11, 77–79.

D. Election of 1948

Abels, Jules. *Out of the Jaws of Victory.* New York, 1959.

Brock, Clifton. *Americans for Democratic Action: Its Role in National Politics.* Washington, 1962.

Campbell, John C. *The United States in World Affairs, 1947–1948.* New York, 1948.

———. *The United States in World Affairs, 1948–1949.* New York, 1949.

Carr, Albert Z. *Truman, Stalin and Peace.* Garden City, N.Y., 1950.

Clay, Lucius. *Decision in Germany.* Garden City, N.Y., 1950.

Daniels, Jonathan. *The Man of Independence.* Philadelphia, 1950.

Druks, Herbert. *Harry S Truman and the Russians, 1945–1953.* New York, 1966.

Dulles, John Foster. *War or Peace.* New York, 1950.

Feis, Herbert. *The Birth of Israel.* New York, 1969.

Ferrell, Robert H. *George C. Marshall.* New York, 1966.

Hamby, Alonzo L. "Henry A. Wallace, the Liberals, and Soviet-American Relations." *Review of Politics,* xxx (April 1968), 153–169.

Hillman, William. *Mr. President.* New York, 1952.

Kennan, George F. *Memoirs, 1925–1950.* Boston, 1967.

Kirkendall, Richard S. "Election of 1948." In Arthur M. Schlesinger, Jr., and Fred L. Israel, eds., *History of American Presidential Elections, 1789–1968.* iv. New York, 1971.

Lubell, Samuel. *The Future of American Politics.* New York, 1952.

MacDougall, Curtis D. *Gideon's Army.* Three volumes. New York, 1965.

Millis, Walter, and **E. S. Duffield, eds.** *The Forrestal Diaries.* New York, 1951.

Paterson, Thomas G., ed. *Cold War Critics: Alternatives to American Foreign Policy in the Truman Years.* Chicago, 1971.

Phillips, Cabell. *The Truman Presidency: The History of a Triumphant Succession.* New York, 1966.

Redding, Jack. *Inside the Democratic Party.* Indianapolis, 1958.

Ross, Irwin. *The Loneliest Campaign: The Truman Victory of 1948.* New York, 1968.

Schapsmeier, Edward L., and **Frederick H.** *Prophet in Politics: Henry A. Wallace and the War Years, 1940–1965.* Ames, Ia., 1970.

Schmidt, Karl M. *Henry A. Wallace: Quixotic Crusade, 1948.* Syracuse, N.Y., 1960.

Smith, Walter Bedell. *My Three Years in Moscow.* Philadelphia, 1950.

Sterling, Claire. *The Masaryk Case.* New York, 1970.

Truman, Harry S. *Memoirs.* Two volumes. Garden City, N.Y., 1956.

Wallace, Henry A. *Toward World Peace.* New York, 1948.

Wechsler, James A. *The Age of Suspicion.* New York, 1953.

Westerfield, H. Bradford. *Foreign Policy and Party Politics: Pearl Harbor to Korea.* New Haven, 1955.

Wittner, Lawrence S. *Rebels Against War: The American Peace Movement, 1941–1960.* New York, 1969.

INDEX

Chamberlain, Neville, 231
Chambers, Whittaker, 236
Chapman, Oscar, 237
Charlottesville, Va., FDR's stab-in-the-back speech, 23, 64
Chiang Kai-shek, 133, 134, 162, 223, 245, 270-271
Chicago: Willkie speeches in, 56, 67, 75; FDR's 1944 speech in, 158; Truman's 1948 speech in, 268; Dewey's 1948 speech in, 269; 1948 vote, 274
Chicago *Tribune*, 155, 158, 248, 256
Childs, Marquis, 36, 83, 88, 244
China: at Dumbarton Oaks, 121, 148; Dewey on, in 1948, 189, 223, 245, 270; Soviet expansion into, 189, 213; Wallace on, 220; as 1948 election issue, 220, 223, 242, 245, 270-271; Nationalist loss of North China and Manchuria, 270-271; reaction to Dewey's 1948 defeat in, 273
Christian Century, quoted, 62, 71
Church, Ralph E., 145
Churchill, Sir Winston, 44, 51, 52, 87, 119, 133, 134, 135, 159, 162; at Teheran Conference, 109, 139; and Polish question, 109, 138, 139; at Quebec Conference, 132-133, 144; at Moscow Conference (1944), 139
CIO (Congress of Industrial Organizations), 33, 72, 130
Cities. *See* Urban vote
Civil rights: Truman's program, and Southern Democratic revolt, 178, 194, 218; 1948 Democratic plank, 218, 235; Wallace as champion of, 248, 249, 272
Clapper, Raymond, 48
Clark, Bennett, 163
Clark, Grenville, 24, 44

Clay, General Lucius D., 180, 215, 222-223, 266
"Clear everything with Sidney," FDR misquoted, 130-131
Cleveland, campaign speeches in: Willkie (1940), 62-63; FDR (1940), 83; Dewey (1948), 269
Clifford, Clark M.: aide to Truman, 172, 183-184, 201, 206, 218, 237, 239; master plan for 1948 campaign, 172-173, 176, 182, 209, 221, 226, 237-238, 240, 274; and Palestine problem, 176, 184, 185, 186, 187, 197-198, 200, 250-251, 253, 264, 266
Cohen, Ben, 149, 198
Cold War, 167, 170, 171, 180-183, 194, 236 (*see also* Berlin crises); as election issue in 1948, 172, 174, 183, 200-205, 207-208, 219-221, 226, 237, 238; Palestine problem and, 186-188, 199-200; Republicans and, 188-189, 226; public apprehensions about, 200-201, 203, 208 (*see also* War scare); U.S. blamed for, by Wallace and Progressives, 219-221, 249-250; institutionalization of, 276
Collier's magazine, 246
Commission on a Just and Durable Peace, 92
Committee of Eight, on world organization, 101-103
Committee of Independent Republicans for Roosevelt, 150
Committee to Defend America by Aiding the Allies, 20, 36, 42
Commonweal (Catholic periodical), 72
Communism, Communists: issue in 1944, 131, 137; Soviet, aggressiveness of, 167, 179, 261, 269 (*see also* Soviet Union); world, containment of, (*see* Containment pol-

icy); Wallace Red-labeled, 171, 173, 183, 220-221, 249, 270, 272; in Chinese civil war, 223, 270-271, 273; election issue in 1948, 173, 183-184, 239, 261, 268, 269, 274; spies in government issue, 236, 239, 242, 244
Communist party (U.S.), 192; endorsement of Wallace by, 221
Congress, U.S. (*see also* House of Representatives; Senate): Republican gains in 1938 election, 3, 13; FDR's relations with (1939/40), 3, 4, 9; conservative coalition of Republicans and southern Democrats, 3, 4, 13, 94, 156; 1939 special session, 5; emergency defense appropriations of 1940, 9-10; and draft bill, 44, 58; by-passed in destroyers-for-bases deal, 45, 51-53; Republican gains in 1942 election, 94, 96, 127; efforts for world organization in, 92-94; 1943 tax bill passed over FDR veto, 94; FDR's relations with (1944), 94, 156; its approval sought for American draft plan for U.N., 101-103; investigations of Pearl Harbor, 147; war-making power of, and U.N. peace force, 148-149, 151, 152; Dewey's relations with, 156-157; Republican losses in 1944 election, 163; Republicans gain control of both houses (1946), 169, 188; special election in Bronx (1948), 174, 176; passage of European Recovery Plan, 180, 182, 183; Truman's address on Soviet threat in Europe, 181-182; Republican 80th, Truman's attacks on, 206, 208, 209, 219, 226, 237, 238, 246, 247, 272; special session of 1948, 219, 226, 236; Democrats capture control of (1948), 272

Connally, Tom, 92, 93, 94, 106, 108, 256; and Committee of Eight, 101-102, 103
Conscription. *See* Draft
Containment policy, 167-170, 201, 205, 239-240, 275-276 (*see also* Marshall Plan; Truman Doctrine); aim of, 201, 259-260; challenged by Wallace, 180, 219, 220, 248, 249, 257, 269-270; Republican support for, 188-189, 230, 240, 247, 249, 275; true national debate on its merits frustrated, 221, 276
Corsi, Edward, 228
Coughlin, Father Charles E., 51
Council of Foreign Ministers Conferences, 204, 229
Country Squire in the White House (Flynn), 11
Cox, Oscar, 155
Crawford, Kenneth, 5
Crossley poll, October 1948, 267-268
Crum, Bartley, 250
Curzon Line (Poland), 109, 111, 139, 140, 141-142
Curzon, Lord George, 109
Czechoslovakia, 159; 1948 Communist takeover in, 179-181, 192, 276

Daniels, Josephus, 133-134
Davenport, Russell, 18, 29, 42, 45, 46, 55, 56, 115, 150
Davies, James Rhodes, 72
Davies, Joseph, 141
Dayton, Ohio, 1940 FDR speech in, 63-65, 72
Debates: offered by Willkie, 48; declined by FDR, 49
Defense, Department of, and Palestine issue, 175, 184. *See also* Forrestal, James

178, 218, 235; Southern revolt within, 178, 188, 194, 195, 209, 216, 218, 235; possible Presidential contenders of 1948, 178, 216-217, 218; Eisenhower mentioned as 1948 Democratic possibility, 178, 190, 194-195, 216-217; dump-Truman movement, 194-195, 209, 216-217; accused of appeasement of Soviets, 189, 192, 223, 227, 246, 261, 269; Republican attacks on foreign policy of, 212-213, 223-224, 227, 246-247, 261; 1948 candidates, 218; election chances improved by Berlin crisis, 226, 272, 275-276; and Vinson episode, 258-259; late campaign resurgence in 1948, 260, 261-262, 266; 1948 election results, 271-272, 275; analysis of 1948 victory of, 274-276

Democrats for Willkie, 42, 72

Denmark, 1940 German occupation of, 7, 15, 19

Destroyers-for-bases deal, 44-46, 47, 51-54, 71, 78

Detroit, 1948 vote, 274

Dewey, Thomas E., 23, 25, 55, 92; background and early career of, 13-14; personality of, 14, 98, 243; as 1940 Republican contender, 13-16, 17, 26, 30; 1940 Gallup poll results on, 13, 15, 19, 26; 1940 foreign policy stand of, 14-15, 19, 26; in 1940 Wisconsin primary, 15, 17; war crisis as blow to chances of, 15-17; campaign effort for Willkie, 67; Governor of N.Y., 97; as 1944 Presidential candidate, 97-100, 117; 1944 poll results on, 97, 100, 126-127, 157-158; in 1944 Wisconsin primary, 97-98; foreign policy views in 1944, 100, 117; and 1944 foreign policy plank, 114; 1944 nomina-tion of, 117; acceptance speech, 117; "tired old men" charge against Democrats, 117, 119; his views on U.N. peace force, 117, 131, 150-151, 152; and Dumbar-ton Oaks Conference on U.N., 122, 148; bipartisan approach to international organization, 122-125, 131-132, 148, 153; his han-dling of Ball's challenge a mis-take, 149, 150-151, 152, 162; handicapped by specter of Har-ding, League of Nations defeat, isolationism, 124, 131, 133-134, 155-157, 160-161, 162; lack of experience charged to, 127, 134, 153; campaign style and tactics, 128-132; Louisville speech as en-dorsement of internationalism, 130-131; foreign policy issues soft-pedaled by, 131-132, 141, 145-146, 147, 150-152, 154; FDR's strongest opponent, 132, 161; Red-baiting speeches against FDR, 137; statements on Poland, 140-141, 154, 155; *Herald Tribune* forum speech of, 141, 150, 154-155; "secret diplomacy" charge against FDR, 141, 154-155; and Palestine issue (1944), 143, 144; bid for Italian vote, 144; avoid-ance of Pearl Harbor issue (se-cret of broken codes), 145-146, 147, 261; congressional relations of, 156; media support for, 156; 1944 campaign speech in New York City, 159-160; "vote for D. is vote for Hitler and Hirohito" innuendo, 161; votes received in 1944, 161; 1944 defeat analyzed, 161-163; and Palestine problem (1948), 177, 223, 252-254, 263-264, 265, 266; criticism of Tru-man's policy toward Soviets, 189,

192, 223-224, 261, 269; foreign policy statements in 1948, 189, 202, 211, 223-224, 227, 244-245, 258, 261, 263-264; and Chinese Communist advances, 189, 223, 245, 270; presidential candidate in 1948, 191-192, 194, 210, 213, 218; in 1948 Wisconsin primary, 191; 1948 nomination of, 213; 1948 acceptance speech of, 214, 263; stand on bipartisanship (1948), 223-224, 225-226, 227, 232, 241-242, 244, 245, 247-248, 261, 266, 270; and Berlin Blockade, 224-226, 232-234, 241, 242, 243, 244, 248, 266-267; and Italian colonies issue, 227-229, 230; 1948 polls on, 236, 239, 242, 248, 261-262, 267-268; 1948 campaign strategy, 242, 273; campaign advisors, 242; campaign tours and speeches, 242, 243-245, 258, 260-261; confidence of winning elections, as influence on his foreign policy stance, 241, 242-245, 248, 258, 266-267; isolationism and appeasement denounced by, 245, 261, 269; media support for, 248; reaction to Vinson episode, 258; breach of bipartisanship in Israel issue, 263-264, 265, 266; Truman's charges of dictatorship and isolationism against, 268-269; votes received in 1948, 271-272; reasons for his defeat, 272-273

Dewey Victory Special, 243

Dillon, Mary, 85

Dixiecrats, 235

Domestic issues: Congressional opposition to FDR policies, 3, 13, 94-95; Republican emphasis on, in 1940 campaign, 5, 13, 18, 57; in 1943, 94; Truman's attack on record of Republican 80th Congress, 206, 208, 209, 219, 226, 237, 238, 246, 272

Donovan, General William, 222

Douglas, William O., 32, 120, 178, 194, 217, 218

Draft, the: need for, 44, 47, 48; bill passed (1940), 58; draft calls of 1940, 59, 66, 68-69; peacetime, Truman's proposal for, 182, 183

Drummond, Roscoe, 135

Dubinsky, David, 232, 265

Duff, James, 192

Dulles, Allen, 242, 252, 264, 267, 273

Dulles, John Foster, 92, 276; as Dewey's foreign policy adviser, 92, 100, 114, 122, 156, 211-212, 214, 258, 267; agreement with Hull on bipartisanship, 122-125, 130, 148, 149, 153, 163; bipartisanship on U.N. continued by, 163-164; and bipartisanship in 1948, 219, 223, 225, 226-227, 228, 229-230, 232, 243, 247, 252, 266; and Berlin crisis, 223, 224-225, 232, 240-241, 243, 244, 247, 266; briefed by Democrats during 1948 campaign, 224, 227, 230; on American U.N. delegation, 227, 240, 252, 267; and Italian colonies issue, 228-230; on Truman's election, 273

Dumbarton Oaks Conference, 121-122, 124, 148, 163

Early, Stephen, 32, 104

Eastern Republicans as interventionists, 13, 154

Eden, Sir Anthony, 109

Edge, Walter, 28, 115

Edison, Charles, 21

Egypt, in 1948 Negev campaign, 262

Eisenhower, Dwight D., 126, 224, 242, 254; mentioned as Democratic candidate in 1948, 178, 190, 194-195, 216-217; and as Republican candidate, 190; 1948 rejection of Presidential candidacy, 190-191, 195, 217; Gallup poll shows popularity of, 190

Election of 1936, 3, 12, 41, 84

Election of 1938 (midterm), 3, 13

Election of 1940:

—issues, 38-40; domestic discontent stressed by Republicans, 5, 13, 18, 57; isolationism, 8-9, 12, 19, 42; inadequate national defense charged, 15, 26, 28, 63, 81; "war party" issue, 21-22, 25, 26, 39; war issue initially avoided, 38-40, 47-48; destroyers-for-bases-deal, 44-46, 47, 52-54; secrecy in government v. public's right to know, 48, 53, 63, 66, 70; war issue forced, 49-51, 61, 62-63; appeasement theme, 49-50, 56-57, 59-61, 62, 73-74; Tripartite Pact, 61-63; war issue clearly drawn with Willkie's antiwar stance, 63, 65, 66-75, 87; war issue exploited by both sides, 79-83

—results, 84; projected effect of war on, 65-66; last-minute forecasts, 83; evaluation of, 84-87; ethnic analysis, 86; foreign reaction to, 87-88

Election of 1942 (midterm), 94, 127

Election of 1944:

—issues, 103, 105, 117; foreign policy, minimized by bipartisanship, 100, 105, 116, 122-125, 130, 131-132, 148; world body, 100, 105, 116, 122-125, 131-132, 148-154; Palestine problem, 105-108, 143-144; Polish question, 105; 108-112, 123, 124, 138-143, 154, 155; Pearl Harbor blame, 105, 112-114, 145-147; FDR's age and fatigue

as, 117, 119, 121, 128, 136; U.S. relations with Russia, 123, 124; isolationist heritage of GOP, 124, 131, 133-134, 136, 155-157, 162-163; "FDR controlled by left-wing labor" innuendos, 130-131; Communism and FDR, 131, 137; lack of war-preparedness charged, 137, 155, 158; "secret diplomacy" charge, 141, 154-155, 160

—results, 161; projected effect of war on, 100, 126-127, 158; last-minute forecasts, 157-158; evaluation of, 161-164; ethnic voting, 142-143, 144-145; foreign reaction to, 162

Election of 1946 (midterm), 169, 188, 189

Election of 1948:

—issues, 171-173, 192, 206, 208, 212-213, 225-226; Cold War, 172, 174, 183, 200-205, 207-208, 219-221, 226, 237, 238, 242, 272; Communism, 173, 183-184, 220-221, 239, 249, 261, 268, 269, 272, 274; Marshall Plan, 173, 174, 192, 218, 223, 224; Palestine, 174, 175-178, 184-188, 194, 196-200, 212, 217-218, 220, 223, 242, 249, 250-254, 262-266; domestic record of Republican 80th Congress, 206, 208, 209, 219, 226, 237, 238, 246, 272; foreign policy, minimized by bipartisanship, 208, 211-212, 219, 223, 224-226, 230, 232-234, 241-245, 247-248, 266, 270, 273, 275-276; foreign policy, injected by Wallace (containment policy), 219-220, 248, 249, 257, 269-270; China, 220, 223, 242, 245, 270-271; Greece and Turkey, 220, 223; foreign policy injected by Dewey, 223-224, 225, 227-229, 263-266; Berlin crisis ruled out as

issue, 224-226, 232-234, 241-243, 244, 266; Italian colonies, 227-230; Communist spies in government issue, 236, 239, 242, 244; peace theme, 237-240, 245, 254-256, 259-260, 261, 262, 268-270, 276
—results, 271-272; last-minute forecasts, 267-268; evaluation of, 272-273, 274-276; foreign reactions to, 273-274; ethnic analysis of, 274-275
Elsey, George M., 207, 237
Emery, Brooks, 57
England. *See* Great Britain
Epstein, Eliahu, 198
Eritrea, 227
Ethiopia, 229
Ethnic vote (*see also* German-American vote; Italian-Americans; Irish-Americans; Jewish vote; Polish-Americans): in 1940, 86; in 1944, 142-143; in 1948, 172, 274-275
Europe: stability seen essential to U.S. security, 12, 21, 43, 88; Allied war progress in, 109, 126, 133; Eastern and Central, in Soviet sphere, 167, 169, 179, 182, 189, 207, 213, 261; Marshall Plan for reconstruction of, 170, 171, 180, 182, 183, 188, 189, 210-211; Western, defense of, 182, 193, 201, 216; 1948 Berlin crisis, 214-216 (*see also* Berlin); Western, U.S. alignment with, 193, 201, 213, 260; reactions to Truman's election in, 273-274
European Recovery Program, 180, 182, 183, 189, 211. *See also* Marshall Plan
Ewing, Oscar, 237
Export controls, U.S., on iron and gasoline, 61

Fala (dog), FDR's reference to, 136

Farley, James A., 4, 6, 32, 36, 37
Farm vote: in 1944, 85; in 1948, 274
Federal spending, FDR's 1932 campaign pledge for control of, 57, 67, 79
Fish, Hamilton, 27, 29, 81, 113, 155, 163
Flynn, Ed, 4, 174; Democratic National Chairman, 64, 73, 75-76, 81
Flynn, John T., 11, 52
Foreign Affairs, 76
Foreign aid, 207 (*see also* Marshall Plan; Military aid); Republican platform of 1948 on, 212
Foreign Policy Association, 153, 155
Foreign policy planks: Republican, of 1940, 27, 28-29, 33, 38; Democratic, of 1940, 34-36, 38, 57, 58-59; Republican, of 1944, 108, 110, 114, 115-116; Democratic, of 1944, 108, 118, 143; Republican, of 1948, 211-212, 263-264; Democratic, of 1948, 217-218, 250, 253, 263, 264; Progressive party, of 1948, 220
Foreign trade, 6, 18, 26
Forrestal, James V., 153, 194, 201, 205, 242, 268, 273, 275, 276; Secretary of the Navy, 146; Secretary of Defense, 175, 181; and Palestine problem, 175, 177, 184, 199; and Berlin Blockade, 215, 232, 233
Fortune magazine, 18; 1940 poll on FDR-Willkie race, 54; 1944 polls on FDR-Dewey race, 126-127, 158; 1948 polls, 236, 262
France, 148, 154, 155, 198; in World War II, 5, 8; 1940 German invasion of, 9; German victory in, 22, 26, 30; appeal for U.S. help, 23-24; liberation of, 126; in Brussels

65, 82; German invasion possibility averted, 66; J. P. Kennedy and, 77, 78; at Dumbarton Oaks, 121, 148; and Palestinian problem, 105, 107, 108, 144, 175, 176, 187, 198, 199, 252; withdrawal from Eastern Mediterranean, 170; withdrawal from Palestine, 176, 184, 185, 186; in Brussels Pact, 193; postwar U.S. relations with, 199, 202, 258; and Berlin Blockade, 214, 216, 221-222, 230, 231, 240, 241

Greece: Italian attack on (1940), 79, 81; postwar military aid to, 170; 1948 election issue, 220, 223

Green, Dwight, 213

Guffey, Ed, 140

Hagerty, James, 129, 130

Hague, Frank, 4

Halleck, Charles, 29-30, 55, 56, 210, 213, 246

Halsey, Admiral William F., 158

Hamilton, John D. M., 18, 24-25, 41, 99

Hanes, John W., 42

Hannegan, Robert, 118, 119-120, 130, 140, 155, 177

Harding, Warren, 115; image haunts Dewey's 1944 candidacy, 124, 131, 134, 156, 160-161

Harness, Forest A., 145

Harriman, W. Averell, 139, 160, 179, 276

Hatch, Carl, 92

Hauge, Gabriel, 242

Hays, Will H., 41

Henderson, Leon, 194, 217

Henderson, Loy, 184

Herter, Christian A., 242

Hill, Lister, 92

Hillman, Sidney, 130-131, 138, 161

Hirohito, Emperor, 161, 268

Hiroshima, 168

Hiss, Alger, 236, 249

Hitler, Adolf, 5, 7, 9, 23, 32, 56, 79, 86, 151, 179, 246, 268; "FDR running against," 39-40, 49-50, 51, 54, 59-61, 73-74; Tripartite Pact announced by, 61-62; meeting with Mussolini, Oct. 1940, 66; persecution of Jews, 105, 175; attack on Russia, 108; "vote for Dewey is vote for H." innuendo, 161

Holifield, Chet, 197

Holland: 1940 German invasion of, 9, 15, 19; in Brussels Pact, 193

Hollister, John, 55

Hoover, Herbert, 15, 24, 67, 213

Hopkins, Harry L., 4, 36, 37, 64, 73, 74, 76, 77, 84, 100, 109, 135, 150, 155, 246; and Pearl Harbor issue, 146-147

House Foreign Affairs Committee, and Zionist Resolution of 1944, 107, 143

House of Representatives, U.S. (see also Congress, U.S.): 1940 emergency defense appropriations, 10; efforts for world organization in (Fulbright Resolution), 93-94; Republican gains in 1942 election, 94; Zionist resolution in, 106, 107, 143; and Pearl Harbor court-martial, 112-113; Republican losses in 1944 election, 163; passage of European Recovery Plan, 182, 183; Kersten/Nixon Resolution, 189; Marshall Plan appropriations cut, 210-211; Democrats capture control of (1948), 272

Howard, Charles P., 219

Howard, Roy, 99

Hull, Cordell, 75-76, 261; as possible 1940 Presidential contender, 4, 6, 10; as Secretary of State, 6, 7, 19, 24, 26, 35, 37, 57, 62, 81,

88, 133, 154, 160, 163; and destroyers-for-bases deal, 45, 51-52; seeks bipartisan approach to foreign policy, 92, 93-94, 100-102, 121-125; possible Presidential contender in 1944, 95; and American draft plan for U.N., 100-105, 121, 123; and Palestine problem, 106, 108; and Polish question, 111, 123; Dumbarton Oaks Conference called, 121; bipartisan agreement with Dulles, 122-125, 130, 148, 149, 153, 163; resignation of, 160, 163
Humphrey, Hubert H., 218, 250

Ibn Saud, King of Saudi Arabia, 106, 144
Ickes, Harold L., 4, 49, 54, 57, 69, 73, 119, 155, 160, 169, 260
Illinois, Polish vote of, 139
Independent vote: decisive in election outcomes, 43, 134, 158, 162; Willkie play for (1940), 42-43; sought by FDR (1944), 134-135, 150, 151-152, 153-154; Truman's appeals to, in 1948, 237; Republican appeals to (1948), 248
Information, Please (radio program), 18
"Insulationism," of Vandenberg, 17
Internationalism (*see also* Interventionism; World federation; World organization): among Eastern Republicans, in 1940, 13, 14; Dewey and, 14-15, 97, 100, 117, 130-131, 152; public mood of 1944, 91, 124; among Republicans in 1944, 92, 93, 96-97, 114-115, 117, 149, 151-152; of Willkie (1944), 96-97, 114-115, 135; of Truman, 120, 156; behind FDR in 1944, 151-154; 1944 triumph of, 162-163; in control at 1948 Repub-

lican Convention, 212-214
Interventionism, and interventionists, of 1940, 7, 8, 10, 23, 25, 50; FDR's leanings, 12, 38, 50, 60-61, 64-65; Willkie's leanings, 19-20, 33, 38, 43, 47-48; Committee to Defend America by Aiding the Allies, 20, 36, 42; Landon's leanings, 27; v. isolationism, at 1940 Republican Convention, 26-30, 38; v. isolationism, at 1940 Democratic Convention, 34-36, 38; destroyers-for-bases deal pressed, 44-45; increased by German raids on London, 57-58; abandoned by Willkie, 62-63; after 1940 election, 88-89, 154
Iowa, 1948 vote in, 274
Irish-Americans, 71-72, 77; FDR's appeal to, 82; 1940 vote of, 86; Truman's appeal for 1948 vote of, 268; 1948 vote of, 274
Isacson, Leo, 174, 176, 272
Isolationism, isolationists: of 1940, 7, 8-9, 10-11, 23, 50 (*see also* "Keep us out of war" sentiment); as 1940 campaign issue, 8-9, 12, 19, 42; among Republicans, 8, 13, 15, 16, 19-20, 25, 52-53; Dewey and, 14-15, 19; Willkie on, 19, 47; among Democrats, 25, 33-34; v. interventionism, at 1940 Republican Convention, 26-30, 38; v. interventionism, at 1940 Democratic Convention, 34-36, 38; Willkie's acceptance-speech concessions to, 47-48, 49; criticism for destroyers-for-bases deal, 52-53; clear rejection by FDR, 64-65; Willkie's appeal for support of, 53, 56, 62-63; behind Willkie, 71-73; America First, 71, 99, 155, 156; Joseph P. Kennedy and, 77-78; ended by Japanese

attack at Pearl Harbor, 91; Republican efforts to shed image of, 91, 92-93, 100, 124, 149; vestiges in Republican ranks, 115, 117, 154, 155, 188-189, 193-194, 210-211; Republicans haunted by image of, 124, 131, 133-134, 136, 155-157, 162-163; FDR's attack on (1944), 155-157; rejected in 1944 election, 162-163; rejected at 1948 Republican Convention, 212-214; denounced by Dewey (1948), 245; Republicans charged with, in 1948, 259, 269

Israel (*see also* Palestine): existence proclaimed, 198; U.S. recognition of, 196-200, 212, 218, 220, 249, 250, 251, 253, 262, 264, 265, 266, 273; U.S. assistance to, 212, 218, 220, 250, 251, 264; Wallace's support for, 220, 249, 250, 263, 270; U.N. membership for, 251; Bernadotte plan for, 251-253, 262, 263, 264, 265; becomes partisan issue in 1948 campaign, 252-254, 263-266; boundary (Negev) question, 251-253, 262-263, 264; occupation of Negev (1948), 262-263, 265; reaction to Truman's election in, 273

Italian-Americans: and FDR's "stab-in-the-back" statement, 64; 1940 vote of, 86; 1944 vote of, 144-145; and Italian colonies issue, 228; 1948 vote of, 274

Italy (*see also* Mussolini, Benito): enters World War II, 22, 23; in Tripartite Pact, 61-62; attack on Greece, 79, 81; surrender and switch to Allies by, 144; U.S. reconciliation policy toward, 144-145; Dewey critical of FDR policy, 154; peace treaty with, 227; African colonies of, 227-229

Jacobson, Eddie, 184-185, 187, 199, 250, 253
Januszewski, Frank, 110, 142-143
Japan, 60, 191; Tripartite Pact with Axis powers, 61-62; attack at Pearl Harbor, 89, 91, 112, 145-147; diplomatic code broken by U.S., 146-147, 261; war reverses in 1944, 126, 158; defeat of, 167, 168
Jefferson, Thomas, 52
Jerusalem, 251
Jewish vote: in 1940, 61, 86; and Palestine issue, 106-107, 143-144, 174, 176-178, 184-187, 194, 196-197, 199-200, 249, 254, 263; in 1944, 144; needed by Democrats in 1948, 172, 174, 177-178, 186, 263; Wallace and, 249, 263, 272; in 1948, 272, 274
Jews (*see also* Israel; Palestine): Hitler's persecution of, 105, 175; Palestinian homeland for, 105-108, 143, 174, 175, 251, 263; Zionist resolution asks free entry to Palestine, 106-107, 143, 144
Johnson, Donald Bruce, 85
Johnson, Gerald W., 131
Johnson, Hiram, 155
Johnson, Hugh, 59, 71
Johnson, Lyndon B., 6, 76
Jones, Lem, 55, 96

Kaltenborn, H. V., 75
Katyn Forest massacre, 109
"Keep us out of war" sentiment of 1940, 8, 11, 20, 43; Gallup poll results, 8, 11, 43; of Vandenberg, 17; of Dewey, 14-15, 26; Willkie statements, 20-21, 26, 30, 38, 56, 63, 67-68, 79-80, 88; at Republican Convention of 1940, 27-29, 30; Republican platform pledge, 28, 38; at Democratic Convention

Military aid: wartime, to Western Allies, 21, 23-24, 26, 38, 47, 64-65, 86 (*see also* Allies; Arms embargo; Great Britain); postwar, to Greece and Turkey, 170; to Western Europe, Truman proposal, 182
Miller, Arthur Lewis, 99
Minneapolis, campaign speeches in: Dewey (1944), 152, 156; Truman (1944), 156
Moley, Raymond, 41, 243
Molotov, Vyacheslav M., 139, 142, 201-202, 230-231, 240
Morgenthau, Henry, Jr., 169
Morgenthau plan, for postwar Germany, 133, 154, 159-160
Mormon Tabernacle, Salt Lake City, Dewey's 1948 speech in, 245
Morse, Wayne, 163
Moscow: Conference and Declaration (1943), 93; Mikolajczyk in, 138, 139; Conference (1944), 139
Moses, Robert, 152-153
Mundt, Karl, 273
Munich agreement of 1938, 21, 49, 56, 179, 231, 245
Murphy, Charles, 237
Murphy, Robert, 222-223
Murray, Philip, 250
Mussolini, Benito, 56, 60, 66, 145, 268; leads Italy into war, 22; attack on Greece, 79; ouster of, 144

Nagasaki, 168
Nation, 11, 71, 153, 257, 258; quoted, 7, 10, 61, 151, 157, 162, 177, 221
National security (*see also* Defense): European stability seen essential to, 12, 21, 43, 88;

balance of power and, 91; dependent on free Western Europe, 182, 193
Navy, Department of the, 112, 113, 145. *See also* Forrestal, James; Knox, Frank
Nazism: interference in 1940 U.S. election, 51, 72-73, 74; Soviet aggressions compared to, in 1948, 179
Nebraska, 1948 primary, 192
Negev, 251, 252, 253, 263; Israeli occupation of, 262-263, 265
Negro vote: in 1940, 85; Wallace and, 249, 272, 274; in 1948, 172, 272, 274
Neutrality Acts, 5, 81
New Deal(ers), 3, 4, 11, 13, 16, 28, 66, 72; Willkie's criticisms of, 17, 30, 57, 67; Willkie's "me-too" line, 86; coalition preserved in 1940 vote, 85; and in 1944 vote, 161; coalition shaky in postwar period, 169-170, 172, 209; revival of support for Truman, 208, 237, 260, 274
New Hampshire, 1948 primary, 190
New Republic, 153, 257; quoted, 12, 105, 136, 194, 219, 260, 274; TRB quoted, 16, 23, 40, 157, 208, 216, 260-261
New York City: Willkie speeches in, 63, 80; 1940 FDR campaign speech in, 80-81; Italian-American vote in 1940, 86; Jewish vote in 1940, 86; 1944 FDR tour and speech, 150, 151, 153, 155; Dewey's 1944 campaign speech in, 159-160; 1944 Democratic rally, 160; Italian-American vote in 1944, 144-145; Jewish vote in 1944, 144; Jewish vote in 1948, 263, 265; Truman's 1948 campaign speech, 265; Wallace's 1948

speech in, 270; Dewey's 1948 speech in, 269; *New York Herald Tribune,* 18; Dewey's speech to 1944 forum, 141, 150, 154-155; quoted, 187

New York State: 1940 ethnic vote of, 64, 86; unsure for Democrats in 1948 third-party situation, 173-174, 270; Wallace's appeal to Jewish vote, 249, 263, 270, 272; Democrats' chances improved in, 265-266; won by Dewey in 1948, 272

New York Times, The, 45, 55, 79, 121, 152, 228, 232, 248, 263; 1940 election forecast, 83; 1948 election forecast, 268; quoted, 8-9, 29, 46-47, 48, 50, 60, 70, 116, 153, 154, 162, 163, 199, 202, 212, 229, 257, 265, 271

Newsweek magazine, 180, 194, 205; 1940 election forecast, 83; 1944 election forecasts, 127, 132, 158; 1948 election forecast, 210; quoted, 23, 50, 53-54, 98, 132, 162, 174, 179, 193-194, 199, 219, 222, 225, 236, 243, 266

Niebuhr, Reinhold, 170

Niles, David, 110, 186, 197-198, 263

Nimitz, Admiral Chester, 126, 128

Nixon, Richard M., 189

Nizer, Louis, 207

Norris, George, 10

Norway, 1940 German occupation of, 7, 8, 15, 19

Noyes, David, 254, 255

Nuclear disarmament, Baruch Plan for, 168-169, 207

Nurczyk, Frank, 139

Nye, Gerald, 155, 163

O'Daniel, Pappy, 272

Ohio: Polish vote of (1944), 139;

1948 vote result, 272

Oil interests, U.S., in Middle East, 106, 144, 176, 184, 187

O'Mahoney, Joseph C., 139

One World (Willkie), 96

Oregon, 1948 primary, 192

PAC. *See* Political Action Committee

Pacific, war in, 126, 128, 133, 158

Palestine (*see also* Israel): as election issue in 1944, 105-108, 143-144; as Jewish homeland, 105-108, 143, 174, 175, 263; Balfour Declaration, 105, 108, 175; British White Paper of 1939, 105, 107; free entry of Jews asked (Zionist resolution), 106-107, 143, 144; as election issue in 1948, 174, 175-178, 184-188, 194, 196-200, 212, 217-218, 220, 223, 242, 249, 250-254, 262-266; Truman's policy, 174, 175-178, 184-188, 194, 196-200, 250-254, 262-266; U.N. partition plan for, 175, 176, 177, 184, 185, 186-187, 196, 263, 264; British withdrawal from, 176, 184, 185, 186, 196; U.S. arms embargo on, 176, 177, 178, 184, 186, 197, 199, 218, 220, 264; U.N. trusteeship proposed, 185-187, 196; recognition of new state of Israel, 196-200, 212, 218, 220, 249, 250, 251, 253, 262, 264, 265, 266; U.N. mediation role, 200, 218, 250, 251, 262, 265-266; Republican foreign policy plank of 1948 on, 212, 263-264; Democratic foreign policy plank of 1948 on, 217-218, 250, 253, 263, 264; Progressive foreign policy plank of 1948 on, 220; Bernadotte plan for, 251-253, 262, 263, 264, 265

101-103; hedge on bipartisan approach to world body, 103-104, 122; bipartisan approach on international organization agreed to, 122-125, 163-164; and Palestine problem (1944), 108, 143, 144; and Polish question, 110, 123, 124, 140-141, 142-143; and question of blame for Pearl Harbor, 112-114, 145-147; internationalist-isolationist tension in 1944, 114, 115-116, 117, 149, 154-157; 1944 candidates, 117; Brownell appointed National Chairman, 117; haunted by image of isolationism, 124, 131, 133-134, 136, 155-157, 162-163; "clear everything with Sidney" smear against FDR, 130-131; and U.N. peace force v. national sovereignty issue, 148-153; liberal, Ball inherits Willkie following, 151-152; 1948 presidential vote results, 161; 1944 Congressional election losses of, 163; bipartisanship in foreign policy after 1944, 163-164, 182, 188-189, 193, 211, 212, 223, 224-227, 230, 232-234, 241-245, 247-248, 266, 275; gain control of Congress (1946), 169, 188; benefits forecast due to Wallace candidacy, 173-174, 188; and U.S. Palestine policy (1948), 177, 199, 212, 242, 252-254, 263-264; outlook for 1948 election, 178, 210, 214, 226, 236, 248; isolationist vestiges in 1948, 188-189, 193-194, 210-211; support for containment policy, 188-189, 230, 240, 247, 249, 275; tensions among, over bipartisan approach to foreign policy, 188-190, 210-211; some opposition to Marshall Plan, 189, 210-211, 218; charges

of appeasement against Democrats, 189, 192, 223, 227, 246, 261; possible Presidential contenders in 1948, 190-194, 210, 213; 1948 primaries, 191-192; domestic record attacked by Truman, 206, 208, 209, 219, 226, 237, 238, 246, 272; isolationism rejected at 1948 Convention, 212-214; criticisms of Truman's foreign policy, 212-213, 223-224, 227, 246-247, 261; Hugh Scott as National Chairman, 214, 230; and Berlin crisis, 224-226, 232-234, 266-267; and Vinson episode, 257-258; charges of isolationism against (1948), 259, 269; last-minute election forecasts in 1948, 261-262, 267-268; 1948 election results, 271-272; 1948 loss in farm votes, 274; bipartisanship in foreign policy after 1948, 276
Reston, James, 202, 225, 261
Roberts, Owen J., 112
Roberts Report (on Pearl Harbor), 112, 113
Rome, Allied liberation of, 144
Roosevelt, Eleanor, 170, 181, 240, 252, 259, 260
Roosevelt, Franklin D., 242, 268, 274-275, 276; 1932 promise to balance the budget, 57, 67, 79; 1936 reelection success of, 3, 84; second term reverses of, 3; congressional relations in 1940, 3, 4, 9; 1940 conservative Democrat attacks on, 3-4; 1940 Gallup poll results on, 4, 11, 31, 41, 43, 54, 58, 62, 65-66, 83; question of seeking third term, 4-6, 10-12, 25, 31-33, 36-38; pro-Allied sentiments of, in 1939/40, 5, 7-8, 12, 21, 23, 38 (*see also below:* aid to Allies); and Neutrality Acts, 5,

Vandenberg, Arthur H., 156, 256; as possible 1940 Presidential contender, 16-17; outspoken isolationist, 16-17, 19; and 1940 campaign, 58, 65, 66, 67; isolationism abandoned, 91, 92-93; and 1944 campaign, 97, 99, 114, 123, 154, 161; on Committee of Eight, 102-103; and plans for world body, 102-103, 114, 115, 148, 163-164; and Palestine problem, 107, 108, 144, 177, 199; and Polish question, 110, 141, 142; Republican leader for bipartisan foreign policy, 163-164, 188, 189-190, 193, 210, 211, 216, 219, 224, 226-227, 229, 230, 232-233, 246, 275; supports Truman Doctrine, 170, 205; champion of Marshall Plan, 180, 188, 210-211; possible Presidential contender in 1948, 191, 192-194, 210, 211, 213; Senate resolution on European defense, 193-194; 1948 foreign policy plank drafted by, 211-212; and 1948 election campaign, 214, 224, 227, 229, 247, 258, 261, 275; and Berlin Blockade, 223, 224-225, 232-233; on Truman's election, 273

Vice-presidential candidates, 1940 Republican, 30; 1940 Democratic, 37, 49-50; 1944 Republican, 117; 1944 Democratic, 119-120; 1948 Republican, 213; 1948 Democratic, 218

Villard, Oswald Garrison, 11, 71

Vinson, Fred, 254; proposed mission to Moscow, 254-259, 260, 262, 268, 273, 276

Vishinsky, Andrei, 267

Voter registration drives, in 1944, 138, 161

Voter turnout: low in 1942, 94, 127; Democrats worried for 1944 election, 127, 137-138; in 1944, 161; in 1948, 273

Wadsworth, James, 44. See also Burke-Wadsworth bill

Wagner, Robert, 34-35, 54, 134, 143, 160, 175

Wall Street influence, in foreign policy, 276

Wallace, Henry A.: 1940 Democratic Vice-Presidential candidate, 37, 62; acceptance speech, 49-50, 56; campaign travels and speeches of, 59, 74; Gallup poll on 1944 chances of, 95; dumped in 1944, 119-120; 1944 speeches for FDR, 134, 155-156; Secretary of Commerce, 167, 169; troubled by postwar U.S. foreign policy, 167-169; and PCA, 169, 171; labor and, 169, 171, 239, 274; opposes Truman Doctrine, 170; opposes Marshall Plan, 170, 180; loss of some non-Communist liberal support, 170-171; "Red dupe" charges against, 171, 173, 183, 220-221, 249, 270, 272, 276; 1948 third-party candidacy of, 171, 194, 201, 203-205, 206, 207, 209, 219-221, 226, 272, 276; *Toward World Peace*, 171; "a vote for W. is a vote for Stalin" innuendo, 173; opinion poll results on, 173, 236, 249, 262; danger of candidacy to Democrats, 173-174, 188, 238, 249, 254, 256, 268, 270, 272; and Communist takeover of Czechoslovakia, 180-181; attacks on bipartisan policy of containment, 180, 219, 220, 248, 249, 257, 269-270; and abortive Soviet peace initiative, 203-205; letter exchange with Stalin, 204-205;

as apologist for Soviets, 205, 220-221, 249; acceptance speech at Progressive Convention, 220-221; strong support for Israel, 220, 249, 250, 263, 270, 272; endorsed by Communist party, 221, 249; election campaign of, 248-250, 269-270, 272; as civil rights champion, 248, 249, 272; foreign policy proposals of, 249, 250, 276; opposition of ADA and liberals to, 260; election results for, 271-272, 274; voter repudiation analyzed, 272, 276

Walsh, David, 35

War Department (*see also* Stimson, Henry L.): and Palestine Resolution in Congress, 106-107; and Pearl Harbor courtmartial, 112, 113, 145

War issue, in 1940 campaign: "war party" label, 21-22, 25, 26, 39; initially avoided, 38-40, 47-48; forced, 49-51, 61, 62-63; emerges clearly with Willkie's antiwar stance, 63, 65, 66-75, 87; exploited by both sides at end of 1940 campaign, 79-83

War-preparedness issue, in 1944, 137, 155, 158

War scare, in 1948, 180, 181-183, 189, 201, 254-255, 258, 262; over Berlin Blockade, 216, 222-223, 225, 232-234, 241-242, 254; called artificially fomented, by Wallace, 249

Warren, Earl, 116, 117, 192; 1948 Vice-Presidential candidate, 213, 246-247, 268

Warren uprising of 1944, 138

Washington, George, two-term tradition set by, 84

Webb, James, 222, 233

Wechsler, James A., 130

Weizmann, Chaim, 184-185, 187, 198, 199, 250, 253, 273

Welles, Sumner, 77

West Germany: formation of (1948), 214-215, 230-231; called war base by Wallace, 220; defense of, 259

Western Republicans, as isolationists, 154

Wheeler, Burton K., 33-35, 93

Wherry, Kenneth S., 188, 193

White, William Allen, 20, 25, 42-43, 45

Willkie, Wendell, 22, 25, 123, 156, 191, 192; background and career of, 17; ex-Democrat, 17, 97; personality of, 17-18, 31, 98; critic of New Deal, 17, 30, 57, 67; 1940 Republican Presidential candidate, 17-21, 26-27, 28, 29-31, 38-39; 1940 Gallup poll results on, 18, 19, 26, 31, 41, 43, 54, 58, 62, 65, 68, 83; attacks on FDR's foreign policy, 19, 23, 47-48, 53, 56-57, 62-63, 66-67, 79-80; pro-Allied stand and interventionism of, 19, 20-21, 26, 30, 33, 38, 43, 47-48; antiwar statements of, 20-21, 26, 30, 56, 63, 67-68, 79-80, 88; nomination of, 29-30; compared to FDR, 31, 38-39, 55; supports aid to England, 39, 47, 57, 63, 86; campaign organization of, 41-42, 85; alienates GOP regulars, 41-42, 55-56; campaign advisors, 42, 55, 56, 85; campaign strategy of, 42-43; acceptance speech, 43, 46, 47-48; and destroyers-for-bases deal, 44-45, 46, 47, 53; endorses draft, 47; challenge of debates to FDR, 47, 49; FDR strategy against, 48-51, 59-61; Ickes's attack on, 49; caught in appeasement issue, 50,